PENGUIN BOOKS

COOKED

Michael Pollan is the author of *Second Nature*, *A Place of My Own*, *The Botany of Desire*, *The Omnivore's Dilemma*, *In Defence of Food* and *Food Rules*. He lives in California.

Cooked

A Natural History of Transformation

MICHAEL POLLAN

PENGUIN BOOKS

PENGUIN BOOKS

Published by the Penguin Group
Penguin Books Ltd, 80 Strand, London WC2R ORL, England
Penguin Group (USA) Inc., 375 Hudson Street, New York, New York 10014, USA
Penguin Group (Canada), 90 Eglinton Avenue East, Suite 700, Toronto, Ontario, Canada M4P 2Y3
(a division of Pearson Penguin Canada Inc.)
Penguin Ireland, 25 St Stephen's Green, Dublin 2, Ireland (a division of Penguin Books Ltd)
Penguin Group (Australia), 707 Collins Street, Melbourne, Victoria 3008, Australia
(a division of Pearson Australia Group Pty Ltd)
Penguin Books India Pvt Ltd, 11 Community Centre, Panchsheel Park, New Delhi – 110 017, India
Penguin Group (NZ), 67 Apollo Drive, Rosedale, Auckland 0632, New Zealand
(a division of Pearson New Zealand Ltd)
Penguin Books (South Africa) (Pty) Ltd, Block D, Rosebank Office Park, 181 Jan Smuts Avenue, Parktown
North, Gauteng 2193, South Africa

Penguin Books Ltd, Registered Offices: 80 Strand, London WC2R ORL, England

www.penguin.com

First published in the United States of America by The Penguin Press,
part of The Penguin Group (USA) Inc., 2013
First published in Great Britain by Allen Lane 2013
Published in Penguin Books 2014

006

Copyright © Michael Pollan, 2013

The moral right of the author has been asserted

A portion of Chapter Two first appeared under the title 'Out of the Kitchen, Onto the Couch'
in *The New York Times Magazine*, 29 July 2009.

All rights reserved

Printed in Great Britain by Clays Ltd, St Ives plc

978-0-141-97562-7

www.greenpenguin.co.uk

FOR JUDITH AND ISAAC
AND FOR WENDELL BERRY

CONTENTS

INTRODUCTION: WHY COOK? • 1

PART I:
FIRE
CREATURES OF THE FLAME • 25

PART II:
WATER
A RECIPE IN SEVEN STEPS • 123

PART III:
AIR
THE EDUCATION OF AN AMATEUR BAKER • 203

PART IV:

EARTH

FERMENTATION'S COLD FIRE • 291

AFTERWORD: HAND TASTE • 405

APPENDIX I

Four Recipes • 417

APPENDIX II

A Short Shelf of Books on Cooking • 437

Acknowledgments • 441

Selected Sources • 447

Index • 459

INTRODUCTION

WHY COOK?

I.

At a certain point in the late middle of my life I made the unexpected but happy discovery that the answer to several of the questions that most occupied me was in fact one and the same.

Cook.

Some of these questions were personal. For example, what was the single most important thing we could do as a family to improve our health and general well-being? And what would be a good way to better connect to my teenage son? (As it turned out, this involved not only ordinary cooking but also the specialized form of it known as brewing.) Other questions were slightly more political in nature. For years I had been trying to determine (because I am often asked) what is the most important thing an ordinary person can do to help reform the American food system, to make it healthier and more sustainable? Another related question is, how can people living in a highly specialized consumer economy reduce their sense of dependence and achieve a greater degree of self-sufficiency? And then there were the more philosophical questions, the ones I've been chewing on since I first started writing books. How, in our everyday lives, can we acquire a deeper understanding of the natural world and our species' peculiar role in it? You can always go to the woods to confront such questions, but I discovered that even more interesting answers could be had simply by going to the kitchen.

I would not, as I said, ever have expected it. Cooking has always been a part of my life, but more like the furniture than an object of scrutiny, much less a passion. I counted myself lucky to have a parent—my mother—who loved to cook and almost every night made us a delicious meal. By the time I had a place of my own, I could find my way around a kitchen well enough, the result of nothing more purposeful than all those hours spent hanging around the kitchen while my mother fixed dinner. And though once I had my own place I cooked whenever I had the time, I seldom made time for cooking or gave it much consideration. My kitchen skills, such as they were, were pretty much frozen in place by the time I turned thirty. Truth be told, my most successful dishes leaned heavily on the cooking of others, as when I drizzled my incredible sage-butter sauce over store-bought ravioli. Every now and then I'd look at a cookbook or clip a recipe from the newspaper to add a new dish to my tiny repertoire, or I'd buy a new kitchen gadget, though most of these eventually ended up in a closet.

In retrospect, the mildness of my interest in cooking surprises me, since my interest in every other link of the food chain had been so keen. I've been a gardener since I was eight, growing mostly vegetables, and I've always enjoyed being on farms and writing about agriculture. I've also written a fair amount about the opposite end of the food chain—the eating end, I mean, and the implications of our eating for our health. But to the middle links of the food chain, where the stuff of nature gets transformed into the things we eat and drink, I hadn't really given much thought.

Until, that is, I began trying to unpack a curious paradox I had noticed while watching television, which was simply this: How is it that at the precise historical moment when Americans were abandoning the kitchen, handing over the preparation of most of our meals to the food industry, we began spending so much of our time thinking about food and watching other people cook it on television? The less cooking we were doing in our own lives, it seemed, the more that food and its vicarious preparation transfixed us.

Our culture seems to be of at least two minds on this subject. Survey research confirms we're cooking less and buying more prepared meals every year. The amount of time spent preparing meals in American households has fallen by half since the mid-sixties, when I was watching my mom fix dinner, to a scant twenty-seven minutes a day. (Americans spend less time cooking than people in any other nation, but the general downward trend is global.) And yet at the same time we're *talking* about cooking more—and watching cooking, and reading about cooking, and going to restaurants designed so that we can watch the work performed live. We live in an age when professional cooks are household names, some of them as famous as athletes or movie stars. The very same activity that many people regard as a form of drudgery has somehow been elevated to a popular spectator sport. When you consider that twenty-seven minutes is less time than it takes to watch a single episode of *Top Chef* or *The Next Food Network Star*, you realize that there are now millions of people who spend more time watching food being cooked on television than they spend actually cooking it themselves. I don't need to point out that the food you watch being cooked on television is not food you get to eat.

This is peculiar. After all, we're not watching shows or reading books about sewing or darning socks or changing the oil in our car, three other domestic chores that we have been only too happy to outsource—and then promptly drop from conscious awareness. But cooking somehow feels different. The work, or the process, retains an emotional or psychological power we can't quite shake, or don't want to. And in fact it was after a long bout of watching cooking programs on television that I began to wonder if this activity I had always taken for granted might be worth taking a little more seriously.

I developed a few theories to explain what I came to think of as the Cooking Paradox. The first and most obvious is that watching other people cook is not exactly a new behavior for us humans. Even when "everyone" still cooked, there were plenty of us who mainly watched: men for the most part, and children. Most of us have happy memories of watching our mothers in the kitchen, performing feats that sometimes looked very much like sorcery and typically resulted in something tasty to eat. In ancient Greece, the word for "cook," "butcher," and "priest" was the same—*mageiros*—and the word shares an etymological root with "magic." I would watch, rapt, when my mother conjured her most magical dishes, like the tightly wrapped packages of fried chicken Kiev that, when cut open with a sharp knife, liberated a pool of melted butter and an aromatic gust of herbs. But watching an everyday pan of eggs get scrambled was nearly as riveting a spectacle, as the slimy yellow goop suddenly leapt into the form of savory gold nuggets. Even the most ordinary dish follows a satisfying arc of transformation, magically becoming something more than the sum of its ordinary parts. And in almost every dish, you can find, besides the culinary ingredients, the ingredients of a story: a beginning, a middle, and an end.

Then there are the cooks themselves, the heroes who drive these little dramas of transformation. Even as it vanishes from our daily lives, we're drawn to the rhythms and textures of the work cooks do, which seems so much more direct and satisfying than the more abstract and formless tasks most of us perform in our jobs these days. Cooks get to put their hands on real stuff, not just keyboards and screens but fundamental things like plants and animals and fungi. They get to work with the primal elements, too, fire and water, earth and air, using them—mastering them!—to perform their tasty alchemies. How many of us still do the kind of work that engages us in a dialogue with the material world that concludes—assuming the chicken Kiev doesn't prematurely leak or the soufflé doesn't collapse—with such a gratifying and delicious sense of closure?

So maybe the reason we like to watch cooking on television and read about cooking in books is that there are things about cooking we really miss. We might not feel we have the time or energy (or the knowledge) to do it ourselves every day, but we're not prepared to see it disappear from our lives altogether. If cooking is, as the anthropologists tell us, a defining human activity—the act with which culture begins, according to Claude Lévi-Strauss—then maybe we shouldn't be surprised that watching its processes unfold would strike deep emotional chords.

The idea that cooking is a defining human activity is not a new one. In 1773, the Scottish writer James Boswell, noting that "no beast is a cook," called Homo sapiens "the cooking animal." (Though he might have reconsidered that definition had he been able to gaze upon the frozen-food cases at Walmart.) Fifty years later, in The Physiology of Taste, the French gastronome Jean Anthelme Brillat-Savarin claimed that cooking made us who we are; by teaching men to use fire, it had "done the most to advance the cause of civilization." More recently, Lévi-Strauss, writing in *The Raw and the Cooked* in 1964, reported that many of the world's cultures entertained a similar view, regarding cooking as the symbolic activity that "establishes the difference between animals and people."

For Lévi-Strauss, cooking was a metaphor for the human transformation of raw nature into cooked culture. But in the years since the publication of *The Raw and the Cooked*, other anthropologists have begun to take quite literally the idea that the invention of cooking might hold the evolutionary key to our humanness. A few years ago, a Harvard anthropologist and primatologist named Richard Wrangham published a fascinating book called *Catching Fire*, in which he argued that it was the discovery of cooking by our early ancestors—and not tool making or meat eating or language—that set us apart from the apes and made us human. According to the "cooking hypothesis," the advent of cooked food altered the course of human evolution. By providing our forebears with a more energy-dense and easy-to-digest diet, it allowed our brains to grow bigger (brains being notoriously energy guzzlers) and our guts to shrink. It seems that raw food takes much more time and energy to chew and digest, which is why other primates our size carry around substantially larger digestive tracts and spend many more of their waking hours chewing—as much as six hours a day.

Cooking, in effect, took part of the work of chewing and digestion and performed it for us outside of the body, using outside sources of energy. Also, since cooking detoxifies many potential sources of food, the new technology cracked open a treasure trove of calories unavailable to other animals. Freed from the necessity of spending our days gathering large quantities of raw food and then chewing (and chewing) it, humans could now devote their time, and their metabolic resources, to other purposes, like creating a culture.

Cooking gave us not just the meal but also the occasion: the practice of eating together at an appointed time and place. This was something new under the sun, for the forager of raw food would have likely fed himself on the go and alone, like all the other animals. (Or, come to think of it, like the industrial eaters we've more recently become, grazing at gas stations and eating by ourselves whenever and wherever.) But sitting down to common meals, making eye contact, sharing food, and exercising self-restraint all served to civilize us. "Around that fire," Wrangham writes, "we became tamer."

Cooking thus transformed us, and not only by making us more sociable and civil. Once cooking allowed us to expand our cognitive capacity at the expense of our digestive capacity, there was no going back: Our big brains and tiny guts now depended on a diet of cooked food. (Raw-foodists take note.) What this means is that cooking is now obligatory—it is, as it were, baked into our biology. What Winston Churchill once said of architecture—"First we shape our buildings, and then they shape us"—might also be said of cooking. First we cooked our food, and then our food cooked us.

If cooking is as central to human identity, biology, and culture as Wrangham suggests, it stands to reason that the decline of cooking in our time would have serious consequences for modern life, and so it has. Are they all bad? Not at all. The outsourcing of much of the work of cooking to corporations has relieved women of what has traditionally been their exclusive responsibility for feeding the family, making it easier for them to work outside the home and have careers. It has headed off many of the conflicts and domestic arguments that such a large shift in gender roles and family dynamics was bound to spark. It has relieved all sorts of other pressures in the household, including longer workdays and overscheduled children, and saved us time that we can now invest in other pursuits. It has also allowed us to diversify our diets substantially, making it possible even for people with no cooking skills and little money to enjoy a whole different cuisine every night of the week. All that's required is a microwave.

These are no small benefits. Yet they have come at a cost that we are just now beginning to reckon. Industrial cooking has taken a substantial toll on our health and well-being. Corporations cook very differently from how people do (which is why we usually call what they do "food processing" instead of cooking). They tend to use much more sugar, fat, and salt than people cooking for people do; they also deploy novel chemical ingredients seldom found in pantries in order to make their food last longer and look fresher than it really is. So it will come as no surprise that the decline in home cooking closely tracks the rise in obesity and all the chronic diseases linked to diet.

The rise of fast food and the decline in home cooking have also undermined the institution of the shared meal, by encouraging us to eat different things and to eat them on the run and often alone. Survey researchers tell us we're spending more time engaged in "secondary eating," as this more or less constant grazing on packaged foods is now called, and less time engaged in "primary eating"—a rather depressing term for the once-venerable institution known as the meal.

The shared meal is no small thing. It is a foundation of family life, the place where our children learn the art of conversation and acquire the habits of civilization: sharing, listening, taking turns, navigating differences, arguing without offending. What have been called the "cultural contradictions of capitalism"—its tendency to undermine the stabilizing social forms it depends on—are on vivid display today at the modern American dinner table, along with all the brightly colored packages that the food industry has managed to plant there.

These are, I know, large claims to make for the centrality of cooking (and not cooking) in our lives, and a caveat or two are in order. For most of us today, the choice is not nearly as blunt as I've framed it: that is, home cooking from scratch versus fast food prepared by corporations. Most of us occupy a place somewhere between those bright poles, a spot that is constantly shifting with the day of the week, the occasion, and our mood. Depending on the night, we might cook a meal from scratch, or we might go out or order in, or we might "sort of" cook. This last option involves availing ourselves of the various and very useful shortcuts that an industrial food economy offers: the package of spinach in the freezer, the can of wild salmon in the pantry, the box of store-bought ravioli from down the street or halfway around the world. What constitutes "cooking" takes place along a spectrum, as indeed it has for at least a century, when packaged foods first entered the kitchen and the definition of "scratch cooking" began to drift. (Thereby allowing me to regard my packaged ravioli with sage-butter sauce as a culinary achievement.) Most of us over the course of a week find ourselves all over that spectrum. What is new, however, is the great number of people now spending most nights at the far end of it, relying for the preponderance of their meals on an industry willing to do everything for them save the heating and the eating. "We've had a hundred years of packaged foods," a food-marketing consultant told me, "and now we're going to have a hundred years of packaged meals."

This is a problem—for the health of our bodies, our families, our communities, and our land, but also for our sense of how our eating connects us to the world. Our growing distance from any direct, physical engagement with the processes by which the raw stuff of nature gets transformed into a cooked meal is changing our understanding of what food is. Indeed, the idea that food has any connection to nature or human work or imagination is hard to credit when it arrives in a neat package, fully formed. Food becomes just another commodity, an abstraction. And as soon as that happens we become easy prey for corporations selling synthetic versions of the real thing—what I call edible foodlike substances. We end up trying to nourish ourselves on images.

Now, for a man to criticize these developments will perhaps rankle some readers. To certain ears, whenever a man talks about the importance of cooking, it sounds like he wants to turn back the clock, and return women to the kitchen. But that's not at all what I have in mind. I've come to think cooking is too important to be left to any one gender or member of the family; men and children both need to be in the kitchen, too, and not just for reasons of fairness or equity but because they have so much to gain by being there. In fact, one of the biggest reasons corporations were able to insinuate themselves into this part of our lives is because home cooking had for so long been denigrated as "women's work" and therefore not important enough for men and boys to learn to do.

Though it's hard to say which came first: Was home cooking denigrated because the work was mostly done by women, or did women get stuck doing most of the cooking because our culture denigrated the work? The gender politics of cooking, which I explore at some length in part II, are nothing if not complicated, and probably always have been. Since ancient times, a few special types of cooking have enjoyed considerable prestige: Homer's warriors barbecued their own joints of meat at no cost to their heroic status or masculinity. And ever since, it has been socially acceptable for men to cook in public and professionally—for money. (Though it is only recently that professional chefs have enjoyed the status of artists.) But for most of history most of humanity's food has been cooked by women working out of

public view and without public recognition. Except for the rare ceremonial occasions over which men presided—the religious sacrifice,
the July 4 barbecue, the four-star restaurant—cooking has traditionally been women's work, part and parcel of homemaking and child
care, and therefore undeserving of serious—i.e., male—attention.

But there may be another reason cooking has not received its
proper due. In a recent book called *The Taste for Civilization*, Janet A.
Flammang, a feminist scholar and political scientist who has argued
eloquently for the social and political importance of "food work,"
suggests the problem may have something to do with food itself,
which by its very nature falls on the wrong side—the feminine side—
of the mind-body dualism in Western culture.

"Food is apprehended through the senses of touch, smell, and
taste," she points out, "which rank lower on the hierarchy of senses
than sight and hearing, which are typically thought to give rise to
knowledge. In most of philosophy, religion, and literature, food is
associated with body, animal, female, and appetite—things civilized
men have sought to overcome with knowledge and reason."

Very much to their loss.

II.

The premise of this book is that cooking—defined broadly enough
to take in the whole spectrum of techniques people have devised
for transforming the raw stuff of nature into nutritious and appealing
things for us to eat and drink—is one of the most interesting and
worthwhile things we humans do. This is not something I fully appreciated before I set out to learn how to cook. But after three years
spent working under a succession of gifted teachers to master four of
the key transformations we call cooking—grilling with fire, cooking

with liquid, baking bread, and fermenting all sorts of things—I came away with a very different body of knowledge from the one I went looking for. Yes, by the end of my education I got pretty good at making a few things—I'm especially proud of my bread and some of my braises. But I also learned things about the natural world (and our implication in it) that I don't think I could have learned any other way. I learned far more than I ever expected to about the nature of work, the meaning of health, about tradition and ritual, self-reliance and community, the rhythms of everyday life, and the supreme satisfaction of producing something I previously could only have imagined consuming, doing it outside of the cash economy for no other reason but love.

This book is the story of my education in the kitchen—but also in the bakery, the dairy, the brewery, and the restaurant kitchen, some of the places where much of our culture's cooking now takes place. *Cooked* is divided into four parts, one for each of the great transformations of nature into the culture we call cooking. Each of these, I was surprised and pleased to discover, corresponds to, and depends upon, one of the classical elements: Fire, Water, Air, and Earth.

Why this should be so I am not entirely sure. But for thousands of years and in many different cultures, these elements have been regarded as the four irreducible, indestructible ingredients that make up the natural world. Certainly they still loom large in our imagination. The fact that modern science has dismissed the classical elements, reducing them to still more elemental substances and forces—water to molecules of hydrogen and oxygen; fire to a process of rapid oxidation, etc.—hasn't really changed our lived experience of nature or the way we imagine it. Science may have replaced the big four with a periodic table of 118 elements, and then reduced each of those to ever-tinier particles, but our senses and our dreams have yet to get the news.

To learn to cook is to put yourself on intimate terms with the laws of physics and chemistry, as well as the facts of biology and microbiology. Yet, beginning with fire, I found that the older, prescientific elements figure largely—hugely, in fact—in apprehending the main transformations that comprise cooking, each in its own way. Each element proposes a different set of techniques for transforming nature, but also a different stance toward the world, a different kind of work, and a different mood.

Fire being the first element (in cooking anyway), I began my education with it, exploring the most basic and earliest kind of cookery: meat, on the grill. My quest to learn the art of cooking with fire took me a long way from my backyard grill, to the barbecue pits and pit masters of eastern North Carolina, where cooking meat still means a whole pig roasted very slowly over a smoldering wood fire. It was here, training under an accomplished and flamboyant pit master, that I got acquainted with cooking's primary colors—animal, wood, fire, time—and found a clearly marked path deep into the prehistory of cooking: what first drove our protohuman ancestors to gather around the cook fire, and how that experience transformed them. Killing and cooking a large animal has never been anything but an emotionally freighted and spiritually charged endeavor. Rituals of sacrifice have attended this sort of cooking from the beginning, and I found their echoes reverberating even today, in twenty-first-century barbecue. Then as now, the mood in fire cooking is heroic, masculine, theatrical, boastful, unironic, and faintly (sometimes not so faintly) ridiculous.

It is in fact everything that cooking with water, the subject of part II, is not. Historically, cooking with water comes after cooking with fire, since it awaited the invention of pots to cook in, an artifact of human culture only about ten thousand years old. Now cooking moves indoors, into the domestic realm, and in this chapter I delve into everyday home cookery, its techniques and satisfactions as well as its discontents. Befitting its subject, this section takes the shape of a single long recipe, unfolding step by step the age-old techniques that grandmothers developed for teasing delicious food from the most ordinary of ingredients: some aromatic plants, a little fat, a few scraps of meat, a long afternoon around the house. Here, too, I apprenticed myself to a flamboyant professional character, but she and I did most of our cooking at home in my kitchen, and often as a family—home and family being very much the subject of this section.

Part III takes up the element of air, which is all that distinguishes an exuberantly leavened loaf of bread from a sad gruel of pulverized grain. By figuring out how to coax air into our food, we elevate it and ourselves, transcending, and vastly improving, what nature gives us in a handful of grass seed. The story of Western civilization is pretty much the story of bread, which is arguably the first important "food processing" technology. (The counterargument comes from the brewers of beer, who may have gotten there first.) This section, which takes place in several different bakeries across the country (including a Wonder Bread plant), follows two personal quests: to bake a perfect, maximally airy and wholesome loaf of bread, and to pinpoint the precise historical moment that cooking took its fatefully wrong turn: when civilization began processing food in such a way as to make it less nutritious rather than more.

Different as they are, these first three modes of cooking all depend on heat. Not so the fourth. Like the earth itself, the various arts of fermentation rely instead on biology to transform organic matter from one state to a more interesting and nutritious other state. Here I encountered the most amazing alchemies of all: strong, allusive flavors and powerful intoxicants created for us by fungi and bacteria—many of them the denizens of the soil—as they go about their invisible work of creative destruction. This section falls into three chapters, covering the fermentation of vegetables (into sauerkraut, kimchi, pickles of all kinds); milk (into cheese); and alcohol (into mead and beer). Along the way, a succession of "fermentos" tutored me in the techniques of artfully managing rot, the folly of the modern war against bacteria, the erotics of disgust, and the somewhat upside-down notion that, while we were fermenting alcohol, alcohol has been fermenting us.

I have been fortunate in both the talent and the generosity of the teachers who agreed to take me in—the cooks, bakers, brewers, picklers, and cheese makers who shared their time and techniques and recipes. This cast of characters turned out to be a lot more masculine than I would have expected, and a reader might conclude that I have indulged in some unfortunate typecasting. But as soon as I opted to apprentice myself to professional rather than amateur cooks—in the hopes of acquiring the most rigorous training I could get—it was probably inevitable that certain stereotypes would be reinforced. It turns out that barbecue pit masters are almost exclusively men, as are brewers and bakers (except for pastry chefs), and a remarkable number of cheese makers are women. In learning to cook traditional pot dishes, I chose to work with a female chef, and if by doing so I underscored the cliché that home cooking is woman's work, that was sort of the idea: I wanted to delve into that very question. We can hope that all the gender stereotypes surrounding food and cooking will soon be thrown up for grabs, but to assume that has already happened would be to kid ourselves.

Taken as a whole, this is a "how-to" book, but of a very particular kind. Each section circles around a single elemental recipe—for barbecue, for a braise, for bread, and for a small handful of fermented items—and by the end of it, you should be well enough equipped to make it. (The recipes are spelled out more concisely in appendix I, in case you do want to try any of them.) Though all the cooking I describe can be done in a home kitchen, only a portion of the book deals directly with the kind of work most people regard as "home cooking." Several of the recipes here are for things most readers will probably never make themselves—beer, for example, or cheese, or even bread. Though I hope that they will. Because I discovered there was much to learn from attempting, even if only just once, these more ambitious and time-consuming forms of cookery, knowledge that might not at first seem terribly useful but in fact changes everything about one's relationship to food and what is possible in the kitchen. Let me try to explain.

At bottom cooking is not a single process but, rather, comprises a small set of technologies, some of the most important humans have yet devised. They changed us first as a species, and then at the level of the group, the family, and the individual. These technologies range from the controlled use of fire to the manipulation of specific microorganisms to transform grain into bread or alcohol all the way to the microwave oven—the last major innovation. So cooking is really a continuum of processes, from simple to complex, and Cooked is, among other things, a natural and social history of these transformations, both the ones that are still part of our everyday lives and the ones that are not. Today, we're apt to think of making cheese or brewing beer as "extreme" forms of cookery, only because so few of us have ever attempted them, but of course at one time all these transformations took place in the household and everyone had at least a rudimentary knowledge of how to perform them. Nowadays, only a small handful of cooking's technologies seem within the reach of our competence. This represents not only a loss of knowledge, but a loss of a kind of power, too. And it is entirely possible that, within another generation, cooking a meal from scratch will seem as exotic and ambitious—as "extreme"—as most of us today regard brewing beer or baking a loaf of bread or putting up a crock of sauerkraut.

When that happens—when we no longer have any direct personal knowledge of how these wonderful creations are made—food will have become completely abstracted from its various contexts: from the labor of human hands, from the natural world of plants and animals, from imagination and culture and community. Indeed, food is already well on its way into that ether of abstraction, toward becoming mere fuel or pure image. So how might we begin to bring it back to earth?

My wager in Cooked is that the best way to recover the reality of food, to return it to a proper place in our lives, is by attempting to master the physical processes by which it has traditionally been made. The good news is that this is still within our reach, no matter how limited our skills in the kitchen. My own apprenticeship necessitated a journey far beyond my own kitchen (and comfort zone), to some of the farther reaches of cookery, in the hopes of confronting the essential facts of the matter, and discovering exactly what it is about these transformations that helped make us who we are. But perhaps my happiest discovery was that the wonders of cooking, even its most ambitious manifestations, rely on a magic that remains accessible to all of us, at home.

I should add that the journey has been great fun, probably the most fun I've ever had while still ostensibly "working." What is more gratifying, after all, than discovering you can actually make something delicious (or intoxicating) that you simply assumed you'd always have to buy in the marketplace? Or finding yourself in that sweet spot where the frontier between work and play disappears in a cloud of bread flour or fragrant steam rising from a boiling kettle of wort?

Even in the case of the seemingly most impractical cooking adventures, I learned things of an unexpectedly practical value. After you've tried your hand at brewing or pickling or slow roasting a whole hog, everyday home cooking becomes much less daunting, and in certain ways easier. My own backyard barbecuing has been informed and improved by my hours hanging around the barbecue pit. Working with bread dough has taught me how to trust my hands and my senses in the kitchen, and to have enough confidence in their reporting to free me from the bonds of recipe and measuring cup. And having spent time in the bakeries of artisans as well as in a Wonder Bread factory, my appreciation for a good loaf of bread has grown much more keen. Same for a wedge of cheese or bottle of beer: What had always been just products, good or bad, now reveal themselves as so much more than that—as achievements, as expressions, as relationships. By itself, this added increment of eating and drinking pleasure would have been enough to justify all the so-called work.

But perhaps the most important thing I learned by doing this work is how cooking implicates us in a whole web of social and ecological relationships: with plants and animals, with the soil, with farmers, with the microbes both inside and outside our bodies, and, of course, with the people our cooking nourishes and delights. Above all else, what I found in the kitchen is that cooking connects.

Cooking—of whatever kind, everyday or extreme—situates us in the world in a very special place, facing the natural world on one side and the social world on the other. The cook stands squarely between nature and culture, conducting a process of translation and negotiation. Both nature and culture are transformed by the work. And in the process, I discovered, so is the cook.

III.

As I grew steadily more comfortable in the kitchen, I found that, much like gardening, most cooking manages to be agreeably absorbing without being too demanding intellectually. It leaves plenty of mental space for daydreaming and reflection. One of the things I reflected on is the whole question of taking on what in our time has become, strictly speaking, optional, even unnecessary work, work for which I am not particularly gifted or qualified, and at which I may never get very good. This is, in the modern world, the unspoken question that hovers over all our cooking: Why bother?

By any purely rational calculation, even everyday home cooking (much less baking bread or fermenting kimchi) is probably not a wise use of my time. Not long ago, I read an Op Ed piece in *The Wall Street Journal* about the restaurant industry, written by the couple that publishes the Zagat restaurant guides, which took exactly this line. Rather than coming home after work to cook, the Zagats suggested, "people would be better off staying an extra hour in the office doing what they do well, and letting bargain restaurants do what they do best."

Here in a nutshell is the classic argument for the division of labor, which, as Adam Smith and countless others have pointed out, has given us many of the blessings of civilization. It is what allows me to make a living sitting at this screen writing, while others grow my food, sew my clothes, and supply the energy that lights and heats my house. I can probably earn more in an hour of writing or even teaching than I could save in a whole week of cooking. Specialization is undeniably a powerful social and economic force. And yet it is also debilitating. It breeds helplessness, dependence, and ignorance and, eventually, it undermines any sense of responsibility.

Our society assigns us a tiny number of roles: We're producers of one thing at work, consumers of a great many other things all the rest of the time, and then, once a year or so, we take on the temporary role of citizen and cast a vote. Virtually all our needs and desires we delegate to specialists of one kind or another—our meals to the food industry, our health to the medical profession, entertainment to Hollywood and the media, mental health to the therapist or the drug company, caring for nature to the environmentalist, political action to the politician, and on and on it goes. Before long it becomes hard to imagine doing much of anything for ourselves—anything, that is, except the work we do "to make a living." For everything else, we feel like we've lost the skills, or that there's someone who can do it better. (I recently heard about an agency that will dispatch a sympathetic someone to visit your elderly parents if you can't spare the time to do it yourself.) It seems as though we can no longer imagine anyone but a professional or an institution or a product supplying our daily needs or solving our problems. This learned helplessness is, of course, much to the advantage of the corporations eager to step forward and do all this work for us.

One problem with the division of labor in our complex economy is how it obscures the lines of connection, and therefore of responsibility, between our everyday acts and their real-world consequences. Specialization makes it easy to forget about the filth of the coal-fired power plant that is lighting this pristine computer screen, or the back-breaking labor it took to pick the strawberries for my cereal, or the misery of the hog that lived and died so I could enjoy my bacon. Specialization neatly hides our implication in all that is done on our behalf by unknown other specialists half a world away.

Perhaps what most commends cooking to me is that it offers a powerful corrective to this way of being in the world—a corrective that is still available to all of us. To butcher a pork shoulder is to be forcibly reminded that this is the shoulder of a large mammal, made up of distinct groups of muscles with a purpose quite apart from feeding me. The work itself gives me a keener interest in the story of the hog: where it came from and how it found its way to my kitchen. In my hands its flesh feels a little less like the product of industry than of nature; indeed, less like a product at all. Likewise, to grow the greens I'm serving with this pork, greens that in late spring seem to grow back almost as fast as I can cut them, is a daily reminder of nature's abundance, the everyday miracle by which photons of light are turned into delicious things to eat.

Handling these plants and animals, taking back the production and the preparation of even just some part of our food, has the salutary effect of making visible again many of the lines of connection that the supermarket and the "home-meal replacement" have succeeded in obscuring, yet of course never actually eliminated. To do so is to take back a measure of responsibility, too, to become, at the very least, a little less glib in one's pronouncements.

Especially one's pronouncements about "the environment," which suddenly begins to seem a little less "out there" and a lot closer to home. For what is the environmental crisis if not a crisis of the way we live? The Big Problem is nothing more or less than the sum total of countless little everyday choices, most of them made by us (consumer spending represents nearly three-quarters of the U.S. economy) and the rest of them made by others in the name of our needs and desires. If the environmental crisis is ultimately a crisis of character, as Wendell Berry told us way back in the 1970s, then sooner or later it will have to be addressed at that level—at home, as it were. In our yards and kitchens and minds.

As soon as you start down this path of thinking, the quotidian space of the kitchen appears in a startling new light. It begins to matter more than we ever imagined. The unspoken reason why political reformers from Vladimir Lenin to Betty Friedan sought to get women out of the kitchen was that nothing of importance—nothing worthy of their talents and intelligence and convictions—took place there. The only worthy arenas for consequential action were the workplace and the public square. But this was before the environmental crisis had come into view, and before the industrialization of our eating created a crisis in our health. Changing the world will always require action and participation in the public realm, but in our time that will no longer be sufficient. We'll have to change the way we live, too. What that means is that the sites of our everyday engagement with nature—our kitchens, gardens, houses, cars—matter to the fate of the world in a way they never have before.

To cook or not to cook thus becomes a consequential question. Though I realize that is putting the matter a bit too bluntly. Cooking means different things at different times to different people; seldom is it an all-or-nothing proposition. Yet even to cook a few more nights a week than you already do, or to devote a Sunday to making a few meals for the week, or perhaps to try every now and again to make something you only ever expected to buy—even these modest acts will constitute a kind of a vote. A vote for what, exactly? Well, in a world where so few of us are obliged to cook at all anymore, to choose to do so is to lodge a protest against specialization—against the total rationalization of life. Against the infiltration of commercial interests into every last cranny of our lives. To cook for the pleasure of it, to devote a portion of our leisure to it, is to declare our independence from the corporations seeking to organize our every waking moment into yet another occasion for consumption. (Come to think of it, our nonwaking moments as well: Ambien, anyone?) It is to reject the de- bilitating notion that, at least while we're at home, production is work best done by someone else, and the only legitimate form of leisure is consumption. This dependence marketers call "freedom."

Cooking has the power to transform more than plants and animals: It transforms us, too, from mere consumers into producers. Not completely, not all the time, but I have found that even to shift the ratio between these two identities a few degrees toward the side of production yields deep and unexpected satisfactions. *Cooked* is an invitation to alter, however slightly, the ratio between production and consumption in your life. The regular exercise of these simple skills for producing some of the necessities of life increases self-reliance and freedom while reducing our dependence on distant corporations. Not just our money but our power flows toward them whenever we cannot supply any of our everyday needs and desires ourselves. And it begins to flow back toward us, and our community, as soon as we decide to take some responsibility for feeding ourselves. This has been an early lesson of the rising movement to rebuild local food economies, a movement that ultimately depends for its success on our willingness to put more thought and effort into feeding ourselves. Not every day, not every meal—but more often than we do, whenever we can.

Cooking, I found, gives us the opportunity, so rare in modern life, to work directly in our own support, and in the support of the people we feed. If this is not "making a living," I don't know what is. In the calculus of economics, doing so may not always be the most efficient use of an amateur cook's time, but in the calculus of human emotion, it is beautiful even so. For is there any practice less selfish, any labor less alienated, any time less wasted, than preparing something delicious and nourishing for people you love?

So let's begin.

At the beginning, with fire.

PART I

FIRE

CREATURES OF THE FLAME

"Roasting is both nothing at all and absolutely
everything."

—*Marquis de Cussy,* L'Art Culinaire

"Once men indulged in wicked cannibal habits,
and numerous other vices; when a man of
better genius arose, who first sacrificed
[animal] victims, and did roast their flesh.
And, as the meat surpassed the flesh of man,
they then ate man no longer. . . ."

—*Athenaeus,* The Deipnosophists

"This art of mine is an empire of smoke."

—*Demetrius,* The Areopagite

I.

AYDEN, NORTH CAROLINA

The divine scent of wood smoke and roasting pig finds you as soon as you make the turn onto South Lee Street, the main artery threading this faded little town, even though the GPS says its source is still half a mile away. For a Wednesday afternoon in May, an impressive number of adults—some white, more black—are doing front-porch duty along Lee Street, sipping amber liquids that might be tea. Why Ayden has faded so is not hard to guess. The town is an hour off the interstate, on the way to not much of anywhere. The national chains set out their big boxes a dozen miles to the north, in Greenville, draining the economic life from Ayden's downtown, much of which stands shuttered. Ayden once supported three barbecue joints; now there is one, though its fame has spread far enough to lure a few hungry travelers off the interstate every day. The agriculture that used to nourish the town's economy has suffered both the decline of tobacco (only the occasional emerald acre of it survives amid the paler fields of corn) and the rise of CAFOs—"Concentrated Animal Feeding Operations."

The coastal plain of North Carolina is one of the sacrifice zones that Big Hog has consecrated to industrial pork production, a business that shrinks the number of farmers in a region even as it massively expands the population of pigs. Long before I registered the pheromone of barbecue, occasional passages of less winning animal odors assailed my nostrils as I navigated the gray roads leading into Ayden.

My destination this sparkling May afternoon is the Skylight Inn, Ayden's lone surviving barbecue restaurant, and even without the perfume of oak and hickory, the place would have been impossible to miss. The Skylight Inn is housed in a cheerfully ridiculous building. A low-slung octagon of brick is crowned with a silver mansard roof that is itself crowned with a replica of the Capitol Rotunda. High above the dome flaps an American flag. The proportions of this ramshackle wedding cake strongly suggest that no architect was involved in its conception, but that, more likely, the design process involved some strong drink and a napkin. The silvery dome went up in 1984, a few years after *National Geographic* declared the Skylight Inn "the barbecue capital of the world." (There is no skylight, which is odd for what is otherwise such a literal building.) A billboard towers over the parking lot, highlighting one of the restaurant's numerous mottos ("If it's not cooked with wood it's not Bar-B-Q") and a drawing of the late Pete Jones, the Skylight Inn's founding father. Jones fired up its pits for the first time in 1947. But the sign will have you know that the family's roots in barbecue go back much further than that: "Upholding a family tradition since 1830." Family legend has it that an ancestor by the name of Skilton Dennis launched the very first barbecue enterprise in North Carolina, and possibly the world, in 1830, when he began selling pit-cooked pork and flat cornbread from a covered wagon not too far from here. Whenever Samuel Jones—Pete's grandson and one of three Jones men now safeguarding the family tradition—speaks of these giants of barbecue, he refers to them, unironically, as "our forefathers."

I know this much (and much more) about the Skylight Inn before even setting foot on the premises because I have read the oral histories and watched the documentaries. These days there is little about Southern barbecue that hasn't been meticulously documented and fulsomely celebrated; for a sleepy vernacular cooking tradition, barbecue has woken up and become notably self-aware. No self-respecting Southern pit master (and self-respect is something most of them have, in bulk) lacks for a sack of sound bites as homespun and well worn as a politician's. He finds plenty of occasions to deploy them, too, whether to visiting journalists or in barbecue competitions or at academic conferences organized by the Southern Foodways Alliance.

What I was chasing here in North Carolina was not a sound bite but a taste, one I'd never experienced before, and also an idea. The idea goes something like this: If fire is the first and most fundamental form of cookery—of the handful of ways humans have devised for transforming the stuff of nature into the stuff of our sustenance and pleasure—then, for an American at least, whole-hog barbecue over a wood fire represents the purest, most unreconstructed expression of that form. By learning what I could about how that work is performed, and how it fits into a community and a culture, I was hoping to learn something about the deeper meaning of this curious, uniquely human activity called cooking. Along the way, I hoped to get a little better at cooking with fire myself. By now, cooking has become so thickly crusted with pretension and gadgetry and marketing hype that the effort to reduce it to its most basic elements, to drive it into a corner and see it plainly, seemed like a good way to take hold of it again. I had reason to believe the Skylight's pit room might offer one such corner.

I know, the quest for authenticity is a fraught and often dubious enterprise, and nowhere more so than in the American South in this time of acute gastronomical self-awareness. When I asked a friend, a chef in Chapel Hill, where she liked to go for barbecue, I could almost hear the sigh in her e-mail: "Driving around NC, I always think that I am about to run into that perfect time-capsule bbq restaurant, but it hasn't happened yet." My friend hadn't yet made it out to Ayden, however, so I allowed myself to hope.

If I wanted to solve for the powerful, primordial equation of pig–plus–wood-smoke–plus–time, the pit behind the Skylight Inn certainly sounded like a place I needed to check out. The Joneses were "barbecue fundamentalists," in the words of one barbecue historian (yes, barbecue now has historians), refusing for several generations to tinker with the basic equation: They cook, exclusively and slowly, whole hogs over "live" oak and hickory coals. They disdain charcoal as a modern-day declension and sauce as "a cover-up for bad cooking." To judge from the captivating smells emanating from their chimneys, the Joneses' fidelity to tradition has served them and their customers well. It has also justified the heroic effort required to defend their "dying art" against the various forces attempting to kill it: the scrutiny of the health department and the fraying patience of the fire department, the convenience of natural gas and stainless steel, the scarcity of firewood, the ubiquity of fast food, and the desire on the part of the pitman for a decent night's sleep, one undisturbed by dreams of conflagration. Or actual sirens. For I had heard that the Skylight Inn's cookhouse has endured more or less regular fires, and in fact has burned to the ground on more than one occasion. The first thing anyone who cooks with live fire will tell you is that it all comes down to one word—"control." But it turns out that that is considerably harder to achieve than you might think, even in the twenty-first century.

8

The control of fire is so ancient and represents such a momentous turn in human history that it has engendered a great many myths and theories to explain how it might have come to pass. Some of these are just plain crazy, and not only the ancient ones, either. Take Sigmund Freud's theory, for example. In a footnote to *Civilization and Its Discontents*, Freud traces the control of fire to the fateful moment when man—and by "man" in this case he really means *man*—first overcame the urge to extinguish whatever fires he chanced upon by peeing on them. For countless millennia this urge apparently proved irresistible, much to the detriment of civilization, the rise of which awaited its repression. Perhaps because putting out fires with one's stream of urine is some-thing women can't do very well, the activity served as an important form of male competition, one that Freud suggests (no surprise here) was homoerotic in character. Cooking with fire remains very much a competitive male preserve, and those of us who do it should probably count ourselves lucky Freud isn't around to offer his analysis of ex-actly what it is we're up to.

The course of human history shifted on the fateful day when it dawned on some fellow possessed of an unusual degree of self-control that he didn't *have* to pee on the fire, and could instead pre-serve the flames and put them to some good use: keeping himself warm, say, or cooking his dinner. Freud believed this advance, like so much else of value in civilization, owed to the unique human ability to govern, or repress, the inner drives and urges before which other animals are powerless. (Not that we have many reports of animals putting out fires with *their* urine.) For him, the control of self is the precondition for the control of fire and, in turn, for the civilization that that discovery made possible. "This great cultural conquest was thus the reward for his renunciation of instinct."

In all the time I've now spent with pit masters, whiling away the hours before the smoldering logs, I've never once brought up Freud's fire theory. I'm just not sure how well it would go over. I have, however, on occasion brought up a second theory, one that, though it is equally outlandish, contains a bright cinder of poetic truth that can usually be counted on to bring a smile to the streaked, perspiring face of a barbecue man.

This is the theory put forward by Charles Lamb, the English writer (1775–1834), in his essay, "A Dissertation upon Roast Pig." Lamb claims that all meat was eaten raw until the art of roasting was accidentally discovered, in China, by a young man named Bo-bo, the dimwitted son of a swineherd named Ho-ti. One day, while Ho-ti was off gathering mast for his pigs, his son—"a great lubberly boy" who liked to play with fire—accidentally burned down his family's cottage, in the process incinerating a litter of piglets. While he was surveying the ruins and deciding what to tell his father, "an odor assailed his nostrils, unlike any scent which he had before experienced." When Bo-bo reached down to feel one of the burnt pigs for any sign of life, he singed his fingers and then instinctively touched them to his tongue.

"Some of the crumbs of the scorched skin had come away with his fingers, and for the first time in his life (in the world's life indeed, for before him no man had known it) he tasted—crackling!"

Bo-bo's father returned to find his cottage in ruins, his piglets dead, and his son gorging himself on their corpses. Ho-ti was sickened by the scene of carnage, until his son exclaimed to him "how nice the burnt pigs tasted," and, bewitched by the extraordinary aroma, he, too, sampled a piece of crackling and found it irresistibly delicious. Father and son decided to keep their discovery secret from their neighbors, whose disapproval they feared; to burn one of god's creatures was, after all, to imply it was less than perfect raw. But in time

> Strange stories got about. It was observed that Ho-ti's cottage was burnt down more frequently than ever. Nothing but fires from this time forward . . . As often as the sow farrowed, so sure was the house of Ho-ti to be in a blaze.

Their secret eventually got out, neighbors tried the technique for themselves and marveled at the results, and the practice caught on. In fact, the custom of burning down houses to improve the taste of piglets grew so widespread that people began to worry that the art and science of architecture would be lost to the world. ("People built slighter and slighter every day," Lamb tells us, and "now there was nothing to be seen but fires in every direction.") Fortunately, a wiser head eventually figured out that the flesh of pigs might be cooked "without the necessity of consuming a whole house to dress it." The invention of the gridiron and then the spit soon followed. And so did humankind discover quite by accident the art of cooking meat over fire—or, rather, we should probably specify, over a *controlled* fire.

"Welcome to the vestibule of hell." Samuel Jones chuckled as he walked me around back of the Skylight Inn to visit the cookhouse where the pits are. There were two cookhouses, actually, cinder-block buildings the size of cottages sited at odd, arbitrary angles to both the restaurant and each other. ("Granddaddy apparently hired a drunk to design everything out here," Samuel explained.) The larger of the two buildings had recently been completely rebuilt, having burned to the ground late one night after one of its brick hearths had failed. "We keep those fires burning twenty-four/seven, and every couple of years even the firebricks lining the inside of the chimneys just give out." He shrugged. "I'd say this cookhouse has caught on fire about a dozen times. But that's just how it goes when you're doing whole-hog barbecue the right way."

Sometimes it's the hog grease that pools in the bottom of the pit that catches fire; other times a burning cinder will climb the column of smoke rising through the chimney and then fall back onto the roof. Just the other night, Samuel happened to be driving by the restaurant a couple of hours after closing time when he noticed a tongue of flame licking out from beneath the smoke-room door. "Now, that was a *real* close call," he smiled. (A surveillance camera in the cookhouse indicated the fire had started only four minutes after the pitman had left for the night.)

Charles Lamb would no doubt be pleased to know that there are still men in North Carolina upholding the tradition of burning down whole buildings in order to improve the flavor of pigs.

Samuel is a cheery, round-faced, goateed man of twenty-nine who has been working in the family business off and on since he was nine years old. He is abundantly proud of the institution his family has built, and feels a profound sense of obligation to keep the tradition not just going but uncontaminated by modern innovations, aka "shortcuts." Southern barbecue is ever looking only backward, but over time that gets harder and harder to do. "It's a fact that our family cannot ever sell this business," he explains, perhaps a bit ruefully, "because, see, we're grandfathered in. With the health department. Anyone who bought it who wasn't a Jones? Well, they would have to bring the place up to code, and right there, that would be the end of it."

As we stepped into the new cookhouse, I could immediately see what he meant. Actually, I couldn't see much of anything at first: The room was wreathed in a thick fog of fragrant wood smoke, and though it couldn't have been more than twenty-five feet from one end of the building to the other, I could barely make out the steel door on the far wall. At either end of the room stands a big, deep brick fireplace, in which a monster-sized grate fabricated from car axles holds a tall stack of flaming logs. Bright-orange cinders drop between the axles, where they're scooped out with a shovel and then fed into the pits. The pits line both of the long walls: a sarcophagus of brick, maybe three feet tall, with iron bars running across them to hold up the hogs and, suspended above each of them by cables, a four-by-eight sheet of black steel, hinged and counterweighted with cinder blocks, to cover them. The pits can hold as many as a dozen two-hundred-pound hogs at a time. On the insides, the pits are caked with an oily black grime that would definitely horrify a health inspector, except perhaps a North Carolina health inspector. It seems that the state has instituted a special, more lenient health code for barbecue establishments; that, and the informal grandfather clause to which Samuel had alluded, is all that stands between a place like this and condemnation.

"Yeah, we clean the pits now and then, depending," Samuel offered when I broached the sanitation issue. "But you don't want to clean them the whole way out, because then you're losing all that good insulation." The problem is, that cake of grime, which a chemist would probably say consists of equal parts saturated pig fat and the particulate matter suspended in wood smoke, is highly flammable. So, it seems, is the smoke we were breathing, which, to my alarm, Samuel claimed could actually ignite if it got sufficiently thick and the room sufficiently hot. "That's called a flash-over," he offered. Samuel has become, perforce, a close if not always entirely successful student of fire. He mentioned he'd joined the Ayden Volunteer Fire Department. Under the circumstances, this would seem like the politic thing to do.

§

The vestibule of hell: The pit room was in fact an infernal chamber, and not a place likely to stimulate an appetite for cooked pig in many people. The residues of fires big and small were everywhere, blackening the bricks, charring the ceiling, puckering the plywood walls. While Samuel and I talked, I could see over his left shoulder a spectral presence emerging out of the smoke, the figure of a slightly bent black man slowly pushing a wheelbarrow topped with a sheet of blood-stained plywood on which the splayed pink carcass of a hog precariously balanced. I could see the hog's eyeless head, bobbing slightly on the lip of the wheelbarrow, and, as it drew closer, the face of the man carefully inching it forward. It was deeply lined, leathery, and missing several teeth.

Samuel introduced me to James Henry Howell, the Skylight Inn's longtime pit master. Howell made it instantly clear he would be leaving all the talking to the Joneses. He had work to do, and indeed it appeared that the lion's share of the physical labor performed at the restaurant—putting on the hogs late in the afternoon, flipping them over first thing the next morning, carrying them, quartered, into the restaurant kitchen for the lunchtime rush, and then chopping and seasoning them on the big wooden block—was work that James Henry Howell did himself, leaving the Jones men free to hold forth. Which was fine by me, except it meant I probably wouldn't be getting any hands-on experience or how-to instruction here in Ayden. That was going to have to wait.

Back and forth across the pit room Mr. Howell slowly wheeled his hogs, melting into the haze to fetch another carcass from the walk-in cooler, then emerging again with his load, which he would tenderly tip onto the iron grates. Howell worked slowly and deliberately, and when he was done putting the hogs on, he had created an arresting tableau: a smoke-dimmed conga line of splayed pink carcasses, laid out skin side up and snout to butt. The interior of the cookhouse now looked like a bunkroom, the sleeping hogs bedded down for the night. Of all the animals we eat, none resembles us more closely than the hog. Each the size of a grown man, hairless and pink, its mouth set in what looks very much like a sly smile, the half dozen pigs laid out in this smoky crypt made me think of many things, but definitely not lunch or dinner.

It was difficult to regard this pit room, filthy and littered with cinders, as a kitchen, but of course that is what it is. And that is why the state of North Carolina has been forced to choose between the equitable enforcement of its health codes and the survival of whole-hog barbecue. Sacred local tradition that it is, barbecue has won, at least for the time being. But this is a most unusual kitchen, one where the principal cooking implements are wheelbarrows and shovels, and the pantry, such as it is, contains nothing but hogs, firewood, and salt. In fact, the entire building is a kind of cooking implement, as Samuel explained: We were inside a giant low-temperature oven for the gentle smoking of pigs. Just how tightly the cookhouse is sealed—even the pitch of its roof—all influence the way the meat cooks.

After the hogs are on, Howell begins shoveling wood coals underneath them, transferring the smoldering cinders, one spade-full at a time, from the hearths, now glowing a deep red, across the room to the pits. Carefully pouring the incandescent coals between the iron bars, he arranges a line of fire roughly around the perimeter of each hog, a bit like the chalk line silhouetting the body at a crime scene. He puts more coals at the ends than in the middle, to compensate for the fact that the different parts of the hog cook at different rates. "That's just one of the challenges of whole-hog cooking," Samuel explained. "Cooking just shoulders, like they do over in Lexington, now, that's a whole lot easier to control." Samuel snorts the word "shoulders" derisively, as if cooking pork shoulders was like throwing frankfurters on the grill. " 'Course, that's not barbecue in our view."

After he's arranged the coals to his satisfaction, Howell splashes water on the backs of the hogs and sprinkles a few generous handfuls of kosher salt—not to flavor it, Samuel said, but to dry out the skin and encourage it to blister, thereby helping to effect its transubstantiation into crackling.

It is a long, laborious way to cook. Mr. Howell will shovel a few more coals around the drip line of each pig every half hour or so until he leaves for the evening at six. Several hours later, around midnight, co-owner Jeff Jones, whom everyone seems to call Uncle Jeff, will have to stop back in to check if the pigs need any more heat on them. The idea behind the line of perimeter fire is to build a lasting, indirect source of heat, so that the hogs cook as slowly as possible through the night. Yet at the same time you want those coals close enough to the pig's drip line so that when its back fat begins to render, some of it will have some nice hot coals on which to drip. The sizzle of those drippings sends up a different, meatier kind of smoke, which adds another layer of flavor to the pork. It also perfumes the air in a way that a wood fire alone does not.

That perfume is what I could smell from the road, and what I was beginning to smell again. Even now, standing here in the middle of this sepulchral chamber slightly starved for oxygen, hemmed between these two serried ranks of the porky dead, I was more than a little surprised to register somewhere deep in my belly the first stirrings of . . . an appetite!

It is a powerful thing, the scent of meat roasting on an open fire, which is to say the smell of wood smoke combined with burning animal fat. We humans are strongly drawn to it. I've had the neighbor's children drift over "for a closer smell" when I've roasted a pork shoulder on the fire pit in the front yard. Another time, a six-year-old dinner guest positioned himself downwind of the same cook fire, stretched out his arms like an orchestra conductor, and inhaled deeply of the meaty-woody perfume, once, twice, and then abruptly stopped himself, explaining that "I'd better not fill up on smoke!"

Apparently the same perfume is equally pleasing to the gods, whose portion of the animals we sacrifice to them has traditionally been not the flesh of these animals but their smoke. There are two good reasons for this. Humans must eat to survive, but gods, being immortal, have no such animal needs. (If they did, they would also need to digest and then, well, eliminate, which doesn't seem terribly godlike.) No, the *idea* of meat, the smoky, ethereal trace of animal flesh wafting up to heaven, is what the gods want from us. They can and do fill up on smoke. And besides, if the gods did demand cuts, how would we ever get their portion of meat to them? The fragrant column of smoke, symbolizing the link between heaven and earth, is the only conceivable medium of conveyance, and also communication, between humans and their gods. So to say this aroma is divine is more than an empty expression.

People have known that the smoke of roasting meat is pleasing to the gods at least since the time of Genesis, where we learn of several momentous sacrifices that altered man's relationship to God and disclosed divine preferences. The first such sacrifice was actually two: the offerings of Cain and Abel. Cain, a tiller of the fields, sacrificed a portion of his crop to Yahweh, and Abel, a shepherd, a choice animal from his flock—and God made it clear it was the sacrifice of domestic quadrupeds he prefers.* The next momentous sacrifice came after the waters of the Flood receded, when Noah, back on dry land at last, made a "burnt offering" to Yahweh. This is a type of sacrifice in which the entire animal is burned to a crisp—i.e., turned to smoke, and thereby offered to God. "And the Lord smelled a sweet savour; and the Lord said in his heart, I will not again curse the ground any more for man's sake . . . neither will I again smite any more every thing living, as I have done." (Genesis 8:21) If there was ever any doubt about the efficacy of animal sacrifice (not to mention the sheer power of scent), Noah's experience should have put it to rest: The aroma of burning meat is so pleasing to God that it tempered his wrath and moved him to take the option of worldwide doom completely off the table for all time.

It's striking how many different cultures at so many different times have practiced some form of animal sacrifice involving the roasting of meat over a fire, and just how many of these rituals conceived of the smoke from these cook fires as a medium of communication between humans and gods. Anthropologists tell us some such practice is very nearly universal in traditional cultures; indeed, you might say it is the *absence* of such a ritual in our own culture that is probably the greater anomaly. Though it may be that the faded outlines of such rituals can still be glimpsed in something like whole-hog barbecue.

But the prominence of smoke in rituals of animal sacrifice suggests we need to add another myth of the origins of cooking to our growing pile: Maybe cookery begins with ritual sacrifice, since putting meat on a fire solves for the problem of how exactly to deliver the sacrificial animals to their heavenly recipients.

*Though later, in Leviticus, rules governing grain sacrifices are spelled out in detail; the commentaries suggest such rituals allowed people who could not afford to sacrifice an animal to nevertheless make an acceptable offering.

8

What the gods have demanded from us in terms of sacrifice has gotten progressively less onerous over time. So what started out as a solemn, psychologically traumatic ritual eventually evolved into a ceremonial feast. Human sacrifice gave way to animal sacrifice, which in turn gave way to partial animal sacrifice in a happy series of dilutions culminating (or petering out) in the modern backyard barbecue, where the religious element is, if not completely absent, then pretty well muffled. It's not a big conceptual leap to go from the observation that the gods seem perfectly happy with a meal of smoke to realizing that maybe we don't have to incinerate the *whole* animal in a burnt offering in order to satisfy them. The gods can enjoy the smoke of the roasting animal, and we can enjoy the meat. How convenient!

But keeping the best cuts of sacrificial animals for human consumption is an innovation hard won, at least in classical mythology, and the figure responsible for it paid a heavy personal price. The Prometheus legend is usually read as a story about man's hubris in challenging the gods, the theft of fire representing the human assumption of divine prerogative—costly yet a great boon to civilization. All this is true enough, but in the original telling, by Hesiod, the story is a little different. Here, it turns out to be as much about the theft of meat as it is about the theft of fire.

In Hesiod's *Theogony*, Prometheus first incurred Zeus's wrath by playing a trick on him during the ritual sacrifice of an ox at Mecone. Prometheus hid the best cuts of beef inside a nasty-looking ox stomach but wrapped the bones in an attractive layer of fat. Prometheus then offered Zeus his choice of sacrificial offerings, and the Olympian, deceived by the "glistening fat," opted for the bones, thereby leaving the tasty cuts of beef for the mortals. This set a new precedent for animal sacrifices—henceforth men would keep the best cuts for themselves, and burn the fat and bones for the gods, as indeed is the custom observed throughout the *Odyssey*. (What Henry Fielding called "Homer's wonderful book about eating.")

Infuriated, Zeus retaliated by hiding fire from man, making it difficult, if not impossible, for men to enjoy their meat. Indeed, without the cook fire humans are no better than animals, which must eat their meat raw.* Prometheus then proceeded to steal it back, hiding the flames in the pith of a giant fennel stalk. In retribution, Zeus chained Prometheus eternally to a rock (where his liver became the unending feast—the raw meat—of another creature) and sent down to mortal men a world of trouble, in the form of Pandora, the first woman.

In Hesiod's telling, the Prometheus story becomes a myth of the origin of cooking, an account of how animal sacrifice evolved into a form of feasting, thanks to Prometheus' daring reapportionment of the sacrificial animal to favor man. It is also a story about human identity—how the possession of fire allowed us to distinguish ourselves from the animals. But the fire in question—the fire that elevates us above the beasts—is specifically a cook fire, and what had been strictly a religious observance—a burnt offering of an entire animal to the gods in a gesture of subservience—becomes a very different kind of ritual, one with the power to bind the human community together in the sharing of a tasty meal.

The dining room of the Skylight Inn could not be much less ceremonial: wood-grain Formica tables scattered beneath fluorescent lights;

---

*In Greek thought, which obsessively worries the distinctions between man and animal, "raw eater" (omophagos) is a cutting epithet, bearing connotations of savagery. Cyclops commits a double outrage against civilization when he eats Odysseus' sailors without cooking them first.

a sign over the counter with old-timey snap-in plastic letters listing your options; faded newspaper and magazine clippings about the establishment, and portraits of the forefathers, decorating the walls. By the door, a glass case proudly displays the restaurant's James Beard Award from 2003.

But there is one ceremonial touch: Directly behind the counter where you place your order sits an enormous chopping block, a kind of barbecue altar where one of the Joneses, or their designated seconds, officiates at lunch and dinner, chopping with heavy cleavers whole hogs in full view of the assembled diners. The maple-wood block is nearly six inches thick, but only at the perimeter. So much pork has been chopped on it that the center of the block has been worn down to a thickness of only an inch or two.

"We flip it over every year or so, and then, when that side wears down, we have to get a new one," Samuel told me, with the glint I'd learned to recognize as a sign that a tasty BBQ sound bite was fast approaching. "Some customers look at our chopping block and say, Hey, there must be a lot of wood in your barbecue. We say, Uh-yeah, and our wood is better than most other people's barbecue!"

The dull rhythmic knock-knock-knock of cleaver hitting wood is the constant soundtrack of the Skylight dining room. ("That's how you know you're getting fresh barbecue," says Uncle Jeff.) Above the chopper's head, the menu board lists a succinct handful of choices: Barbecue sandwich ($2.75); barbecue in trays (small, medium, and large, from $4.50 to $5.50) and barbecue by the pound ($9.50); along the bottom, the sign promises "all orders with slaw and cornbread." A few soft drinks, and that's it. The only things on the menu that have changed since 1947 are the prices, and those not by all that much. (The price of a barbecue sandwich at the Skylight Inn undercuts that of a Big Mac—$2.99—at the McDonald's in Ayden, one of the few instances where slow food beats fast food on price.) The next Skylight sound bite goes like this: "We got barbecue, slaw, and cornbread, that's all," Samuel recites. "When you come here, it's not what you want, it's how much of it you need."

As I waited at the counter to place my order (a barbecue sandwich and an iced tea), I watched Jeff chop and season barbecue. Seasoning consists of salt and red pepper, a generous splash of apple cider vinegar, and a few dashes of Texas Pete, a red-hot sauce that, curiously, is made in North Carolina. (I guess "Texas" is a superior signifier for spicy and authentic.) Wielding a cleaver in each hand, Jeff roughly chops big chunks of meat from different parts of the hog. This is what makes whole-hog barbecue special.

"See, you got your ham, which is lean meat but can be a little dry, and then you got your shoulder, which is greasier [pronounced greazier] but more tender and moist, and of course there's the belly meat, which is probably your juiciest cut. 'Course, there's always some nice bark here and there." Bark is BBQ terminology for the singed outer edges of the meat. "And then you got your skin [skeen], which lends some nice salty crunch. Chop them all together, not too fine, throw some seasoning on there and mix it in good, and that's it right there: whole-hog barbecue."

Uncle Jeff insisted that I also take a tray of unseasoned barbecue, so I could see for myself that what's going on here at the Skylight Inn does not in any way, shape, or form depend for its flavor or quality on "sauce." This is a word he pronounces with an upturned lip and a slight sneer, suggesting that the use of barbecue sauce was at best a culinary crutch deserving of pity and at worst a moral failing.

I tried the unseasoned barbecue first and it was a revelation: moist and earthy, with an unmistakable but by no means overpowering dimension of smoke. In fact, the meat had a flavor far subtler than what you would think could ever have issued from the smoking inferno of oak wood and hog out back. The variety of textures was especially nice—ham, shoulder, belly, bark—but it was the occasional mahogany shard of crackling dispersed through the mixture that really made the dish extraordinary: a tidy, brittle, irreducible packet of salt, fat, and wood smoke. (Bacon gives you some idea, but only an idea.) I suddenly understood, at a deep level, exactly what had overcome young Bo-bo when he touched the irresistible substance to his tongue: There is something life-altering about pork crackling.

Though I think I enjoyed the seasoned barbecue in the sandwich even more. The sharpness of apple cider vinegar provides the perfect counterweight to the sweet unctuousness of the fat, of which there was plenty melted right into the meat, and also balances out the heaviness of the wood smoke. Together, the acid and red pepper brightened and elevated a dish that otherwise might have seemed a little too earthy.

So this was barbecue. Right away I realized I had never before tasted the real thing, and I was converted. This was easily one of the tastiest, most succulent meat dishes I had ever eaten, and certainly the most rewarding $2.75 I'd ever invested in a sandwich. Barbecue: My first bite made me realize, with a cringing pang, that, as a Northerner, I'd already spent more than half of my life as a serial abuser of that peculiar word, which is to say, as a backyard blackener of steaks and chops over too-hot fires—over flames!—with a pitiable dependence on sauce. Even before I had finished my sandwich, I resolved to figure out how to make barbecue like this, to try to redeem that noble word, at home.

There was so much going on in this sandwich. It wasn't just all the different cuts of pork, which kept things interesting bite after bite, but also all that wood and time and tradition. This was the way barbecue had been prepared for generations here in eastern North Carolina, and, having done my reading in BBQ history, I could appreciate what an accurate reflection of this place and its past this sandwich offered. If a sandwich can be said to have terroir, that quality of place that the French believe finds its way into the best wines and cheeses, this sandwich had it, a sense of place and history you could taste.

Since the Europeans first set foot on these shores, the pig has been the principal meat animal in this part of the country. Indeed, the words "meat" and "pork" have been synonymous for most of Southern history. The Spanish conquistador Hernando de Soto brought the first pigs to the American South in the sixteenth century. For centuries, the descendants of those hogs ranged freely in the Carolinas, feeding themselves on the abundant mast produced by the oak-and-hickory forest. This means that, at least before pigs were confined to farms, the flavors of the Eastern hardwood forest could find their way into their meat by two routes: first as acorn and hickory nuts and then as wood smoke. (Three ways, if you count the wood contributed by the chopping block.) These feral hogs were hunted as needed, or rounded up in the fall by the porcine equivalent of the cowboy. Hogs were so abundant that even slaves could enjoy them from time to time. And because a single animal yielded so much meat, to "cook a pig" in the South has always implied a special occasion, a gathering of the community.

The practice of grilling whole pigs over wood fires came to the American South with the slaves, many of whom passed through the Caribbean, where they observed Indians cooking whole animals split and splayed out on top of green branches stretched over fire pits. Along with this technique, which the Indians called barbacoa (or at least that's how it sounded to African and European ears), the slaves brought with them from the islands seeds of the red chili pepper, which became a key ingredient of barbecue seasoning.

In the Carolinas the tradition of whole-hog barbecue has long been bound up with the rhythms of the tobacco harvest, which enlisted the entire community for a few crucial weeks every fall. After the men hauled the tobacco into the curing sheds, the women sorted and "poled" the big leaves on frames, and oak-wood fires were burned through the night to slowly dry them. Retrieving the hot coals produced by these fires and shoveling them into a pit to barbecue a whole hog became an autumn tradition, a way to celebrate the completion of the harvest and thank the workers for their labors. The patient rhythms of hanging and curing tobacco meshed neatly with the rhythms of slow cooking a pig over wood coals. I met black pit masters in North Carolina whose own childhood reminiscences of barbecue are tightly braided with memories of bringing in the tobacco in the fall, one of the rare occasions when blacks and whites worked, and feasted, side by side.

Though barbecue is largely an African American contribution to American culture, it has always been equally prized by white Southerners, most of whom will freely acknowledge that the best pitmen have always been black. (And were called "pit boys" until uncomfortably recently.) The arrangement in place at the Skylight Inn—a white-owned establishment with a black pitman out back—is not atypical. But "good barbecue" has always been one subject on which black and white Southerners could agree, as the salt-and-pepper composition of the clientele here at the Skylight Inn attested. Even during the darkest days of segregation, blacks and whites patronized the same barbecue joints, despite the fact that, prior to the passage of the Civil Rights Act in 1964, they could not eat their barbecue in the same dining room. If the best barbecue in town happened to be at a black establishment, whites would line up at the take-out window; if it happened to be at a white joint, then blacks would line up at the window. Nowadays, barbecue restaurants are, in the words of John Shelton Reed and Dale Voldberg Reed, the preeminent historians of North Carolina barbecue, "a good deal more integrated than most other places of worship."

A large weight of significance for any one plate of food to bear, it is true, but there it all was: the beloved pig, the smoky traces of the local forest, the desultory rhythms of Southern life and labor, and the knotted strands of race—all that, and probably more I didn't know, seasoning this most delicious and democratic sandwich, one that just about anybody could afford.

And yet. I'm sorry to report that all was not sweetness and light here at the Skylight Inn. Well, sweetness, maybe: The slaw, finely ground and snowy white, was tooth-achingly sweet; so was the tea. The cornbread, steeped in grease, was imposingly leaden, albeit tasty. (Lard will do that.) But there was something else that threw a shadow over my meal, tasty as it was, something I was forcibly reminded of by Jeff Jones when he told me a little story about the lard in the cornbread. It made me realize that the Joneses' proud efforts to stand their ground against the tide of modernity had failed in one important respect. Something *had* changed since 1947, and though it wasn't so easy to see, it could not be overlooked.

While we were in the cookhouse, Jeff had mentioned how in the old days he could put a pan beneath a pig roasting on the pit and by morning have collected all the lard he needed to make his cornbread. Not anymore. Now the pigs had so little fat on them that the restaurant had to purchase the lard for its cornbread. His point was that the hog had been reengineered in recent years to be a much leaner and faster-growing animal, one that, thanks to genetics, modern feed, and pharmaceuticals, is ready for slaughter several months before its first birthday. Jeff didn't much like the modern hog—it wasn't nearly as flavorful as the ones he remembered—but he reckoned we were stuck with it.

"Pigs today, they live their whole lives indoors, standing on concrete, and they eat only what they're fed. No wonder they don't taste like they used to." Samuel chimed in: "They're all bulked up on steroids, too"—the hormones farmers often use to speed their growth.

The Joneses seemed to know all about the brutal efficiencies of industrial pork production; it would be hard not to, living here on the coastal plain of North Carolina. In the CAFOs that have sprung up around Ayden, hundreds of thousands of pigs live accelerated lives jammed up against one another in gridded steel pens suspended over cesspools of their waste—animals, keep in mind, that are the equal of dogs in intelligence and sensitivity. To make them easier to inseminate, the breeding sows spend their lives in metal crates too small for them ever to turn around in. Following standard industry practice, farmers dock their piglets' tails—clip them off with a pair of pliers—to create stubs so sensitive that the discouraged creatures will raise an objection when their fellow pigs, driven mad by the stress of their confinement, attempt to cannibalize them. I once paid a visit to such a CAFO—one not too far from here, in fact—and it was a place I won't soon forget: a deep circle of porcine hell the stench and shrieking squeals of which I can still vividly recall.

I suppose it is a testament to the Joneses, and all the signifiers of an earlier time they have so lovingly preserved, that I was able to suppress these thoughts and images long enough to enjoy my barbecue sandwich. We moderns are great compartmentalizers, perhaps never more so than when hungry. But there it is, the question I wanted very much to avoid since I'd first learned that the Skylight Inn was serving commodity pork: How authentic could "authentic barbecue" really be if the object of its tender ministrations was now this re-engineered and brutalized animal—the modern creation of science, industry, and inhumanity? Had the Skylight Inn's elaborate fetish of tradition— the wood fires burning through the night, the smoldering coals so carefully arranged in the pits, the old-timey pitman tending to the pigs—become a cover for something very different, the moral and aesthetic equivalent of barbecue sauce?

The Joneses didn't think there was much to be done about the modern pig, and in this they fall very much into the mainstream of modern barbecue men: By now, "commodity pork" is the rule in Southern barbecue, and people old enough to remember something better, people like Jeff Jones, are few and far between. Sure, there are still a handful of farmers in North Carolina raising hogs outdoors the old-fashioned way, and, as I would discover, their meat was superior in every respect (yield of lard included). But there was just no way a restaurant could afford that kind of pork and still charge $2.75 for a barbecue sandwich. Today, that most democratic sandwich is under-written by the most brutal kind of agriculture.

But I guess that, with enough smoke, time, and maybe a little bar-becue sauce, you can redeem any kind of pork, or at least seem to, be-cause that sandwich did taste awfully good. One way to think about cooking, or the cooking of meat anyway, is that it is always doing something like this: effecting a transformation, psychological and chemical, that helps us (or at least most of us) enjoy something we might otherwise not be able to stomach, whether literally or figura-tively. Cooking puts several kinds of distance between the brutal facts of the matter (*dead animal for dinner*) and the dining-room table set with crisp linens and polished silver. In this, CAFO meat may be just an extreme instance of the general case, which has never been pretty. "You have just dined," Ralph Waldo Emerson once wrote, "and however scrupulously the slaughterhouse is concealed in the graceful distance of miles, there is complicity."

The problem is not a new one, and we flatter ourselves if we think we're the first people to feel moral or spiritual qualms about killing animals for our supper. The ancient and widespread practice of ritual animal sacrifice suggests that such qualms have assailed humans for a very, very long time. Before drawing knife against throat, the Greek priests would sprinkle water on the sacrificial animal's brow, causing it to shake its head in a gesture they chose to interpret as a sign of assent. Indeed, viewed in the coldest light, many of the elements of ritual sacrifice begin to look like a set of convenient rationalizations for doing something we feel uneasy about, but need or want to do anyway. The ritual lets us tell ourselves that we kill animals not for our dining pleasure but because God demands it; that we cook their meat over a fire not to make it tastier but because the rising smoke conveys the offering to the heavens; and that we eat the prime cuts not because they're the most succulent, but because the smoke is all the gods really want.

Alone among the animals, we humans insist that our food be not only "good to eat"—tasty, safe, and nutritious—but also, in the words of Claude Lévi-Strauss, "good to think," for among all the many other things we eat, we also eat ideas. Animal sacrifice has been a way to make animal flesh "good to think"—to help people feel better about killing, cooking, and eating animals, which has never been anything less than a momentous, spiritually freighted, and deeply ambivalent occasion. That might explain why, whether in Homer or Leviticus, the work of slaughter, butchery, and cooking all had to be performed by a priest; these were all equally solemn operations. Nowadays, we think of sacrifice as a primitive rite, and snicker at the underlying rationalizations, but the cultures that practiced such rituals before eating were at least acknowledging that something important was going on, something that demanded their full attention. Just because we no longer pay that kind of attention when we eat meat doesn't mean that something momentous—in fact, a kind of sacrifice—hasn't taken place. You have to wonder, who is really the more "primitive" character here? In our failure to attend to the processes that put meat on our plates, we moderns eat more like the animals than the ancients did.

This points to something else ritual sacrifice did for people: It drew sharp lines of distinction between humans and other animals on the one side, and between humans and the gods on the other. Other animals don't clothe their killing or eating in ritual; nor do they cook their food over fires they control. When people participate in a ritual sacrifice, they're situating themselves in the cosmos at a precise point halfway between the gods, whose power over them they acknowledge by making the sacred offering, and the animals, over whom the ceremonial killing demonstrates their own godlike powers. The recipe for the ritual tells us exactly where we stand.

One way to approach cooking of any kind is as a secular and somewhat faded version of the same operation, helping us to locate ourselves in nature and deal with our ambivalence about eating other beings. Like fire itself, which destroys what photosynthesis has created, all cooking begins with small or large acts of destruction: killing, cutting, chopping, mashing. In that sense, a sacrifice is at its very heart. But cooking also helps put Emerson's "graceful distance of miles"—or time, or smoke, or seasoning, or chopping, or sauce—between the eaters and the eaten, its various transformations helping us to forget, or suppress, the violence of the underlying transaction. At the same time, the wonderful refining alchemies of the kitchen demonstrate how far we have come as a species, affirming that we have indeed lifted ourselves out of nature red in tooth and claw, achieved a kind of transcendence. Cooking sets us apart, helps us to mark and patrol the borders between ourselves and nature's other creatures—none of which can cook.

"My definition of Man is a 'Cooking Animal,'" James Boswell wrote. "The beasts have memory, judgment, and all the faculties and passions of our mind, in a certain degree, but no beast is a cook." Boswell was not alone in regarding cooking as a faculty that defines us as human. According to Lévi-Strauss, the distinction between "the raw" and "the cooked" has served many cultures as the great trope for the difference between animals and people. In The Raw and the Cooked, he wrote, "Not only does cooking mark the transition from nature to culture, but through it and by means of it, the human state can be defined with all its attributes." Cooking transforms nature and, by doing so, elevates us above that state, making us human.

If the human enterprise involves transforming the raw of nature into the cooked of culture, the different techniques we've devised for achieving this transformation each embody a different stance toward both nature on the one side and culture on the other. After studying the foodways of hundreds of peoples around the world, Lévi-Strauss (who apparently never saw a dualism he didn't like) distinguished two basic methods for turning the stuff of nature into something that is not only more tasty and digestible but more human (i.e., good to think) as well: cooking directly over a fire and cooking in a pot with liquid.

To barbecue or to braise? To roast or to boil? That, apparently, is the question, and much—about who we think we are—depends on the answer. Compared with cooking over a fire, braising or stewing implies a more civilized approach to the transformation of nature. The braise or boil, since it cooks meat all the way through, achieves a more complete transcendence of the animal, and perhaps the animal in us, than does grilling over a fire, which leaves its object partly or entirely intact, and often leaves a trace of blood—a visible reminder, in other words, that this is a formerly living creature we're feasting on. This lingering hint of savagery isn't necessarily a strike against fire cooking, however. To the contrary, some believe a bloody slab of beefsteak augments the power of the eater. "Whoever partakes of it," Roland Barthes wrote in *Mythologies*, "assimilates a bull-like strength." By comparison, the braise or stew—and particularly the braise or stew of meat that's been cut into geometric cubes and rendered tender by long hours in the pot—represents a deeper sublimation, or forgetting, of the brutal reality of this particular transaction among species.

Certainly this kind of forgetting has its advantages, especially in everyday life, where cooking in pots is the norm. Who wants to be confronted with existential questions of life and death and human identity on a daily basis? And yet there are times when that is exactly what we're looking for, when we *want* to be reminded, if only a little, of what's really going on just beneath the thin crust of civilization. This is, perhaps, the same impulse that compels some people to endure the discomforts of sleeping out in the woods, or to go to the unnecessary lengths of hunting their own meat or growing their own tomatoes. All these activities are forms of adult play that also serve as ceremonial acts of remembering—who we are, where we came from, how nature works. (And, perhaps, of a time when men were still indispensable.) Cooking meat over a fire—whether a few steaks thrown on the backyard barbecue or, more spectacularly, a whole animal roasted all night over a wood fire—is one of the most stirring of those ritual acts, usually performed outdoors, on special occasions, in public, and by men. And what, exactly, does such cooking commemorate? No doubt many things, including male power (for isn't the triumph of the hunt at least implied?) and ritual sacrifice (for this is cooking-as-performance, exerting the kind of gravitational force that draws people out of the house to watch). But I suspect that, as much as anything else, grilling meat over a fire today commemorates the transformative power of cooking itself, which never appears so bright or explicit as when wood and fire and flesh are brought together under that aromatic empire of smoke.

II.

CAMBRIDGE, MASSACHUSETTS

"Homo sapiens is the only animal that . . ."

How many flattering clauses have philosophers tacked on to that cherished construction, only to watch them eventually crumble? One by one, the faculties on which we thought we could stake the flag of our specialness science has shown belong to other animals as well. Suffering? Reason? Language? Counting? Laughter? Self-consciousness? All have been proposed as human monopolies, and all have fallen before science's deepening understanding of the animal brain and behavior. James Boswell's nomination of cooking as the defining human ability seems more durable than most, though perhaps an even sturdier candidate would be this: "Humans are the only species that feels compelled to identify faculties that it alone possesses."

But here's why cooking may stand a better-than-average chance of surviving this silly game: Only the control of fire and consequent invention of cooking can explain the evolution of brains big and self-conscious enough to construct sentences like "*Homo sapiens* is the only species that . . ."

That at least is the import of "the cooking hypothesis," a recent contribution to evolutionary theory that throws a wonderfully ironic wrench into the scaffold of our self-regard. Cooking, according to the hypothesis, is not merely a metaphor for the creation of culture, as Lévi-Strauss proposed; it is its evolutionary prerequisite and biological foundation. Had our protohuman ancestors not seized control of fire and used it to cook their food, they would never have evolved into *Homo sapiens*. We think of cooking as a cultural innovation that lifts us up out of nature, a manifestation of human transcendence. But the reality is much more interesting: Cooking is by now baked into our biology (as it were), something that we have no choice but to do, if we are to feed our big, energy-guzzling brains. For our species, cooking is not a turn away from nature—it *is* our nature, by now as obligatory as nest building is for the birds.

I first encountered the cooking hypothesis in a 1999 article in the journal *Current Anthropology* titled "The Raw and the Stolen: Cooking and the Ecology of Human Origins" by Richard Wrangham, a Harvard anthropologist and primatologist, and four of his colleagues. Wrangham subsequently fleshed out the theory in a fascinating 2009 book, *Catching Fire: How Cooking Made Us Human*. Soon after it came out, we began corresponding by e-mail, and eventually we had the opportunity to meet, over a lunch (of raw salads) at the Harvard Faculty Club.

The hypothesis is an attempt to account for the dramatic change in primate physiology that occurred in Africa between 1.9 and 1.8 million years ago, with the emergence of Homo erectus, our evolutionary predecessor. Compared to the apelike habilines from which it evolved, Homo erectus had a smaller jaw, smaller teeth, a smaller gut— and a considerably larger brain. Standing upright and living on the ground, Homo erectus is the first primate to bear a stronger resemblance to humans than apes.

Anthropologists have long theorized that the advent of meat eating could account for the growth in the size of the primate brain, since the flesh of animals contains more energy than plant matter. But as Wrangham points out, the alimentary and digestive apparatus of Homo erectus is poorly adapted to a diet of raw meat, and even more poorly adapted to the raw plant foods that would still have been an important part of its diet, since a primate cannot live on meat alone. The chewing and digestion of raw food of any kind requires a big gut and big strong jaws and teeth—all tools that our ancestors had lost right around the time they acquired their bigger brains.

The control of fire and discovery of cooking best explain both these developments, Wrangham contends. Cooking renders food much easier to chew and digest, obviating the need for a strong jaw or substantial gut. Digestion is a metabolically expensive operation, consuming in many species as much energy as locomotion. The body must work especially hard to process raw foodstuffs, in which the strong muscle fibers and sinews in meat and the tough cellulose in the cell walls of plants must be broken down before the small intestines can absorb the amino acids, lipids, and sugars locked up in these foods. Cooking in effect takes much of the work of digestion outside the body, using the energy of fire in (partial) place of the energy of our bodies to break down complex carbohydrates and render proteins more digestible.

Applying the heat of a fire to food transforms it in several ways—some of them chemical, others physical—but all with the same result: making more energy available to the creatures that eat it. Exposure to heat "denatures" proteins—unfolding their origami structures in such a way as to expose more surface area to the action of our digestive enzymes. Given enough time, heat also turns the tough collagen in the connective tissues of muscle into a soft, readily digestible jelly. In the case of plant foods, fire "gelatinizes" starches, the first step in breaking them down into simple sugars. Many plants that are toxic eaten raw, including tubers such as cassava, are rendered harmless as well as more nutritious by heat. Other foodstuffs the cook fire purifies, by killing bacteria and parasites; it also retards spoilage in meat. Cooking improves texture and taste as well, making many foods more tender, and others sweeter or less bitter. Though which comes first—an inborn taste for cooked food or nearly two million years of familiarity with it—is hard to say.

True, cooking can have some negative, seemingly maladaptive, effects, too. High heat produces carcinogenic compounds in some foods, but the danger of these toxins is outweighed by the sheer increase in energy that cooking makes available to us—and life is at bottom a competition for energy. Taken as a whole, cooking opened up vast new horizons of edibility for our ancestors, giving them an important competitive edge over other species and, not insignificantly, leaving us more time to do things besides looking for food and chewing it.

This is no small matter. Based on observations of other primates of comparable size, Wrangham estimates that before our ancestors learned to cook their food they would have had to devote fully half their waking hours simply to the act of chewing it. Chimps like to eat meat and can hunt, but they have to spend so much of their time in mastication that only about eighteen minutes are left each day for hunting, not nearly enough to make meat a staple of their diets. Wrangham estimates that cooking our food gives our species an extra four hours a day. (This happens to be roughly the same amount of time we now devote to watching television.)

"Voracious animals . . . both feed continually and as incessantly eliminate," the Roman physician Galen of Pergamum pointed out, "leading a life truly inimical to philosophy and music, as Plato has said, whereas nobler animals neither eat nor eliminate continually." By freeing us from the need to feed constantly, cooking ennobled us, putting us on the path to philosophy and music. All those myths that trace the godlike powers of the human mind to a divine gift or theft of fire may contain a larger truth than we ever realized.

Yet having crossed this Rubicon, trading away a big gut for a big brain, we can't go back, as much as raw-food faddists would like to. Wrangham cites several studies indicating that in fact humans don't do well on raw food: They can't maintain their body weight, and half of the women on a raw-food regimen stop menstruating. Devotees of raw food rely heavily on juicers and blenders, because otherwise they would have to spend as much time chewing as the chimps do. It is difficult, if not impossible, to extract sufficient energy from unprocessed plant matter to power a body with such a big, hungry brain. (Our brains constitute only 2.5 percent of our weight yet consume 20 percent of our energy when we're resting.) By now, "humans are adapted to eating cooked food in the same essential way as cows are adapted to eating grass," Wrangham says. "We are tied to our adapted diet of cooked food, and the results pervade our lives, from our bodies to our minds. We humans are the cooking apes, the creatures of the flame."

How do we know if the cooking hypothesis is true? We don't. It's just a hypothesis, and not an easy one to prove. The fossil evidence that humans were cooking when Homo erectus walked the earth is not yet there, though it has recently gotten stronger. When Wrangham first published, the oldest known fossil remains put the date for controlled fire at around 790,000 B.C., but Wrangham's hypothesis suggests cooking must have begun at least a million years earlier. In his defense, Wrangham pointed out that evidence of fires that old would be unlikely to survive. Also, cooking meat doesn't necessarily leave behind charred bones. But recently archaeologists found a hearth in a cave in South Africa that pushed the likely date for cooking back considerably further,* to one million years B.C., and the hunt for even older cook fires is on.

So far at least, Wrangham's most convincing arguments are deductive ones. Some new factor of natural selection changed the course of primate evolution about two million years ago, expanding the brain and shrinking the gut; the most plausible candidate for this new selective pressure is the availability of a new, higher-quality diet. Meat by itself could not have supplied that diet. Primates, unlike dogs, don't digest raw flesh efficiently enough to thrive on it. The only diet that could have yielded such a dramatic increase in energy is cooked food. "We are," he concludes, "cooks more than carnivores."

To demonstrate how the advent of cooking could have supplied a caloric boon sufficient to change the course of our evolution, Wrangham cites several animal-feeding studies comparing raw and cooked or otherwise processed food. When researchers switch a python's diet from raw beef to cooked hamburger, the snake's "metabolic cost of digestion" is reduced by nearly 25 percent, leaving the animal that much more energy to put to other purposes. Mice grow faster and

---

*Berna, Francesca, et al., "Microstratigraphic Evidence of In Situ Fire in the Acheulean Strata of Wonderwerk Cave, Northern Cape Province, South Africa," Proceedings of the National Academy of Sciences 109 No. 20 (May 15, 2012), E1215–20.

fatter on a diet of cooked meat than on a diet of the same meat raw.[*] This might explain why our pets tend toward obesity, since most modern pet food is cooked.

It would seem that all calories are not created equal, or, as a proverb quoted by Jean Anthelme Brillat-Savarin in *The Physiology of Taste* puts it, "A man does not live on what he eats, an old proverb says, but on what he digests." Cooking allows us to digest more of what we eat, and to use less energy doing it.[†] What is curious is that animals seem instinctively to know this: Given the choice, many animals will opt for cooked food over raw. This shouldn't surprise us: "Cooked food is better than raw," Wrangham says, "because life is mostly concerned with energy"—and cooked food yields more energy.

It may well be that animals are "pre-adapted" to prefer the smells, tastes, and textures of cooked food, having evolved various sensory apparatus to steer them toward the richest sources of energy. Attractive qualities such as sweetness, softness, tenderness, and oiliness all signify abundant, easy-to-digest calories. A hardwired preference for high-energy foods would explain why our evolutionary ancestors would immediately have appreciated cooked foods. In speculating as to exactly how early humans would have discovered all the good things fire does to food, Wrangham points out that many animals scavenge burned landscapes, enjoying particularly the roasted rodents and seeds. He cites the example of chimpanzees in Senegal, who will eat the seeds of the *Afzelia* tree only after a fire has passed through and toasted them. It seems likely that our ancestors would also have scavenged among the remains of forest fires, looking for tasty morsels and, perhaps occasionally, getting lucky enough to have the sort of

---

[*]Carmody, Rachel N., et al. "Energetic Consequences of Thermal and Nonthermal Food Processing." *Proceedings of the National Academy of Sciences* 108 No. 48 (November 2011): 19199–203.
[†]Ninety percent of a cooked egg is digested, whereas only 65 percent of a raw egg is; by the same token, the rarer the steak, or more al dente the pasta, the less of it will be absorbed. Dieters take note.

transformative experience that Bo-bo, the swineherd's son in Charles Lamb's story, did when he first touched that bit of crackling to his tongue.

Like any such theory—indeed, like evolution itself—the cooking hypothesis is not subject to absolute scientific proof. For that reason, some will no doubt dismiss it as another "just so" story, Prometheus in modern scientific garb. But, really, how much more can we expect when trying to account for something like the advent of ourselves? What the cooking hypothesis gives us is a compelling modern myth— one cast in the language of evolutionary biology rather than religion— locating the origins of our species in the discovery of cooking with fire. To call it a myth is not to belittle it. Like any other such story, it serves to explain how what is came to be using the most powerful vocabulary available, which in our case today happens to be that of evolutionary biology. What is striking in this instance is that classical mythology and modern evolutionary theory both gazed into the flames of the cook fire and found there the same thing: the origins of our humanity. Perhaps that coincidence is all the confirmation we can hope for.

III.

INTERMISSION:
A PIG'S PERSPECTIVE

I can attest from personal experience to the fact that animals are just as attracted as humans and gods are to the aroma of food cooked over a fire, barbecue included and perhaps especially. This story is hard to believe, but it is true in every particular. The first particular is that, as a teenager, I briefly owned a pig, a young white sow by the name of Kosher. My father gave me the pig; he also gave the pig its perverse name. I'm still not entirely sure why my father gave me a pig. We lived in Manhattan, in an apartment on the eleventh floor, and I certainly hadn't asked for one. But ever since reading *Charlotte's Web*, I had liked the idea of pigs, and collected pig books and pig figurines and such. Yet as is sometimes the way with even mild predilections like mine, other people take them far more seriously than you do. Before long, I found myself with a bedroom-full of pig paraphernalia to which, at least by the time I was sixteen, I was more or less indifferent.

But my father got it into his head that a real live pig was just what I wanted, so he had his secretary track down a piglet on a farm in New Jersey and one evening brought it home in a shoe box. This was not a pot-bellied pig, not a miniature pig of any kind. No, Kosher was a standard Yorkshire sow, destined to grow to a quarter of a ton or more if nothing was done to stop her. At the time, we lived in a door-man building, a co-op on the Upper East Side; the co-op allowed pets, but I was fairly sure a full-grown pig didn't qualify.

Luckily, for most of the time I had Kosher, it was summer and we were living in a cottage on the beach. The cottage stood on stilts in the sand, and Kosher lived beneath the deck; pigs are susceptible to sunburn (one of the reasons they like mud so much), so I fenced in the shaded area beneath the house as her pen. Kosher was the size of a football when I got her; she could, and did, fit in a shoe box. However, that didn't last very long. To paraphrase Galen the Physician, she was a voracious animal, feeding constantly and eliminating incessantly. Often in the middle of the night, Kosher would empty her bowl of pig chow, flip it over with an expressive clatter, and then unleash a chorus of deep guttural grunts to alert me to her hunger. When that didn't produce a biped at her gate with a bucket of lunch,

Kosher would take to butting the wooden posts with her powerful snout until the seismic shaking of the cottage woke me. Some nights, having run out of pig chow, I was forced to empty the entire contents of the refrigerator into her bowl, not just the produce and leftovers, but everything, down to the eggs, milk, soda, pickles, ketchup, mayonnaise, and cold cuts, including once (I'm ashamed to admit) a few slices of Virginia ham. Kosher ate it all, with a gusto that never failed to impress me. She ate like a pig.

But that isn't the story. The story is of the evening Kosher's Falstaffian appetite got us both into trouble with the neighbors. Every now and then, when Kosher was feeling peckish or had caught a whiff of something good to eat, she would make a break for it, forcing her snout under the fencing and squeezing her muscular body through the gap. Usually she would head for the nearest garbage can, topple it, and feast on its contents. The neighbors were getting used to this sort of thing, and I was getting used to apologizing, cleaning up after her, and then corralling her back into her pen with the promise of a tasty morsel. But on this particular summer evening, just before sunset, Kosher must have raised her snout into the breeze and detected a few molecules of something even better than garbage: the scent of the smoke of meat on the grill. She made her escape and began working her way up the line of cottages along the beach, until she had located the source of the aroma.

What happened next I learned from the neighbor in question within a few minutes of his visit from Kosher. When it happened, this fellow was sitting on his deck, sipping a gin and tonic, and taking in the last pastel light of the summer day as his dinner sizzled on the grill. Like just about everyone on our strip of beach, this man was a well-to-do New Yorker or a Bostonian, maybe a lawyer or businessman, but likely not a person with much experience of hogs, except perhaps in the form of hams, chops, and strips of bacon. Hearing the clatter of hoof on wood, he looked up from his summer reverie to find a pinkish-white creature the size of an extremely short-legged Labrador bounding up the steps to his deck, grunting furiously. This was no dog. Kosher had evidently locked on to the scent of grilling meat, and when she arrived at last at its source, she worked with the efficiency and speed of a commando, knocking over the barbecue and making off with the man's steak.

Only a few minutes earlier, I had stepped outside to feed Kosher and discovered she had gone missing. I tracked her movements up the beach—most of the neighbors were on their decks, and had spotted her heading north—and arrived at the scene of the crime only a few minutes after Kosher had scurried off with a partially grilled steak clamped between her jaws. To my great good fortune, either Kosher's victim had an excellent sense of humor or his gin-and-tonic had put him in particularly high spirits, because he was doubled over with laughter as he recounted what Kosher had done. I apologized profusely, offered to drive to town to replace his dinner, but he waved me off, declaring the story was worth far more than the price of any steak. The man was still cracking up when I left him to go track down my fugitive hog.

It was long overdue: the Pig's Revenge on Barbecue. I have to think that if hogs had their own mythology, in which they passed down tales of heroism from one generation to the next, the daring achievement of my pig would figure prominently in it: Kosher, the porcine Prometheus.

IV.

RALEIGH, NORTH CAROLINA

Now, of course, to a Southerner, Kosher's theft wasn't a theft of barbecue, not really: Only a deluded Northerner would ever refer to a steak grilled over an open fire as "barbecue." Southerners will argue without end about the precise definition of the word—and in fact any comprehensive definition of barbecue would have to include the fact that it is a food the definition of which is endlessly being contested—but to qualify for the term this cooking must include at a minimum meat, wood smoke, fire, and time. Beyond that, the definition of barbecue changes state by state, and even county by county. I have a map over my desk called "The Balkans of Barbecue." It purports to depict the different barbecue regions of the Carolinas, and superimposed over a map of the two states are the outlines of five distinct barbecue cantons: whole-hog here, shoulders there, strictly vinegar east of this line, tomato-based sauce to the west, mustard-based sauce to the south and east.

And that's only the Carolinas. The map stops before you get anywhere near the ribs of Tennessee or the smoky briskets of Texas, which, because they're beef, no Carolinian would deign to call barbecue. Every one of these barbecue nations regards the practices of every other as an abomination. As you might expect, the trash talking among pit masters is endlessly inventive. Damning with faint praise is one common rhetorical strategy. Once, when I asked someone in Texas to assess the quality of a fellow Texan's barbecued brisket, he allowed, in a drawl, that though his brisket was "goooood, it wasn't knock-your-dick-in-the-dirt good."

Perhaps the most generous definition of barbecue I've come across attempts to bridge all these regional differences. Put forward by a black pit master from Alabama named Sy Erskine, this definition diplomatically elides the whole vexed issue of sauce; it also hints at the sacramental quality of barbecue. Barbecue, he told a writer, is "the mystic communion among fire, smoke, and meat in the total absence of water."* I suspect most Southerners could rally under that broad banner. But the other thing they could agree on? That my own Northerner's conception of barbecue—which wasn't even clear as to whether the word referred to the cooking process or the apparatus used in that process or the resulting food or the accompanying sauce— was just wrong. I had been in North Carolina long enough now to know at least this: "Barbecue" is a noun (not a verb) that refers either to a social event or to the kind of food prepared and served at that event.

Thus far my own experience of Southern barbecue had been limited to observer and eater. Though I had now tasted the food, I had not yet been to a real barbecue. So I left Ayden with an aspiration: to see if I could learn at least a few of the secrets of barbecue, by apprenticing myself to one of its masters, and not in a kitchen but at a barbecue. I didn't want to watch anymore. I wanted to do.

Before I came to North Carolina, I thought I had done and knew something about how to barbecue; I do it all the time at home. As for most American men, the cooking of meat outdoors over fire constitutes one of my most exalted domestic duties. And like most American men, I do a fine job of mystifying what is at bottom a very simple process, such a fine job, in fact, that my wife, Judith, is by now convinced that grilling a steak over a fire is as daunting a procedure as changing the timing belt on the car.

---

*I'm not sure why he even brings up water—perhaps because it is the enemy of fire? Or because it's a feminine principle and barbecue is a male domain?

Indeed, North or South, it is remarkable how much sheer bullshit seems to accrete around the subject of barbecue. No other kind of cooking comes even close. Exactly why, I'm not sure, but it may be that cooking over fire is actually so straightforward that the people who do it feel a need to baste the process in thick layers of intricacy and myth. It could also be that barbecue is performed disproportionately by self-dramatizing men. For my own part, I made much of my special talent for determining the doneness of a chunk of grilled meat, which involved touching the meat on the grill and then, with the same finger, touching various sectors of my face. If the meat responds to pressure like my cheek does, that means it is rare; if it feels more like my chin, it's medium; if like my forehead, then it's well done. I'd seen some chef demonstrate the technique on television and it seemed to work, not just as a handy metric but, much more important, as a further aid to mystification. Judith has come to doubt her own face could possibly work as well.

It's a pretty good racket. Or at least I thought it was until someone let me in on the secret that many women play dumb around the whole subject of fire, in order to make sure that men do at least some of the cooking.

But that barbecue sandwich at the Skylight Inn had persuaded me that my definition of barbecue was faulty and that there was a lot more involved in cooking over a fire than I knew—which was, basically, how to throw meat on a blazingly hot grill and then, after a while, poke at it knowingly. What I needed was a pit master willing to let me work as his sous chef, or whatever the barbecue cognate of that role was. James Howell was clearly too taciturn and inaccessible to be that mentor, and the Joneses didn't seem inclined to let me get my hands dirty (or burned) in their cookhouse.

As it happened, the pit master I was looking for would appear in my life the very next day. That's when I had an interview scheduled with a celebrated North Carolina barbecue man who had a restaurant in Raleigh called The Pit. Ed Mitchell is his name, and I had heard a great deal about him before flying out to North Carolina—in fact had seen his picture on the front page of the *New York Times*, after he had wowed the crowd with his whole-hog barbecue at the first Big Apple Barbecue Block Party in New York City in 2003. By now Ed Mitchell was nationally famous, had been all over television, had had his oral history taken by the Southern Foodways Alliance, among others, and been profiled over the years in several national magazines, including *Gourmet*.

None of this boded well for eliciting more than a few well-sanded sound bites from the guy, who in the pictures looked like quite the showman, a big black Santa Claus in denim overalls and a baseball cap. Of concern, too, was the fact that his barbecue joint served wine and had valet parking, and that a wag on one of the restaurant blogs had dismissed the place as "a barbecue zoo." But I had learned that over the following weekend Mitchell would be cooking a pig at a benefit barbecue in Wilson, his hometown, some distance from the putative zoo in Raleigh. So I decided that I would call Mitchell, and if he seemed even remotely amenable, I would ask him if I might tag along and assist.

Ed Mitchell just might be the first pit master in history to have handlers. Before I could talk to him I had to go through his people at Empire Eats, the Raleigh restaurant group that owned The Pit, or 51 percent of it anyway. The backstory, I quickly learned, was complicated. Ed Mitchell had lost his original restaurant, Mitchell's Ribs, Chicken & Barbecue, in Wilson, after a legal tussle with the bank and the State of North Carolina, which in 2005 had charged him with embezzlement for his failure to remit various state taxes. (Later, I would hear Mitchell refer to his legal and financial difficulties as a case of "orchestrated turbulence.") The charges against him were eventually reduced to tax evasion, but Mitchell spent some time in jail and the bank foreclosed on his restaurant. After his release, Mitchell was approached by Greg Hatem, a young local real-estate developer who'd made a reputation revitalizing Raleigh's faded downtown district. The key to luring people back downtown, Hatem had figured out, was to open some good restaurants there. Now, in Ed Mitchell, he recognized a rare opportunity: one of the most famous barbecue men in the country down on his luck and without a stage. Hatem proposed a 51–49-percent partnership; Ed would run the pits and the front of the house, while Greg's people would manage the business side—evidently Ed's Achilles' heel. The Pit would be a whole new kind of barbecue restaurant, an upscale place with good lighting, a wine list, and valet parking.

To many in the barbecue world, this seemed a dubious concept at best, the most withering appraisal being the one I'd read online suggesting the South's greatest black pitman had been caged in a barbecue zoo. Someone else said Ed Mitchell had become the Colonel Sanders of barbecue. The Pit seemed to put the whole question of authenticity, never far from discussions of barbecue and always vexed, in deeper doubt than ever. Yet there was no denying the dubious concept was working. The Pit was packed for both lunch and dinner, and the barrier of the $10 barbecue sandwich had been successfully breached.*

When I finally got Ed on the phone, I had the feeling I often did

---

*In 2011, Ed Mitchell left The Pit, in a split with Greg Hatem's restaurant group described in the press as amicable. But Ed told me there had been battles over philosophy and economics and he could "no longer put Ed Mitchell's face and reputation on something where I had no control." Ed plans to open a new barbecue restaurant in Durham, North Carolina.

when talking to an experienced pitman—that I'd opened the spigot on a hydrant of barbecue blarney. This one positively gushed. Mitchell was evangelical on the subject of whole-hog barbecue, and strict in his construction of it. He dropped the word "authentic" into every third or fourth sentence, something that I was getting used to here in North Carolina but which raised an uncomfortable question. To wit, can authenticity be aware of itself as such and still be authentic?

I was beginning to suspect that barbecue had become something of a hall of mirrors. Mitchell himself seemed to embody the culture of Southern barbecue as reflected back at itself in the celebration of Southern barbecue by Northern food writers, professors of cultural studies, and the Southern Foodways Alliance, which had gotten behind Ed Mitchell in a big way. This possibly explained his habit of speaking of himself in the third person ("And that's when the story of old Ed Mitchell really began to spiral ever upward . . ."). Mitchell talked about The Pit as his new "stage," and how he and Greg Hatem were taking whole-hog barbecue upscale, and making it "a little bit more trendy" while "keeping it real." The Pit had an executive chef, and I got the feeling Ed was doing a lot more talking than cooking nowadays.

Delivering his practiced patter, Ed was upbeat in the automatic mode of the salesman or evangelist. And yet I also detected a real sweetness in the man, a passion for cooking for people, and, somewhere deep down there beneath all the talk about authenticity, the kernel of something that felt a lot like . . . authenticity.

I asked Ed about the event in Wilson, which some of the PR people at the restaurant group had discouraged me from attending. Maybe it would turn out to be as boring as they promised ("I just have to warn you, it's a long hot day in a parking lot with a lot of sitting around") or maybe they wanted to keep the focus on the restaurant, but to me it sounded perfect. Ed would be cooking a couple of hogs himself in his hometown, assisted by his younger brother Aubrey. He planned to start the hogs on the pit at his old restaurant Friday night, and then finish them in the parking lot Saturday on portable cookers. I asked Ed if I could help out.

"I don't see why not. Come on down, we'll put you to work, show you how old Ed Mitchell cooks whole-hog barbecue."

8

When I showed up at The Pit Friday afternoon to meet Ed Mitchell for the drive out to Wilson, the pit master was not in the kitchen. He was in the dining room, getting his picture taken with a customer, something that clearly happened all the time. Ed was a slow-moving bear of a man with the build of a linebacker (in fact, he attended Fayetteville State on a football scholarship), but a sixty-three-year-old linebacker, with a prosperous belly. His complexion was dark as coal, and his full-moon face was fringed in a nimbus of snow-white beard. Ed had on his trademark outfit—crisp denim overalls and baseball cap—and after finishing up with the customer, he asked a server to take a picture of the two of us, with our arms wrapped around each other's shoulders like old friends.

On the ride out to Wilson in one of The Pit's catering vans, I got "the Ed Mitchell story," complete with that title. Listening to him tell his story was very much like déjà vu. More than once, I could swear I had heard this exact sentence somewhere before. And I had—usually in one of the oral histories I had read before coming to North Carolina. The version of "the Ed Mitchell story" that follows draws on both those oral histories (especially the one done for Southern Foodways Alliance) and my own interviews with Ed.

Cooking barbecue had never been part of Ed's life plan, though because he was the oldest of three boys his mother, Doretha, had insisted he learn how to cook. She worked while he was growing up, first for a tobacco company, and then as a domestic in the home of one of the tobacco executives who lived in the grand houses on the west side of Wilson. "I stayed home to cook for my brothers, and I hated it. Hated it! Cooking just wasn't something boys did. But I'm a mama's boy, always been, and Mama insisted on it."

Cooking barbecue was different, however. It was something the men did on special occasions: at Christmastime and other holidays, and for "the quarterlies"—family reunions. Ed remembers getting to cook his first pig at fourteen, and how he relished the privilege of spending long hours around the fire pit with the men of the family.

"Moonshine was always an important part of barbecue, because, you see, the men were not allowed to drink in the house. So this kind of whole-hog cooking that had to be done outside and went on all night long—well, that was just perfect for passing the jar!" To Ed, the great appeal of cooking a whole pig was not so much the meal as the occasion it provided, for time around a fire, for talk, and for camaraderie. The food was almost incidental to the ritual work of producing it.

After a couple of years playing football at Fayetteville State, Ed was called up to serve in Vietnam, where he spent eighteen harrowing months. When he got home he finished his degree, graduating in 1972, and was recruited by Ford Motor Company to join a minority-dealer development program. After some training in Michigan, Ford sent him to Waltham, Massachusetts, where he worked as a regional manager in customer service for twelve years, until the day he got word that his father, Willie, had taken ill. Ed decided to return to Wilson to help his parents out.

At the time, Ed's parents ran a mom-and-pop grocery story on the east side of town, but after his father passed in 1990, business took a turn for the worse. Every day, Ed would escort his mother to and from the store, and he remembers coming by one afternoon to find his mother looking downcast. He asked her why. "Well, I've been here all day," she told him, "and I haven't made but seventeen dollars, and twelve dollars of that was in food stamps."

"I wanted to cheer her up, so I asked her, what did she want to eat for lunch? She thought about it and said, 'I know what I want. I've got a taste for some old-fashioned barbecue.' Well, I knew what that meant, so I went down to the Super Duper and I bought a small little pig, maybe thirty-two pounds or so, and I bought five dollars' worth of oak wood to give it the flavor I wanted. I pulled the old barrel cooker out of the shed, put the pig on, and gave it about three hours to cook. When the pig was done, I chopped it up, Mama seasoned it, and she and I sat down in the back of the store for a late lunch.

"While we were enjoying our barbecue, someone came into the grocery story wanting some hot dogs, which was something Mom and Dad offered. But when the man saw the pail of barbecue, he said, "Mrs. Mitchell, y'all got barbecue, too?" Mother looked over at me. I had my mouth full, so I couldn't speak, but I nodded, uh-huh. I figured what she needed was to make some money, so, yeah, sell the man some barbecue! She made the guy a couple of sandwiches and he left.

"When I came back that evening to escort her home, Mama was all bubbly, happier than she'd been in all the time since Daddy passed. I asked her, why the change in mood? 'I made some money today,' she said. 'I sold all that barbecue.' Get out of here! But it seems the man had gone out in the community with his sandwiches and told somebody, and that somebody told somebody else, and the news got around like wildfire, until all the barbecue was sold.

"Anyway, as we were locking up for the night, a stranger came to the front door.

" 'Mr. Mitchell?' I thought maybe the man was here to rob us, so I put a little bass in my voice:

" 'Yeah, who is it?'

" 'Oh, I just want to know if y'all got any more of that barbecue.'

" 'No, we don't have no more today, but we'll have some more tomorrow.' And that is how Ed Mitchell got into the barbecue business. The good Lord had brought me right back to where I started, cooking for my mom."

Within a few months, they had phased out the groceries and built some pits, and Ed had persuaded James Kirby, an elderly pit master in town, to come out of retirement to help man the pits and teach him the old ways. "Because, by the late nineties, you couldn't find the kind of traditional barbecue we wanted to cook. It had died out when everyone switched to gas units. But there's a most definite distinction between wood- or charcoal-cooked barbecue and gas-cooked barbecue. You can taste the difference." Mr. Kirby was a purist of the old school, committed to cooking with live fire, and he had a few tricks to teach Ed, including a technique he called "banking."

The first time he and Mr. Kirby put a big pig on to cook, Ed had figured they'd be up all night tending to the fire, so he laid in a supply of sandwiches and coffee. "But after we got the pig on, and I was settling in for the night, Mr. Kirby got up, went to the door, and put on his hat. I asked him where he was going.

" 'You can sit here all night if you want to, but I'm going home.' He explained to me that if you bank the coals right—place them strategically around the pit—and then shut down all the drafts, that pig'll sit there and simmer all night, without you having to add more coals.

"Well, I couldn't sleep a wink that night because I just knew that pig was going to burn down the store. But when I came back to check on it at four in the morning and opened the grill, I could not believe my eyes. It was the prettiest pig you ever laid eyes on! This beautiful honey color, and the meat was so done it was literally falling off the bone." Mr. Kirby taught Ed the finer points of banking coals; he also showed him how to crisp the pigskin into crackling.

It wasn't long before Mitchell's Ribs, Chicken & Barbecue had earned a reputation, and the national food writers and then the academics found their way to Wilson, a town of fifty thousand located on I-95, "halfway between New York and Miami," as the visitors' bureau likes to point out. The attention had a curious effect on Mitchell, altering his understanding of who he was and what he was doing in a way that perhaps only an outsider bearing fresh context can do. A turning point came in 2001, when Ed read an oral history—of Ed Mitchell—done by a historian named David Cecelski. The history here was Ed's own—Cecelski had taken down the skeletal first draft of the narrative you've just read—but reading it helped Ed to see his story in a new light.

"I did not fully realize that what I was doing—which to me was just old-fashioned barbecue, the fabric of our lives but nothing all that special—was really a part of the larger African-American story, of our contribution. And that felt very good."

Ed Mitchell's barbecue was becoming aware of itself, a process that deepened in 2002, when the Southern Foodways Alliance recognized Mitchell as a leading eastern North Carolina, whole-hog pit master by inviting him to cook at a symposium on barbecue. The Alliance is a program at the University of Mississippi established in 1999 and run by historian John T. Edge to chronicle and celebrate, and thereby help to preserve, Southern foodways. Edge had found that talking about food—something Southerners could always talk (and argue) about even when it was too uncomfortable to talk (and argue) about anything else—was a good way to broach some of the more difficult issues of Southern history. "Food," Edge told me, "is one of the ways the South is working through its race quandaries."

Edge invited Mitchell to the barbecue symposium at the university in October of 2002. "So we went down to Oxford, Mississippi, and it opened my eyes," Mitchell told me. There were pit masters from every region, every tradition, as well as scholars, journalists, and panels on the history, techniques, and regional variations of barbecue. "The symposium was very informative to me. I realized this thing was a lot bigger than just Wilson, North Carolina. I mean, there was a national movement going on about barbecue, something that I literally took for granted. But I learned there how what I was doing fit into the bigger picture, that barbecue was an African American contribution and I was part of that tradition. So that was very exciting. It made me proud, very proud."

Southern Foodways wanted to tell the story of barbecue as an important African American contribution to American culture. The only problem was that most of the faces of Southern barbecue were now white, like the Joneses in Ayden, even when a black pitman like James Howell might be working out back. Ed was the exception: a black man who owned the pits he cooked on. (Or at least did then, before his troubles.) So Ed Mitchell was as important to the Southern Foodways Alliance as the Foodways Alliance was to Ed Mitchell.

As part of the symposium, the pit masters were invited to cook their specialty and then submit to judging by the food writers; competitive cooking has become an important part of barbecue culture over the last few years. Ed tells a story about how the truck carrying his rigs made a wrong turn at Tupelo and arrived hours late. "Everybody else had these fancy rigs set up—you know, with canopies and shining lacquer. Some of these guys had invested hundreds of thousands of dollars! So everybody's waiting to see what sort of equipment Ed Mitchell's got, but it hasn't shown up. Then, finally, the truck pulls up, this big eighteen-wheeler, and they're expecting something fancy to come out of the back when we open the doors. Well, I roll out my equipment—and it's just these three rusty old barrel cookers, that's all! And everybody just laughed.

"But you see, that's all I've ever needed. So I cooked my pig—a little faster than I normally would, because we started so late—and when it was done I pulled all the meat and chopped it up and seasoned it. I put the skin back on the fire to crisp, and then chopped that into real fine pieces and mixed it all together. And lo and behold, when people started eating it, they started talking, and then literally everyone started running over to taste my barbecue. We were bombarded! Everybody thought we'd just hung the moon. We may have had the least impressive equipment, but it turned out the tastiest product.

"And then, from there on, old Ed Mitchell's story has been spiraling ever upward since." Ed left the Oxford symposium the most famous pit master in America.

At the time, Ed was, like the Joneses, cooking standard commodity hogs, but now he had entered a world where the provenance of pork actually mattered. One of the food writers he met at the symposium was Peter Kaminsky, who was researching a book about old breeds of pigs that would be published a few years later under the title Pig Perfect. Kaminsky, who is from Brooklyn, pointed out to Ed Mitchell, gently, that his barbecue was not quite as authentic as it might be.

"Peter Kaminksy told me Mitchell's Ribs, Chicken & Barbecue had two out of the three big things people were looking for in authentic barbecue: traditional cooking, a black-owned establishment, and traditional hogs." Kaminsky helped arrange for Ed to cook an older breed of hog that had been raised outdoors. "I tell you, I was hooked from the first bite. This was the taste I remember from my childhood, sweet and succulent and very, very good even without seasoning."

Kaminsky introduced Mitchell to some people at North Carolina A&T State University, in Greensboro, who were organizing a group of black farmers, many of them former tobacco growers. The idea was to bring back some of the older breeds of pigs, rearing them humanely on pasture without hormones or antibiotics. An eye-opening visit to a hog-confinement operation solidified Mitchell's commitment to supporting this new/old kind of hog farming in North Carolina. So did a comparative tasting of industrial and pastured hog barbecue that John T. Edge helped arranged for him to cook at an event in Oxford. Ed realized that if he could promote these pigs at his restaurant and then get other barbecue restaurants to join him, he could do something for the state's small farmers, who were struggling to stay above water after the fall of tobacco.

"Peter set me on this path," Ed said. Here again was the foodways feedback loop at work, in which a Jewish writer from Brooklyn ends up helping to restore the authenticity of Southern barbecue. By now, Ed had taken ownership of the project and was eloquent on the subject: "You see, this cooking is really all about interdependence and community, and that extends to the farmers who grow the food and the little slaughterhouses they depend on. That sense of interdependence is what we've lost."

We were talking about slaughterhouses because we had pulled off the highway in Sims to pick up our hogs at a small custom meat plant, George Flowers Slaughterhouse. As we drove up, Mr. Flowers himself was sitting beneath a tree out front, having a smoke. He was a wiry old white guy with the most unusual facial hair I had ever laid eyes on. If in fact it *was* facial hair, because it wasn't quite that simple. Mr. Flowers's prodigious muttonchops, once white but now stained yellow by tobacco smoke, had somehow managed to merge with the equally prodigious yellowish-white hair sprouting from his chest. I didn't want to stare, but they appeared to form a single integrated unit, and if so represented a bold advance in human adornment.

Mr. Flowers greeted Ed warmly, ribbing him about a recent TV appearance, in which Mitchell had roundly defeated Bobby Flay in a "throwdown" on the Food Network. (I was surprised how deep into the sticks of eastern North Carolina news of this epic confrontation had penetrated.) After a while, Flowers showed us into the plant, which wasn't a whole lot bigger than an old-time gas station with a garage. A sign posted on the loading dock spelled out the services and prices: $100 to cut up a deer; $150 to break down a cow, and $18 to dress a hog for a barbecue. Inside, Flowers's sons were cleaning up. The killing was done for the day, and they were pushing blood into drains in the floor with brooms. The severed heads of several different species—pig, sheep, cow—were piled high in a barrel by the door. The Flowers boys threw our split pigs over their shoulders, carried them outside, and flipped them into the back of the van.

When exactly does the cooking process begin? is a question I sometimes wonder about. Does it start when you take your ingredients out of the fridge and begin chopping? Or does it begin before that, when you go shopping for those ingredients? Or is it earlier still, when the meat for your meal is being raised and taken to the slaughterhouse and killed? In ancient Greece the name for the man who did the cooking, the butchery, and the slaughter was the same—the *mageiros*—since all were steps in a single ritual process. Ed Mitchell had evidently decided his own cooking would now start all the way back on the farm. For barbecue to be truly authentic, he was saying, it should pay at least as much attention to the pigs as it did to the seasoning or the sauce.

V.

WILSON, NORTH CAROLINA

When we pulled up at the back door of the restaurant formerly known as Mitchell's Ribs, Chicken & Barbecue,* at the corner of Singletary and 301 Highway South, in the black part of Wilson, Ed's younger brother Aubrey was standing there waiting for us, impatiently. "Aubrey is always getting places very early," Ed explained, "but to him, see, early is on time." (I would discover as much the next morning, when Aubrey was scheduled to pick me up in front of my Holiday Inn at six; I found him fidgeting in the lobby at five.) Aubrey was an intense man, a decade or so Ed's junior, and built on a stouter frame, which made the shiny gold crucifix he wore loom large on his chest. Ed introduced him to me as his indispensable second, "the man behind the man, the vice president of operations. Aubrey here is my Scottie Pippen"—i.e., to his Michael Jordan. This wasn't the first time Aubrey had heard these compliments, and he seemed to take them in stride.

It was time to start cooking. While Ed supervised, Aubrey and I lifted the split hogs onto big sheet trays, carrying them as if on stretchers into the kitchen. The sink was long enough to accommodate an entire split pig, and we began by washing down the carcasses with water, trimming stray bits of fat, and removing any blood. ("You never want to eat blood," Ed explained. The injunction is biblical: Blood is the animal's soul, and that belongs exclusively to God.) The

---

*The name itself is a mini-polemic about what barbecue is and is not. Since the word "barbecue" is reserved for pork, that need not be mentioned; however, the word may not be used to modify ribs or chicken, which, whatever else they are, are not barbecue. At least here in North Carolina east of Lexington.

pigs were heavy—about seventy-five pounds each half—and extremely slippery when wet. The first time I tried to hoist my end out
of the sink after we'd rinsed it, I lost my grip. The pig fell to the floor
and had to be rinsed all over again, a humiliating start to my barbecue career.

The four pits, which occupied one long wall of the kitchen, were
built out of brick and resembled the ones in Ayden, except that they
had sleek, stainless-steel covers and a sophisticated system for venti-
lating the smoke. Ed was very proud of the kitchen's design, which
included a redundant ventilation system and sprinklers that allowed
him to safely and legally bring wood-burning barbecue pits into a
restaurant kitchen—the first time, he claimed, this had ever been
done in North Carolina.

Ed was happy to give orders and let me work. I never did figure
out whether he had decided I had some potential as a pitman, or was
just happy to have someone else do the heavy lifting. He handed me
a shovel and told me to remove the ashes from the floor of the pits,
ashes probably left over from the last barbecue Ed cooked here, before
the foreclosure in 2004. What he instructed me to do next came as a
surprise, and a disillusioning one at that. He asked me to empty two
twenty-pound bags of charcoal into the center of each pit. Ed cooked
with Kingsford!—those little rectangular black pillows of compressed
charcoal made from sawdust and who knows what else. How authentic is that? Ed explained that Kingsford gave him a long, slow burn that
"allowed me to get some sleep at night." But it was tasteless! What
about the wood smoke? "You'll see in due course."

After I mounded the briquettes in the center of each pit, Aubrey
squirted copious amounts of lighter fluid onto them, waited a moment for it to soak in, and tossed a match that instantly ignited an
impressive conflagration. This wasn't exactly the primordial fire I'd
come in search of. It was more like the suburban backyard barbecue

blazes of my childhood. Everyone, it seems, makes his own compromises, whether in the interest of convenience or cost, but everyone else's compromises are abominations. Though I uncovered a reservoir of mutual respect between the Joneses and Mitchells, the former regards Mitchell's charcoal as a sad declension, and the latter feels the same way about the Joneses' commodity pigs. ("I would say they're eighty percent of the way there," Ed told me.)

While we waited for the briquettes to catch fire and then mellow, Ed showed me around the building, parts of which had been leased to a woman who was operating it as a cafeteria. The structure was a somewhat bewildering warren of rooms that had been added on, piecemeal, to the original mom-and-pop grocery store. The former store survives as the comparatively tiny, windowless heart in the middle of what has grown into a sprawling cinder-block complex. Proudly, Ed showed me the upstairs lecture hall, where he had planned to start a barbecue college for aspiring pit masters; the "pig bar," where customers could have a drink while watching Ed or Aubrey chop barbecue; and the dining room, the walls of which were covered with a remarkable mural depicting the role of barbecue in Southern history. It was an ambitious piece of folk art, at least fifty feet in length, and painted over the course of a few years by an autistic man who worked in the kitchen as a dishwasher. (It took me the longest time to realize Ed was not saying an "artistic man," which seemed self-evident.) "He offered to do the whole thing for ten dollars," Ed told me. "That didn't seem right, so I gave him twenty dollars and bought the paint."

Ed made sure I looked at every scene closely. The mural depicted a myth of the origins of barbecue in the traditions of the tobacco harvest. Its theme was community. You saw carts laden with tobacco; men stripping the big leaves, women poling them, then handing the long poles to men to hang in the barn; wood fires burning in the barns to cure the tobacco; men slaughtering hogs outside, hanging their carcasses from trees; women making sausages and soap from the lard; men digging the barbecue pits, which looked like fresh graves, and passing jars of moonshine. And then the climactic scene: On a broad lawn in front of a big white mansion, an improbably long table stretches out in the shade of a great oak. This is the site of the celebratory feast that marked the end of the harvest.

"Now look at the faces of the people at that table: black and white. *Together.* This was practically the only time that happened back then. We needed each other and everyone knew it, even if we went back to our separate lives afterward. But whether you were picking cotton or putting in the tobacco, everyone worked together and then everyone feasted together at a barbecue."

Ed spoke of the tobacco harvest as if it had been part of his own childhood, but his nostalgia was for a world that was already fading into myth by the time he was a boy. (His parents left the land in 1946, the year he was born.) Yet such memories don't necessarily have to be in the first person to shape our lives. For Ed, the mural underscored what was most meaningful to him about barbecue: that it brought people together as a community, and that, even if only temporarily, it transcended race. As far as he is concerned, it still does.

"There's something about cooking a whole animal that makes people feel happy. It's usually a special occasion, a celebration of some kind, and it never fails. Barbecue brings people together, it always did and always will. Even in the sixties, during the race movements, barbecue was one of the things that held down the tensions. At a barbecue, it didn't matter who you were.

"Only two things in my experience have had the power to transcend race: Vietnam and barbecue. There's no other dish that powerful. And don't ask me why, because I don't know."

Ed appeared to grow melancholy as he showed me around the

building, much of which felt hastily abandoned. I asked him to tell me how he'd lost Mitchell's Ribs, Chicken & Barbecue.

Though it wasn't something he could prove, Ed was convinced that his outspokenness on the subject of industrial hog farming had led directly to his troubles.

"We held a press conference here in Wilson in 2004, and John T. came up and spoke. We announced the A&T project with the farmers, and my plans for bringing natural pigs back into barbecue. I didn't think anything of it at the time, but two men I didn't recognize stood up and asked me, very grumpily, 'Are you trying to start something?'

"'No, I'm not trying to start anything.'

"'Oh yes, you are. You're getting ready to tell people not to buy my product, and that isn't good.'"

Thus began what Ed refers to as a period of "orchestrated turbulence." Within weeks of the press conference, he claims, the state launched an audit of his books, which quickly turned into an investigation. Then the bank suddenly notified him he was in foreclosure. Soon after that he was charged with embezzlement. True, Ed had fallen behind on his payments, both to the bank and the state, but the speed and severity of the actions taken against him seemed suspicious.

"In less than thirty days of my press conference, I had my business closed and was charged with embezzlement. The arraignment was all over the television and newspapers. I can only think it was an orchestrated effort to ruin Ed Mitchell's reputation, because I had become a viable spokesman for an alternative kind of product." Ed Mitchell had become a threat to one of the state's most powerful industries—industrial hog farming—and was raising uncomfortable questions—questions of authenticity—about one of its proudest traditions: whole-hog barbecue.

But is this really what happened? I talked to people in Raleigh who don't buy Ed's version of events, and believe that his troubles stemmed from his business failings, nothing else. Others aren't so sure. John T. Edge, for his part, thinks it entirely plausible that Ed was the victim of a campaign to discredit him. "Here was a black man in North Carolina telling people he was cooking the best barbecue in the state and promoting an alternative to the commercial hog industry. I'm sure there are some people in North Carolina who thought Ed Mitchell had gotten uppity and needed to be taken down a peg."

Since the time of his troubles, Ed has taken pains to tone down his rhetoric about the commercial hog industry. He speaks more about "the chef's personal taste" in pork and less about the evils of agribusiness. But he has also received a partial vindication: A judge ruled that the bank had improperly foreclosed on Mitchell and did not have "clean hands." The ruling came too late to do Mitchell much good, however. Mitchell's Ribs, Chicken & Barbecue is no more, and it may be that Ed's travails will stand as the exception to the lovely rule that barbecue never fails to bring people together.

When we got back to the kitchen, the coals were ready, glowing red and dusted with white ash. Ed handed me the shovel again and explained how to properly bank the coals: You arrange them in the rough outline of your pig, a six-inch-wide line of coals all around except at the top and bottom, beneath the butt and shoulders, which, being thicker, need more fire. There, you want more like twelve inches of coals. Ed then took an oak log that had been soaking in vinegar and tossed it on the coals. That one log would supply all the smoke the pig would need. Now Aubrey and I each took one end of the big grates, placed them over the pits, and then lifted the split hogs onto the grates, skin side up; we would flip them in the morning. I began to lower the covers over the pigs, but Ed stayed my hand.

"This is where I like to stop and salute the pigs. They've given the ultimate sacrifice so that people can eat, and we should at least acknowledge that." He gave them each a fond little pat on the ham, the kind of affectionate butt-pat athletes give one another. Then he lowered the steel covers over the pigs and closed down the vents, and that was it. We were done for the night.

Over the course of our conversations, Ed had gone back and forth on the relative difficulty and mystery of his art. More than once he had alluded tantalizingly to "trade secrets," but other times he disclaimed there were any such thing. This was one of those times. "It's hard work, but there's really nothing all that complicated about making good barbecue." Which might be the deepest, darkest secret of all.

When the three of us reconvened in the kitchen at seven the next morning, you could tell immediately that something had changed. The chemical scent of lighter fluid was gone, replaced by the seductive aromas of roasting meat. Something very good was going on under those stainless-steel pit covers. I lifted one of them and marveled at the transformation: What had been a flabby white carcass was now a considerably smaller side of pork with a deep, rich color and some muscle tone. Its skin was gorgeous: lacquered brown, the color of strong tea. The animal was still leathery to the touch, though now its flesh put up some resistance, like cooked meat. It wasn't quite done, but I couldn't wait to taste it.

So what exactly had happened in the night, to transform these more or less odorless, flaccid hunks of hog flesh into delicious-smelling and -looking meat? How was it that some burning coals and a single oak log had turned something you would never think to eat—dead pig—into something you couldn't wait to eat?

Actually, a great many things had happened in the night, transformations both physical and chemical. The heat had driven off much of the water in the meat, altering its texture and concentrating its flavors. It had also rendered much of the substantial layer of fat directly under the skin. Some of that fat had dripped onto the hot coals and turned into smoke, sending up a whole range of aromatic compounds that rejoined the surface of the meat, adding new layers of flavor. But because the pork was cooking at such a low temperature, much of the back fat had slowly melted into the meat, helping to keep it moist and adding its own rich flavor to the muscle, which in the absence of fat has relatively little flavor of its own. The muscle fibers themselves had undergone a transformation, as the heat broke down the collagen that bound them together, turning it to gelatin, which tenderized and further moistened the meat.

Chemically, what had been simple the fire had rendered complex. According to a flavor chemist I consulted, putting smoke and fire to the proteins, sugars, and fats in meat creates anywhere between three thousand and four thousand entirely new chemical compounds, complex and often aromatic molecules forged from the simple building blocks of sugar and amino acids. "And those are just the compounds we can name; there are probably hundreds more we haven't identified." In this, cooking, even though it may start by breaking things down, is the opposite of entropy, erecting complex new molecular structures from simpler forms.

Several different chemical reactions are responsible for these creations, but one of the most important is the one named for the French doctor who identified it in 1912: Louis-Camille Maillard. Maillard discovered that when amino acids are heated in the company of sugar, the reaction produces hundreds of new molecules that give cooked food its characteristic color and much of its smell. The Maillard reaction is responsible for the flavors in roasted coffee, the crust of bread, chocolate, beer, soy sauce, and fried meats—a vast amount of chemical complexity, not to mention pleasure, created from a handful of amino acids and some sugar.

The second important reaction working on our pigs during the night was caramelization. The heating of odorless sucrose until it browns generates more than a hundred other compounds, with flavor notes reminiscent not just of caramel but also of nuts, fruits, alcohol, green leaves, sherry, and vinegar.

Together these two reactions produce a vast encyclopedia of scents and flavors. The question that arises is, why should it be that we prefer this complexity to the comparatively monochromatic flavor of uncooked meat? Richard Wrangham would say it's because evolution has selected for humans who happened to like the complex flavors of cooked foods; those who did ate more of it and produced more offspring. Harold McGee, the food-science writer, proposed another intriguing theory in his 1990 book, *The Curious Cook*. He points out that many of the aromatic compounds generated by the two browning reactions are similar or identical to compounds found in the plant world, such as the flavor notes that we think of as nutty, green, earthy, vegetal, floral, and fruity. It might be expected that caramelizing sugars would produce some of the same compounds found in ripe fruit, since fruits contain sugars; however, it is curious to find so many phytochemicals—plant compounds—showing up in something like roast meat.

"The mingling of the animal and vegetable, the raw and the cooked, may seem like a remarkable coincidence," McGee writes, and it is. But it makes sense that this particular canon of scents would move us, since it is the one we encountered every day in the world of edible plants long before we discovered how to cook. In that uncooked world, this particular group of aromatic compounds amounts to a kind of universal interspecies language, one of the principal systems of communication between plants and animals. Already familiar, those plant scents and flavors were precisely the ones you did well to pay attention to, since they could direct you to good things to eat and away from bad.

Plants have become, by necessity, the great masters of biochemistry in nature. Rooted in place, they evolved the ability to manufacture these aromatic compounds because chemistry can do for the plants what locomotion, vocalization, and consciousness do for animals. So the plants produce molecules that warn and repel and poison some creatures, and others that attract them, whether pollinators to assist them with reproduction or mammals and birds to move their seeds over distances. When their seeds are ready for transport, plants summon mammals with the strong scents and tastes of ripe fruit, a sensory language to which we have become particularly sensitive, since it alerts us to the presence of food energy—sugars—and other plant chemicals we need, like vitamin C. But all animals learn to operate in the information-rich chemical environment that plants create. Fluency in the molecular language of plants would have been particularly important for humans before the advent of agriculture reduced our diet to a small handful of domesticated species. When we still ate hundreds of different plant species, we relied on our senses of smell and taste to navigate a far more complicated food landscape.

So it is no wonder that those types of cooking (such as meat over fire) that happen to generate scents and flavors borrowed from the plant world's extensive chemical vocabulary (and perhaps especially from the rich dialect of ripe fruit) would stimulate us as much as they do. They recall us to a time before agriculture, when our diet was far more diverse, not to mention more interesting and healthy.

"Our powerful response to [these] odors may in part be a legacy of their prehistoric importance for animals, which have used them to recall and learn from their experiences," McGee writes. That these plant scents and flavors provoke us is no accident. Cooked food, he suggests, is Proustian through and through, offering a rich trove of sensory evocations that take us off the frontier of the present and throw us back on the past, our own and, possibly, our species'. "In a sip of coffee or a piece of crackling there are echoes of flowers and leaves, fruit and earth, a recapitulation of moments from the long dialogue between animals and plants." The fact that we are omnivores, creatures who need to consume a great many different substances in order to be healthy, might also predispose us to complexity in the scent and taste of our food. It signals biochemical diversity.

It may also be that, quite apart from any specific references one food makes to another, it is the very allusiveness of cooked food that appeals to us, as indeed that same quality does in poetry or music or art. We gravitate toward complexity and metaphor, it seems, and putting fire to meat, or fermenting fruit and grain, gives us both: more sheer sensory information and, specifically, sensory information that, like metaphor, points away from the here and now. This sensory metaphor—*this stands for that*—is one of the most important transformations of nature wrought by cooking. And so a piece of crisped pigskin becomes a densely allusive poem of flavors: coffee and chocolate, smoke and Scotch and overripe fruit and, too, the sweet-salty-woodsy taste of maple syrup on bacon I loved as a child. As with so many other things, we humans seem to like our food overdetermined.

These particular pigs were still somewhat underdetermined, however. The plan was to finish them at the barbecue, which was taking place in a parking lot downtown across from the old vaudeville theater for which the event was raising money. Aubrey and I rolled the pigs onto the hotel pans—they were considerably lighter now, much of the water having evaporated and the fat rendered out—and then carried them outside to a flatbed truck. Chained to the flatbed were three big pig-cookers, the same kind that had elicited gales of derision from the pit masters assembled in Oxford, Mississippi. These were simply 275-gallon steel oil tanks that had been laid on their side, cut in half, and hinged. A short chimney stuck out of the top of the thing; an axle with two wheels had been welded to the bottom on one end, and a trailer hitch on the other, so the cooker could be towed.

The business district of downtown Wilson consists of a small grid of handsome streets, dominated by a handful of restored Beaux Arts buildings. These stolid limestone banks and office blocks were built in the first decades of the twentieth century, the city's heyday. For a time, Wilson was one of the biggest tobacco markets in the region, but downtown today seems underutilized, at least on a Saturday, and our barbecue inconvenienced nobody. A big white tent had been erected on the empty parking lot; we rolled out and arranged the cookers along one side of it.

I was surprised to see propane tanks mounted on the trailer hitches of the cookers. Ed lit them, and we put the pigs on to finish. Propane had somehow gone from barbecue abomination to convenience overnight. When I asked him about it, Ed explained, somewhat defensively, that he was using the gas not to cook the pigs but merely to keep them warm.

The barbecue was still several hours off, but the sight of the big cookers, and the fine smells already emanating from them, began drawing people as if out of thin air almost right away. Already it seemed clear that the mere sight of Big Ed in the company of a smoking pig cooker put the people of Wilson in an exceptionally good mood. It was Saturday and there was going to be a barbecue.

Actually, there were going to be two barbecues: a lunch and a dinner. Fifteen dollars bought you barbecue, coleslaw, rolls, and sweet tea. By noon, a crowd of two hundred or so had gathered for the first seating. When a critical mass of eaters had settled in, Aubrey and I opened the cookers and, wearing heavy black fireproof gloves, lifted off the first pig and brought it to the chopping block. Ed was shmoozing with the crowd that had gathered around us. We were going to be doing our cooking in public.

Aubrey gave me the front half of the animal to work on while he went to work on the back. The first step was to pull all the meat from the skin, which we would later put back on the cookers to crisp. The fat fingers of the gloves permitted only the crudest manual operations: pulling big hunks of pork off the bones and blades in the shoulder, digging out chunks of cartilage, extracting the ribs, and removing various tubular structures and other anatomical anomalies present in the meat. Even through the big fat gloves, the steaming meat was almost unbearably hot, and I had to stop and remove them every so often to let my hands cool. Mostly, the meat fell easily off the bone, and before long we had before us a big pile of various pork parts—hams, loins, shoulders, bellies.

It was time for Aubrey to start chopping. He wielded a big cleaver in each hand, and the knock-knock-knocking sound of steel on chopping block brought more people around to watch us. When the pile of meat he was chopping seemed too dry, Aubrey would ask me to toss in some shoulder or belly, and when it seemed too fatty, he'd call for more ham or loin, until the mixture seemed about right. Seasoning came next. Aubrey continued to mix the pork with his gloved hands while I added whatever ingredient he called for: nearly a gallon of apple cider vinegar, followed by fat handfuls of sugar, salt, and pepper, both red and black. I sprinkled the dry ingredients over the pork with an even, wrist-flicking motion that Ed had taught me: just like sowing seeds. Aubrey kneaded the seasoning into the mass of meat, pushing it back, then folding it forward, over and again, until he nodded at me to taste it. It tasted a little flat, which meant more vinegar. I splashed on another third of a gallon or so, and another handful of red-pepper flakes, which I figured couldn't hurt since I knew Ed liked some spice in his barbecue. This did the trick.

Now Ed showed me how to crisp the skin, which was nicely browned on one side but still rubbery and white with curds of fat on the other. I sprinkled several handfuls of salt on the fatty side, and threw the skin on the grill, while Ed cranked up the heat. "Keep flipping it or it's liable to burn," he warned. "When it won't bend anymore and begins to blister, that means it's ready." Using a long pair of tongs, I flipped the broad page of skin, first this way then that. It took awhile, and the heat—of the day but especially of the hellish exhalation that hit me full in the face every time I lifted the lid on a cooker—was getting brutal. And then, all at once, the skin lost its pliability and turned to glass. Crackling!

I moved the skin to the chopping block and, after it had had a moment to cool, took a cleaver to it. People were swarming us now—they knew all about crackling and didn't want to wait for us to serve it. "*Can I get me some of that skeeeen?!*" became the question of the hour; we would hear it a hundred times before it was all over. "It's coming, don't worry, it's coming." The crackling shattered at the mere touch of the cleaver. I added handfuls of the brittle little shards into the meat. Another taste: perfect! Aubrey concurred; the barbecue was ready.

By now I was drenched with perspiration, struggling in fact to keep the sweat beading on my brow from raining onto the meat, but this was fun, an adrenaline rush. These people were treating all three of us, and not just Ed, like we were some kind of rock stars. They *really* loved barbecue, we had the barbecue (plus the precious skeen) and we were in a position to give them what they craved. The man who mediates between the fire and the beast, and the beast and the beast eaters, has projected onto him a certain primal power: This is basic stuff, Anthro 101, but now I could actually feel it, and it felt pretty good.

In my room at the Holiday Inn the night before, I had put myself to sleep reading a book called *The Cuisine of Sacrifice Among the Greeks*, by a French and a Belgian classicist. The word "barbecue" never appears in the book, but the more I read about the role of the sacrificial feast in ancient Greece, the more it seemed to unlock what Ed had called "the power of this dish." I became convinced that even today wisps of the smoke of ritual sacrifice linger over barbecue—indeed, shadow us, however faintly, whenever we cook a piece of meat over a fire.

I don't know about you, but I always skipped over the big eating scenes in Homer, barely even stopping to wonder why there were so many of them, or why Homer took the trouble to spell out so many seemingly trivial details: the ins and outs of butchery ("They flayed the carcass . . . and divided it into joints"), fire management ("When the flame had died down, [Patroclus] spread the embers, laid the spits on top of them"), the parceling out of portions ("Achilles served the meat"), table manners ("Face-to-face with his noble guest Odysseus . . . he told his friend to sacrifice to the gods"), and so forth. But according to *The Cuisine of Sacrifice Among the Greeks*, there was good reason for Homer to dwell on these ritual meals. The sharing of cooked meat constituted the communal act among the ancient Greeks, as indeed it has done in a great many other cultures before or since. And doing it right takes some doing. Quite apart from its spiritual significance, the ritual sacrifice had three worldly purposes, purposes that will seem familiar to anyone who has cooked at a barbecue:

To regulate the potentially savage business of eating meat,

To bring people together in a community,

And to support and elevate the priestly class in charge of it.

Eating animals is, at least for humans, seldom anything less than a big deal. Being both desirable and difficult to obtain, meat is naturally bound up with questions of status and prestige, and because killing is involved, eating it is an act steeped in moral and ethical ambiguity. The cooking of meat only adds to the complexity. Before the advent of cooking over fire, "the meal" as we think of it probably didn't exist, for the forager of raw food would have fed him- or herself on the go and alone, much like the animals do. Surpluses were probably shared, but what you found was yours, and you ate it when you got hungry. The cook fire changes all that, however.

"The culinary act is from the start a project," according to Catherine Perlès, the French archaeologist. "Cooking ends individual self sufficiency." For starters, it demands collaboration, if only to keep the fire from dying out. The cook fire itself draws people close together, and introduces the unprecedented social and political complexity of the shared meal, which demands an unprecedented degree of self-control: patience while the meat is cooking, and cooperation when it is ready to be divided. Competition for cooked meat needs to be carefully regulated.

This might help to explain why, in both ancient Greece and the Old Testament, the only time meat is eaten is as part of a carefully prescribed religious observance. It was either a ritual sacrifice, or more nuts and berries for dinner. And though the rules governing the ritual differ from culture to culture, even from occasion to occasion, one of them is universal. And that is simply the rule that there must be rules for cooking and eating meat, ideally a whole bunch of them. Rules, like salt, are the proper accompaniment for meat. For shadowing the eating of meat is always the horrific imagery of animals eating animals: lawlessness, unbridled greed, savagery, and, most frightening of all, cannibalism.

Writing about the kashrut, or kosher rules, Leon R. Kass, the doctor and philosopher, points out, "Although not all flesh is forbidden, everything that is forbidden is flesh." The rules spell out which kinds of animals must not be eaten, which parts of the permissible animals must not be eaten, and what foods can't be eaten in the company of the permitted parts. Yes, there are kosher rules governing the consumption of plant foods, but none of them are outright prohibitions. The Greeks were equally legalistic about eating meat: Only domestic species could be sacrificed, the consumption of blood was forbidden (as it is in the kashrut), and elaborate protocols governed the apportioning of the different cuts.

Beyond guarding against various forms of savagery, the rules governing ritual sacrifice are designed to promote community. *The Cuisine of Sacrifice Among the Greeks* describes the Greek ritual as an act of "alimentary communion." Eating from the same animal, prepared according to the agreed-upon rules of the group, strengthens the ties binding the group together.* Sharing is at the very heart of ritual sacrifice, as indeed it is in most forms of cooking.

Many, if not most, modern commentators on the Old Testament regard the specific rules that constitute the kashrut as more or less arbitrary; so do most anthropologists. Contrary to what I was taught as a child, pork is no more dangerous to eat than any other meat. Yet however arbitrary such prohibitions may be, they retain the power to knit us together, help forge a collective identity: *We are the people who don't eat pork.* Many of the rules regulating sacrifice in Leviticus make little

---

*Much the same can be said of the Christian Eucharist, in which all communicants symbolically eat from the body and blood of Christ.

sense unless understood in this light—as forms of social glue. For example, in one kind of sacrifice, it is specified that all the meat must be eaten before the second day is over, an injunction that ensures it will be shared among the group rather than hoarded by any individual.

Perhaps this is the best light in which to make sense of the endlessly intricate legalisms of the various schools of Southern barbecue: as rules governing "acts of alimentary communion" that help to define and strengthen the community. Whole-hog barbecue stands out as a particularly powerful form of communion, in which the meat is divided among the eaters according to a notably democratic protocol. Everyone gets a taste of every cut, eating not just from the same animal but from every part of that animal, the choice and the not-so-choice. But at bottom most of the rules of barbecue, spelling out what is and is not acceptable in species of animal, animal part, sauce, fuel, and fire, are as arbitrary as the kashrut, rules for the sake of rules, with no rational purpose except to define one's community by underscoring its differences from another. *We are the people who cook only shoulders over hickory wood and put mustard in our barbecue sauce.* Prohibitions multiply like weeds. *No propane, no charcoal, no tomato, no ribs, no chicken, no beef.*

"So barbecue is basically like kashrut for goys," a friend put it as I labored to explain the subtle distinctions between the various denominations of Southern barbecue. The sentence I heard more than any other from the pit masters I interviewed, from the Carolinas to Texas and Tennessee, would have to be the one they wielded when speaking of any other tribe's cooking rituals: "Okay, but that's not barbecue." Whatever else the food in question might be, it didn't conform to the traditional rules of the group. It wasn't kosher.

The third function of ritual sacrifice is to elevate and support the priestly or noble class that performs it. In this, the ritual is no different from any other political institution. It is concerned foremost with the perpetuation of its own power. Great prestige accrues to the man who officiates at the ritual sacrifice, killing the animal, cutting it up, cooking it, and dividing the meat. In ancient Greece, women and slaves did most of the everyday cooking, but when the occasion called for a ritual meal, whether to mark the beginning or conclusion of a military campaign, or the arrival of an honored guest, or a day otherwise made large by history, the men performed the honors. Odysseus, Patroclus, even Achilles man the cook fires themselves, at no cost to their prestige; to the contrary, this sort of festal cooking enhances it. The rules in Leviticus all serve to enhance the authority of the priest performing the sacrifice, taking special care to specify precisely which portion of the animal should be allotted to the priest himself. The commentators suggest that the requirement that ritual accompany all meat eating was, among other things, a way to make sure the community supported its priestly class—by feeding it.

The pit master seasoning his barbecue at the altar of the chopping block—indeed, even the husband presiding over his Weber in the backyard—is drawing on whatever remains of this age-old cultural capital. That any such capital endures more than two millennia hence strikes me as both marvelous and slightly absurd. Which is why you've really got to hand it to these latter-day masters of fire, smoke, meat, and community. The barbecue men have done a masterful job keeping the old show going.

My own solo turn on the barbecue stage came that evening, during the second seating in Wilson. Aubrey, it seems, was only being paid for a twelve-hour shift, so when six o'clock rolled around he simply disappeared. I never got to say good-bye. Since part of the event's draw was supposed to be a barbecue lecture and demo by local hero Ed Mitchell, this meant I would be on my own at the chopping block while he took the microphone. Ed seemed surprisingly unperturbed by this turn of events, and since no one had told me Aubrey had gone off the clock, I barely had time to get nervous.

It seems to me that authentic whole-hog barbecue (if I may use that term) is not something you ever want to pay someone to do by the hour. In fact, it's hard to imagine that this method of cooking, which demands so much more time than effort, would ever have taken root in a society where wage labor was the norm. The rhythms of barbecue are much better suited to the premodern economics of sharecropping or slavery. Such an economy, combined with the heat, helped make a certain slowness—as much as pork or wood smoke— a key ingredient in Southern cooking, and Southern culture more generally. "Southerners have been known to be slow traditionally in doing certain things," Sy Erskine, the Alabama pit master, told a journalist. "It transfers right on to the cooking of the food. They sit down and take their time and let that meat cook instead of rushing things on and off the fire. It is a tradition strictly of the South."

I now knew exactly what he meant. Ed and I had spent one of the laziest, most desultory afternoons I can remember, standing and sitting around the cookers, getting as close to doing absolutely nothing as you can get while still ostensibly "cooking." We were "letting that meat cook," low and slow, and there really wasn't much to do while it happened.

But now that the guests had arrived and Ed had taken the stage, things were speeding up—getting a tad frantic, in fact. Before me on the chopping block was an entire steaming half of a pig. While Ed explained the procedure to the audience, seasoning his rap with tales of Bobby Flay and the Food Network throwdown, I picked out the ribs and other bones with my cartoony black propylene fingers, and pulled the meat from the carapace of pigskin. Now, wielding a cleaver in each hand, I went to work on the pile of pig parts, reducing it to a roughly chopped mass of pork, leaving some of the belly in reserve so I could adjust for fat and moisture content. The cleavers were heavier than they looked, and the repetitive motion soon exhausted the muscles in my forearms. Aubrey's chop had looked like pork hash, uniform and fine. I decided to go for something a little rougher, partly because I preferred the texture and partly because my arms were about to fall off. Now, as Ed narrated what I was doing and the crowd watched, I seasoned the great mound of pork. First the gallon of vinegar, then the handfuls of sugar, salt, and pepper, black and red, all of it sown like seeds across the sprawling heap of meat.

A voice in the crowd erupted: "Now, don't you go forgetting the skeen!" Then another: "Yeah, give us some of that nice crackling!" Fortunately, Ed had crisped a side's worth of skin before he took the stage, because, from the sound of it, this hungry crowd might not have waited for me to do it now. I shattered the brittle skin with my cleaver and scooped several big handfuls of crackling onto the mound of pork. The rest I piled on trays for the servers to pass around plain, since the crowd seemed mad for the stuff, their energies focused less on the beer and wine now flowing than on these mahogany shards of hog skin. I don't want to think what would have happened if I had left out the crackling or—God forbid!—burned it beyond a crisp.

VI.

MANHATTAN, NYC

A few weeks after my star turn in Wilson, I got a chance to join the barbecue road show one last time, but now on a much bigger stage. Ed and Aubrey and their crew from The Pit were driving up to Manhattan for the eighth annual Big Apple Barbecue Block Party, and Ed invited me to come to New York and lend a hand. After Wilson, North Carolina, this sounded like opening on Broadway.

Manhattan has never been much of a barbecue town, something the restaurateur Danny Meyer realized soon after he added an upscale barbecue joint called Blue Smoke to his roster of successful Manhattan restaurants. New Yorkers just didn't get it, and those who actually knew something about barbecue were skeptical such a place could possibly be authentic. So Meyer and Blue Smoke's executive chef, Kenny Callaghan, hit on the idea of bringing America's best pit masters to New York City for a weekend in June. The event would teach New Yorkers, who probably own the smallest number of grills per capita in America, about "authentic barbecue," and at the same time showcase Blue Smoke's own pit master in the company of such barbecue luminaries as Chris Lilly (Decatur, Alabama); Jimmy Hagood (Charleston, South Carolina); Joe Duncan (Dallas, Texas); Skip Steele (St. Louis, Missouri); and Ed Mitchell (Raleigh, North Carolina). The idea was for some of the authenticity of these pit masters to rub off on Blue Smoke. In exchange, the visiting pit masters would sell a ton of barbecue and get some national media exposure. Seven years later, New York City has evidently discovered a taste for barbecue. One hundred twenty-five thousand people were expected in Madison Square

Park for this year's event, coming to hang around the pits and sample barbecue over two days, at $8 a sandwich.

When I showed up early Saturday morning, Ed and his crew had already set up their tents, cookers, and chopping blocks on the south side of 26th Street just off Fifth Avenue. Parked around the corner on Fifth, taking up nearly half a city block, was a white eighteen-wheel tractor trailer with a billboard-sized image of Ed Mitchell's smiling face painted on the side. The night before, the truck had disgorged eight 275-gallon cookers, sixteen pigs, several tables and chopping blocks, cleavers, shovels, bag upon bag of Kingsford charcoal, and countless gallons of (premixed) barbecue sauce. Ed and Aubrey had put the pigs on the fire at six the night before, and a couple of guys from the restaurant had stayed up all night looking after them. Madison Square Park had never smelled so good, the smoke of fifteen different barbecue pits mingling in the soft air of an early-summer evening.

The guys were running two chopping blocks simultaneously, and Aubrey invited me to take over one of them, working next to Ed's grown son, Ryan. It was only 11:00 a.m., but a crowd had already begun to gather, drawn by the auspicious smoke as well as Ed's reputation. Since the first Big Apple Barbecue Block Party in 2003, Ed Mitchell has been its biggest draw. He is the only pit master doing whole-hog barbecue, and the only black pit master at the event. You could almost see, floating over the crowd forming at Ed Mitchell's corner of Madison Park, the thought bubble: "Authenticity."

By now I knew the drill, or thought I did, and got right to work pulling pork from a nicely browned side of pig that Aubrey had delivered to my chopping block. There was something unexpectedly powerful about the sight of a whole hog cooked on the streets of Manhattan, a collision of realms or times. Yet there is nothing Manhattan cannot absorb, and the scene didn't take long to feel almost normal. I flattered myself into thinking I knew what I was doing, but it soon became clear I wasn't in Wilson, North Carolina, anymore—and in fact was in way over my head. At 11:00 a.m. sharp, The Pit crew had begun selling sandwiches, and they sold out the first batch so quickly that the sandwich-making crew began calling, with mounting insistence, for more pork. I was chopping as fast as I could, but there was a limit to how fast you could go. Not only were my arms growing rubbery, but I wanted to be sure there were no little bones or bits of cartilage left in the meat before I released another pile of barbecue to the servers. What if someone chomped down on an overlooked vertebra? Manhattan might have the lowest number of barbecue grills per capita, but surely it has the highest number of lawyers. Yet the clamor from the sandwich crew wouldn't let up. "More pork, please! We need more pork up here!" I was chopping pork as fast as my arms would let me, then pouring gallons of sauce over the pile, all the while scanning and sifting the meat for suspicious bits of white. As soon as I passed a sheet tray heaped with barbecue to the sandwich crew, Aubrey deposited another steaming pig on my chopping block, and the process started all over again.

(What about the crackling? Sorry you asked. Our assembly line was moving so quickly now that there simply wasn't time to crisp the skin and add it in. But, luckily for us, only a handful of people in this crowd knew enough to ask for it, and even they didn't want to wait. So: no crackling today.)

The few moments I could steal to look up from my chopping block, I spotted the big round black-and-white head of Ed Mitchell schmoozing with the crowd, which looked to be happy but also, it seemed to me, collectively insatiable. Behind the velvet rope line snaking down 26th Street, there must have been several thousand people waiting to get their barbecue sandwich, more people than we could ever hope to feed. I redoubled my chopping, working now at a furious pace that (among other problems of quality control) spattered my clothing with hot fat. And then, all at once, I noticed that my feet, of all things, felt simultaneously wet and on fire. I looked down to see that the scalding-hot juice from the pigs was streaming off the chopping block and soaking my sneakers and feet. So it came as sweet relief when Aubrey offered to spell me.

Gratefully, I stepped away from the blazing heat of the cookers, putting some cool air between myself and the smoke and spatter of chopped pig, as well as the hunger of the crowd and the clamor of the sandwich makers. ("More barbecue! We need more barbecue up here!") I could see Ed moving serenely through the sea of New Yorkers, giving interviews, but couldn't get close enough to say goodbye. He was charming the congregation with his shtick, which surely never gleamed so brightly as it did in Manhattan. Ed was clearly enjoying himself, playing the role of the barbecue rock star in New York City, but I found the whole happy scene also just a little harrowing. There was obviously not going to be enough barbecue for everyone, and I wondered how the crowd would react when the disappointment dawned.

I found out later we sold out by 1:00 p.m., eight whole hogs and two thousand sandwiches snapped up in something less than two hours. Ed would likely have promised the crowd there would be more barbecue tomorrow, eight more pigs, and eventually they must have drifted off to other stands, other sandwiches. But I was long gone by then, eager to escape the crowd and the heat.

I made a slow circuit of Madison Square Park, checking out the other pits and pit masters. It was a United Nations of barbecue, with all the important denominations represented: South Carolina with its eccentric mustard-based sauce, Memphis with its ribs, smoked links and brisket from Texas. All the pit masters were men, all had a gleaming rap, and many of them also had an equally gleaming rig. But by far the best of these was Jimmy Hagood's fire-engine-red double-decker barbecue-joint-on-wheels, up from Charleston: a full-scale kitchen with a half dozen pig cookers at street level linked by a circular stairway to a deck with tables upstairs. Chatting up Jimmy, I learned he had been an insurance agent in Charleston, bored with life until he discovered his inner pit master. This struck me as still a work in progress, with something of the indoors—the office, even—not yet completely expunged. "You've got to work your persona," he explained. "It's called marketing."

The second-floor platform on Jimmy Hagood's rig commanded a fine treetop view of the whole festival. I sat myself down for a few minutes to sip a cold drink and catch my breath. Barbecue, barbecue as far as the eye could see, tens of thousands of people wending their way among the fragrant curls of hickory smoke, carrying their cardboard trays of pork ribs and barbecue sandwiches. How many years had it been since Manhattan had seen so many pigs—I guessed that more than three hundred hogs had been sacrificed to feed the weekend's crowd—or so many wood fires?

Manhattan these days is a world capital of gastronomy, but these barbecue men cut figures that could hardly be more different from that of the typical New York chef. In a place where chefs regard themselves as artists, and diners prize novel tastes and experiences, the world of the pit master seems premodern, almost epic in its directness and lack of shading or irony. Getting it right counts for more than making it new, which to these men is an utterly alien concept. How could you improve on barbecue? Theirs was an outdoor and completely externalized world, everything in it brightly lit and foregrounded, with plenty of smoke, sure, but no shadows—no subtleties or shades of gray. The pit masters worked exclusively with the ancient, primary colors of cooking—wood, fire, smoke, and meat—and strove not for originality or even development but for faithfulness.

Compared with the contemporary chef, the pit masters present themselves less as artists than as priests, each with his own congregation and distinctive liturgy, working, scrupulously, in forms passed down rather than invented. What chef would ever boast, as Samuel Jones, trotting out one of his most cherished sound bites, did to me in Ayden, "Our barbecue is like the King James Bible"? In their work and their food as much as in their patter, the pit masters are as formulaic as Homer. They present themselves as outsized, heroic characters, but full of themselves in the specific way epic heroes are—boastful rather than merely egotistical. They're allowed to boast, because they don't stand for themselves so much as for an ideal or, better yet, a tribe—the community defined by their style of barbecue. "I am the old keeper of the flame," Ed Mitchell told the oral historian from the Southern Foodways Alliance, putting more than a little of the King James into his diction. "And I don't want anyone to forget that you did not take sausage out of the hog and barbecue those sausages and call it barbecue, you did not take ribs out of that hog and call it barbecue, you did not take the shoulders out of that hog and call it barbecue. You first cooked the whole hog, and everything derived from cooking the whole hog."

It's almost as though these men fixed their personae at a time before novels were invented. So could there possibly be a better stage for such brightly drawn characters, or for the elemental drama of pig meets wood fire and time, than twenty-first-century Manhattan? From my perch atop Jimmy Hagood's shiny red barbecue rig, I gazed across Madison Square Park and caught my last glimpse of Ed Mitchell, his great round head rising out of the crowd like a black-and-white moon, lighting up a whole sea of New Yorkers.

VII.

BERKELEY, CALIFORNIA

I didn't realize how much I'd learned in North Carolina about cooking with fire until I got home and ran a few experiments. I ordered a whole pork shoulder from an Iowa hog farmer I knew named Jude Becker. Jude raises traditional breeds outdoors and finishes them on acorns in the fall. I also ordered a cord of wood, oak and almond, and began cooking with it in the fire pit in my front yard. In fact, I began burning shamefully large quantities of wood, because I now understood that it was not the fire but the remains of the fire, the smoldering wood coals, that you really wanted to cook with. (Well, Ed Mitchell's Kingsford compromise to the contrary notwithstanding.) I probably could have cured an entire barn's worth of tobacco with all the wood I burned before I ever put a piece of meat on to cook. What I had learned—not only from the Southern pit masters but also from all the other fire cookers I met in my travels, people working in traditions and places as far-flung as Patagonia and the Basque Country—is simply this: You have to cook the wood before you can cook the food.

The pork shoulder arrived in a surprisingly big box and wasn't at all what I expected. Say "pork shoulder" to a butcher, and he'll wrap you a five- or six-pound cut of meat, a portion of the shoulder, or top of the front leg, that is sometimes referred to, confusingly, as a picnic ham or Boston butt. But apparently the same order in the wholesale trade means an entire front leg of a hog, complete with hide and dainty hoof, and that's exactly what greeted me when I pried opened the box. I suppose I could have cooked the whole thing, but a failure of nerve (and shortage of eaters) prompted me instead to call in a chef friend for help butchering it. She showed me how to bone out the shoulder and cut it into three manageable parts. The good thing about working from the whole leg is that we could divide it in such a way that each section still wore its skin. Which meant I could try for crackling. We scored the leathery skin with a sharp knife in a tic-tac-toe pattern; this would help the fat to render and the skin to crisp.

My fire pit is an old, shallow hammered-iron bowl about four feet in diameter; the guy who sold it to me said he found it in India, where it was used to cook street food. The pit is wide enough at the bottom that you can build a fire on one side and then shovel the ripe coals under a grill set up on the other; however, covering such a big area for barbecue is a problem. So far, the best solution anyone has come up with is something less than elegant: Bend a few pieces of rebar into an igloo-tent frame and cover that with one of those silvery insulation blankets people use to wrap their water heaters or engine blocks. The result resembles a redneck Martian's spacecraft, but it does the trick when cooking a large segment of animal.

Cooking barbecue in my front yard involves a great deal of time staring into a fire, waiting for the flames to subside and the wood to break down into smoldering coals that I can shovel under the meat. Gazing into the flames of a wood fire is mesmerizing; the flames seem to take control of your thoughts, deflecting them from any linear path. Gaston Bachelard, the idiosyncratic French philosopher, claims that philosophy itself began in front of the fire, flowing from the peculiar reverie that a fire inspires.

Bachelard offers not a shred of evidence for his claim, but there is a certain poetic truth to it, and poetic truth is the only kind he's interested in. In 1938, he wrote a slim, oddly elusive book called The Psychoanalysis of Fire, essentially to protest modern science's reductive understanding of fire.* Fire once obsessed the scientist as much as the poet. It seemed to be the key to all transformation. But no longer. What humans have believed since belief began—that fire is a great and powerful thing, one of the constitutive elements of reality—science now tells us is merely an epiphenomenon: the visible trace of a straightforward chemical process, also known as "rapid oxidation."

But though fire "is no longer a reality for science," in our everyday experience, as in our imaginations, it remains what it was for Empedocles, who more than two thousand years ago counted it, with earth, air, and water, as one of the elements: the four underived and indestructible substances from which the world is made. Modern science has long since replaced the classical quartet with a periodic table of 118 elements, but, as the literary critic Northrup Frye writes in his preface to Bachelard's book, "For the poet, the elements will always be earth, air, fire and water."

But whether or not fire is constitutive of physical reality, we can say—and science now seems prepared to accept—that the control of fire is constitutive of us, of our humanity. "Animals need food, water, and shelter," Richard Wrangham writes in *Catching Fire*. "We humans need all those things, but we need fire too." We are the only species that depends on fire to maintain our body heat, and the only species that can't get along without cooking its food. By now, the control of fire is folded into our genes, a matter not merely of human culture but of our very biology. If the cooking hypothesis is correct, it is fire that—by unlocking more of the energy in food and partly externalizing human digestion—fed the spectacular growth of the human brain. So, in this sense at least, Bachelard is correct to credit fire with

---

*In the introduction, Bachelard helpfully warns us, "When our reader has finished reading this book he will in no way have increased his knowledge."

the invention of philosophy. He might have added music, poetry, mathematics, and books about fire itself.

The cook fire in particular, the kind of fire I'm tending in my front yard, also helped form us as social beings. "Fire's power of social magnetism," as the historian Felipe Fernández-Armesto puts it, is what first drew us together, and in doing so probably shifted the course of human evolution. The cook fire selected for individuals who could tolerate other individuals—make eye contact, cooperate, and share. "When fire and food combined," writes Fernández-Armesto, "an almost irresistible focus was created for communal life." (In fact, the word "focus" comes from the Latin word for "hearth.") The social gravity of the cook fire seems undiminished, as I'm reminded every time my guests drift outdoors to watch their dinner sizzle and brown, or when the neighbor's children drift over into my yard to find out what it is that smells so good.

As fire's presence in our everyday lives has diminished, the social magnetism of the cook fire seems, if anything, to have only grown more powerful. One way to tell the history of cooking is as the story of the taming of the cooking fire followed by its gradual disappearance from our lives. Contained first in stone fireplaces and brought indoors, it was then encased in iron and steel, and in our time replaced altogether by invisible electric currents and radio waves confined to a box of glass and plastic. The microwave oven, which stands at the precise opposite end of the culinary (and imaginative) spectrum from the cook fire, exerts a kind of antigravity, its flameless, smokeless, antisensory cold heat giving us a mild case of the willies. The microwave is as antisocial as the cook fire is communal. Who ever gathers around the Panasonic hearth? What reveries does its mechanical whir inspire? What is there even to look at through the double pane of radiation-proof glass, except the lazy rotation of the "single-serving portion" for the solitary eater? To the extent there has been a revival of fire cooking in recent years, it may be the microwave we have to thank, for driving us back outdoors into the fire's orbit and once again into one another's company. . . .

8

. . . But back to this particular cook fire, the one now burning in my front yard.

I wait for the flames to subside and the logs to crumble before I even think about putting on the meat. This is true whether I'm grilling in the open air or slow cooking barbecue under cover. The smoke of wood coals is much gentler than the smoke of burning woods. All but invisible, this "second smoke," as I've come to think of it, has none of the tarry, acrid compounds that the initial combustion of wood releases, and therefore imparts a subtler set of woody flavors.

For barbecue, what seems to work best is to build a fire in the pit and then shovel the coals into a kettle grill that can be covered. I keep the vents almost completely closed, aiming for a temperature somewhere between 200°F and 300°F—much hotter and the meat will sear; much cooler and it won't cook through. Ideally, you would keep the original "mother fire" going, because you may need to add more coals later. Before I put the meat on the fire, I clear just enough space in the bed of coals to place a disposable tinfoil tray directly beneath it in order to catch the dripping fat. I pour an inch or so of water into the tray to prevent flame-ups and help keep the atmosphere in there moist.

Now comes the time—and there will be plenty of it—for doing nothing, except keeping one eye on your roast. (Which is why you can't leave home.) This is where, if alone, you launch your reverie, or, if with friends, some conversation and drinking. Inevitably, I find that at some point in the afternoon I have either too much fire or not enough fire. The key, as every pit master I've ever met has told me, is control, but control is easier to achieve than it is to maintain for any sustained period of time. Opening or closing the vents may do the trick, but if it doesn't, you'll have either to add or to remove hot coals, which can be a messy, dangerous business.

Here is when one's easy condescension toward those who cook with gas or charcoal will be tested.

And in fact I must confess that the best results I have achieved to date have involved: propane. A pork shoulder needs at least six hours, and ideally a couple more, to attain perfection, and it's hard to keep a gently smoldering fire gently smoldering quite that long. So, rather than keep a mother fire burning all that time, and then have to lift up a hot grate and shovel fresh coals underneath it, I take the meat off the wood fire once the temperature in the grill has dropped below 225°F or so. By then, I figure the meat has received most of the blessing of wood smoke, the flavor of which cooked meat can't absorb anyway. Now the meat just needs more heat and time: a couple more hours at 250°F to 300°F. And besides, by now I've acquired from Ed Mitchell and his colleagues a much more supple and forgiving concept of authenticity.

When I move the shoulder onto the gas grill, its internal temperature hovers around 160°F, and the skin, which is pulling apart into little cubes, has a nice wood-toned finish, though it still feels rubbery to the touch. At this temperature, the meat is cooked through but dry and tough. If I took the shoulder off now, I would have not barbecue, just overcooked pork.

But a miraculous transformation occurs once the internal temperature of the meat reaches 195°F. If you've been poking the shoulder along the way, you will feel it. The muscles, which had earlier felt as though they had seized up tight, have suddenly relaxed. The slow, steady heat has dissolved the collagen into moist gelatin and freed the muscle fibers, which now separate into tender, succulent, pullable threads. And if everything has gone according to plan, the skin by now will have crisped into precious little cubes of crackling.

There you have it, all but the chopping and seasoning: authentic-enough barbecue. It's not whole-hog, true, but the shoulder, which consists of a few different muscle groups as well as plenty of fat, is the next best thing. The first time I achieved delicious, quasi-authentic results—crackling included—I wanted to call Ed Mitchell with the news, practice my boasting—as indeed I am now doing—and look seriously into entering a competition. But eventually I settled down. I called up some friends to come over for an impromptu dinner, and together we enjoyed one of the tastier sandwiches I had ever made, and without a doubt the very proudest.

VIII.

CODA: AXPE, SPAIN

There is one last cook fire I need to tell you about, one that made me think that, even after some two millions years of practice, the possibilities of cooking with fire may not be exhausted yet. I found this fire in the microscopic town of Axpe, in the Basque Country of Spain, high in the rocky hills between the cities of San Sebastián and Bilbao. This is where, in an undistinguished but ancient stone house on the town square, a self-trained chef in his fifties by the name of Bittor Arguinzoniz, a former lumberjack and electrician, has been quietly and intently reinventing what it means to cook with fire in the twenty-first century.

I met Arguinzoniz within twenty-four hours of cooking with Ed Mitchell in Manhattan, and the contrast between the two men and their worlds could not be starker. Bittor does not like to give interviews, or for that matter even talk much, at least not while he's cooking, a process demanding such fierce concentration that a visitor to his kitchen feels at first like an intruder and then utterly invisible. He is a modest, ascetic man, tall, slender except for a compact paunch, and gray as smoke. Bittor likes to work in solitude, seldom leaves Axpe (where he grew up in a house with no running water or electricity; his mother heated and cooked exclusively with wood), and is not given to pronouncements, except perhaps one: *"Carbón es el enemigo"*—"Charcoal is the enemy." He believes cooking is all about sacrifice, though I soon realized he was referring to the sacrifice of the chef himself, rather than that of the creatures he cooks.

The kitchen at Asador Etxebarri (which in the Basque tongue means "New House") combines the gleaming, controlled geometry of stainless steel—six grills of Bittor's own design lining one wall—with the raw power of a raging wood fire. On the opposite wall, at waist height, two open ovens each hold a stack of blazing logs. Every morning, Bittor and his sous-chef, a loquacious but protective Australian named Lennox Hastie, begin the day by cooking a large quantity of the local oak, citrus, olive, and grape logs in the two ovens, to produce the wood coals with which Bittor cooks exclusively.

Bittor flavors all his food with wood, a different species and even a different kind of ember (glowing red or ashy white, intensifying or fading) for each dish. Grapevines, which burn hot and aromatic, he matches with beef, whereas a single dying ember of oak would be used to more subtly inflect the flavor of a scallop. A black plunger jutting from the wall above each of the wood ovens allows him to precisely control the amount of oxygen feeding the fire, and thereby the temperature, and the life span, of the wood coals it produces.

By the kitchen's screened back door stands a little lean-to, neatly stacked with different species of firewood and, on top of the wood-piles, crates of produce—tomatoes, leeks, onions, fava beans, and ar-tichokes. Most of it has been grown a few miles up the hill, on a plot tended by Bittor's eighty-nine-year-old father, Angel, mainly because he could find nothing worth cooking in the market. ("Everything is prostituted," he tells me, with a little snort of disgust. "With chemi-cals.") Most of the seafood he cooks—lobsters, eels, sea cucumbers, oysters, clams, fishes of various kinds—is kept alive in saltwater tanks (a challenge up here in the mountains) in a room off the kitchen until the appointed moment when the fire is ready and the creature is pulled from the water to meet it.

The afternoon I spent in his kitchen, Bittor had on a black T-shirt and gray slacks. He wore no apron, yet remained spotless: Liquids of any kind scarcely enter into his cooking. I had planned to ask if I could pitch in with the cooking, as I had done in North Carolina, but I quickly realized that, here, that would be tantamount to asking a brain surgeon if I might assist. Lennox made it clear I was lucky just to get into the kitchen.

Everything at Etxebarri is cooked to order, not a moment sooner. When the first order came in, I watched Bittor use a small stainless-steel scoop to retrieve a fist-sized pile of oak embers with which to cook a sea cucumber. Sea cucumbers are striated, slightly rubbery white sea creatures, reminiscent of squid, that live on the ocean floor. They require brief but intense heat to break down their leathery skin. Before he puts one on the grill, Bittor watches his coals intently, pa-tiently waiting for them to ripen. A stainless-steel wheel above each grill, and connected to it by a system of cables and counterweights, allows him to make microadjustments in the distance between food and fire. When Bittor determines the coals are ready—strictly by eye; I never once saw him pass his hand over the fire to judge its heat—he places the sea cucumber over them. Now he spritzes it with a fine mist of oil, which he believes helps the food better absorb the aromatic compounds in wood. And then he silently waits, staring at the sea cucumber as if lost in a trance. He's looking for the slightest suggestion of a grill mark to form across the striations before flipping it, just once.

Next I watched Bittor "cook" an oyster, a process that involved choosing a single, perfect ember and placing it beneath the plump dove-gray ovoid with a pair of forceps, just so. I flashed back to James Howell, in Ayden, shoveling smoky wood coals under a pig. Here was the same basic operation, yet could this cooking possibly be more different? Fire, it seems, is protean; smoke, too. Bittor didn't actually want to cook his oyster, just wreathe it in the merest wisp of orange wood smoke, a process that took less than thirty seconds. The whole time, Bittor looked to be in a staring contest with the oyster. I can only infer—because he would not speak, and never touched the oyster—that he was watching for a change in the reflectivity of its surface, a certain shift in the quality of its glistening, that told him it was done, or, rather, ready for the table. He then passed the oyster to Lennox, who gently slid it back into its shell. Bittor bent down and sprinkled several grains of sea salt over it, and then a spoonful of an off-white froth that Lennox had made by whipping the liquid that the oyster had left behind when it was shucked a few moments before.

I tasted twelve courses that Bittor had cooked, and all of them, up to and including the butter and the desserts, had in some way been touched, more or less, by wood smoke. This probably sounds like a recipe for monotony. That it was nothing of the kind remains something of a mystery to me. That oyster? It tasted more like an oyster than any oyster I have ever tasted. Somehow, the taste of smoke didn't merge with the oyster but coexisted alongside it, held in a perfect balance, so that it underscored the oyster's meaty brine, in the way that a frame or window can deepen our appreciation of a view we might otherwise overlook. Many of the dishes seemed to work that way, the native flavor of an octopus or tuna belly intensified by just the right note of the right kind of smoke, much as a careful deployment of salt can bring out the flavors of a food without announcing its own salty presence.

By the end of the meal, I began to think that Bittor had figured out how to use smoke as a sixth flavor principle, entitled at last to equal billing with salt, sour, sweet, bitter, and umami. And maybe smoke is that, one of the irreducible, primary colors of taste. Or so at least it can seem, perhaps because wood smoke was cooked food's first flavor, the taste we gave to raw nature when we first introduced it to fire. This, anyway, was the sort of speculation inspired by Bittor's cooking, at once so elemental and so delicate that it becomes a meditation on the nature of cooking itself.

When Bittor and I sat down to talk at a picnic table outside, he spoke of cooking with wood as the "best way to honor the product." For him fire is not about the transformation of nature—of the animals and plants and fungi he works with—but about achieving something more like an italicization of nature, making the food more like itself rather than something else.

"What the grill is going to do is reveal the excellence or mediocrity of the product," Bittor explained, which is why he must go to such lengths to secure the freshest and best produce. For him the grill is a tool for exploring the natural world, the creatures of the sea and the meadows (the steak he grilled for me was too good to be true: a cut from a fourteen-year-old dairy cow that he quickly charred on both sides at once in a blazing-hot fire of grapevines) but also of the woods: the various trees he cooks with. For the trees are clearly this former forester's first love, and their flavors inflect everything he touches. Though to my surprise, Bittor insisted that his medium is not smoke, a taste and a smell he regards as crude; rather, he flavors his food with the "perfume" or "fragrance" of wood. But isn't that communicated to the food by means of smoke? "No, no, no smoke," he insisted. It was here I got lost, either in the vagaries of translation or in the metaphysics of burning trees.

In Bittor's view, there is no food that cannot be enhanced by fire, by this quality of that-which-is-not-smoke, though exactly how to achieve this enhancement is not always obvious. "My cooking is a work in progress; I am still experimenting." At the moment, he's on a quest to figure out how to grill honey. A metalworker, Bittor has fabricated pans with stainless-steel meshes so fine he can "cook" something as delicate and minuscule as caviar. Lennox said it had pained him to watch Bittor experiment with kilo after kilo of caviar (at $3,200 per kilo) until he was ready to add it to the menu. To cook mussels, he built a kind of Bundt pan that conducts smoke through a central funnel to flavor the briny liquor without letting so much as a drop of it escape. For his butters and ice cream, Bittor briefly warms cream in unglazed crockery that admits only the most indirect hint of smoke—or, rather, the perfume of wood.

In fact, my meal at Etxebarri began and ended with variations on smoked cream, and for me these remain the most memorable tastes of the afternoon, if not of my whole exploration of fire to date. Bittor churns his butter himself and serves it without bread. It is meant to be eaten plain, like a fine cheese, and his butters—there were both cow's milk and goat—become a study in contrasts, of these two different methods nature has evolved for transforming grass into butterfat. But that hint of smoke, or whatever you want to call it, brought out something else in the cream, something entirely unexpected, even poignant.

Cream—the richest, sweetest part of milk—is of course our first flavor, the taste, in a spoon, of life's first freshness and innocence, long before we ever encounter the taste of cooked food. And what is smoke—or ashes, with which one of the butters has been dusted—if not the very opposite of that freshness? There it is, innocence and experience mingled in a spoonful of ice cream. Bittor, whom no one would describe as a sunny man, has figured out a way to pass a fleeting, chill shadow of mortality over the formerly uncomplicated happiness of ice cream.

A dark dessert, you might say, and rightly so, yet the fact that anyone could do so much with so little—with some superlative produce and a wood fire—strikes me as a most happy and hopeful discovery. In Bittor's kitchen I got to witness, and to taste, the apotheosis of the control of fire. The cook fire, which had seemed so ancient in North Carolina, here in Spain seemed new again, fresh with possibility.

This is certainly not what you expect to find in contemporary Spain, a country that has become known for "molecular gastronomy"—for an elaborate kind of cooking that leans more heavily on science and technology than on nature, or, as the chefs now call it, "product." As it happens, Ferran Adrià, perhaps the world's most famous exponent of molecular gastronomy, a chef known for cooking with liquid nitrogen, xanthan gum, synthetic flavors and textures, and all the other tools of modern food science, is an admirer of Bittor's cooking and comes often to Axpe to dine at Etxebarri. Adrià was once quoted in Gourmet magazine saying, "Bittor probably couldn't be doing what he's doing if I hadn't done what I did first." It is a claim of breathtaking arrogance, and when I read it back to Bittor, he bristled slightly, then waved it away like a fly.

"Ferran cooks for the future," he tells me. "I am more interested in going backward. But the further back we can go, the more we can then advance.

"At this point there are people trying to cook with no product at all"—with nothing whatever derived from nature. This he believes is a dead end. "You can fool the palate," he says, "but you cannot fool the stomach."

And yet Ferran Adrià may be right to put his cooking before Bittor Arguinzoniz's in this one sense: It may be that a taste for Bittor's cooking, for his obsessive, slightly mad investigation into the nature of wood and fire and food, has been prepared by our culture's ongoing attempt to transcend all those things, not just with molecular gastronomy, but with artificial flavors and colors, synthetic food experiences of every kind, even the microwave oven. High and low, this is an age of the jaded palate, ever hungry for the next new taste, the next new sensation, for mediated experiences of every kind. It's unclear how far that quest can take us, or when it might lose its savor. But isn't it always precisely when we are most at risk of floating away on the sea of our own inventions and conceits that we seem to row our way back to the firm shore that is nature? And though the shore we return to is never quite the same one we left, it has not let us down yet.

"This kind of cooking is as old as man himself," Bittor Arguinzoniz says when I ask him why in a world such as ours the power of cooking over a wood fire should still transfix us. It isn't very complicated. "We carry it in our genes. When you come into a room—it could be a clearing—and you notice the smell of wood smoke, it is a powerful thing. You ask, What is cooking? And then your senses open!"

PART II

WATER

A RECIPE IN SEVEN STEPS

"The transformation which occurs in the
cauldron is quintessential and wondrous,
subtle and delicate. The mouth cannot express
it in words."

— I Yin, *a Chinese chef, 239 B.C.*

"Water is H2O, hydrogen two parts, oxygen
one, but there is also a third thing, that makes
it water, and nobody knows what it is."

—D. H. Lawrence, *Pansies*

I.

STEP ONE:
FINELY DICE SOME ONIONS

Is there anyone alive who actually enjoys chopping onions? Oh, there may be some Buddhists who give themselves over to the work, even to the tears, on the principle that, "when chopping onions, just chop onions"—i.e., don't resist or complain about it, just be there in the moment, doing it. But most of us are not so Zen. When chopping onions, we bitch about chopping onions. It's no wonder everyday home cooking is in trouble, now that there are so many cheap and easy ways to outsource the work, chopping included. Prepare dinner yourself from scratch and, more often than not, the recipe will begin with a dice of onions, and the onions, more often than not, will resist.

In fact, there are few things we eat that defend themselves against us quite as effectively as an onion. From the onion's point of view, the blade of your knife might as well be the incisor of a rodent: a mortal threat that elicits a chemical reaction cleverly designed to thwart the would-be attacker. Hoping to make chopping onions more interesting, if not more pleasant, I looked into the onion's strategy, and was surprised to learn that the plant does not mount its defense until the moment tooth or blade pierces cell wall.

If you could shrink yourself down to the size of a mitochondria or nucleus and swim around inside an undamaged onion cell, you would find the environment surprisingly benign, the taste of the ambient fluid sweet, certainly no cause for tears. Although there are four different defense molecules floating all around you, you probably would not notice them. What you might notice floating around you are these vacuoles, little balloonlike storage structures that in onions contain an enzyme that functions as a kind of trigger. When a blade or tooth breaks open a vacuole, the enzyme escapes, locates one of the defensive molecules, and breaks it in two. The volatile new chemical compounds that result are what give raw onions their powerfully sulfurous and irritating smell. One of the most volatile of these compounds is, aptly, called "the lachrymator"–tear maker. It escapes from the damaged cell into the air and proceeds to attack the nerve endings in a mammal's eyes and nasal passages, before breaking down into a noxious cocktail of sulfur dioxide, hydrogen sulfide, and sulfuric acid. "A very effective molecular bomb!" is how Harold McGee describes it. Indeed. Imagine a "food plant" that greets its eater with a hit of sulfuric acid and tear gas. That is the onion.

Lately I've gotten plenty of practice chopping onions, because I've been spending time in the kitchen learning how to cook pot dishes— soups, stews, braises—and it seems like almost all of these dishes, no matter what the culinary tradition, begin with a chopped onion or two or six. This is one of the many differences between cooking with fire and cooking with water, or for that matter with any liquid: Pot dishes make much more use of plants—vegetables, herbs, spices— and usually depend for their flavor on the reactions that occur when plants are combined with one another, and with meat, in a hot liquid medium. More often than not, onions constitute the foundation of these dishes, usually in combination with a small handful of other aromatic but equally unprepossessing vegetables, including carrots, celery, peppers, or garlic. Homely in the best sense, pot dishes are about marrying lots of prosaic little things rather than elevating one big thing.

In fact, it is the precise combination of these chopped-up plants that usually gives a pot dish its characteristic flavor and cultural identity. So if you start with a dice of onions, carrots, and celery sautéed in butter (or sometimes olive oil), you've made a mirepoix, which marks the dish as French. But if you begin by sautéing a mince of diced onions, carrots, and celery in olive oil (and perhaps add some garlic, fennel, or parsley), you've made a soffritto, the signature of an Italian dish. However, a "sofrito"—when spelled with one "f" and one "t"—is a dice of onions, garlic, and tomato in place of celery, and identifies the dish as Spanish. (Cajun cooking begins with a dice of onions, garlic, and bell pepper—"the holy trinity.") If a recipe calls for a base of diced spring onions, garlic, and ginger, you've left the West entirely and made what is sometimes called an "Asian mirepoix," the foundation of many dishes in the Far East. In India, pot dishes usually begin with a "tarka," a dice of onions and spices sautéed in clarified butter, or ghee. Even if we're unfamiliar with these terms or techniques, the aroma of these chopped-up plant bases instantly tells us where in the world we are, culinarily speaking.

But wherever we go, we have to do a lot of chopping to get there. On the plus side, chopping leaves you plenty of time for reflection, and one of the things I've been thinking about while doing it is, appropriately enough, the "drudgery" of everyday cooking. Curiously, you never hear that word around the grill. When men cook outdoors over a fire, it's usually a special occasion, so by definition cannot be "drudgery." Grill work itself is less prosaic, too: less detailed (no recipe needed) but also more social, more public, more like performance.

Fire! Smoke! Animals!—This is drama, drudgery's antithesis, and about as far from dicing and mincing, from the fine work of fingers, as a cook can get. Indeed, the only time the grill man or pit master deploys a knife is at the very end of his show, to carve or chop the animal, and that qualifies as ceremony.

There's nothing ceremonial about chopping vegetables on a kitchen counter, slowly sautéing them in a pan, adding a liquid, and then tending the covered pot for hours. For one thing, there's nothing to look at. (And please don't even try, since a watched pot never boils.) For another, this sort of cooking takes places indoors, in the prosy confines of a kitchen. No, this is real work.

So why would you—why would anyone?—do it if you didn't have to? When you could go out or order in or pull "a home meal replacement" from the freezer and nuke it in the microwave? This is of course precisely what more and more people *are* doing today instead of cooking. Cooking is no longer obligatory, and that marks a shift in human history, one whose full implications we're just beginning to reckon. No one *has* to chop onions anymore, not even the poor. Corporations are more than happy to chop them for us, and often at bargain rates. In many ways this has been a blessing, especially for women, who in most cultures for most of history have chopped most of the onions. Today, the typical American spends a mere twenty-seven minutes a day on food preparation, and another four minutes cleaning up. That's less than half the time spent cooking and cleaning up in 1965, when I was a boy. Somewhat more than half of the evening meals an American eats today are still "cooked at home," according to the market researchers. That sounds like a lot, until you discover that the meaning of the verb "to cook" has been defined radically downward in the last few years.

I learned this from a veteran food-industry market researcher named Harry Balzer, a blunt Chicagoan with whom I've now spent several illuminating, if discouraging, hours discussing the future of cooking. Balzer has been studying American eating habits for more than thirty years; the NPD Group, the market-research firm he's worked for since 1978, collects data from a pool of two thousand food diaries to track American eating habits. A few years ago, Balzer noticed that the definition of cooking held by his respondents had grown so broad as to be meaningless.

"People call things 'cooking' today that would roll their grandmother in her grave," he explained. "Like heating up a can of food or microwaving a frozen pizza." So the firm decided to tighten up, at least slightly, the definition of what it means to cook, in order to capture what was really going on in American kitchens. To cook "from scratch," they decreed, means to prepare a main dish that requires some "assembly of ingredients." So microwaving a pizza does not count as cooking, though washing a head of lettuce and pouring bottled dressing over it does. Under this generous dispensation (no chopping required), you're also cooking when you spread mayonnaise on a slice of bread and pile on some cold cuts or a hamburger patty. (Home or away, a sandwich is today the most popular meal in America.) At least by Harry Balzer's none-too-exacting standards, we Americans are still cooking up a storm: 58 percent of our evening meals qualify, though even that figure has been falling steadily since the 1980s.

Like most people who study consumer behavior, Balzer has developed a somewhat cynical view of human nature, which his research suggests is ever driven by the quest to save time or money or, if possible, both. He puts it less delicately: "Face it: We're basically cheap and lazy." Over the course of several conversations, I kept asking him what his research had to say about the prevalence of the activity I referred to as "real scratch cooking"—the kind of cooking that begins with chopping onions. But he wouldn't even touch the term. Why? Apparently the activity has become so rarefied as to elude his tools of measurement.

"Here's an analogy," Balzer offered. "A hundred years ago, chicken for dinner meant going out and catching, killing, plucking, and gutting a chicken. Do you know anybody who still does that? It would be considered crazy! Well, that's exactly how cooking will seem to your grandchildren. Like sewing, or darning socks—something people used to do when they had no other choice. Get over it!"

Maybe we should get over it. But before we do, it's worth considering for a moment how even something as tedious as chopping onions gets, paradoxically, more interesting, and more problematic, as soon as doing it is no longer obligatory. When cooking is optional, a person can elect not to do it, a choice that may reflect one's values or simply a desire to use the time in some other way. Yet for the person who believes home cooking still has *some* value, its new status as optional sets up a conflict—between competing desires—that may never have surfaced when cooking was simply what had to be done if the family was to eat. As soon as we have choices about how to spend our time, time is suddenly in much shorter supply, and it becomes that much harder to be in the kitchen, in either the literal or the Buddhist sense. Shortcuts suddenly seem more attractive. (*I can buy a bottle of chopped garlic, or a bag of prechopped mirepoix!*) Because you could be doing something else, something more pressing or simply more fun. This is certainly how I've usually felt when chopping onions.

By the same token, though, the not-cook option—for which we have food manufacturers and fast-food restaurants to thank—means that people can also, for the first time, choose to cook purely for the pleasure of doing it. A form of "work" can now be approached as a "leisure activity." But this is not a choice Harry Balzer is willing to take very seriously, either because he thinks we're just too lazy to enjoy doing any unnecessary work, or because he is, finally, in the business of helping food companies profit from the decline of every-day home cooking. Or it could simply be that he subscribes to the general view in a modern specialized consumer culture that "leisure activities" should involve consumption, whereas any activity involv-ing production is leisure's opposite: work. Put another way, a leisure activity is one you can't conceive of paying someone else to do for you. (Watching television, for example, or reading a book, or doing the crossword puzzle.) Everything else—everything that the market has figured out a way to do for us—becomes a species of work, some-thing that any rational actor would presumably outsource just as soon as he or she could afford to.

This at least is how economists seem to view the question of work and leisure: as antithetical terms that neatly line up with the equally antithetical categories of production and consumption. But perhaps that view says more about them, and consumer capitalism, than it does about us. For one of the most interesting things about cooking today—optional cooking—is how it confounds the rigid categories of work and leisure, of production and consumption. The Buddhists are probably right about chopping onions: It's all a matter of how you choose to see and experience it, as a chore to resist or a kind of path—a practice, even. Depending on the context, the very same activity can have diametrically opposed meanings. Is cooking a form of oppres-sion, as many feminists argued (with some justification, I might add) in the 1960s? Back in the 1970s, KFC ran billboards depicting a family-sized bucket of fried chicken under the slogan "Women's Liberation." And so perhaps it was, and still is for many women even now, and especially when both partners work at jobs outside the house. Yet even with those demands, today there are more and more people, men and women both, who view home cooking—and even raising and killing chickens!—as a means of liberation from the influence, on our lives and culture, of corporations like KFC. Which raises an interesting question: As a political matter, is home cooking today a reactionary or a progressive way to spend one's time?

At the moment, it's all up for grabs. Which is one reason I was curious to spend some time in the kitchen learning how to cook the very kinds of dishes that throw these sorts of questions into sharp relief. "Grandma cooking," as it's sometimes called: the formerly mundane (now "special") dishes that are cooked in pots and, more often than not, begin with onions and take considerably more than twenty minutes to put on the table. I seriously doubted I would ever get to the stage of enlightenment where, when chopping onions, I was just chopping onions. (You'll know I succeeded if the rest of these pages are blank. Oh—guess not.) But perhaps I could at least get to a place where I was completely at home in the kitchen, and where whatever lies on the other side of the "end of cooking" would come into sharper focus.

Here's the first thing I learned: In the same way that the procedure for cooking over fire, if viewed from a sufficient distance, can be reduced to a single basic recipe (animal plus wood fire and time), so, it turns out, can cooking with water in pots. If you thumb through cookbooks from every imaginable culinary tradition, the variations seem infinite, and though there *are* a million different ways to make a stew or braise or soup, the underlying structure, or syntax, of all these dishes is very nearly universal. Let me propose a radically simplified version of that structure, something that might serve as a kind of template or Ur-recipe for dishes organized around the element of water:

Dice some aromatic plants
Sauté them in some fat
Brown piece(s) of meat (or other featured ingredient)
Put everything in a pot
Add some water (or stock, wine, milk, etc.)
Simmer, below the boil, for a long time

As a practical matter, the virtue of this sort of skeleton recipe, for me anyway, is that it makes cooking any such dish much less daunting—and daunted is how I usually feel when confronted by a multistep recipe. But once you get a feel for the basic theme, all the variations become much easier to master.

Paring away the dense undergrowth of culinary detail from a whole genre of recipes has the added virtue of helping to expose what a particular mode of cooking—of transforming the stuff of nature into the occasion of a meal—might have to say about us and our world. Do it often enough, and you begin to see that cooking with fire implies a completely different narrative, about the natural world on one side and the social world on the other, than does cooking with water. Cooking with fire tells a story about community, and, perhaps, about where we fit in the cosmic order of things. Like the column of smoke that rises from the pit, it's a story that unfolds on a vertical axis, with all sorts of heroic (or at least mock heroic) flourishes. There's a priest, sort of, and a ritual, too, even a kind of altar; death is confronted, and the element of fire is brought under control.

To turn from the bright sunlight of this Homeric world and come into the kitchen of covered pots and simmering liquids feels like stepping out of an epic and into a novel. So, if every recipe tells a story, what kind of tale might cooking with the element of water have to tell?

II.

STEP TWO:
SAUTÉ ONIONS AND OTHER AROMATIC VEGETABLES

I knew I needed some help finding my way in the kitchen, and I found it in a young local cook by the name of Samin Nosrat. As it happens, I was Samin's teacher before she became mine. I met Samin five years ago, when she asked to sit in on a food-writing class that I was teaching at Berkeley. She had graduated from the university a few years before and, though working as a chef in a local restaurant, she also had ambitions to write. Samin has a big personality and soon became a figure in the class, sharing her deep knowledge about food as well as her cooking. Each week, a different student would bring in a snack for the class—maybe a favorite childhood cookie or an unusual heirloom variety from the farmers' market—and share a story about it. When Samin's turn to do snack came around, she showed up in class with several hotel pans of piping hot lasagna, both the tomato sauce and the pasta handmade from scratch, and proceeded to serve it to us on china with silverware and cloth napkins. The story Samin told us was about learning to cook, first at Chez Panisse, where she'd worked her way up from bussing tables to prep cook, and then in Tuscany, where she'd spent two years learning how to make fresh pasta, butcher meat, and master the kind of "Grandma cooking" she loves best. Samin's lasagna was probably the most memorable thing about that semester.

That's the first time I can recall ever hearing that phrase, "Grandma cooking." For Samin, this was the sort of traditional food that emerged from her mother's kitchen, which was nominally in San Diego but in every other sense—and especially those of taste and smell—in Tehran. Her parents had emigrated from Iran in 1976, three years before the revolution; as a follower of the Baha'i faith, her father feared persecution from the ascendant Shia. Samin was born in San Diego in 1979, but her parents, nourishing a dream of someday returning, treated their home as sovereign Iranian territory. The family spoke Farsi at home, and Mrs. Nosrat cooked Persian food exclusively. "The moment you come home from school and step over that threshold," Samin remembers being told as a young child, "you are back in Iran."

Samin was definitely not the kind of child of immigrants who could be embarrassed by the old-world dishes her mother would tuck into her lunch box. To the contrary, she loved Persian food: the aromatic rice dishes, the kabobs, the rich stews made with sweet spices, nuts, and pomegranates. "One time at school I was made fun of for my weirdo lunch. But my food tasted so much better than theirs! I refused to be insulted." Her mother, who "definitely wore the pants in our house," would drive all over southern California in search of a particular taste of home: an unusual variety of sweet lime called for in a particular dish, or a kind of sour cherry associated with a seasonal feast. Growing up, Samin never gave much thought to cooking— though her mom would occasionally recruit the children to squeeze lemons or shell big piles of fava beans—"but I was very interested in eating. I loved my mom's cooking."

It was during college in Berkeley that the seed of the idea of cooking as a vocation was planted—in the course of a single memorable meal eaten at Chez Panisse. Samin told me the story one afternoon, while we were standing around the island in my kitchen, chopping vegetables. I had asked her if she would be willing to teach me how to cook, and we had started having lessons once or twice a month, four- or five-hour sessions that invariably began around this island, each of us at a cutting board, chopping and talking. Conversation, I soon came to realize, was the best way to deal with the drudgery of chopping onions.

As usual, Samin had a white apron tied around her waist, and the thicket of her black hair raked partway back. Samin is tall and sturdily built, with strong features, slashing black eyebrows, and warm olivey-brown skin. If you had to pick one word to describe her, "avid" would have to be it; Samin is on excellent terms with the exclamation point. Words tumble from her mouth; laughter, too; and her deep, expressive brown eyes are always up to something.

"I had never even *heard* of Chez Panisse! In fact, the whole concept of a 'famous restaurant' was totally alien to me, because my family never went to fancy restaurants. But my college boyfriend had grown up in San Francisco, and when he told me all about Alice Waters and Chez Panisse, I was like, dude, we *have* to go! So, for that entire school year, we saved our money in a shoebox, throwing in loose change, quarters from the laundry, money from bets we made between us. And when we had collected two hundred dollars, which was just enough to pay for the prix-fixe meal downstairs, we set the alarm on a Saturday morning to make sure we'd get through the *minute* they started answering the phone, so we could make a reservation for the Saturday night exactly one month later.

"It was an incredible experience, the warm and glittering dining room, the amazing care they took of us—these two kids! They served us a frisée salad with 'lardons of bacon'—and I remember thinking, *What is this?!* The second course was halibut in a broth, and I had never eaten halibut before, so I was really nervous about that. But what I remember most vividly was the dessert: a chocolate soufflé with raspberry sauce. The waiter had to show us how to punch a hole in the dome and pour in the sauce. It was *really* good, but I thought it would be even better with a glass of milk, and when I asked for one, the waitress started laughing! Milk was a total faux pas, I now realize— you're supposed to drink a dessert wine, duh—but the waitress was so nice about it. She brought me my glass of milk. And *then* she brought us a glass of dessert wine—on the house!

"The food was beautiful, but I think it was the experience of being totally taken care of that evening that made me fall in love with the restaurant. I decided right then that, someday, I wanted to work at Chez Panisse. It seemed so much more special than a normal job. Plus, you'd get to eat all this amazing food all the time!

"So I sat down and wrote a long letter to the manager. I talked about how I'd had this life-changing meal, and could I please, please, please work as a busser. And by some crazy fluke, they called me in and I was hired on the spot."

Samin reorganized her schedule at school so she could work several shifts a week at the restaurant. She remembers her first one vividly. "They walked me through the kitchen, and everyone had on these immaculate white coats, and they were making the most beautiful food. Someone showed me where to find this old-school vacuum cleaner, and I started vacuuming the dining room, and I remember thinking, 'I can't believe they're trusting me to vacuum the downstairs dining room at Chez Panisse!' I felt so honored. And that's the way I felt every day I went to work there.

"I'm sort of obsessive-compulsive, in case you haven't noticed, and this was the first place in my life where everybody seemed just as OCD as I am. Everyone there was seeking perfection in whatever they were doing, whether it was the way they tied up the trash or made the best soufflé they could ever hope to make, or polished the silver just so. I could see how every task, no matter how trivial, was being done to the fullest, and that's when I began to feel at home.

"It clicked for me the first time I was taught how to load the dumbwaiter. You had to load the dishes in it just so: Keep the hot plates away from the salads, use the space superefficiently, and arrange things in such a way that the china would make the least amount of noise. It's a tiny, rickety old building that has to feed five hundred people every day, and give them the best possible experience, so everything has been carefully thought through over the years, and developed into a system. Which means that if you take a shortcut it can mess things up for everyone else.

"When, eventually, I started cooking, this whole approach translated seamlessly into how I approached food. For me, cooking is about seeking the deepest, farthest, richest flavors in everything I make. About extracting the absolute most out of every ingredient, whether it is a beautiful piece of salmon or a plain old onion. And that way of thinking about food started the day I was taught how to load the Chez Panisse dumbwaiter."

Sundays with Samin—our usual day together—always began the same way, with her bursting into the kitchen around three in the afternoon and plopping a couple of cotton market bags onto the island. From these she would proceed to pull out her cloth portfolio of knives, her apron, and, depending on the dish we were making, her prodigious collection of spices. This notably included a tin of saffron the size of a coffee can. Her mom sent her these eye-popping quantities of saffron, which whenever a recipe called for it Samin would sprinkle as liberally as salt.

"I'm soooo excited!" she'd invariably begin, in a singsong, as she tied her apron around her waist. "Today, you are going to learn how to brown meat." Or make a soffritto. Or butterfly a chicken. Or make a fish stock. Samin could get excited about the most mundane kitchen procedures, but her enthusiasm was catching, and eventually I came to regard it as almost a kind of ethic. Even browning meat, an operation that to me seemed fairly self-evident if not banal, deserved to be done with the utmost care and attention, and so with passion. At stake was the eater's experience. There was also the animal to consider, which you honored by making the very most of whatever it had to offer. Samin made sure there was also a theme undergirding each lesson: the Maillard reaction (when browning meat); eggs and their magical properties; the miracle of emulsification; and so forth. Over the course of a year, we made all sorts of main course dishes, as well as various salads and sides and desserts. Yet it seemed our main courses always came back to pot dishes, and we probably cooked more braises than anything else.

Much like a stew, a braise is a method of cooking meat and/or vegetables slowly in a liquid medium. In a stew, however, the main ingredient is typically cut into bite-sized pieces and completely submerged in the cooking liquid. In a braise, the main ingredient is left whole or cut into larger pieces (with meat ideally left on the bone) and only partially submerged in liquid. This way, the bottom of the meat is stewed, in effect, while the exposed top part is allowed to brown, making for richer, more complex flavors as well as, usually, a thicker sauce and a prettier dish.

Samin and I braised duck legs and chicken thighs, roosters and rabbits, various unprepossessing cuts of pork and beef, the shanks and necks of lamb, turkey legs, and a great many different vegetables. Each of these dishes called for a braising liquid, and at one time or another we used them all: red wine and white, brandy and beer, various stocks (chicken, pork, beef, fish), milk, tea, pomegranate juice, dashi (a Japanese stock made from seaweed and flaked bonito), the liquid left over from soaked mushrooms and beans, and water straight from the tap. We also made dishes that were not, technically, stews or braises, but were built on the same general principle, including sugo or ragù (or ragoût), bouillabaisse, risotto, and paella.

More often than not, the general principle called for a foundational dice of onions and other aromatic vegetables, which I would try to get ready before Samin showed up. And more often than not, Samin would take one look at the neat piles of chopped onions, carrots, and celery on my cutting board (the height of said piles conforming to the prescribed ratio of 2:1:1) and tell me to rechop them, because my dice wasn't fine enough.

"In some dishes, a rough dice like that is fine." I tried not to take offense, but I didn't think of my neat cubes as "rough" at all. "But in this dish, you don't necessarily want to be able to see any evidence of the soffritto," she explained. "You want it to melt away into nothingness, become this invisible layer of deliciousness. So . . . keep chopping!" And so I did, following her example of rocking a big knife back and forth through the piles of diced vegetables, dividing and subdividing the little cubes until they became mere specks.

On the subject of sautéing onions, another operation I wrongly assumed to be fairly straightforward, Samin had definite opinions. "Most people don't cook their onions nearly long enough or slow enough. They try to rush it." This was apparently a major pet peeve of hers. "The onions should have no bite left whatsoever and be completely transparent and soft. Turn down the flame and give them a half hour at *least*." Samin had been a sous-chef in a local Italian restaurant where she had sixteen young men working under her. "I was constantly walking down the line, turning down their burners, which were always on high. I guess it's some kind of guy thing to crank your flame all way to the max. But you need to be *gentle* with a mirepoix or soffritto."

Whether you "sweated" your onions at a low temperature or "browned" them at a higher one yielded a completely different set of flavors in the finished dish, Samin explained. Her ultimate authority on such matters was Benedetta Vitali, the chef she had worked for in Florence, who wrote a whole book about soffritto, called—what else?—*Soffritto*. "Benedetta makes three different soffrittos, depending on the dish—and all of them start with the exact same onions, carrot, and celery. But it can be made darker and more caramelized, or lighter and more vegetal, all depending on the heat and speed you cook them at." (In fact, the word "soffritto" contains the key cooking instruction: It means "underfried.")

Spend half an hour watching onions sweat in a pan and you will either marvel at their gradual transformation—from opaque to translucent; from sulfurous to sweet; from crunchy to yielding—or go stark raving mad with impatience. But this was precisely the lesson Samin was trying to impart.

"Great cooking is all about the three 'p's: patience, presence, and practice," she told me at one point. Samin is a devoted student of yoga, and she sees important parallels in the mental habits demanded by both disciplines. Working with onions seemed as good a place to develop those habits as any—practice in chopping them, patience in sweating them, and presence in keeping an eye on the pan so that they didn't accidentally brown if the phone rang and you permitted yourself a lapse in attention.

Unfortunately, not one of the "p"s came easily to me. I tend toward impatience, particularly in my dealings with the material world, and only seldom do I find myself attending to one thing at a time. Or, for that matter, to the present, a tense I have a great deal of trouble inhabiting. My native tense is the future conditional, a low simmer of unspecified worry being the usual condition. I couldn't meditate if my life depended on it. (Which—believe me, I know—is the completely wrong way to approach meditation.) Much as I like the whole concept of "flow"—that quality of being so completely absorbed in an activity that you lose the thread of time—my acquaintance with it is sorely limited. A great many boulders get in the way of my flow, disturbing the clarity of the mental waters and creating lots of distracting noise. Occasionally when I'm writing I'll slip into the flow for a little while; sometimes while reading, too, and of course sleeping, though I doubt that counts. But in the kitchen? Watching onions sweat? The work just isn't demanding enough to fully occupy consciousness, with the result that my errant, catlike thoughts refuse to stay where I try to put them.

One thought I did have, watching the onions sweat before we added the carrots and celery to the pan, took the form of an obvious question. Why is it that onions are so widespread in pot dishes? After salt, I can't think of another cooking ingredient quite as universal as the onion. Worldwide, onions are the second most important vegetable crop (after tomatoes), and they grow almost everywhere in the world that people can grow anything. So what do they do for a dish? Samin suggested that onions and the other commonly used aromatics are widely used because they are cheap and commonly available ingredients that add some sweetness to a dish. When I gently pushed for a more fulsome explanation, she offered, "It's a chemical reaction." I soon discovered that that's her default answer to all questions about kitchen science. Her second is "Let's ask Harold!" meaning Harold McGee, the kitchen-science writer who, though she had never met him, nevertheless serves as one of the god figures in her personal cosmology.

But what kind of chemical reaction? It turns out a comprehensive scientific investigation of mirepoix remains to be done; even Harold McGee, when I wrote to ask him about it, was uncharacteristically vague on the subject. The obvious but incorrect answer is that the sugars in the onions and carrots become caramelized in the sauté pan, thereby contributing that whole range of flavor compounds to the dish. But Samin (like most other authorities) recommends taking pains not to brown a mirepoix, whether by reducing the heat or adding salt, which by drawing water out of the vegetables serves to keep the browning reaction from kicking in. The caramelized-sugar theory also doesn't account for the prominent role in mirepoix and soffritto of celery, a not particularly sweet vegetable that would seem to contribute little but water and cellulose. What all this suggests is that there must be other processes that come into play in sautéing aromatic vegetables besides caramelization (or the Maillard reaction), processes that contribute flavors to a dish by other means not yet well understood.

One afternoon in the midst of slowly sweating a mirepoix, I risked ruining it by doing some Internet research on what might be going on in my pan just then. I know, I was multitasking, failing utterly at the "p" of presence, possibly patience as well. I found a fair amount of confusion and uncertainty about the subject online, but enough clues to conclude it was likely, or at least plausible, that the low, slow heat was breaking down the long necklaces of protein in the vegetables into their amino acid building blocks, some of which (like glutamic acid) are known to give foods the meaty, savory taste called "umami"—from the Japanese word umai, meaning "delicious." Umami is now generally accepted as the fifth taste, along with salty, sweet, bitter, and sour, and like each of the others has receptors on the tongue dedicated to detecting its presence.

As for the seemingly pointless celery, it, too, may contribute umami to a pot dish, and not just by supplying lots of carbohydrate-stiffened cell walls and water to a mirepoix. My Web surfing eventually delivered me to an article in the *Journal of Agricultural and Food Chemistry* written by a team of Japanese food scientists and titled, fetchingly, "Flavor Enhancement of Chicken Broth from Boiled Celery Constituents."[*] These chemists reported that a group of volatile compounds found in celery called phthalides, though completely tasteless by themselves, nevertheless enhanced the perception of both sweetness and umami when they were added to a chicken broth. Way to go, celery.

Abstracted soul that I am, patiently cooking a mirepoix became much more interesting, or bearable at least, now that I had a theory. Now, knowing what was at stake, I paid close attention to the satisfying sizzle—the auditory evidence of water escaping from the plant tissues—and then, as it subsided, to the softening of the vegetables, indicating that the scaffold of carbohydrates that held the cell walls rigid was breaking down into sugars that it was up to me to keep from browning. I now understood that, even before I introduced the meat or liquid to the pot, the depth of flavor in my braise, the very savoriness of it, hung in the balance of these gently simmering onions, carrots, and celery.

One more scientific fact contributed to my deepening admiration for mirepoix and soffritto, and especially for the onions in them, which this fact single-handedly rendered considerably less irritating. It seems that adding onions to foods, and to meat dishes in particular, makes the food safer to eat. Like many of the most commonly used spices, onions (garlic, too) contain powerful antimicrobial compounds that survive cooking. Microbiologists believe that onions, garlic, and

---

[*]Vol. 56 (2008): 512–16.

spices protect us from the growth of dangerous bacteria on meat. This might explain why the use of these plants in cooking becomes more common the closer you get to the equator, where keeping meat from spoiling becomes progressively more challenging. Before the advent of refrigeration, the bacterial contamination of food, animal flesh in particular, posed a serious threat to people's health. (In Indian cooking, recipes for vegetarian dishes typically call for fewer spices than recipes for meat dishes.) Purely through trial and error, our ancestors stumbled upon certain plant chemicals that could protect them from getting sick. Onions happen to be one of the most potent of all antimicrobial food plants. That the flavors of such plants "taste good" to us may be nothing more than a learned preference for the taste of molecules that helped to keep us alive.

What this suggests is that cooking with these aromatic plants may involve something more than simply overcoming their chemical defenses so that we might avail ourselves of a source of calories other creatures can't. It's much more ingenious than that. Cooking with onions, garlic, and other spices is a form of biochemical jujitsu, in which the first move is to overcome the plants' chemical defenses so that we might eat them, and the second is to then deploy their defenses against other species to defend ourselves.

I was beginning to appreciate how the marriage of plant and animal foods in a liquid medium offers a great many advantages over simply cooking either kind of foodstuff by itself over a fire. Now the cook can improve meat by incorporating the flavors (and antimicrobial properties) of aromatic plants such as onions, garlic, and spices, something difficult, if not impossible, to do when cooking directly over a fire. In a slowly simmering liquid, vegetables and meat can exchange molecules and flavors, in the process creating new end products that are often much more than the sum of their humble parts. One such end product is a sauce, probably the richest dividend of pot cooking.

Cooking in a pot is all about economy. Every last drop of the fat and juices from the meat, which over a fire would be lost, are conserved, along with all the nutrients from the plants. Pot cooking allows you to make a tasty dish from a third-rate or over-the-hill cut of meat, and to stretch a small amount of meat so that, with the addition of vegetables and sauce, it might feed more mouths than that same meat ever would by itself. It also allows you to dispense with meat altogether, or use it simply as a flavoring.

"This is food for when you're poor," Samin pointed out one afternoon, while we were trimming a particularly gnarly piece of lamb shoulder. "Braising is a wonderful way to cook, because it yields powerfully flavored food from relatively inexpensive ingredients." In fact, the tastiest braises and stews are made from the "worst" cuts. The older the animal, the more flavorful its meat. Also, tough cuts come from muscles that have worked the hardest, and so contain the greatest amount of the connective tissues that, after a long, slow cooking, dissolve into succulent gelatin.

The covered pot—covered to conserve moisture and heat for the long haul—symbolizes the modesty and economy of this kind of cooking. By comparison, roasting a big piece of meat over an open fire—Homeric cooking—looks like an extravagance: a form of conspicuous display of one's wealth, generosity, or hunting skill. And so it has been, at least until our own era of extravagantly cheap meat. The British, famous for roasting impressive joints over fires, traditionally looked down on the "humble pots" of the French, with their plebeian cuts hidden beneath dubious sauces. Prosperous and blessed with good grass for grazing cattle and sheep the year round, the English enjoyed access to high-quality meat that required little more than fire to taste good. Whereas the less well-to-do and well-provisioned French were thrown back on their wits in the kitchen, developing techniques that allowed them to make the most of meat scraps and root vegetables and whatever liquid might be handy.

That we now think of such peasant fare as fancy or elite, while regarding the tossing of pricey filets of meat on the grill as simple food for the masses, represents a complete reversal of the historical situation. There has always been a trade-off between time and technique in the kitchen and the quality of the raw ingredients. The better the latter, the less of the former is required to eat well. But the opposite is equally true. With a modicum of technique and a little more time in the kitchen, the most flavorful food can be made from the humblest of ingredients. This enduring formula suggests that learning one's way around the kitchen—knowing what to do with the gnarly cut, the mirepoix, and the humble pot—might still be a good recipe for eating delicious food without spending much to make it. These are skills that confer a measure of independence.

But there are ethical implications here as well, about the way to approach the eating of animals, and the environmental issues that practice raises. If we're only going to eat the prime cuts of young animals, we're going to have to raise and kill a great many more of them. And indeed this has become the rule, with disastrous results for both the animals and the land. Nowadays, there is no market for old laying hens, since so few of us know how to cook them, with the result that much of this meat ends up in pet food or landfills. If we are going to eat animals, it behooves us to waste as few and as little of them as we possibly can, something that the humble cook pot allows us to do.

III.

STEP THREE:
SALT THE MEAT; THEN BROWN IT

The other task I usually tried to get done before Samin arrived on Sunday was to salt the meat we were planning to cook, an operation she regarded as absolutely critical and urged me to tackle early and in a spirit of shocking extravagance. "Use at least three times as much salt as you think you should," she advised. (A second authority I consulted employed the same formulation, but upped the factor to five.) Like many chefs, Samin believes that knowing how to salt food properly is the very essence of cooking, and that amateurs like me approach the saltbox far too timorously.

Before we learned to cook food in pots, humans never had to think about adding salt to their food. Animal flesh contains all the salt our bodies need, and roasting meat preserves most of the salt in it. It was only with the advent of agriculture, when people began relying on a diet of grain and other plants, and took to boiling much of their food (leaching the salt from it in the process), that deficiencies of sodium became a problem. This is when salt—the only mineral we deliberately eat—became a precious commodity. Yet in a modern diet completely saturated with sodium, deficiencies are not exactly a problem, so why would we want to salt meat at all, let alone so extravagantly?

Samin prefaced her defense of the practice by pointing out that the salt we add to our food represents a tiny fraction of the salt people get from their diet. Most of the salt we eat comes from processed foods, which account for 80 percent of the typical American's daily intake of sodium. "So, if you don't eat a lot of processed foods, you don't need to worry about it. Which means: Don't ever be afraid of salt!"

Judiciously applied, Samin explained, salt brings out the intrinsic flavors of many foods and can improve their texture and appearance. But it is not only the amount of salt that matters; the timing of its application is important, too. Some dishes (like meat) should get salted early, some in the middle of the cooking process, some only immediately before serving, and still others at every step along the way. In the case of meat that will be stewed or braised, you can't salt too soon or too liberally. At least one day before cooking was good; two or three days were even better.

But doesn't salting dry out a piece of meat? Yes, it can, if you don't salt it far enough in advance. Initially, salt draws moisture out of the cells of muscles, which is why, if you haven't salted your meat well in advance of cooking it, you're probably better off not doing it at all. But as the salt draws water out of the meat, a kind of osmotic vacuum forms in the cells. Once the salt has been diluted by the water it has attracted to it, this salty liquid is drawn back into the cells (along with any spices or other flavorings present in it), greatly improving the meat's flavor. Put simply, salting early helps meat later absorb flavors, including but not limited to the flavor of salt.

It took me awhile, but eventually I got comfortable salting meat to Samin's ultraliberal specifications. "Sprinkling" does not do justice to the practice she taught me, though "pouring it on" might be putting matters a bit too strongly. She taught me how to pick up quantities of kosher salt by dipping all five fingers into the box like a crane and then, with a rhythmic rubbing together of thumb against fingers (a bit like sowing tiny seeds), I found I could spread a nice, even layer of salt all over a piece of meat, making sure to coat any crevices and cavities. Sowing this much salt felt all wrong, I have to admit, and yet, when I discovered the meat didn't come out tasting particularly salty, I succumbed. Now I, too, am a proud, indulgent liberal with the salt.

The last important step before putting the ingredients of a braise or stew into the pot is to brown the meat in a little fat. This is done for two reasons: to add another layer of flavor to the dish by incorporating the hundreds of tasty compounds created by the Maillard reaction and caramelization, and to make the dish more appealing to look at, browned meat being more attractive than gray. Without browning, Samin explained, both the flavor and color of the meat would be paler.

The problem is that meat won't ever brown in a liquid that consists mostly of water. In order for the Maillard reaction to take place, meat needs to reach a higher temperature—250°F at least—than water can ever attain, since water can never exceed the boiling point— 212°F. To caramelize the sugars in meat requires an even higher temperature, in excess of 330°F. Because oil can reach these temperatures that water can't, the best way to brown meat is in a pan with a little fat. (Browning can be accomplished in a hot oven, too, and often is in restaurants, but at some risk of drying out the meat.)

Many recipes recommend patting dry the exterior of the meat to promote better browning. Some are particular as to what kind of fat to brown meat in: Julia Child liked to use bacon fat, which adds another layer of flavor to a dish. Sometimes, Samin and I would brown the meat while the mirepoix or soffritto cooked in another pan; other times, we'd brown the meat first, leaving us a pan coated with flavored fat and browned bits of meat in which to cook, and enrich, the mirepoix.

A few of Samin's tips for browning: Big chunks of meat are better than small; bone in is better than out. Use just enough oil to coat the pan and conduct heat evenly; too much, and you'll be frying the meat, too little, you're apt to scorch it over patches of dry, naked pan. Cast iron is best. Watch carefully to prevent any blackening, which can render the whole dish bitter. But brown every surface you can reach, the sides included. Take your time to do it thoroughly. And stop as soon as the color is "toasty beautiful."

In short, another straightforward kitchen procedure improved by patience and presence.

Whether we were browning a duck leg or a lamb neck or a shoulder of pork, this was the point when the kitchen would begin to fill with the complex and captivating aromas of the browning reactions: savory and meaty, but also earthy, floral, and sweet, the precise mix and balance of them all depending on the type of meat being browned. Outwardly, browning looks like a fairly simple operation, but at the molecular level it adds a great deal of complexity to the dish, hundreds of new compounds and, taken together, a whole other layer of flavors. And there was yet another layer still to add: After we removed the browned meat from the pan, we would deglaze it with a little wine, boiling off the alcohol while freeing up the browned bits stuck on the bottom of the pan with a spatula. This liquid would end up in the braise, too, adding "one more little layer of deliciousness"—this on top of the mirepoix layer and the Maillard layer we had already laid down. I was beginning to understand what Samin meant when she talked about "building" the flavor of a simple dish by extracting the deepest, furthest, richest flavors from even the humblest of ingredients. And that's before we put anything into the pot.

IV.

STEP FOUR:
PLACE ALL THE INGREDIENTS
IN A COVERED POT

In 1822, a German art historian and gastronome by the name of Baron Karl Friedrich von Rumohr published a book called *The Essence of Cookery* that, among other things, sought to elevate the prestige of the humble stockpot, and see it for the revolutionary development in human history that it was. "Enough of the fire," the Baron declared. "Innumerable natural products were rendered edible by the invention of the cooking pot," he wrote, a method of cooking he deemed more highly evolved and richer in possibilities than cooking over a fire. "Man had finally learned the arts of boiling and stewing and was now able to combine animal products with the nutritious and aromatic products of the plant kingdom, creating a new end product. For the first time, it was possible for the art of cookery to be developed in all directions."

Perhaps because a German is bound to have less credibility on matters of gastronomy than a Frenchman, Rumohr is not nearly so well known or widely read today as his more flamboyant contemporary, Jean-Anthelme Brillat-Savarin. But in some ways *The Essence of Cookery* holds up better than *The Physiology of Taste*, in which much of the science and history is pure fancy. Compared with Brillat-Savarin, Baron Rumohr has his feet firmly planted on the ground, or, rather, on the floor of the everyday domestic kitchen, a place where water commands as much respect as fire. In fact, his definition of cooking includes it: "To develop, with the aid of heat, water and salt, the nu-

tritional, refreshing, and delectable qualities of those natural substances which are suitable for the nourishment or restoration of
mankind." Rumohr's aim in writing The Essence of Cookery was to return
cooking, which he felt had fallen into a "state of over-refinement and
exaggeration," back to basics, and nothing symbolized straightforward, honest cooking better than the stockpot.

Historically, cooking in pots with water comes much later than
cooking with fire, since it awaited the development of watertight and
fireproof containers in which to do it. Exactly when these appeared,
however, is uncertain. Some archaeologists put the advent of ceramic
pottery as early as twenty thousand years ago in Asia. Cooking pots
show up in many places around the world, including the Nile River
delta, the Levant, and Central America, between ten thousand and
seven thousand years ago. All of these dates fall hundreds of thousands of years after humankind domesticated fire, and it is generally
agreed that the practice of cooking in pots didn't become widespread
until the Neolithic era, when humans settled into patterns of life organized around agriculture. The technologies of agriculture and clay
pottery—both of which make different uses of earth and fire—turn
out to be closely linked.

Yet there is reason to believe that food was being boiled even before the invention of cooking pots. In numerous ancient sites around
the world, archaeologists have dug up burned stones and fired clay
balls the purpose of which was for many years a mystery. In the
1990s, a young Native American archaeologist named Sonya Atalay
was working in a ninety-five-hundred-year-old site called Çatalhöyük,
one of the earliest known urban centers in Turkey, when she found
thousands of round fist-sized fired-clay balls. Stumped, she brought a
couple of the balls to an elder in her tribe, the Ojibwa, hoping he
could identify them. He took one look and told her: "You don't need
a Ph.D. to know that these are cooking stones."

Archaeologists believe the stones were heated in a fire and then dropped into an animal skin or watertight basket that had been filled with water. The hot cooking balls allowed the cook to bring water to a boil without having to expose its container to the direct heat of a fire. This method, which is still employed today by some indigenous tribes, allowed people to soften seeds, grains, and nuts and render many toxic or bitter plant foods edible long before there were pots.

Boiling water vastly expanded the horizons of edibility for our species, especially in the world of plants. All kinds of formerly inedible seeds, tubers, legumes, and nuts could now be rendered soft and safe—and therefore the exclusive nutritional property of Homo sapiens. In time, boiling stones gave way to clay pots, a transition Atalay has documented at Çatalhöyük. The invention of fired, watertight pots, which made boiling food safer and easier, represented a second gastronomic revolution, the first having been the control of fire for cooking. All this revolution lacked is its own Prometheus, though perhaps that is as it should be for a method of cooking generally thought of as more domestic than heroic.

But without the cook pot, just how far would agriculture have gotten? Many of the important crops humankind has domesticated require boiling (or at least soaking) for us to be able to eat them, especially the legumes and the grains. The cook pot is a kind of second human stomach, an external organ of digestion that allows us to consume plants that would otherwise be inedible or require elaborate processing. These auxiliary clay stomachs made it possible for humans to thrive on a diet of stored dry seeds, which in turn led to the accumulation of wealth, the division of labor, and the rise of civilization. These developments are usually credited to the rise of agriculture, and rightly so, but they depended as much on the cook pot as on the plow.

Cooking food in pots also helped expand the human population, by allowing for earlier weaning of children (thereby increasing fertility) and a longer life span, since both the very young and the very old could now be fed soft foods and nutritious soups out of the pot, no teeth required. (So pots functioned as external mouths as well.) In all these ways, the pot, by domesticating the element of water, helped us to leave behind hunting and to settle down. According to the historian Felipe Fernández-Armesto, the invention of the cook pot (and its offshoot, the frying pan) is the last innovation in the history of cooking until the advent in our own time of the microwave oven.

In drawing his bright line between roasting and boiling as the two principal modes of food preparation, Claude Lévi-Strauss characterized them, respectively, as "exocuisine" and "endocuisine"—that is, "outside" and "inside" cooking. Lévi-Strauss wants us to take these terms figuratively as well as literally, since he regarded the methods as recipes for something much bigger than a meal: Each also tells a different story about our relationship to both nature and other people. So cooking over fire was "outside" cooking in two senses: Not only was the cooking done outside, in the open, with the meat exposed to the flames, but the process itself was exposed to the larger social world—it was a public ritual conducted by men and open to outsiders. By comparison, endo-, or inside, cooking took place within the confines of the closed pot and, more often than not, within the private space of the household. The interior of the cook pot itself, concave and shielding its contents from view, symbolized the home and the family, its lid a kind of roof over a domestic space presided over by women. Lévi-Strauss describes New World tribes where "a man never boils anything," and others in which boiling was associated with the strengthening of family ties, and roasting with the weakening of those ties, since guests, including strangers, were often invited to partake.

Boiled food also stands at a further remove from uncivilized nature than does roasted food, which requires nothing more than the element of fire (and perhaps a stick) to cook the meal. In addition to a fire, boiling depends on a cultural artifact—the pot—and the process involves not just one but two mediations—a layer of clay and the medium of water—between food and flame. The pot also allows for a more complete cooking of foods, which is why Aristotle rated boiling "higher," or more civilized, than roasting, "on the grounds that it was more effective in destroying the rawness of meat." (Evidently he was unfamiliar with slow-cooked Southern barbecue.) If all cooking is a process of transforming the stuff of nature into culture, boiling achieves a more complete transformation of the animal being eaten by (among other things) eliminating any trace of blood.

After the meal, the cooking implements used to boil food are all carefully cleaned and preserved, Lévi-Strauss points out, while the wooden frame used to barbecue meat was traditionally destroyed after the feast. Why? For fear that the vengeful animals would use it to turn the tables and roast one of us. This superstition speaks to the fact that roasting is more closely associated with violence and danger, which might explain why in many cultures women—traditionally identified with giving life rather than taking it—are prohibited from doing it. "Boiled food is life," Lévi-Strauss writes, "roast food death." He reports finding countless examples in the world's folklore of "cauldrons of immortality," but not a single example of a "spit of immortality."

Is there anyone who takes the trouble to clean and care for a grill, or grilling implement, the way we do an old casserole or serving spoon from our childhood? It's not just the elements that account for the differential survival rates of outdoor grills and cooking pots. The former get tossed as soon as the baked-on grime becomes too thick to face; the latter become cherished family heirlooms.

There's not a lot I can recall of my mother's kitchen when I was growing up, but one image I can easily summon is of the turquoise casserole from which she ladled out beef stews and chicken soups. Made by Dansk, it was Scandinavian in design, sleek and thinly walled, though its unexpected heft suggested steel beneath the aquamarine enamel. Crowning the casserole was a lid that you lifted using a slender X-shaped handle; the handle was cleverly designed to allow the inverted top to double as a trivet. Every chip and scratch of its bright enamel is precisely recorded in my memory; I'm sure even today I could pick my mother's casserole out of a lineup of otherwise identical ones.

The captivating smells that emanated from that pot, their never-once-broken promise of something rich and satisfying to eat, seeped out to fill the house and lure us from our separate rooms toward the kitchen as dinnertime approached. In our modern, all-electric 1960s kitchen, that pot with its centripetal energies was the closest thing we had to a hearth, a warm and fragrant synecdoche for domestic well-being.

In fact, my attempt to reconstruct that kitchen in memory fifty years later starts from an image of the aquamarine casserole perched on top of the stove, and gradually builds out from there, to take in the yellow porcelain sink, the rectangular white Formica table in the corner with the curvy Jetsons-style chairs, the tan rotary phone on the wall, the birdcage hanging (unwisely) next to that, and the picture window overlooking the great, two-trunked oak tree in the front yard that loomed benevolently over the house. When it was time for dinner, my mother would carry the casserole from the range to the table, set it down dead center on its trivet, lift the turquoise lid, and serve us, one by one, from the rising cloud of fragrant steam.

A comfortable old pot like that one, filled with a thick stew still hatching bubbles from its surface, is a little like a kitchen in miniature, an enclosed pocket of space in which a hodgepodge of cold ingredients get transformed into the warm glow of a shared family meal. What more do you need? Like the kitchen, the pot bears the traces of all the meals that have been cooked in it, and there is a sense (even if it is only a superstition) in which all those past meals somehow inform and improve the current one. A good pot holds memories.

It also holds us, or that's the hope. To eat from the same pot is to share something more than a meal. "To eat out of the same cauldron" was, for the ancient Greeks, a trope for sharing the same fate: *We're all in this together.* In the same way that the stew pot blends a great many different ingredients together, forging them into a single memorable flavor, it brings the family together as well. (Or at least it did, until my sisters declared themselves vegetarians, splintering the one-pot family meals into a menu of different entrées.) This might sound like a sentimental conceit, but compare the one-pot dinner to the sort of meal(s) that typically emerge from the microwave: a succession of single-serving portions, each attempting to simulate a different cuisine and hit a different demographic, with no two of those portions ever ready to eat at the same time. If the first gastronomic revolution unfolded under the sign of community, gathered around the animal roasting on the fire, and the second that of the family, gathered around the stew pot, then the third one, now well under way, seems to be consecrated to the individual: *Have it your way.* Whereas the motto hovering over every great pot is the same one stamped on the coins in our pocket: *E pluribus unum.*

The symbolic power of the pot—to gather together, to harmonize— might begin in the home, but it reaches well beyond it, all the way into the political realm. The ancient Chinese conceived of the well-governed state as a cauldron, specifically a three-legged one called a *ding*. In this monumental pot the skilled chef-cum-administrator deploys his culinary skills to forge a diversity of clashing interests into a single harmonious dish. Closer to home, the "melting pot" sought to achieve a similar result in the social sphere, resolving the diverse flavors of our far-flung immigrant histories into a single American stew. The common pot is always pushing against the sovereignty of individual taste. Which might help explain why its popularity is in decline today while the microwave's is ascendant.

But it would be a mistake to overlook the darker side of cooking in pots. Another Greek saying—"To boil in the same cauldron"—suggests a less happy take on the shared destiny. There is, too, the witch's cauldron, also presided over by women, yet producing the very antithesis of comfort food. Who knows *what* is cooking down there in that scary pot? Bubbling away beneath the murky swamp of sauce might be eye of newt or tail of rat. All pot cooking is occult in some degree, the precise identity of the ingredients hidden from inspection, more or less illegible. "Mystery meat" is how children refer to it, and rightly so.

Given what a classicist once called "the Homeric horror of formlessness," it's no wonder that roasting is the only kind of cooking ever described in Homer. The pot dish, lidded and turbid, has none of the Apollonian clarity of a recognizable animal on a spit; it trades that brightly lit, hard-edged object and its legible world for something darker, more fluid and inchoate. What emerges from this or any other pot is not food for the eye so much as for the nose, a primordial Dionysian soup, but evolving in reverse, decomposing forms rather than creating them. To eat from the pot always involves at least a little leap into unknown waters.

I don't own a cauldron, unfortunately, but we do own a couple of heavy-duty casseroles made from cast iron (and coated in a blue enamel) and a red porcelain tagine, one of those Moroccan pots with stovepipe lids that look like festive hats. Recently I bought two clay casseroles: a La Chamba handmade in Colombia from unglazed black clay, and a wide terra-cotta casserole from Tuscany glazed the color of winter wheat. I like to think of these new pots as future heirlooms, provided I don't crack or drop them before they've had a chance to become venerable. Such pots might begin life as ordinary commodities, but in time the ones that endure accumulate rich sediments of family history, until they become one of the very least commodified objects in our possession.

The weight and thickness of these receptacles make them ideal for slow-cooked braises and stews, as well as for soups and beans. They warm up slowly and diffuse their heat evenly through the dish, gently blending flavors without developing hot spots that might cause some ingredients to cook too fast or burn. The advantage of the cast-iron casserole, by comparison, is that you can put it directly on the flame to brown meat or sweat a soffritto. Most earthenware pots can be used only in the oven, which means dirtying a second pot or pan to prepare ingredients. But clay pots are the gentlest cookware there is, and the most conserving of both heat and memory: Many cooks claim that over time they build up flavors in their clay that will improve anything you cook in them. Earthenware pots can also be brought to the table, where they will keep their contents piping hot as long as guests care to linger.

The vegetables go into the cook pot first, the mirepoix or soffritto (and/or any other vegetables called for by the recipe) spread out evenly across the bottom of the dish to form a nice cushion for the larger, chunkier ingredients. You don't want pieces of meat sitting directly on the pot's hot floor, where they might stick or burn, and have that much less opportunity to mingle productively with the other ingredients. Only after the meat has been comfortably settled on its bed of vegetables should the braising liquid be introduced: the all-important medium that will unify the ingredients, and in time become itself something much greater than the sum of whatever it was and everything it now connects—sauce!

V.

STEP FIVE:
POUR THE BRAISING LIQUID
OVER THE INGREDIENTS

"Whatever it was" might be wine or stock or a purée or juice or milk or beer or dashi or plain old water from the tap, depending on the recipe and its cultural reference or the cook's desire. But in fact all of these liquids are really just enhanced forms of water, H_2O serving as what the chemists call the "continuous phase" in which various other molecules disperse to great and flavorful effect.

In the story of a stew, the pot is the stage and water the hero (or the nonhuman hero, anyway), the elemental actor that supplies unity of character and makes things happen. True, there are a few braises that call for no added liquid, but, as long as they cook slowly in a covered pot, liquid will soon appear anyway, in the form of juices seeping from the meat or the vegetables, and these liquids will perform ably in the role of water.

Which in cooking is protean: creative and destructive and ultimately transformative. Water that has been domesticated by being confined to a pot might not seem as potent as the wild water that carves canyons and coastlines, but its powers are impressive even so. Consider some of the things water can do once it has been captured in a cook pot and that pot has been put on a fire:

First, the water will conduct the fire's heat, evenly and efficiently, conveying it from the walls of the pot into every cranny of whatever's being cooked in it. If that happens to include dried seeds, water will bring them back to life—sometimes literally, by inspiring them to germinate, or figuratively, by making them soft and plump enough to eat. But water, sufficiently heated, can kill, too, dispatching dangerous bacteria in our food. It will sterilize meat and detoxify plants and fungi. It will leach out salt and bitterness. Water in a pot can bring together far-flung taxonomic kingdoms, marrying plants and animals and fungi, so that they might act on one another—swap flavors, alter textures. Given enough time and the proper amount of heat, water will break down the toughest fibers in both plants and animals, transforming them into food. Given still more time, it will break these foodstuffs down into a rich paste and, eventually, into a tasty, nutritious liquid: a dispersed phase of its continuous self. But what water breaks down it also reassembles along new lines.

Water will extract molecules from one ingredient and diffuse them so that they might encounter and act on the molecules in another ingredient, breaking some chemical bonds and forging new ones, which might be aromas, flavors, or nutrients. In a pot, water is the medium of flavor as well as heat, allowing spices and other seasonings to get around and make their presence felt. It also dilutes the effect of the most pungent spices, like peppers, making them more amenable. Given heat and time, water softens, blends, balances, harmonizes, and marries.

With so much going for it, you would think water alone would be more than adequate as a braising liquid. And it is, sometimes. In fact, Samin was of the opinion that tap water was underrated as a braising liquid, while chicken stock, the default in most kitchens, was used way too much.*

"I don't understand why you would want everything you braise to taste like chicken, unless you're braising chicken," Samin mentioned one afternoon, when we were getting ready to put a Moroccan lamb stew into the oven. The dish already promised plenty of flavor. To its base of mirepoix and garlic, we had added a bunch of toasted Moroccan spices, and then laid out some orange peels, dried apricots, cilantro stems, and, on top of that fragrant bed, the well-browned cuts of lamb. So we dispensed with stock and used some water, and a splash of white wine, instead. "Eventually that liquid is going to turn into something rich and delicious—it doesn't need to taste like chicken!"

As the continuous phase in our lamb stew, water's role is to blend and balance some pretty wild flavors, forging them into a familiar sense experience: the flavor of Moroccan food. Most of us instantly recognize such basic flavor profiles, and indeed depend on them to figure out what we're eating and to feel comfortable doing so. If the omnivore's dilemma is to determine what is good and safe to eat amid the myriad and occasionally risky choices nature puts before us, then familiar flavor profiles can serve as a useful guide, a sensory

---

*Marcella Hazan, the Italian cookbook writer, was on the same page: "Water is the phantom ingredient in much Italian cooking," she wrote. "One of my students once protested, 'When you add water, you add nothing!' But that is precisely why we use it. Italian cooking is the art of giving expression to the undisguised flavors of its ingredients. In many circumstances, an overindulgence in stock, wine or other flavored liquids would tinge the complexion of a dish with an artificial glow."

signal of the tried and true. To an extent, these familiar blends of flavor take the place of the hardwired taste preferences that guide most other species in their food choices. They have instincts to steer them; we have cuisines.

This at least is the theory of culinary flavor advanced by Elisabeth Rozin, the cookbook writer, and her former husband, Paul Rozin, the social psychologist. "Flavoring a dish with soy sauce, for example, almost automatically identifies it as Oriental," she points out in her book *Ethnic Cuisine: The Flavor-Principle Cookbook*. But the sprawling Eastern empire of soy has many nations within it: "If you add garlic, molasses, ground peanuts and chilies to the basic soy sauce, you will create a taste characteristically Indonesian," she points out. And if fish sauce and coconut milk are added instead, the dish becomes Laotian, and so forth. Every cuisine has its characteristic "flavor principle," Rozin contends, whether it is tomato-lemon-oregano in Greece; lime-chili in Mexico; onion-lard-paprika in Hungary, or, in Samin's Moroccan dish, cumin-coriander-cinnamon-ginger-onion-fruit. (And in America? Well, we do have Heinz ketchup, a flavor principle in a bottle that kids, or their parents, use to domesticate every imaginable kind of food. We also now have the familiar salty-umami taste of fast food, which I would guess is based on salt, soy oil, and MSG.) But as soon as we encounter a familiar flavor principle, we know what we're eating and can relax in the knowledge that our dinner has been prepared according to a set of time-tested rules, and so probably won't kill us or make us sick.

These flavor principles always involve the marriage of at least two aromatic plants and often many more. That may be because no single seasoning can ever mark a food as having completed the necessary journey from the risky realm of raw nature to the safety of cooked culture. What we seem drawn to is the combination of flavors that only *Homo sapiens*, experimenting over time, could concoct from whatever nature has to offer locally. And much like any other artifact of culture—a vase, a melody—these combinations most appeal to us when they exhibit a kind of balance or symmetry—in this case, between sweet and sour, say, or bitter and salty.

Particularly in the case of the more elaborate combinations of flavor, such as in our Moroccan stew, the greatest conductor of flavor principles is the element of water: it is what weaves together the differently colored threads of taste into a familiar pattern, gives them their unity. A cooking oil can achieve somewhat similar results (and is often itself an important element in a flavor principle), but water is the principle medium of taste; indeed, for the tongue to taste any molecule, it must be soluble in water. (Strictly speaking, "taste" is limited to one or more of the five senses perceptible to the tongue: sweet, salt, sour, bitter, and umami. Flavor is a broader category, encompassing smells as well as taste, with the result that our response to it depends less on our genes than on our experience.)

But if plain old water can do all this for the flavor of a stew or soup or sauce, then why do so many cuisines resort so often to animal-enhanced waters, in the form of a stock or broth? Cooks will tell you that stocks add a quality of richness or intensity or "depth" to a braise or stew or sauce, making a savory dish that much more savory. It also adds "body," or substance. "Stock is everything in cooking," the great French chef Auguste Escoffier famously declared, "Without it, nothing can be done." This is why many great restaurants employ a "saucier," a cook whose entire job consists of making stocks. To buy such a foundational ingredient would be out of the question.

It's curious that this one ingredient of a dish consists, in effect, of a whole other dish—one with its own recipe, its own cook pot, its own liquid, and its own foundation of aromatic vegetables, notably including our old friends onion, carrot, and celery. To make a stock to add to a braise or a sauce, which Samin and I did on several occasions, feels like embarking on an infinite culinary regression, taking us all the way back, again, to the chopping of onions, browning of meat, and adding of liquid. But this process of repeating reductions—cooking things down in water, extracting their essences, and then reducing them yet again—seems to be how the deepest, purest layers of flavor are formed.

So what exactly is it about stock that makes it so indispensable? What does it really mean to say it gives "body" or "depth" to a pot dish or sauce, or makes something taste more "savory," as stocks undeniably do? What, in other words, is so special about this particular liquid we call stock?

I suspect it's something more than the flavor of the animal (or vegetables) on which the stock is based. As Samin's feelings about chicken stock suggest, the flavor of chicken is not necessarily a plus, and often goes unnoticed in the finished dish anyway. Indeed, one of the reasons that chicken or veal is usually the default stock owes to their relative lack of flavor, at least when compared with beef or pork, as well as to the fact that their young bones contribute comparatively more gelatin to a dish or sauce, thereby adding to their body. But there had to be something more to it than that, and after I spent some time researching the chemistry of meat stocks and the physiology of our sense of taste, it became (you'll forgive me) clear as consommé: The most important quality that a long-simmered stock contributes to any dish to which it has been added is the seductive and still somewhat mysterious fifth taste called umami.

Umami has been recognized as a full-fledged taste in Japan since 1908. That was the year that a chemist named Kikunae Ikeda discovered that the white crystals that form on dried kombu, a kind of seaweed that has been used as a base for soups and stocks in Japan for more than a thousand years, contained large amounts of glutamate, and that the savory taste of this molecule was sui generis—was not sweet or sour or bitter or salt. Ikeda decided to call the taste umami— the Japanese word for "deliciousness." Today, most of us encounter glutamate on ingredient labels in the form of a salt called monosodium glutamate, or MSG.*

The idea of a fifth taste was controversial in the West until 2001, when American scientists identified a dedicated taste receptor for glutamate on the human tongue. Now umami is generally recognized as a distinct taste, as is the fact that, in addition to glutamate, at least two other molecules, including the nucleotides inosine (found in fish) and guanosine (found in mushrooms) also contribute to a perception of umami. When combined, these chemicals seem to have a synergistic effect, dramatically intensifying the umami taste.

Like the other four tastes that have been identified in mammals, umami is actually a discrete sense. In each case, we are born with dedicated receptors that are wired to regions of the brain primed to respond in a specific way. Thus no one needs to "learn" the taste of sweetness or recognize it as positive. It is innate. Olfaction operates quite differently: Humans can sniff out some ten thousand smells and how we respond to each of them is largely the result of learning, individual and cultural. A smell that is appealing in one culture—that of rotted tofu, say, to which I was treated in China—may be absolutely disgusting in another. The difference between innate taste and learned smell is encoded in our language, which makes clear that smell is more associative, or metaphoric, than taste: We say something smells "like" something else, while we say that something simply is sweet or bitter or whatever—no simile required.

---

*MSG is a food additive synthesized by microbes from various natural materials. Glutamate also finds its way onto ingredient labels as "hydrolyzed vegetable protein," "protein isolate," "yeast extract," and "autolyzed yeast."

Each of the five tastes has been selected by evolution for its survival value. Either it guides us toward nutrients we need to survive, or it steers us away from ingesting things that might endanger us. For example, the taste of sweetness steers us toward particularly dense sources of energy in our environment, which is what sugars are. Salt is an essential nutrient we have been wired to like. Bitter happens to be how many plant toxins taste, which probably explains why babies instinctively frown when it is introduced on their tongues. (And why pregnant women in particular are often repelled by bitter foods.) Sour elicits an instinctive negative reaction, too, perhaps because when food rots it generally becomes more acidic, and rotten food is generally a risky thing to eat (stinky tofu notwithstanding). But even though they are innate, these last two responses can be "overridden": many of us learn to like sour or bitter foods.

So what about the taste of umami, or savoriness? Like salt and sugar, it evokes a universally positive response and, also like them, it signals the presence of an essential nutrient, in this case protein. Curiously, umami receptors have been found in the stomach as well as on the tongue. Their purpose, presumably, is to prepare the body to digest meat, alerting it to produce the necessary enzymes, hormones, and digestive acids. The most important chemical known to stimulate the umami receptors is the amino acid glutamate and the nucleotides inosine and guanosine, all of which are by-products of the breakdown of protein.

Which is of course precisely what is going on in a long-simmered stock: The long protein chains in the meat are breaking down into their various amino acid building blocks, glutamate chief among them. In fact, chicken stock is loaded with glutamate, which has been contributed not only by the protein-rich meat but by the slow cooking of the aromatic vegetables as well. Also present in meat stocks is inosinate, which when combined with glutumate creates a perception of umami much greater than the sum of its chemical parts.

But though umami can make a food taste "meaty," meat is only one of the many sources of glutamate. (That's why "savoriness" is probably a better translation for umami than "meatiness" or "brothiness.") Ripe tomatoes, dried mushrooms, Parmesan cheese, cured anchovies, and a great many fermented foods (including soy sauce and miso paste) contain high levels of glutamate, and can be added to a dish to boost its quotient of umami. This property of ripe tomatoes surely explains why so many of the braises I made with Samin called for a "tomato product"—canned tomatoes, or tomato paste—in addition to stock or wine. Occasionally we threw in a Parmesan rind, too, or some dried porcini or a squirt of anchovy paste. (And the reason we sometimes, à la Julia Child, browned our meat in bacon fat? Because bacon is a veritable umami bomb, containing all of the umami compounds that have thus far been identified.) I didn't know it at the time, and nor did Samin, but all these additions were ways to augment the umami in our dish, and the reason there was always more than one of them—tomato plus Parmesan, or stock plus dried mushrooms—was no doubt to exploit the synergistic properties of this particular taste. Umami, I realized, is the quasi-secret heart and soul of almost every braise, stew, and soup.

I say "secret" because umami works in somewhat mysterious ways, at least compared with sweet, salt, bitter, and sour. Encountered in the purified form of monosodium glutamate (MSG), glutamate doesn't taste particularly good, or for that matter much like anything at all. To work its magic, umami needs to be in the company of other ingredients. A bit like salt, glutamate seems to italicize the taste of foods, but, unlike salt, it doesn't have an instantly recognizable taste of its own.

The other mystery about umami is how it alters the texture as well as the taste of many foods—or, more accurately, our perception of its texture. Add umami to a soup and eaters will report it is not just "heartier" but actually thicker, too; the umami taste appears to have synesthetic properties. It makes a liquid seem less like water and more like food. It's possible that the umami chemicals activate not only the sense of taste in our mouths, but also trip the sense of touch as well, creating an illusion of "body."

What I learned about the properties of umami made me want to run some experiments with dashi, the classic Japanese stock. If pot dishes owe so much of their power to umami, then making them with dashi—a cooking water designed, albeit unwittingly, to contain as much umami and as little of anything else as possible—seemed worth trying. It sounded to me like the Ur–cooking liquid. So, naturally, I wanted to make some.

At least until you understand the science of umami, dashi seems like a thoroughly improbable concept: a stock made from dried seaweed, shavings from a cured fish, and, optionally, a dried mushroom or two. But it so happens that each of those items contains a different one of the three principal umami chemicals. Put all three together in water and you get synergies that vastly amplify the umami effect. Dashi, which has been made in Japan for more than a thousand years, is a classic example of the wisdom of cuisines: how, strictly by trial and error, a traditional culture can perfect a chemistry in food that is not fully appreciated until long after the fact.

With my dashi experiments, I was venturing well outside Samin's culinary orbit. She doesn't have much experience of Eastern foodways. But she was able to direct me to someone who did: a young Japanese

American cook by the (unsurpassed) name of Sylvan Mishima Brackett. When I e-mailed him to say I was interested in learning how to make dashi, Sylvan invited me over to the tiny, converted garage behind his house where he cooks, using little more than a hot plate.

What Sylvan did have, and what is difficult to find in this country, is a block of katsuobushi, or cured bonito, that he had brought back with him from a recent trip to Japan. Katsuobushi looks like a toy submarine carved out of a block of hardwood, perhaps walnut. It is as hard and fine-grained as walnut, too, making it impossible to cut with any tool less sharp than a woodworker's plane. Which is in fact what is traditionally used to coax shavings from Katsuobushi.

Sylvan had been to a katsuobushi factory in Japan, and he described the absurdly laborious process by which it is made. After the bonito is filleted into quarters, the fillets are simmered in water for two hours and then put on racks in a room in which an oak fire is burned for part of each day for a minimum of ten days. After that, the dried blocks of fish are scraped, taken out in the sun, and then inoculated with a fungus called koji (*Aspergillus oryzae*), before spending ten more days in a "molding room." That process—scraping, sun-drying, inoculating—is repeated three times, before the block—now completely desiccated and as hard as rock—is ready to be used. Here was an extreme instance of a pot-dish ingredient that was itself a complicated dish with a long recipe that called for an ingredient that itself had an unbelievably complicated recipe.

Sylvan used a whetstone to sharpen the blade on his plane and put me to work shaving katsuobushi. The block was actually considerably harder than wood, and it took a strenuous effort to accumulate even a small pile of shavings. The grain that the plane raised was a beautiful shade of salmony pink; how is it, I wondered as I worked, that the flesh of a fish and a tree could have so similar a structure? Meanwhile, Sylvan cranked up his hot plate and put a pot of water on to boil, to which he added a foot-long section of kombu. Kombu is air-dried kelp, one of the richest sources of glutamate in nature. Out of the package, it wears a cloak of white salt that is basically monosodium glutamate. Sylvan said the very best-quality kombu comes from (wouldn't you know it?) a specific beach on the northern coast of Hokkaido. He also mentioned that soft water was best for extracting the maximum flavor from the ingredients, and that in fact the word "dashi" means "extraction."

But if the backstory of the ingredients in dashi is complicated, the recipe for making it is fairly straightforward and, for a stock, quick and easy—less than ten minutes from start to finish. Sylvan dropped a sheet of kombu into a pot of cold water, heated it to a point just shy of the boil, and then removed the now green and floppy length of kombu with a pair of tongs. If the kombu reaches a full boil, he explained, the dashi will turn out bitter. At this point, the liquid gave off only the faintest scent of brininess. Unlike the kombu, the bonito flakes need to be boiled to release their flavor, so, as soon as the pot began to roil, Sylvan dropped in a big handful. The pinkish shavings danced crazily on the surface and then, as they rehydrated, began to sink to the bottom. They had only been in the water five or six minutes when Sylvan poured the stock through cheesecloth and discarded the residual flakes. The resulting liquid resembled very weak tea, an almost perfectly transparent pale gold. As the liquid cools, you have the option of adding a dried shiitake mushroom. But that's all there is to it.

I bent over to smell the finished dashi. It reminded me of a tide pool: briny, with the faintest suggestion of decay—the beach at low tide. I dipped a finger into the cooling liquid. It had very little taste to speak of; some saltiness, but not too much—sort of like a freshwater version of the ocean. Brackish. Compared with a real stock, it was pallid stuff; you would never think of sipping it as a soup. But the pale liquid contained large amounts of the three main umami chemicals—

glutamate from the kombu, inosinate from the bonito, and guanylate from the mushroom—each of them extracted by the water.

Sylvan gave me some bonito flakes and kombu to take home, and over the course of the next several days I made my own dashi and experimented with it. The first thing I tried was a dipping sauce. To a small bowl of dashi I added a tablespoon each of soy sauce, mirin, and rice wine vinegar, as well as a small handful of chopped scallions and ginger. It was remarkable stuff: Anything dipped in it—a chicken breast, some soba noodles, a piece of pork—received an uncanny boost in flavor, somehow tasted more platonically itself. (And more platonically Japanese.) Next, I tried the dashi as a braising liquid, for beef short ribs and then for a pork loin, combining it, again, with some soy sauce, mirin, vinegar, and sake, as well as some miso paste. The result in both cases was a rich and satisfying dish, somewhat lighter than the braises that Samin and I had made, though no less intensely flavored. I have not yet tried dashi in a non-Asian dish; that might be crazy, I don't know, and Samin would probably flip if I proposed it. But dashi itself is not a flavor principle, exactly—it's more like an italicizer of flavors—so it might well work with another cuisine. Nothing about dashi, when tasted by itself, prepares you for what it does in concert with other flavors. I'm starting to think of it as magic water: hydrogen and oxygen and amino acids and something no one knows.

One curious fact I stumbled on in my umami research was that human breast milk is rich in this particular taste, and contains relatively large amounts of glutamate—as it happens, nearly the same amount of glutamate as an equivalent amount of dashi. It stands to reason that everything in milk is there for an evolutionary reason; since every chemical compound in it comes at a metabolic cost to the mother, natural selection would quickly dispense with any constituent of milk that didn't do the infant some good. So what good does all that glutamate do?

There are a couple of possible explanations. Bruce German, a food chemist at the University of California, Davis, who analyzes human milk in order to better understand our nutritional needs, believes that the glutamate supplies an important nutrient to the growing infant. Besides being a flavor, this particular amino acid is a cellular fuel and molecular building block of special value to the stomach and intestines of the growing infant. In the same way that glucose is an ideal food for the brain, glutamate is a perfect food for the gut, which might explain why we're born with taste buds in the stomach that can detect it.

All that glutamate in breast milk might be doing something else as well: conditioning the baby to like the taste of umami, that being (along with sweetness) one of the first and most abundant tastes it encounters in mother's milk. This preference is highly adaptive for *Homo sapiens*, since we require a diet rich in the proteins that umami helps us to recognize and seek out.

But could it be that, for us, the taste of foods rich in umami also sounds deep Proustian echoes, bearing us back to memories, however faint, of our very first food? Is it merely a coincidence that so many of the things we think of as "comfort foods"—everything from ice cream to chicken soup—traffic in tastes of either sweetness or umami, the two big tastes first encountered on the breast?

This bit of speculation was very much on my mind during a recent Sunday afternoon with Samin, when we set out to make an ancient Roman dish called *maiale al latte*—pork braised in milk. I was skeptical about this one, and not only because it was so radically unkosher. The fact that I eat pork should by now be well established, but there does seem something slightly perverse about cooking it in milk, and I wondered if there might not be some good practical reason behind the Old Testament's taboo on mixing milk and meat. But apparently not: The rabbinical commentators say that particular taboo falls under the heading of "hukkim," which are laws for which there is no obvious explanation.

My guess? The kosher laws are all about drawing and defending crisp lines of demarcation between various realms, and what line is sharper than the one between life and death? You don't mix a symbol of death, such as animal flesh, with a symbol of life as powerful as mother's milk. Also, cooking meat in milk mingles the male realm of the hunt with the female realm of nurturing—a taboo in many cultures. As the anthropologist Mary Douglas has written, a rule against mixing meat and milk "honors the procreative function."

Well, not today. "This is one of my all-time favorite dishes," Samin said, when I expressed my doubts about it. "I know, it sounds really weird, and I have to prepare you: it looks sort of gross when you're cooking it. But I promise, it will be the most delicious, succulent comfort food you've ever tasted in your life!"

As a cooking liquid, milk presents special challenges. Of all the pot dishes we cooked, this one had to be watched the most closely, lest the sugars in the milk begin to burn on the bottom of the pot. Yet, at the same time, *maiale al latte* was also the very simplest recipe we'd made. In fact, it can be written out in a sentence: Brown chunks of pork in butter; add some milk, a few cloves of garlic, a handful of sage leaves, and the juice (and peel) of a lemon; simmer for several hours. That's it. *No soffritto?* I asked Samin. *No chopped onions?*

"Nope. Weird, I know. But I think this dish must be even older than soffritto is. It might even go back to Etruscan times."

The biggest challenge is keeping the milk at a gentle simmer just below the boil—the braising liquid should merely "smile," as the French say, rather than bubble. So we peeked in at regular intervals, taking advantage of the established fact that a watched pot will never boil. (Probably because in order to watch you lift the lid, which drops the temperature.) After a while the milk began to yellow slightly and form curds—and to look very much like baby vomit. Which is not at all unlike what it was: warm milk that has curdled after having been exposed to an acid. The age-old conceit of the cauldron as an external organ of digestion had never seemed so apt, but that of course was precisely what was going on here, the proteins in the milk being broken down and rearranged by the acids.

"I know, it's sort of disgusting," Samin allowed. "But this is exactly what we want. You'll see, those curds are going to be super-delicious."

And so they were, eventually. After several hours the cooking liquid turned a gorgeous shade of ochre, and the golden curds no longer looked like mistakes. The lemony milk had gone to work on the proteins in the meat, breaking it down until it was so tender it fell apart at the prodding of a fork. The meat was as succulent and tasty as Samin had promised, but it was the sauce that was most incredible, with its creamy layers of savory and sweet. Actually, all five tastes were represented in that silky liquid: besides the savory-saltiness from the meat and the sweetness from the milk, the sauce bore traces of sourness and bitterness contributed by the lemon peel and sage leaves, all of it harmoniously dispersed in the milk. To concoct so much flavor from such a small number of ordinary ingredients—pork, garlic, lemon, sage, and milk—seemed like a miracle of transubstantiation. "The transformation which occurs in the cauldron is quintessential and wondrous, subtle and delicate," wrote a Chinese chef named I Yin in

239 B.C., no doubt moved by a similar eating experience. "The mouth cannot express it in words."

◉◉

Gaston Bachelard, the somewhat obtuse French philosopher of the elements, wrote a book called *Water and Dreams*, in which he attempts to "psychoanalyze" water and other liquids in much the same way he attempted a psychoanalysis of fire. "For the imagination, everything that *flows* is water," Bachelard writes in a chapter called "Maternal Water and Feminine Water." Water is always feminine in the imagination, he contends, just as its opposite, fire, is always masculine. But he then goes a step further, suggesting that, to the imagination, "all water is a kind of milk," though a moment later he confines this claim to the kinds of water we like: "More precisely, every joyful drink is mother's milk," and, a bit farther on, "water is a milk as soon as it is extolled fervently."

As an example Bachelard offers an image of the "nourishing waters" of the sea, in which the resident fish effortlessly feed themselves from the particles of fat and other nutrients dispersed in the liquid medium, floating along without care as if in amniotic fluids. "For the material imagination, water, like milk, is a complete food."

Bachelard has little else to say about food in *Water and Dreams*, and nothing at all about stews and soups, but my guess is that they would all qualify in his imagination as "milks"—as a medium much like the nourishing sea, in which the fish, like babies on the breast, never want for anything they need or desire. The nourishing liquid that forms in a pot dish starts out as thin and transparent as water, then clouds and colors as it absorbs and disperses substance and flavor, ending up eventually as a more or less complete and milklike food. In the imagination, at least, this kind of cooking qualifies as a transubstantiation of matter, in this instance not of water into wine but of something no less miraculous: water into milk.

"Stone Soup" is the ancient parable of this everyday miracle, of turning water into food. In the story, which has been told for centuries in many different cultures (sometimes as "Nail Soup" or "Button Soup" or "Ax Soup"), some poor, hungry strangers come to town with nothing but an empty pot. The villagers refuse them food, so the strangers fill their pot with water, drop a stone in it, and put it on to boil in the town square. This arouses the curiosity of the villagers, who ask the strangers what it is they're making.

"Stone soup," the strangers explain. "It's delicious, as you'll soon see, but it would taste even better if you could spare a little garnish to help flavor it." So one villager gives them a sprig of parsley. Then another remembers she has some potato peelings at home, which she fetches and drops into the pot. Someone else throws in an onion and a carrot, and then another villager offers a bone. As the kettle boils, one villager after another comes by to throw in a scrap of this, a bit of that, until the soup had thickened into something nourishing and wonderful that everyone—villagers and strangers—sits down to enjoy together at a great feast.

"You have given us the greatest gift," one of the village elders declares, "the secret of how to make soup from stones."

VI.

STEP SIX:
SIMMER, BELOW THE BOIL, FOR A LONG TIME

Braise: the sound of that lovely word itself suggests a certain slow un-folding, the final "z" sound trailing off with no hard consonant to stop it. And in fact nothing is more important to a successful braise than allowing it to take its sweet time. This period of simmering is in many ways the easiest step of the process, since it requires nothing of the cook but patience. As one wise cookbook advises when one is making a braise, "If you wonder whether it's done, it's not."

Yet most recipes try to rush the process, promising to wrap things up and get the dish on the table in a couple of hours. These days, recipes are steeped in the general sense of panic about time, and so have tried to speed everything up, the better to suit "our busy lives." In the case of braises and stews, this usually means cranking up the cooking temperature, often to 325°F or 350°F. Not a good idea—in fact, not really braising at all. At those temperatures, all but the fatti-est meats will dry out and toughen, and the gradual transformations and meldings of flavors, the chemical reactions and synergies of taste that make so many slow-cooked foods so delicious, simply won't have a chance to unfold. Time is everything in these dishes, and in most cases, more is more. (The word "braise" comes from a "brazier," a metal cook pot sort of like a Dutch oven that, since it is heated by placing a few coals on top of and below it, never gets very hot.)

Harold McGee recommends never allowing a braise to exceed the boiling point—212°F. Even at 300°F, liquid in a covered pot will boil, and likely damage the meat. You want the cooking liquid merely to "smile"—hatch a tiny bubble now and then, but never boil. McGee goes so far as to suggest starting a braise at 200°F with the lid off, which should bring the liquid to around 120°F, scarcely warmer than a hot tub. But two hours at such a temperature "amounts to a period of accelerated aging" that tenderizes the muscle by allowing enzymes to break down the connective tissues. (It also preserves the reddish pigmentation of the meat even after it's been completely cooked—a color that the pit masters I met prized as proof of low and slow cooking.) After that, cover the pot and bump the temperature to 250°F, and keep it there until the meat has reached 180°F. At that point, which could take three or four hours, all the collagen will have melted into succulence, and the meat should tremble at the approach of a fork.

The first time I asked Samin how long some dish we were cooking should cook, she offered this slightly gnomic answer: "Until the meat relaxes." Here was one way that slow cooking with water or fire had the same effect. "When you're cooking a muscle, which is basically what meat is, first it tenses up like this"—she scrunched her shoulder, drew in a breath, and grimaced—"but then, at a certain point, it suddenly unclenches"—she released her shoulders and her breath—"so that when you touch it you can *feel* that it has relaxed. *That's* when slow-cooked meat is done."

Time is the missing ingredient in our recipes—and in our lives. I'm not going to pretend that the Ur-braise I've described here can be made in just twenty minutes of "active cooking time," as the recipes now like to promise. There's at least a half hour of that (chopping onions, sweating the mirepoix, browning the meat, etc.), and probably more if you cook the onions as slowly as they should be cooked. On the other hand, once that work is done, you can put the pot on low (or just throw everything in a Crock-Pot) and do something else for the rest of the afternoon—make the sides and a dessert, check your e-mail, take a walk—while the pot works its leisurely magic. But unless you make your braise in a Crock-Pot (which is always an option), you do need to be around to keep an eye on it, which for most of us today is a lot to ask, at least during the week. In households where both partners work outside the home, it is difficult, if not impossible, to weave this sort of cooking into the rhythms of weekday life.

Yet even on the weekends, most of us are moving too fast for slow cooking, even unattended slow cooking. So if we cook at all we clip ten- and twenty-minute recipes from the newspaper and throw expensive filets on the grill. This is certainly what Judith and I do most nights, and it took me awhile to get accustomed to the idea of spending several hours at a time in the kitchen, even on a weekend day. Coming into the kitchen, I always felt divided against myself, torn, because there was always something else, something more pressing, I could be doing with that time—household errands, exercise, reading, watching television. But knowing Samin was going to be here for four hours of cooking, I eventually found that I could (like some of the meat we were cooking) relax into it, clear my mind of competing desires, and give myself over to the work. *When chopping onions, just chop onions.*

This time became a kind of luxury, and that is precisely when I began truly to enjoy the work of cooking.

You could argue that this sort of cooking was a special case, and it was. Our cooking was luxuriously optional, not obligatory. It didn't happen every day, either. It was also not time spent alone, which I've come to think is a big part of the "drudgery problem" with cooking, and one of the reasons so many of us happily abandoned the kitchen as soon as that became a real option. Cooking can be isolating in households where one person is expected to do it all—typically the woman in a nuclear family. Yet it's worth remembering that it is cooking alone that is the historical exception. Historically, cooking has been a much more sociable activity than it became after World War II, when so many people moved to the suburbs and the nuclear family with a wife who didn't go off to work became the norm.

Before that, multiple generations of women in a family would often cook together. And before the industrial revolution, when men first left the home to earn wages, men and women commonly worked together (at different tasks, it's true) to put food on the table. The household was a more self-sufficient unit before the rise of the market and the division of labor. Going back still further, the women in small, traditional communities would perform food work as a group, grinding grain or making bread in what anthropologists call "the conversational circle." Even today, in many Mediterranean villages, you find communal ovens, where people bring their proofed loaves, roasts, and braises, and pass the time in conversation while waiting for their dishes to come out of the oven. Sundays with Samin had some of that flavor. Sooner or later, Judith and Isaac, our son, would drift into the kitchen and pick up a knife to help, and conversation became a more or less constant companion to the soothing, rhythmic sounds of kitchen business.

It is true that this cooking was purely elective. But nowadays, what cooking isn't? With fast- and convenience food so cheap and ubiquitous, cooking is hardly ever obligatory anymore, even among the poor. We all get to decide whether to cook, and increasingly, we decide not to. Why? Some people will tell you they find it boring or daunting. But the most common reason people offer is, they don't have the time.

And for many of us, that is true. For years now Americans have been putting in longer hours at work and enjoying less time at home. Since 1967, we've added 167 hours—the equivalent of a month's full-time labor—to the total amount of time we spend at work each year, and in households where both parents work, now the great majority, the figure is more like 400 hours. Americans today spend more time working than people in any other industrialized nation—an extra two weeks or more a year. This probably owes to the fact that, historically, the priority of the American labor movement has been to fight for money, whereas the European labor movement has fought harder for time—a shorter workweek, longer vacations. Not surprisingly, in those countries where people still take home cooking seriously, as they do in much of Europe, they also have more time to devote to it.

It's generally thought that the entrance of women into the work-force is responsible for the collapse of home cooking, but the story turns out to be a little more complicated, and fraught. Yes, women with jobs outside the home spend less time cooking—but so do women without jobs. The amount of time spent on food preparation in America has fallen at the same precipitous rate among women who don't work outside the home as it has among women who do: In both cases, it has fallen about 40 percent since 1965.* In general, spending on restaurant and take-out food rises with income. Families where both partners work simply have more money to pay corporations to do their cooking, yet all American families now allow corporations to cook for them when they can. There is an irony in the fact that many of the women who have traded time in the kitchen for time in the workplace are working in the food-service industry, helping to produce meals for other families who no longer have time to cook for themselves. These women are being paid for this cooking, true, yet a substantial part of their pay is going to other corporations to cook their families' meals.

---

*Though for married women who don't have jobs the amount of time spent cooking is greater: 58 minutes a day, as compared with 36 for married women who do have jobs.

Now, whenever anyone—but especially a man—expresses dismay at the decline of home cooking, a couple of unspoken assumptions begin to condense over the conversation like offending clouds. The first assumption is that you must be "blaming" women for the decline in cooking, since (and here is assumption number two) the meals no longer being cooked are women's responsibility. It's not hard to identify the basis for these assumptions: Women have traditionally done most of the household food work, so to defend cooking is automatically to defend those roles. But by now it should be possible to make a case for the importance of cooking without defending the traditional division of domestic labor. Indeed, that argument will probably get nowhere unless it *challenges* the traditional arrangements of domesticity—and assumes a prominent role for men in the kitchen, as well as children.

Even so, the decline of cooking remains a fraught subject, and there are many people who don't think a man has a leg to stand on talking about it. But the very touchiness of the subject turns out to be an essential element of the story. When women left the house to go to work, there was a problem: Who would now do the housework? The women's movement plopped that difficult question onto kitchen tables all over the world. How fair was it to expect women who now worked to continue taking care of the children, cleaning the house, and putting meals on the table? (In the 1980s, one sociologist calculated that, when you added up work at work and work at home, working women were putting in fifteen hours more work a week than men.*) The time had come, clearly, for a renegotiation of the division of labor in the family.

This promised to be a very difficult and uncomfortable conversation. No one was looking forward to it. And then we found a way to

---

*Arlie Russell Hochschild, *Second Shift* (New York: Penguin Books, 1989).

avoid having it. Several ways, actually. Couples who could afford to defused the conflict by paying other women to clean the house and take care of the children. And instead of arguing about who should get dinner on the table, or how that work might be equitably shared, the food industry stepped into the breach with an offer that proved irresistible to everyone, male or female, rich or poor: *Why don't you just let us cook for you?*

Actually food manufacturers had been working to convince us they should do the cooking since long before large numbers of women entered the workforce. Beginning after World War II, the food industry labored mightily to sell Americans—and American women in particular—on the processed-food wonders it had invented to feed the troops: canned meals, freeze-dried foods, dehydrated potatoes, powdered orange juice and coffee, instant and superconvenient everything. As Laura Shapiro recounts in her social history, *Something from the Oven: Reinventing Dinner in 1950s America*, the food industry strove to "persuade millions of Americans to develop a lasting taste for meals that were a lot like field rations." The same process of peacetime conversion that industrialized our farming, giving us synthetic fertilizers made from munitions and new pesticides developed from nerve gas, also industrialized our eating.

Shapiro shows that the shift toward industrial cookery began not in response to a demand from women entering the workforce, or even from feminists eager to escape the drudgery of the kitchen, but was mainly a supply-driven phenomenon. Processing food is extremely profitable—much more so than growing it or selling it whole. So it became the strategy of food corporations to move into our kitchens long before many women had begun to move out.

Yet for years, American women, whether they worked or not, strenuously resisted processed foods, regarding them as a dereliction of their "moral obligation to cook," something they viewed as a parental responsibility on par with, and part of, child care. And though second-wave feminist writers like Betty Friedan depicted all housework as a form of oppression, many women drew a distinction between cooking, which they regularly told food-industry researchers they enjoyed, and other domestic tasks. As author and nutritionist Joan Gussow has said, "There is absolutely no evidence that cooking is, or was, a hated chore from which the food processors—as they claim—liberated women." But though it may not have been a hated chore, it was one of the easier chores to hand over to the market when time became short and the household workload too burdensome.

In fact, many second-wave feminists were ambivalent on the gender politics of cooking. Simone de Beauvoir wrote in *The Second Sex* that, though time spent in the kitchen could be oppressive, it could also be a form of "revelation and creation; and a woman can find special satisfaction in a successful cake or a flaky pastry, for not everyone can do it: one must have the gift." We can read this as either a special (very French) exemption for the culinary arts, or as a bit of genuine wisdom that some American feminists thoughtlessly trampled in their rush to get women out of the kitchen. But this ambivalence about the value of cooking raises an interesting question. Has our culture devalued food work because it is unfulfilling by its very nature or because it has traditionally been women's work?

Either way, it appears that the food industry—along with the falling wages of American families, which is what drew most women into the workforce beginning in the 1970s—probably had more to do with the decline of cooking than feminist rhetoric. Not that feminist rhetoric didn't help. It did, especially when food marketers began deploying it themselves, as a clever way to align their products, and interests, with the rising feminist tide. Kentucky Fried Chicken was not the only convenience food that promised "women's liberation" from cooking. The industry was only too happy to clothe itself in feminist ideology if that would help it insinuate itself into the kitchen and onto the dinner table.

Yet running just beneath the surface of food-industry feminism was an implicit antifeminist message. Then as now, ads for packaged foods were aimed almost exclusively at women, and so reinforced the retrograde idea that the responsibility for feeding the family fell to Mom. The slick new products would help her to do a job that was hers and hers alone. The ads have also helped manufacture a sense of panic about time, depicting families so rushed and harried in the morning that there is no time to make breakfast, not even to pour some milk over a bowl of cereal. No, the only hope is to munch on a cereal bar (iced with synthetic "milk" frosting) in the bus or car. (Tell me: Why can't these hassled families set their alarm clocks, like, *ten minutes* earlier?!) Like so much of modern advertising, the commercials for convenience food simultaneously stoke an anxiety and promise to relieve it. The food industry's marketing message has the added benefit of letting men completely off the hook. For the necessary and challenging questions about *who* should be in the kitchen, posed so sharply by Betty Friedan in *The Feminine Mystique*, ultimately got answered for us by the food industry: *No one! Let us do it all!* With that, we welcomed the food industry into our kitchens as a way to head off the conflict brewing between Mom and Dad.

Yet it took years of such clever, dedicated marketing to wear down the resistance of many women to the farming-out of food preparation to corporations. They first had to be persuaded that opening a can or cooking from a mix really *was* cooking. Honest. This took some doing. In the 1950s, just-add-water cake mixes languished in the supermarket until the marketers figured out that if they left *something* for the "baker" to do—specifically, crack open an actual egg—she could take ownership of the cake, feel as though she had discharged her moral obligation to cook. But in the years since, our resistance has crumbled as the food scientists have gotten better and better at simulating real food while making it look attractive and seemingly fresh. At the same time, the rapid penetration of microwave ovens—which went from being a fixture in 8 percent of American households in 1978 to 90 percent today—opened up a vast new field of home-meal replacements by slashing the time it takes to, um, "cook" them.

The idea of cooking as a solemn parental obligation has not been completely vanquished, but, as Harry Balzer's research suggests, the corporate project of redefining what it means to cook and serve a meal to your family has succeeded beyond the industry's wildest expectations. People think nothing of buying frozen peanut-butter-and-jelly sandwiches for their children's lunch boxes. The march of packaged foods into our pantries and freezers has also undermined our willingness to buy fresh ingredients, Balzer has found, since they oblige us to do something with them before they go bad—yet another pressure of time. A wilting head of broccoli in the fridge is "a guilt trip," Balzer says, whereas a frozen entrée loyally stands by us indefinitely. "Fresh is a hassle."

"We've had a hundred years of packaged foods," Balzer told me, "and now we're going to have a hundred years of packaged meals." Already today, 80 percent of the cost of food eaten in the home goes to someone other than a farmer, which is to say, to industrial cooking and packaging and marketing. More than half the money we spend to eat goes to food prepared outside the home. Balzer himself is unsentimental about this development; in fact, he looks forward to the next frontier in the industrial revolution of dinner.

"We're all looking for someone else to cook for us. The next American cook is going to be the supermarket. Take-out from the supermarket, that's the future. All we need now is the drive-through supermarket." In the end, women did succeed in getting men into the kitchen, just not their husbands. No, they've ended up instead with the men who run General Mills and Kraft, Whole Foods and Trader Joe's.

◉◉

The whole question of time begins to look a little different when you consider what we're doing with the half hour a day that the food industry has so generously granted us. Longer hours at work are part of the answer. Another is more time spent in the car, on longer commutes. We're also spending more time shopping—for take-out food, among other things. (We forget how much time it can take simply to avoid cooking: all that time spent driving to restaurants or waiting for our orders, none of which gets counted as "food preparation.") But much of the half hour saved by not cooking is being spent in front of screens: watching television (nearly thirty-five hours a week on average), surfing the Web (about thirteen hours a week), and playing games on our smart phones. During the last few decades, we have somehow managed to find nearly two more hours in our busy lives to devote to the computer each day. In a day that still has exactly twenty-four hours in it, where in the world did we find all that time?

Well, we've gotten much better at multitasking, a phenomenon that makes this whole business of measuring how we budget our time much trickier. Multitasking also counts against cooking as an acceptable use of our time, since it is harder to check e-mail while chopping onions than it is to, say, eat while shopping online. And yet what's to keep us from looking at this "problem" as one of the great virtues of cooking?

One multitasking activity that has increased substantially as cooking has declined is a new human behavior called "secondary eating." When asked what Americans are doing with the time that industrial food preparation has freed up, Karen S. Hamrick, an economist at the USDA, said, "People spend more time eating. Eating while they're watching TV; eating while driving; eating while getting dressed; eating while they're doing almost everything else." A USDA study that Hamrick wrote found that Americans are now spending seventy-eight minutes a day engaged in secondary eating and drinking—that is, eating or drinking while doing something else.* This is now more time than they spend engaged in "primary eating"—aka meals. Who would ever have predicted that cooking less would actually lead us to eat more? But that is precisely what has happened.

The rise in "secondary eating" points up one of the subtler ways that not cooking might be deleterious to our health. There is good reason to believe that the outsourcing of food preparation to corporations and sixteen-year-old burger flippers has taken a toll on our physical and psychological well-being. But the reason is not simply because corporations and fast-food franchises cook poorly, true as that is. Rather, it's because the time that people used to spend cooking had a substantial, invisible, and generally positive effect on the way that they and their families ate.

That at least is the conclusion of some intriguing recent research

---

*From the study: On an average day during 2006–8, Americans age 15 and older spent 78 minutes in secondary eating and drinking, that is, while doing something else considered to be the primary activity. Secondary eating and drinking was reported as occurring in all 400-plus detailed activities, except sleeping and primary eating and drinking. The two most popular activities that accompanied secondary eating or drinking were watching television and engaging in paid work. Travel related to work or travel related to shopping was also a frequent activity that accompanied secondary eating and drinking. (*How Much Time Do Americans Spend on Food?*, EIB-86, November 2011.) http://www.ers.usda.gov/publications/eib-economic-information-bulletin/eib86.aspx.

on the links between time spent cooking and dietary health. A 2003 study by a group of Harvard economists led by David Cutler* found that most of the increase in obesity in America over the last several decades could be explained by the rise of food preparation outside the home. Mass production has driven down the cost of many foods, not only in terms of purchase price but, perhaps even more important, in the amount of time required to obtain them.

Consider the french fry. Fried potatoes did not become the most popular "vegetable" in America until the food industry relieved us of the considerable time, effort, and mess required to prepare them ourselves. Similarly, the mass production of cream-filled cakes, fried chicken wings and taquitos, exotically flavored chips and dips, or cheesy puffs of refined flour has transformed all these hard-to-make-at-home foods into the sort of everyday fare we can pick up at the gas station on a whim for less than a dollar. And the fact that we no longer have to plan or even wait to enjoy these foods, as we surely would if we were making them ourselves, makes us that much more likely to indulge impulsively.

Economics teaches that when the cost of something goes down, consumption of it goes up. But cost is measured not only in money; it can be measured in time, too. Cutler and his colleagues make a strong case that the decline in the "time cost" of food has had a substantial effect on our eating. Since the 1970s, we're consuming five hundred more calories a day, and most of them consist of precisely the sort of foods (like snacks and convenience foods) that are typically cooked outside the home. The study found that when we don't have to cook meals ourselves we eat more of them. As the amount of time Americans spend cooking has dropped by half, the number of

*Cutler, David M., et al., "Why Have Americans Become More Obese?," Journal of Economic Perspectives, 17 No. 3 (2003): 93–118.

meals Americans eat in a day has climbed; since 1977, we've added roughly half a meal's worth of food to our daily intake, most of it in the form of secondary eating.

Cutler and his colleagues surveyed cooking patterns across several cultures and discovered that obesity rates are inversely correlated with the amount of time spent on food preparation. The more time a nation devotes to food preparation at home, the lower its rate of obesity. In fact, the amount of time spent cooking predicts obesity rates more reliably than female participation in the labor force or even income. Other research supports the idea that home cooking is a better predictor of a healthful diet than social class. A 1992 study in the *Journal of the American Dietetic Association* found that poor women who routinely cooked were likely to eat a more healthful diet than well-to-do women who did not.[*] A 2012 *Public Health Nutrition* study of the elderly in Taiwan found a strong correlation between regular cooking and superior health and longevity.[†]

So time spent cooking matters—a lot. Which, when you think about it, should come as no surprise. When we let corporations cook for us, they're bound to skimp on quality ingredients and go heavy on the sugar, fat, and salt. These are three tastes we've been hardwired by natural selection to favor; they also happen to be dirt cheap and to do a good job masking the shortcomings of processed foods. Industrial cookery also increases the range of the tastes and cuisines available to us; we may not know how to cook Indian or Moroccan or Thai, but Trader Joe's does. Although such variety might seem like a good thing, as Cutler suggests (and any buffet table proves), the wider the choice of food, the more of it we will consume. And then there is dessert: If

[*]Haines, P. S., et al., "Eating Patterns and Energy and Nutrient Intakes of US Women," *Journal of the American Dietetic Association* 92 No. 6 (1992): 698–704, 707.
[†]Chia-Yu Chen, Rosalind, et al., "Cooking Frequency May Enhance Survival in Taiwanese Elderly," *Public Health Nutrition* 15 (July 2012): 1142–49.

you make special-occasion foods cheap and easy enough to eat every day, we will eat them every day. The time and work involved in cooking, as well as the delay in gratification built into the cooking process, serve as an important check on our appetite. Now that check is gone, and we're struggling to deal with the consequences.

The question is, can we ever go back? Once it has been dismantled, can a culture of everyday cooking (and "primary eating") be rebuilt? Because it's hard to imagine ever reforming the American way of eating unless millions of us—women and men both—are willing to make cooking and eating meals a part of daily life. The path to a healthier diet of fresh, unprocessed food (not to mention to a revitalized local food economy) passes right through the home kitchen.

If this strikes you as an appealing idea, you might not want to call Harry Balzer to discuss it.

"Not going to happen," he told me. "Why? Because we're basically cheap and lazy, and the skills are already lost. Who is going to teach the next generation how to cook?"

Crusty as a fresh baguette, Harry Balzer insists on dealing with the world, and human nature, as it really is, or at least as he finds it in the survey data he has spent the last three decades poring over. But for a brief moment, I was able to engage him in the project of imagining a slightly different reality. This took a little doing. Most of his clients, who include many of the big chain restaurants and food manufacturers, profit handsomely from the decline of cooking in America; indeed, their marketing has contributed to it. Yet Balzer himself clearly recognizes what industrial cookery has cost us. So I asked him how, in an ideal world, we might begin to undo the damage that the modern diet of industrially prepared food has done to our health.

"Easy. You want Americans to eat less? I have the diet for you. Cook it yourself. Eat anything you want—just as long as you're willing to cook it yourself."

Toward the end of my year of cooking with Samin, I began braising and stewing solo, regularly devoting my Sunday afternoons to cooking various pot dishes on my own. The idea was to make a couple of dinners at a time and freeze them to eat during the week: my own home-meal replacements, homemade. Weeknights, it's often hard to find more than a half hour or so to fix dinner, so I decided to put in a few hours on the weekend, when I would feel less rushed. I also borrowed a couple of minor mass-production techniques from the food industry: I figured that if I was going to chop onions for a mirepoix or soffritto, why not chop enough for two or three dishes? That way, I'd only have to wash the pans, knives, and cutting boards once. Making pot dishes in this way has proved to be the single most practical and sustainable skill—both in terms of money and time spent to eat well—I acquired in my cooking education.

Sundays without Samin have become a pastime I look forward to most weekends. Isaac usually keeps me company, bringing his laptop down to the kitchen so he can do his homework while I chop and sauté, season and stir. Sometimes he'll wander over to the pot on the stove with a tasting spoon, and offer some unsolicited seasoning advice. But mostly we work in parallel, both of us absorbed in our respective tasks, with occasional breaks for conversation. I've learned that the very best time to talk to a teenager is while doing something else, and our hours at the kitchen island, during what is his last year at home, have become some of the easiest, sweetest times we've had together. I believe he feels the same way. One Sunday, Isaac answered the phone while I stirred a sugo; we were planning to make some fresh pasta together a little later in the day. It was my parents on the line.

"It's cold and drizzly here, but really cozy inside," I heard Isaac tell them. "Dad's cooking and the house smells so good. This is my perfect kind of Sunday."

Once I committed a couple of hours to being in the kitchen, I found my usual impatience fade and could give myself over to the afternoon's unhurried project. After a week in front of the screen, the opportunity to work with my hands—with all my senses, in fact—is always a welcome change of pace, whether in the kitchen or in the garden. There's something about such work that seems to alter the experience of time, helps me to reoccupy the present tense. I don't want you to get the idea it's made a Buddhist of me, but in the kitchen, maybe a little bit. *When stirring the pot, just stir the pot.* I get it now. It seems to me that one of the great luxuries of life at this point is to be able to do one thing at a time, one thing to which you give yourself wholeheartedly.

Unitasking.

VII.

STEP SEVEN:
REMOVE POT FROM OVEN. IF NECESSARY, SKIM FAT AND REDUCE LIQUID. BRING TO THE TABLE AND SERVE.

All that first winter of Sundays without Samin, and several of the weekdays thereafter, we enjoyed a variety of tasty pot dishes: sugo over homemade pasta, braised short ribs in dashi, a pork-and-chili stew, braised duck legs, a vegetable tagine, coq au vin, beef stew, osso buco, and so on. After some practice, I found that two hours of so-called active cooking time followed by a few more of unattended simmering could produce three or four nights' worth of good and—I don't mind saying—occasionally exceptional home cooking. I'm counting leftovers; stews and braises are infinitely more delicious the second or third night.

But one Sunday afternoon that winter, while Isaac and I were at work in the kitchen, we cooked up a little experiment, a plan for a family dinner later that week that would constitute the precise nega-tion of all the cooking we'd been doing to that point: "Microwave Night." The deal was, we would each choose whatever entrée most appealed to us in the frozen-food case and make a dinner of them. How much time would we save? What would it cost? And what would the meal be like? Isaac saw it as a chance to indulge his desire for fast food. I was indulging a more journalistic curiosity.

So the next afternoon, after school, we drove to the Safeway, grabbed a shopping cart, and wheeled it down the long, chilly aisle of freezer cases holding the microwavable dinners. The choices were stupendous—almost stupefying, in fact. It took us more than twenty minutes just to decide among the bags of frozen Chinese stir-fry, the boxed Indian biryanis and curries, the fish-and-chip dinners, the multiflavored mac-and-cheese options, the Japanese gyoza and Indo-nesian satays, the Thai rice bowls, the old-timey Salisbury steaks, the roast-turkey and fried-chicken dinners, the beef Stroganoff, the bur-ritos and tacos and fully loaded hero sandwiches, the frozen garlic bread and sliders, and the cheeseburgers preinstalled on their frozen buns. There were whole product lines targeted at women trying to minimize their caloric intake, and others at men looking to maximize theirs (the "Hungry Man" promises "a full pound of great-tasting food"), and still others aimed at kids dreaming of an authentic fast-food restaurant experience at home. I hadn't spent much time on this aisle in years, so had no idea just how many advances there had been in the technology of home-meal replacement. Every genre of fast food, every ethnic cuisine, every chain-restaurant menu item known to man and commerce now has its facsimile in the freezer case.

Judith was willing to go along with our dinner plans but declined to join us shopping for it. She had requested a frozen lasagna, and Isaac spotted a bright-red box of Stouffer's that looked halfway appetizing. Dubious about eating meat under the circumstances, I first checked out a vegan "chicken cacciatore" entrée, but the lengthy list of ingredients—most of them ultraprocessed permutations of soy—put me off the mock meat. So I opted for an organic vegetable curry from Amy's that seemed fairly straightforward in composition; at least, I recognized all the ingredients as food, which is saying a lot in this sector of the supermarket. Isaac agonized for a good long time, but his problem was the opposite of mine: There were just too many tempting entrées he wanted to try. Eventually it came down to a call between the bag of P. F. Chang's Shanghai Style Beef stir-fry and Safeway's own frozen French onion soup gratinée. I told him he could get them both, as well as some frozen molten (sic) chocolate cookie he'd been eyeing for dessert.

The total for the three of us came to $27—more than I would have expected. Some of the entrées, like Isaac's stir-fry, promised to feed more than one person, but this seemed doubtful given the portion size. Later that week I went to the farmers' market and found that with $27 I could easily buy a couple pounds of an inexpensive cut of grass-fed beef and enough vegetables to make a braise that would feed the three of us for at least one night and probably two. (The variable, as ever, is Isaac's appetite.) So there was a price to pay for letting the team of P. F. Chang, Stouffer's, Safeway, and Amy's cook our dinner.

I don't think it's boastful of me to say that none of these entrées did anything to undermine my growing confidence in the kitchen.

True, I don't yet know how to engineer dishes that can withstand months in the freezer case, or figure out how to build little brown ice cubes of hoisin sauce, designed to liquefy just in time to coat the vegetables after they've defrosted but not a moment sooner. And nothing I learned from Samin could help me design the consecutive layers of cheese curds and croutons topping the chocolate-colored cylinder of frozen onion soup like a Don King fright wig.

So how did it all taste? A lot like airline food, if you can remember what that was like. All the entrées tasted remarkably similar, considering how far-flung the culinary inspirations. They were all salty and had that generic fast-food flavor, a sort of bouillon-y taste that probably can be traced to the "hydrolyzed vegetable protein" that several of the dishes contained. This is an ingredient-label euphemism for monosodium glutamate (MSG)—basically, a cheap way to boost the perception of umami. The dishes all tasted better on the first bite—when you might be tempted to think, *Hey, not half bad!*—than on the second or third, when those words would be unlikely to cross your mind. There is a short half-life to the taste of a frozen dinner, which I would peg somewhere around bite number three, after which the whole experience rapidly deteriorates.

Oh, but wait: I've skipped over the cooking, or not cooking, segment of our meal. Which you probably assumed, as I certainly did, would be nominal, and so not worth going into in this account. That is, after all, the reason people buy these frozen dinners in the first place, isn't it? Well, if it is they're sorely mistaken, because it took nearly an hour to get our entrées on the table. For one thing, you could only microwave one of them at a time, and we had four to defrost and heat, not counting the molten frozen cookie. Also, one of the packages warned that we would not get optimal results in the microwave: The various stages that made up the frozen brown rocket of onion soup would meld together pointlessly in the microwave. If we wanted the gratinée effect promised on the package, then we had to bake it in the oven (at 350°F) for forty minutes. I could make onion soup from scratch in forty minutes!

Isaac didn't want to wait that long, so we ended up taking turns standing in front of the microwave. Is there any more futile, soul-irradiating experience than standing before the little window on a microwave oven watching the carousel slowly revolve your frozen block of dinner? Time spent this way might be easier than cooking, but it is not enjoyable and surely not ennobling. It is to feel spiritually unemployed, useless to self and humanity.

Anyway, as soon as the first dish was hot, we swapped it out for the second, but by the time the fourth entrée was hot enough to eat, the first one had gotten cold and needed re-nuking. Isaac finally asked permission to start eating his onion soup before it got cold again. The advent of the microwave has not been a boon to table manners. He was already down to the bottom of his bowl when Judith's lasagna emerged from the oven.

Microwave Night turned out to be one of the most disjointed family dinners we have had since Isaac was a toddler. The three of us never quite got to sit down at the table all at once. The best we could manage was to overlap for several minutes at a time, since one or another of us was constantly having to get up to check the microwave or the stovetop (where Isaac had moved his stir-fry after the microwave got backed up). All told, the meal took a total of thirty-seven minutes to defrost and heat up (not counting reheating), easily enough time to make a respectable homemade dinner. It made me think Harry Balzer might be right to attribute the triumph of this kind of eating to laziness and a lack of skills or confidence, or a desire to eat lots of different things, rather than to a genuine lack of time. That we hadn't saved much of at all.

The fact that each of us was eating something different completely

altered the experience of (speaking loosely) eating together. Beginning in the supermarket, the food industry had cleverly segmented
us, by marketing a different kind of food to each demographic in the
household (if I may so refer to my family), the better to sell us more
of it. Individualism is always good for sales, sharing much less so. But
the segmentation continued through the serial microwaving and the
unsynchronized eating. At the table, we were each preoccupied with
our own entrée, making sure it was hot and trying to decide how
successfully it simulated the dish it purported to be and if we really
liked it. Very little about this meal was shared; the single-serving portions served to disconnect us from one another, nearly as much as
from the origins of this food, which, beyond the familiar logos, we
could only guess at. Microwave Night was a notably individualistic
experience, marked by centrifugal energies, a certain opaqueness,
and, after it was all over, a remarkable quantity of trash. It was, in
other words, a lot like modern life.

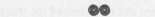

I thought about that at dinner the following night, when we sat down
together to eat one of the pot dishes I'd made the previous Sunday.
Duck, which I had braised following Samin's recipe, with red wine
and sweet spices in my new terra-cotta pot. Since the dish had been
in the fridge since Sunday, it was easy to skim off the fat before putting the pot in the oven to reheat. By the time the sweet smells of
allspice, juniper, and clove began to fill the house, Isaac and Judith
had gravitated to the kitchen; I never had to call them to dinner. I
brought the pot out to the table, and began serving everyone from it.

The energies working on the three of us at the dinner table this
evening were the precise opposite of the ones that had been loosed in
the house on Microwave Night. The hot, fragrant casserole itself ex-

erted a gravitational force, gathering us around it like a miniature hearth. It was no big deal, really, a family sharing a meal from a common pot on a weeknight, and yet at a time when so many of the forces working on a household are so individualistic and centrifugal—the screens, the consumer goods, the single-serving portions—it's a wonder such a meal ever happens anymore. It certainly doesn't have to, now that there are easier ways to feed a family.

There's something about a slow-cooked dish that militates against eating it quickly, and we took our time with dinner. Isaac told us about his day; we told him about ours. For the first time all day, it felt like we were all on the same page, and though it would be overstating things to credit that feeling entirely to the delicious braise, it would also be wrong to think that eating the same thing from the same pot, this weeknight communion of the casserole, had nothing to do with it, either. Afterward, when I lifted the lid from the pot, I was glad to see there would be leftovers for lunch.

PART III

AIR

THE EDUCATION OF
AN AMATEUR BAKER

"There is not a thing that is more positive
than bread."

—*Fyodor Dostoevsky*

"Bread is older than man."

—*old Albanian saying*

I.

A GREAT WHITE LOAF

One way to think about bread—and there are so many: as food or Food, matter and Spirit, commonplace, communion, metaphor, and medium (of exchange, transformation, sociality, etc.)—is simply this: as an ingenious technology for improving the flavor, digestibility, and nutritional value of grass. True, the technology doesn't work for all grasses, mainly just wheat, and it really only works for the seeds of that particular grass, not the leaves or stems. So it's not quite as ingenious as the ruminant's system for processing grass. The cow carries around a whole other stomach for the sole purpose of fermenting all parts of all kinds of grass into usable food energy. Our single stomach can do no such thing, but when, about six thousand years ago, we learned how to leaven bread, we joined the grass eaters of the world in earnest, much to the benefit of our species (not to mention the grasses).

Ruminant or human, the advantages of being able to eat grass are many. Grasses occupy some two-thirds of the planet's landmass and, among plants, are especially good at collecting solar energy and transforming it into biomass—"primary productivity," in the ecologist's jargon. Before we learned to eat grass directly, we availed ourselves of its energy by eating the ruminants that could eat grass or, sometimes, the predators that ate them. Yet second- or third-hand is a wasteful way to eat grass. Only about 10 percent of the energy consumed by an animal passes up the food chain to an eater of that animal. (Among other things, a lot of that energy is "wasted" by the animal in trying to avoid being eaten.) In fact, for every step up a food chain (or "trophic pyramid"), 90 percent of the food energy is lost, which is why big predators are so much more rare than ruminants, which in turn are so much more rare than blades of grass.

Even as Paleolithic hunters we ate whatever grass seeds we could gather, but figuring out a way to consistently get enough of the little things to make a staple meal represented a momentous development for our species. (It may also have been an obligatory development, since we were running out of grass eaters to hunt.) Learning how to eat lower on the food chain gave us access to more solar energy than ever before, and by doing so allowed us to create many more humans than would otherwise exist. Agriculture—which consists mainly of growing edible grasses like wheat, corn, and rice—is our term for this revolutionary new approach to getting food from the soil and the sun.

In working with edible grasses, our ancestors concentrated on collecting and eventually planting the biggest, most easily accessible seeds, since the seed is the most energy-dense part of the plant, and the only part that a single-stomached creature can readily digest. In time, the plants evolved to gratify our desires, developing ever-bigger seeds and refraining from "shattering"—dropping off the plant—in advance of harvest. We in turn altered the environment to suit the plants: tilling the soil and defending them from competitors—trees, weeds, insects, pathogens.

The new relationship between grasses and people led to evolutionary changes on our end, too, notably the ability to produce the enzymes needed to digest the starch in grass seeds. Yet the seeds of even these domesticated grasses go to some lengths to protect their precious cache of nutrients (intended to nourish their offspring, after all, not ours) and so require some degree of processing to unlock them, whether by soaking, grinding, boiling, toasting, acidifying, alkalizing, or some combination of these steps.

These rudimentary forms of "food processing" worked well enough for the first few thousands years of the agricultural era. Depending on the region, various kinds of grass seed were toasted on a fire or ground between stones and then boiled in water to create a simple mash—a porridge. The inert mush that resulted might not have made for inspiring meals, but it was simple enough to prepare, and nutritious enough to eat, providing us with the energy of starch as well as some protein, vitamins, and minerals. To make these mashes more appetizing, people would sometimes spread them on a hot stone to cook, creating a kind of unleavened flat bread.

And then, one day, once upon a time somewhere in ancient Egypt, probably about six thousand years ago, something seemingly miraculous happened to one of these porridges. We don't know exactly how it happened, but some observant Egyptian must have noticed that a bowl of porridge, perhaps one off in a corner that had been neglected for a couple of days, was no longer quite so inert. In fact, it was hatching bubbles from its surface and slowly expanding, as if it were alive. The dull paste had somehow been inspired: The spark of life had been breathed into it. And when that strangely vibrant bowl of porridge— call it dough—was heated in an oven, it grew even larger, springing up as it trapped the expanding bubbles in an airy yet stable structure that resembled a sponge.

It must have seemed a miracle, for a food to double or triple in volume on its own, or at least appear to (prefiguring, perhaps, the miracle of the loaves that Christ would perform four thousand years later). Though that increase proved to be an illusion—the volume added was only air—the reality, once tasted, was almost as impressive. The food had acquired a whole range of interesting new flavors and a delicate texture that made it much more interesting to eat. Bread! In time people would discover that the new food was also more nourishing than the mash from which it was made, so in that sense the miracle of the multiplying loaves was real. No longer mere cooks—putting fire to plants and animals, or boiling them in water—the Egyptians were now the masters of a far more complicated (and in some ways more powerful) technology for transforming nature into nourishment. So was born bread baking, the world's first food-processing industry.

I really love good bread. In fact, even bad bread is pretty good. I'd much prefer to eat a slice of fresh bread than a piece of cake. I especially love the contrast between a rugged crust and a moist, tender, alveolate interior—the "crumb," as I've learned to call it, now that I've been hanging around bakers. Alveoli are what bakers call the pockets of air that make up the crumb. The gases trapped in those curvaceous voids carry much of the aroma of bread, that rich complex of scents—roasty-yeasty-hazelnutty and faintly alcoholic—that, to me, is more captivating even than the smell of wine or coffee. Though I see no reason why I should have to choose between them, since bread goes so well with both.

One reason to bake bread is to fill your kitchen with that aroma. Even if the bread turns out badly, the smell of it baking never fails to improve a house or a mood. People trying to sell their homes are often advised to bake a loaf of bread before showing it. The underlying idea here is that freshly baked bread is the ultimate olfactory synecdoche for hominess. Which, when you think about it, is odd, since how many of us grew up in homes where bread was ever baked? Yet somehow that sense memory and its association with a happy domesticity endure. The trick has helped move quite a few houses.

To fill my house with that wonderful air is not why I took up baking, however. Nor was it to eat good bread, a desire that today can easily be gratified by simply buying it from one of the many good bakeries that have sprung up in recent years. Baking is one case where outsourcing the work to professionals has served humanity pretty well for much of the last six centuries. (Except, perhaps, during the last century, aka the Wonder Bread Era, a notably bad time for bread.) No, I began baking bread as a way to learn what I could about how it is made and what it means to us—its enduring uncanny power. Few things are as ordinary as a loaf of bread, yet the process by which it is made is extraordinary—and still something of a mystery even to those who study it or practice it every day.

Compared with earlier and simpler methods humans have devised for turning plants and animals into foods—the roasted chunk of meat, say, or pot of stew, either of which an individual or a small group can pull off—a loaf of bread implies a whole civilization. It emerges only at the end of a long, complicated process assuming settlement and involving an intricate division of human, plant, and even microbial labor. In addition to an agriculture and a culture of milling and baking, the loaf of bread depends on a nonhuman culture as well: It won't rise without the active contribution of some highly specialized living creatures besides the baker, the miller, and the farmer. The work of these yeasts and bacteria is the reason that the airy loaf of bread coming out of the oven cannot be inferred from a wet mash of powdered grass seed in the way that, say, a pork roast or stew can be inferred from a pig. By comparison, the delicate spongelike structure that rises in a loaf of bread to trap the gaseous waste products of those microbes has the complexity of an emergent system: something that is much more than, and qualitatively different from, the sum of its simple parts.

I took up baking because I was determined to know bread. If I somehow managed to bake a decent loaf along the way, great, but my impetus, quite frankly, was more journalistic curiosity than a deep-seated desire to bake my own bread. I simply wanted to get a feel for the process by getting my hands into dough at home and in any bakery that would have me. I had little reason to believe I'd be, or ever become, any good at it.

To the contrary. I had baked one or two loaves years before with only middling results, and had concluded baking was probably not for me. As a form of cooking, it seemed way too demanding—of exactitude and of patience, neither a personal strong suit. Baking was the carpentry of cooking, and I've always gravitated toward pursuits that leave considerably more room for error. Gardening, cooking, writing, all are roomy in that way, amenable to revision and mid-course correction. Baking by comparison seemed unforgiving, not to mention mysterious. Leavening dough depended on managing unseen and unpredictable forces. The recipes looked daunting. Messy, too. Plus, all the books and the bakers I consulted told me I would need to buy a kitchen scale to measure out ingredients. In *grams*.

But I would do it for the book, to learn whatever I could about this most extraordinary ordinary food and gather enough material to write about it. Then I would put away my scale and move on to other things.

That's not what happened. Long after I gathered all the material I needed to write these pages, I'm still baking. In fact I've got a loaf in the oven now, and another proofing in a basket. I can't seem to stop.

I've come to love the feel of the dough in my hands as it develops, the way, on the third or fourth turn, the inert, sticky paste begins to cohere and then gradually become elastic, as if sinews and muscles were forming inside it. I love (and a little bit dread) the moment of truth when I lower the oven door to discover how much "oven spring" (if any) my loaf has achieved. And I love the muffled static the bread emits while it cools, as the interior steam crackles the crust during its escape, filling the kitchen with that matchless air.

And yet the breads themselves, while occasionally handsome and flavorful, have never quite lived up to the expectations that the baking process, with its admixture of magic and possibility, seems to inspire. The Next Loaf always promises to rise higher, taste more complex, caramelize more gorgeously, alveolate more idiosyncratically, and throw a more distinctive "ear" where I scored it. So there came a point in my education as a baker when an image of the perfect loaf took shape in my head. This was not just a visual image, either. I could imagine how this ultimate loaf would smell and taste and feel in the hands, too, the precise ratio of weight to volume—said volume having been exalted by a most spectacular oven spring. Now I'm not sure I'll be able to put away my kitchen scale until I've actually baked, and tasted, that perfect loaf.

The best bread I ever tasted was a big country loaf shot through with holes the size of marbles and golf balls—easily more air than bread. It had a tough hide of a crust, very nearly burned, but held inside a crumb so tender, moist, and glossy it made you think of custard. There was something sensual about the strong contrast between these two realms—outside and inside, hard and soft. The bread was so powerfully aromatic that, had I been alone, I would have been tempted to push my face into it. But I was at a dinner party in Oakland with people I didn't know very well, so I limited myself to eating as much of it as possible and asking questions about it. One of our hosts worked in San Francisco and had stopped by a bakery in the Mission District to pick it up on his way home. It seemed that the bread made at this bakery didn't come out of the oven till late in the afternoon, which explained why when I first tasted it the bread was still slightly warm.

When I started baking bread, this memorable loaf loomed large in my mind, as an unattainable ideal, perhaps, but a loaf to shoot for anyway. By then I knew the name of the bakery—Tartine—and the name of the baker—Chad Robertson. (I live in a part of the world where bakers can be celebrities.) Here and there I picked up bits and pieces of intelligence about the man. I heard that the reason the bread came out so late in the day was that he was a surfer; he wanted to keep his mornings free in case the waves were good off Ocean Beach. (This turned out to be only slightly apocryphal.) I read that he baked just 250 loaves a day, and refused to bake more, even though on most afternoons a line of customers snaking down Guerrero Street snaps up all the loaves before they have had a chance to cool. People phone ahead to reserve a loaf.

So it came as very good news when I learned that Chad Robertson was publishing a book that would reveal the recipe for his iconic country loaf. I managed to get hold of an advance copy of *Tartine Bread*. It was an unusually handsome volume, bound like a textbook with a cover that somehow managed to be simultaneously hard and soft—like his bread. I cracked the big book open, my sense of anticipation rising. It quickly collapsed, however, as soon as I began reading the "basic recipe." The recipe started on page 42 and didn't arrive at the point of putting a loaf in an oven until page 69. Along the way were plenty of helpful pictures, mostly of dough but a few of Robertson himself shaping loaves. He looked to be in his thirties, slender, bearded, and monkishly intense. After the twenty-seven-page recipe came another ten pages titled "The Basic Loaf in Depth," a scientifico-Talmudic explication of the principles behind the recipe. I was daunted. This was going to be a project.

Yet even if I had felt dauntless enough to jump in on it right away, I couldn't, not according to the recipe. I needed first to build a "starter"—a culture of wild yeasts and bacteria to leaven the bread, a process the book said could take weeks. Why not leaven the bread with instant yeast from the supermarket, as in most bread recipes? Robertson explained that a sourdough culture contributed not just air to a bread but much of the texture and the flavor—precisely what I felt was missing from my earlier efforts to bake bread. So, if I was really serious about this baking project, a starter was apparently somewhere in my future.

It would be a few weeks before I felt sufficiently mentally prepared to embark on my Tartine loaf. In the meantime, I built up to the undertaking by wading out into what turned out to be a deep, fermenting pool of online chatter inspired by the recently disclosed Tartine recipe. TheFreshLoaf.com, a chat group for amateur bakers, was abuzz with reports on people's earliest efforts to bake the legendary loaf, and on Facebook, somebody had started a page ("Recipes from Tartine Bread") to help hobbyist bakers struggling to master the recipe.

I noticed that most of the posts were from men, many of them sounding less like home cooks than twenty-something computer geeks trying to master a new software platform. (I found out later than in fact both the Web site and the Facebook group had been started by young Web developers.) Only a few of these amateur bakers had ever tasted the bread they were striving to emulate, but this didn't seem to slow them down—they had seen pictures and video. They posted pictures of their starters, Tupperware containers bubbling over with masses of pearly glop—or, all too often, masses of grayish slime that stubbornly refused to bubble at all. They compared notes on "feeding schedules" for their starters as if they were caring for new kittens. Portraits of finished loaves of every size, shape, and alveolation were posted, sometimes as boasts, other times as plaintive cries for help.

"How do you adjust when it's very humid?" went one. "It's 88% humidity here and I just experienced some impressive TBF." It took me a few visits to the page before I figured out that "TBF" was short for total bread failure. (PBF meant partial bread failure.) Someone else was struggling with a "cavitation" problem, and posted a cross-section picture, known in this subculture as a "crumb shot," of a loaf disfigured by vast caverns of air that had formed directly beneath the crust.

The chatter of the online bakers made me only more anxious about the prospect of attempting a Tartine loaf. Here was exactly what I worried about: baking as carpentry or, even more intimidating, computer code. Yet when I finally sat down to read through Robertson's entire opus, I was surprised to discover that the recipe read nothing like code. Instead of a precise set of instructions, he offered a fairly casual, open-ended set of guidelines. Sure, he specified how many grams of flour and water and starter to use, but after that, the recipe was more narrative than numbers. It left a lot up in the air. Robertson made ample allowance for the vagaries of weather and humidity, flour, and even one's personal schedule.

Robertson encouraged bakers to be observant, flexible, and intuitive. Rather than specify exactly how many hours the bulk fermentation stage should last, he offered a few indicators of dough development to look and feel for: Does the dough feel "dense and heavy" or "cohesive"? To someone accustomed to computer code or carpentry, this sort of advice must have seemed frustratingly vague and subjective.

"If the dough seems to be developing slowly, extend the bulk fermentation time." Okay, but, *by how much?!* Robertson refused to say. "Watch your dough and be flexible." He talked about dough as if it was a living thing, local and particular and subject to so many contingencies that to generalize or make hard-and-fast rules for its management was impossible. Robertson seemed to be suggesting that success as a baker demanded a certain amount of negative capability—a willingness to exist amid uncertainty. His was a world of craft rather than engineering, one where "digital" referred exclusively to fingers.

Clearly Robertson's loose, novelistic approach to the whole notion of baking was driving a certain kind of person absolutely crazy. And then all at once, I was buoyed by this thought: *I am not that kind of person!* This was the moment when I decided I was ready to jump in. It was time to start my starter.

Considering what it is (a living thing) and what it does (leaven and flavor a bread), the instructions for starting a sourdough culture could not be much simpler. Take some flour, preferably a fifty-fifty mixture of white and whole grain, and mix it by hand in a glass bowl with some warm water until you have something that feels like a smooth pancake batter. Cover the bowl with a cloth and leave it in a cool spot for two or three days. If by then nothing has happened, wait a few more days and check it again.

Simple maybe, but not foolproof: My first attempt at starting a starter didn't start. After a week of inactivity, the batter separated into a layer of cement beneath a layer of perfectly clear water. It remained absolutely inert and odorless. I did some reading to figure out what was supposed to be happening but wasn't. Wild yeasts and bacteria were supposed to find their way into the batter, take up residence, and eventually organize themselves into a more or less stable microbial community. Curiously, none of the authorities I consulted could say with certainty just where these yeasts and bacteria came from or how they got here, if and when they did. They might already be in the flour, or on my hands (which is why Robertson suggests mixing by hand), or in the air. Indeed, one of the many mysteries of sourdough culture is the origin of its resident microbes, some of which— like the all-important *Lactobacillus sanfranciscensis*—have never been found anywhere on earth *except* in a sourdough bread culture.* This suggests these "wild" microbes are actually in some sense domesticated— dependent upon us (and our love of bread) to create and maintain their highly specialized ecological niche. But either I had failed to create a niche to their liking or the bugs had failed to find it, because even after two weeks my starter was as lifeless as plaster.

I started a new culture, but this time after mixing it I gave the bowl an hour or two outside in the sun, hoping to snag some airborne microbes. I also gave it some vigorous stirs whenever I remembered to, in order to work some oxygen into the mixture. Within a week, my batter was showing tentative signs of life in what seemed very much like an instance of spontaneous generation: proposing the occasional bubble and giving off a faint, not-unpleasant scent reminiscent of rotten apples. But a couple of days later, the odor had taken an unpleasant turn, veering toward strong cheese or worn sock. Something bacterial was definitely afoot. So, following Robertson's directions, I discarded 80 percent of the starter, more or less, and fed what remained a couple tablespoons of fresh flour and warm water. Within a day, the bowl was burbling contentedly. I had a starter! Whether it

---

*Hammes, Walter P., et al., "Microbial Ecology of Cereal Fermentations," *Trends in Food Science & Technology* 16 No. 1-3 (2005): 4–11.

was lively enough to leaven a dough, I wasn't yet sure, but it was definitely alive.

A couple weeks later, when my starter seemed to be settling into a predictable daily rhythm, rising in the hours after its morning feeding and then subsiding again overnight, I embarked on my first loaf of naturally leavened bread.

Step one is to turn a small amount of the starter into a "sponge" or "leaven"—basically, use it to inoculate a much bigger mass of sourdough culture, which in turn would inoculate and leaven the entire dough I would mix the next morning. Placing a glass bowl on my new (digital) kitchen scale, I zeroed it out and added two hundred grams of flour (the same fifty-fifty mix I used to feed my starter), then an equal amount of warm water. To this I introduced a heaping tablespoon of my starter, mixed it all together, covered the bowl with a dish towel, and went off to bed.

I faced a test in the morning, one that many of the participants in the chat rooms and discussion groups on line had struggled to pass. To wit: Would this so-called sponge take on enough air overnight so that, when dropped into a bowl of water, it would float? If instead it sank, that would indicate there wasn't enough microbial activity to leaven a loaf of bread.

The question would be decided while I slept: There was nothing to do now but wait, while my culture either did or failed to do its fermentative thing. Already this felt like a radically different way of "cooking" than I had done up to now, but not because it was any more exacting or precise. To the contrary: I'd delegated my accustomed kitchen powers and responsibilities to this invisible cohort of unidentified microbes.

Up to now, most of the things I'd cooked and ingredients I'd cooked with had been dead, after all, and therefore more or less tractable. The raw materials responded in predictable ways to physical and chemical processes that I controlled; whatever did or didn't happen to them could be explained in terms of either chemistry or physics. Obviously those laws play an important part in baking, too, but the most important processes unfolding in a naturally leavened bread are biological. Though the baker might be able to influence and even manage those processes, "control" would be far too strong a word for what he does. It's a little like the difference between gardening and building. As with the plants or the soil in a garden, the gardener is working with living creatures that have their own interests and agency. He succeeds not by dictating to them, as a carpenter might to lumber, but by aligning his interests with theirs. To use a metaphor a little closer to Chad Robertson's frame of reference, what the baker does is a little like the surfer's relationship to the wave.

This lack of control has never sat well with our species, which probably explains why the modern history of bread baking can be told as a series of steps aimed at taking the unruliness, uncertainty, and comparative slowness of biology out of the process. Milling white flour was the first such step. Whole-grain flours, as I would soon learn, are much more complex and biologically active than white flour. That's because white flour consists chiefly of dead starch, whereas the germ and the bran removed in milling it contain living cells. Whole grains teem with enzymes and volatile oils that make their flours more perishable and fermentation more difficult to manage.

Around the same time that the advent of roller mills made white flour widely available in the 1880s, the introduction of commercial yeast gave bakers an even more decisive gain in control. Now, instead of having to rely on an unruly community of unidentified fungi and bacteria to leaven bread, as had been the case for thousands of years, they could enlist a single species of yeast to do the job on command. Called *Saccharomyces cerevisiae*, this species had been (as its name suggests) found in beer, selected over countless generations, and optimized for the role of putting gas in dough. Commercial bread yeast is a purified monoculture of S. *cerevisiae*, raised on a diet of molasses, then washed, dried, and powdered. Like any monoculture, it does one thing predictably and well: Feed it enough sugars and it will promptly cough up large quantities of carbon dioxide.

Though commercial yeast is alive, its behavior is linear, mechanical, and predictable, a simple matter of inputs and outputs—which is no doubt why it so quickly caught on. S. *cerevisiae* can be counted on to perform the same way everywhere and give the same results, making it supremely well suited to industrial production. Yeast could now be treated simply as another ingredient rather than as a locally variable community of organisms in need of special care and feeding. In fact, as microbes go, S. *cerevisiae* is notable for not playing well with others, especially bacteria. Compared with wild yeasts, commercial yeast cannot survive very long in the acidic environment created by lactobacilli.

While scientists have known about yeast since Louis Pasteur first identified it in 1857, the intricate microbial world within a wild sourdough culture like mine was a complete mystery until fairly recently—and remains at least a partial mystery even today. In 1970, a team of USDA scientists based in Albany, California, collected samples of sourdough starter from five San Francisco bakeries and conducted a kind of microbial census. Why San Francisco? Because the city was famous for its sourdough bread. The scientists were hoping to identify the local microbes responsible for the bread's distinctive qualities. Their landmark 1971 paper, "Microorganisms of the San Francisco

Sour Dough French Bread Process," helped to spur a revival in naturally leavened breads and almost single-handedly established the (albeit still minor) field of sourdough microbiology.*

The USDA team discovered that unlike what happens in the
straightforward fermentation performed by S. cerevisiae, no single yeast
species was responsible for what takes place in a sourdough culture.
Rather, the process depended on a complex, semisymbiotic association
between a yeast (Candida milleri†) and a previously unknown bacterium.
Assuming—wrongly, as it turned out—that the bacterium they had
identified was unique to San Francisco's famed sourdoughs, they
named it Lactobacillus sanfranciscensis. It has since been found in bakeries all
over the world. Oh well.

Though not exactly dependent on each other, the yeast and the
bacteria are ideally suited to living together. Each microbe consumes
a different type of sugar, so they don't compete for food. And when
the yeasts die, their proteins break down into amino acids that the
lactobacilli need to grow.

At the same time, the lactobacilli produce organic acids that shape
the environment in ways agreeable to C. milleri (which is acid-tolerant),
but disagreeable to other yeasts and bacteria. L. sanfranciscensus also produces an antibiotic compound that prevents competing microbes
from gaining a toehold in the culture, but which doesn't trouble C.
milleri in the least. Thus the sourdough culture defends itself from
colonization by outsiders. This biochemical defense is a boon to us as
well, since it extends the shelf life of the bread.

Perhaps the USDA team's most important contribution was to

---

*Sugihara, T. F., et al., "Microorganisms of the San Francisco Sour Dough Bread Process I. Yeasts
Responsible for the Leavening Action," Applied Microbiology 21 No. 3 (1971): 456–8. Kline, L., et al.,
"Microorganisms of the San Francisco Sour Dough Bread Process II. Isolation and Characterization
of the Undescribed Bacterial Species Responsible for the Souring Activity," Applied Microbiology 21
No. 3 (1971): 459–65.
†Candida milleri is sometimes also referred to as Saccharomyces exiguous.

demonstrate that a sourdough culture functions as a kind of ecosystem, with the various species performing distinct roles that lend stability to the culture over time. Once established, the system exhibits more cooperation than competition, so that no one organism ever dominates. Subsequent research in other parts of the world has greatly expanded the list of species found in sourdough cultures—at least twenty types of yeast and fifty different bacteria—but most of them seem to fall into similar niches, organize themselves into similar relationships, and perform similar functions. Same play, different actors. Presumably these yeasts and bacteria coevolved with one another, which might explain why many of them have been found nowhere *except* in sourdough cultures, their "natural habitat." Which in turn suggests these microbes probably coevolved with us: Their culture depends upon our culture of bread making, and (until recently) vice versa.

In the microuniverse of a sourdough culture, the baker performs in the role of god, or at least of natural selection. It may well be that the requisite microbes are everywhere, but by shaping their environment—the food and feeding schedule, the ambient temperature, the amount of water—the baker, wittingly or unwittingly, selects which microbes will thrive and which will fail. Frequent feedings and warm temperatures tend to favor the yeasts, for example, creating an airier, milder loaf, whereas skipping meals and refrigerating the culture favors the bacteria, leading to a more acidic environment, and a more strongly flavored bread.

"Baking well really comes down to managing fermentation," according to Robertson. The flavor and quality of a naturally leavened bread depends to a great extent on how skillfully the baker governs this invisible microbial world. And if the baker fails to care for his culture? It may take awhile, but once the sun of his attention goes dark, the culture eventually dies.

The morning after starting my sponge, I woke up eager to head down to the kitchen to see what, if anything, had happened overnight. When I'd mixed the stuff the night before, the heavy paste of flour and water filled a two-cup measuring bowl halfway to the top. Incredibly, it had doubled in volume overnight, and I could feel it had lightened considerably, achieving a consistency reminiscent of marshmallow. Through the glass I could see that the paste had become a gassy foam, shot through with millions of air bubbles. I felt certain it would float.

So into a larger bowl I measured out the quantity of warm water called for in the recipe (750 grams), and then, using a spatula, scooped out the sponge. It slid into the warm bath and then bobbed up to the surface of the water like a raft, buoyant. I was in business! Next I added 900 grams of white flour and 100 grams of whole-wheat flour. I mixed everything together by hand, squeezing the flour and water through my fingers to make sure there were no unhydrated lumps of flour—what bakers call "chestnuts." The result was a dough wetter than anything I had ever worked with before. This promised to be a challenge.*

Before any salt is added, the dough gets to rest for twenty minutes or so. Called the "autolyse," this period gives the flour a chance to fully hydrate, the gluten to begin to swell and get itself organized, the enzymes to begin cleaving complex starches into simpler sugars, and the fermentation of those sugars to commence. Salt acts as a check on all these processes, which in its absence would proceed too rapidly.

---

*I would learn later that the dough at Tartine is even wetter than what the published recipe calls for; in the book Robertson reduced the amount of water by 10 percent or so, fearing that home bakers confronting a dough too wet to knead would "freak out."

The goal is a long, slow fermentation in order to build maximum flavor. As one nineteenth-century cookbook put it, salt serves as the bridle on the wild horse of fermentation.

After I mixed in the twenty grams of salt, the dough felt dull and sticky to the touch—a wet, heavy, lifeless clay. I covered the bowl with a towel and went back to work, setting my phone to alert me in forty-five minutes. "Bulk fermentation" was now under way—a period of between three and four hours during which the principal development and fermentation of the dough takes place.

A complex drama unfolds during the bulk fermentation, one that the baker cannot see but can infer by the evolving texture, smell, and taste of his dough. Within the dough, a spongiform structure is taking shape, a three-dimensional lacework of air. The structure is the result of two separate developments—one chemical in nature, the other biological—that in a dough made from wheat flour happen, fortunately for the panivore, to coincide and intersect just so.

The chemical development is the formation of gluten (the word means "glue" in Latin), an interesting if somewhat problematic substance that is found primarily in wheat, and to a much lesser extent in rye, another species of grass. To be precise, gluten as such is not found in wheat itself, but, rather, its two precursors are, the proteins gliadin and glutenin, which when moistened in water combine to form the mesh of proteins known as gluten. Unprepossessing on its own, each of these proteins contributes a different but equally important quality to a bread: extensibility on the part of gliadin, and elasticity on the part of glutenin. As in the fibers of a muscle, these qualities exist in a productive tension, the former allowing the dough to be stretched and shaped, while the latter impels it to bounce back to something close to its original form. In fact, the Chinese call gluten "the muscle of flour," and all bakers speak in terms of a dough's "strength" or "weakness," qualities that correspond to the amount of gluten in it.

The pliable yet rubbery properties of gluten make it the ideal medium for trapping air, which happens to be the crucial by-product of the second, biological development under way in a wet mass of fermenting dough. While the gluten network is forming and gaining strength, the community of yeasts and bacteria introduced by the starter are dining on starches "damaged" during milling, when some of them are broken into sugars. Various enzymes (some of which are present in the flour, others produced by the bacteria and yeasts) go to work on the undamaged starches and proteins, breaking them down into simple sugars and amino acids to feed the microbes. Thus fed, the bacteria proliferate, producing lactic and acetic acids, which help to strengthen the gluten while contributing new flavors. And, most important of all, the yeasts are busy transforming each molecule of glucose they consume into two molecules of alcohol and two of carbon dioxide. The carbon dioxide gas, which is a by-product of alcohol production, would simply escape into the atmosphere if not for the rubbery matrix of gluten, which stretches like a balloon to contain it. Without the extensible and elastic gluten to trap the carbon dioxide, bread would never rise.

The properties of gluten have commended wheat to humanity since the Egyptians first recognized what it could do. Before that, wheat was just one edible grass among many, part of a crowded field that included millet, barley, oats, and rye and, later, corn and rice. Barley barely registers in our eating lives today, but before the invention of bread it was just as important a staple food in the West. It grows more quickly than wheat, and in more places, from the tropics to the Arctic Circle. Highly nutritious, it was the food of choice of the Roman gladiators, who were in fact called *hordearii*, the barley eaters. But though barley made nourishing porridges and flat breads (and beer, as I would discover), no amount of leavening could raise it off an oven floor.

Wheat's own ancestors couldn't rise, either. Einkorn, the earliest known form of wheat, has been cultivated in southeastern Turkey for nearly ten thousand years, but eaten mostly as a porridge or brewed as beer. It has too much gliadin and not enough glutenin to trap fermentation gases. The ancestry of bread wheat is tangled and still a subject of botanical debate, but it took thousands of years of accidental crosses and mutations before a civilization-altering curiosity showed up in a farmer's field somewhere in the Fertile Crescent: a stalk of wheat with big fat seeds that just happened to contain the proteins gliadin and glutenin in just the right proportions. Gluten, and with it the possibility of leavened bread, had come into the world.*

What had been one edible grass among many became the imperial grass, spreading from the Fertile Crescent of the Middle East to Europe by 3000 B.C., to Asia two thousand years later, and then, soon after 1492, to both continents of the New World. Bread wheat spread because people liked to eat bread, but also because of its central place in the Christian liturgy; priests needed bread to give communion, and in the New World would plant it expressly for that purpose.† The

---

*What gluten offered human wheat eaters is obvious enough, but what, if anything, did it offer the plant? I've put this question to several wheat breeders and botanists, and the consensus answer seems to be: nothing special. All seeds store proteins for the future use of the new plant by locking up amino acids in stable chains called polymers. The default storage protein in most grasses is globulin, over which gliadin and glutenin offer no advantages—except, that is, for the one tremendous advantage of happening to gratify the desires of an animal as well traveled and influential as *Homo sapiens*.

†In his book *1493*, Charles Mann suggests that the first bread wheat was planted in the New World in Mexico, after Cortés found three kernels in a bag of rice sent from Spain. He ordered the seeds planted in a plot by a chapel in Mexico City. Two of them took and, according to a sixteenth-century account, "little by little there was boundless wheat"—much to the delight of the clergy, who needed bread to properly celebrate mass.

only continent where wheat had not made significant inroads until well into the twentieth century was Africa. But after World War II the United States began giving food aid to Africa in the form of wheat, and then promoted its consumption in cultures where it had never before been eaten. It caught on, completing the plant's global triumph.

Today, wheat is planted more widely than any other single crop, waving its golden seed heads over more than 550 million acres worldwide; there is no month of the year when wheat is not being harvested somewhere in the world. It is true that, by weight, the world's farmers produce more corn than wheat, but most of that crop ends up in the stomachs of animals or the gas tanks of automobiles (in the form of ethanol). As a food for humans, no crop is more important than wheat. (Rice comes second.) Worldwide, wheat flour accounts for a fifth of the calories in the human diet. And that's low by historical standards: For most of European history, bread represented more than half the calories in the diet of the peasantry and the urban poor, according to French historian Fernand Braudel.

When you consider that other cereal crops produce more calories per acre (corn, rice) and others are easier to grow (corn, barley, rye) and still others are more nutritious (quinoa), triticum's triumph appears even more unlikely and impressive. The secret of wheat's success? Gluten. Which is another way of saying, the human love of leavened bread. Yet to put it that way is not to have found a case-closing answer so much as another question. Because what in the world is so wonderful about aerated porridge?

An hour into the bulk fermentation, the dough already felt slightly different to the touch—still flabby but slightly less yielding, and maybe a little lighter. Robertson recommends "turning" the dough in a container rather than kneading it on a flat surface—nearly impossible anyway with a dough this wet. A turn involves reaching your fingers down along the inside wall of the bowl, lifting the mass of dough up from the bottom, and then folding it over the top; repeat the move three or four times as you rotate the bowl with your other hand, so each quadrant gets at least one fold. That's one complete turn. (Wetting your fingers helps keep the dough from sticking to them.) Robertson advises a complete turn every half hour to start, and then with diminishing frequency, and a gentler touch, as the dough begins to billow with air. The folds help to exercise and so strengthen the gluten, while trapping a certain amount of ambient air in the dough— each fold creating minuscule pockets that will later balloon with carbon dioxide and ethanol.

By the third or fourth turn, the character of the dough has changed substantially. No longer clinging to the sides of the bowl, it has cohered into a distinct mass and developed what feels like muscle tone. When you pull it upward for a fold, it stretches without tearing and then pulls back down. The dough now feels less like clay than living flesh, something in possession of will, seemingly, and an identity. It's also begun to smell yeasty, and what was tasteless before is now sweet on the tongue.

Nowadays, I usually get some writing done during bulk fermentation. The intervals between turns are just right for getting up from my desk to take a break, and the process is sufficiently forgiving in the event I get so absorbed in my work that I miss a turn. The dough is largely developing itself—or, rather, my sourdough culture is developing the dough while I develop something else, like this chapter. As I've heard some bakers say, baking takes a lot of time, but for the most part it's not your time.

As a means of processing a raw foodstuff, a sourdough fermentation is a wonder of nature and culture, an example of an ancient vernacular "technology" the ingenuity of which science is just now coming to appreciate. "You could not survive on wheat flour," Bruce German, the food chemist at UC Davis, told me, "but you can survive on bread." The reason you can is largely due to the work of these microbes going about their unseen lives. And though modern food science can simulate many of their effects in commercial bread production, by using commercial yeasts and other leavening agents, sweeteners, preservatives, and dough conditioners, it still can't do everything a sourdough culture can do to render grass seeds nourishing to humans.

The waste products of the various microbes are the key to this transformation. Carbon dioxide gases produced by both the yeasts and bacteria are what leaven the bread, while the ethanol excreted by the yeasts contributes aromas. The organic acids produced by the lactobacilli have a whole range of crucial effects: They contribute flavor, strengthen the dough, and, perhaps most important, help to activate various enzymes already present in the seed.

Think of a seed as a well-stocked pantry for the future plant: Energy, amino acids, and minerals are stored there in the form of stable, hard-to-access molecules called polymers. The various enzymes are molecular keys that unlock the pantry by breaking down the various polymers so that the developing embryo will have something to eat in the period before it puts down roots. But the seed can also be tricked into unlocking all that sequestered food for the microbes in the starter and, in turn, for us.

The acids produced by sourdough bacteria rouse the sleeping enzymes and put them to work. Amylase attacks the complex carbohydrates, breaking the tightly wound (and tasteless) balls of yarn that starches resemble into shorter, more accessible snippets of sugar. The proteases break the long protein chains into their amino acid building blocks. These sugars and amino acids contribute to the flavor and beauty of the bread, by feeding the chemical reactions (both Maillard and caramelization) that, in the oven, will brown the crust. They also feed the yeasts, thereby helping to make the bread airier. But airiness in bread does more than make it attractive. The air pockets provide a place for steam to form, and since steam gets considerably hotter than water (which never exceeds the boiling point), it helps to more completely cook (or "gelatinize") the starches, rendering them both tastier and more digestible.

Sourdough fermentation also partially breaks down gluten, making it easier to digest and, according to some recent research from Italy (a nation of wheat eaters with high rates of celiac disease and gluten intolerance), destroying at least some of the peptides thought to be responsible for gluten intolerance. Some researchers attribute the increase in gluten intolerance and celiac disease to the fact that modern breads no longer receive a lengthy fermentation. The organic acids produced by the sourdough culture also seem to slow our bodies' absorption of the sugars in white flour, reducing the dangerous spikes of insulin that refined carbohydrates can cause. (Put another way, a sourdough bread will have a lower "glycemic index" than a bread leavened with yeast.) Lastly, the acids activate an enzyme called phytase, which unlocks many of the minerals that, in a seed, have been carefully locked up (or "chelated") for the eventual use of the germinating plant.

To learn about the many beneficial transformations taking place in my lump of dough during its bulk fermentation is to gain a deeper appreciation for the genius of human culture—for having "figured out" how to process grass this way—but equally for the ingenuity of the microbial culture that actually does the most important work of bread making. The dance of mutual exploitation that these two cultures have performed for six thousand years now has served both of us well, and required no conscious awareness on our part beyond the recognition and remembering of what seemed to work. Much like a soil, which it in some ways resembles, a sourdough culture can be nurtured and cultivated without having to be understood. But now that science has given us a belated understanding of all that a sourdough fermentation can do to render grass seed so nourishing and tasty, we can only marvel that we would have so blithely abandoned it, for no good reason other than our impatience—and, perhaps, our desire to control rather than to dance or surf.

I decided the bulk fermentation was complete after about six hours, when my dough was soft and billowy and showed more interest in clinging to itself than to me or its container. What had felt reluctant in my hands now felt willing and lively. Fat marbles of gas had formed directly beneath its snowy skin, and the dough gave off a nice, yeasty aroma tinged with alcohol and vinegar. I sampled a pinch of dough; it tasted sweet and slightly acidic. To let it go any longer was to risk too sour a bread, so I decided the time had come to move on to the next step: shaping the dough into loaves.

Here is where my difficulties began. The book said to scoop the mass of dough onto a floured work surface, divide it into two pieces with a bench knife (basically a big plastic knife), and shape each piece of the still sticky but now perky mass into a globe, or *boule*, the French word for a round country loaf. (Also the root of the French word for baker, *boulanger*.) The dough was so wet that this proved difficult and messy, but after dusting my hands and the cutting board and every other surface in the kitchen with white flour, I was able to coax the dough into a pair of vaguely globular shapes. The instructions said to take a round of dough in both hands and rotate it while maintaining contact with the work surface; the bottom of the dough should cling, slightly, to the countertop, thereby creating some tension in the surface of the sphere as it takes shape. At first my globe resembled an attractive white buttock with some muscle tone, but it soon relaxed into something considerably more flaccid and pancakelike.

The two rounds of dough now got another twenty or so minutes of rest, covered with a dish towel to keep the air from crusting them. I peeked under a few times and could see that the dough was continuing to percolate and expand even as it relaxed and subsided.

Now it was time to execute the set of shaping maneuvers I'd been dreading since I first studied the instructions and accompanying sequence of how-to photographs in the book. Unless you're the kind of person who can learn a dance step from a diagram or figure out how to diaper a baby from a book, printed instructions for properly shaping a loaf of Tartine bread are nearly impossible to follow.

Why bother shaping at all? you might legitimately wonder at this point. Because a dough as wet and flabby as this one will not achieve a good oven spring unless the baker endows it with some internal tension and structure. This is achieved as follows: With your fingers, take hold of each quadrant of the dough in turn, stretch it outward, and then fold it back over the center, until it forms a neat rectangular package, a bit like a papoose. Do this again with each of the four corners. Then roll the package of dough away from you until the seams come around to the bottom and the surface has grown smooth and tight. Each fold builds structural tension in the gluten at a different point within the loaf, while the rolling creates surface tension in the crust. At least that's the idea.

It took me several aborted attempts and another kitchenwide blizzard of flour, but eventually I was able to form the dough into taut rounds of powdery-white flesh. The impulse to cup the soft globes in my hands was irresistible. I have to say, not one of the bakers I had read or talked to had adequately prepared me for the erotics of leavened, shaped dough.

I carefully slipped the shaped loaves, seam side up, into bowls lined with kitchen towels that I had rubbed with flour to keep them from sticking. I wrapped the corners of the towel over the top to keep the loaves from exposure to drafts, which might dry out their skins and so impede their rise. Now came the second fermentation. Called "proofing," this final step takes between two and four hours, depending on the temperature and the degree of sourness the baker desires. The dough is ready for the oven when its volume has expanded by a third or so but looks like it still has some life left in it. An overproofed loaf is liable to be sour and sticky, and, its yeasts having exhausted their supply of sugars, incapable of much oven spring.

Toward the end of the proofing process, I preheated the oven to 500°F with a cast-iron Dutch oven in it. Baking in a covered pot represents something of a breakthrough in home bread making. A steamy oven is the key to achieving a good oven spring as well as a chewy crust. The steam delays the moment when the bread forms a crust, allowing the dough to expand as long as possible before solidifying. Professional bakers inject steam into their ovens for precisely this reason, but home ovens have been designed to vent steam. By baking bread in the sealed environment of a Dutch oven or covered casserole, the home baker can closely approximate the steamy interior of a bakery oven without having to add any water: The moisture from the dough creates all the steam needed for a good spring.

When the oven temperature reached 500°F, I removed the Dutch oven with oven mitts and rested it on top of the stove. Now came Moment of Truth Number One: I flipped the bowl over the open pot, dropping the ball of dough onto its blazingly hot bottom. My aim was a few degrees off, however, because the dough caught the edge of the pot and landed lopsidedly, wrecking its perfect symmetry and no doubt disturbing its hard-won internal structure. My poor loaf suffered a second insult when it came time to score it with a razor blade—Moment of Truth Number Two. The idea here is that slashing the loaf's skin will release some of its surface tension and by doing so facilitate a greater spring. The slash also serves as a kind of baker's signature, especially when, in Robertson's words, it "opens elegantly."

One mark of a good loaf is a pronounced "ear"—a crisp edge of crust thrust up, like a tectonic plate, by the bread's sudden expansion in the oven. Two problems here: Since my Dutch oven is much deeper than the ball of dough is tall, it was tricky to reach in there for the scoring without burning the meat of my hand on its 500-degree edge. Second, I failed to be as "decisive" in my scoring as Robertson had advised. I'm sorry, but after all the time spent coddling this gorgeous round of dough, slashing it with a razor blade was just hard to do. It seemed reckless, violent even. I hesitated—fatally, as it turned out: Some dough snagged on the corner of the blade, and tore as I tried to draw my line. The result was a sloppy signature.

Having thus mangled my gorgeous dough, I had little hope for the finished bread. But when the third and biggest Moment of Truth arrived, twenty minutes after the loaf went into the oven, I was pleasantly surprised. I lifted the lid to find that the loaf had mostly self-corrected for its lopsidedness, and had sprung up—not spectacularly but respectably. Here was a round, puffy, fawn-colored pillow easily twice as large as the flop of dough I'd dropped in the pot only twenty minutes before.

I closed the oven door gently to make sure I didn't deflate the risen loaf while it finished baking. I needn't have worried: By now, the starches in the dough had "gelatinized"—stiffened enough to formalize the matrix of gluten, which had itself stiffened. During the early moments of baking, the cells in that matrix had ballooned under the pressure of gases expanding in the heat. At least for the first six to eight minutes of oven time, new alveoli continue to form, since the yeasts keep working until the temperature reaches a lethal 130°F. During this period, provided there remain enough sugars to feed them, the rapid flush of heat inspires one last, climactic burst of fermentation.

When I took the bread out of the oven twenty-five minutes later, it smelled better than it looked, but it didn't look too bad. It had thrown no ear to speak of: My too-tentative slash had merely opened a pale scar in the crust. The crust was smoother and more tentatively colored than a Tartine loaf, but it was handsome even so, marred only slightly by these two curious blackened humps. A roasty aroma filled the kitchen. Still wearing oven mitts, I tapped on the bottom of the loaf and listened for the hollow, woody timbre indicating the bread was cooked through. It was. I held the loaf up to my cheek to feel its radiating warmth. The bread gave off a pleasing low static as it cooled.

The sense of accomplishment surprised me. I hadn't done much, after all, except mix together some flour, water, and a little sourdough starter, and then babied it for several hours. And yet—here was this substantial thing that hadn't existed before, this fragrant risen form. I might as well have pulled a rabbit out of a hat, and indeed my family, whose expectations for this latest project of mine were modest, reacted as if I had. *Something from nothing:* You can see why the prescientific mind (and the skeptics in Jesus's audience) might have been impressed. Bread science would eventually offer a material explanation for this apparent miracle, but even now that we have it, the fresh-baked loaf still feels like a creation ex nihilo, its from-mud-wrested form a refutation of cosmic entropy, its sheer plusness a tasty proof of the nonzero sum or, to put it in more homely terms, the free lunch.

But before I get carried away congratulating myself . . . there were, let's not forget, those two unsightly black protuberances, rising like volcanic islands from the smooth, tan sea of crust. It wasn't until the loaf had cooled that I could slice it open and find out what lay beneath them: two yawning caverns of air that reached deep into the center of the loaf. Cavitation! A really bad case, too. Chubby pockets of air are part of the charm of a country loaf, but these were far too big and far too close to the surface to be charming. "The room where the baker sleeps" is what bakers call such cells—in derision.

PBF: Any professional baker would toss this loaf on the reject pile, a case of partial bread failure. But it smelled absolutely delicious, and when I tasted a slice, I was once again pleasantly surprised. The crust was thin and chewy, and the moist crumb had plenty of flavor—wheaty, sweet, and fragrant. This was not a half bad loaf of bread, I decided, especially if you ate it with your eyes closed.

I had a ways to go, certainly, but I didn't feel discouraged in the least. To the contrary: I felt determined to make another, better loaf, and soon. The final product might be no triumph, but something about the process had captivated me—the mysteries of fermentation, the sweetly sweaty smell of my sourdough culture, the feel of the dough in my hands, the suspense surrounding the climactic oven spring. But before I ventured another loaf, I decided it would probably be a good idea to spend some time in the company of someone who actually knew what he was doing. So I got in touch with Robertson and asked if I could come by the bakery, talk to him about how he had learned to bake bread, and maybe work a shift or two at his side.

Chad Robertson looks less a baker than the surfer he also is. He has a swimmer's long, sleek torso and a certain litheness about him. Chad is equally economical with his words, his movements, and his smiles. On my first visit to the bakery, I spent an hour watching him shape bâtards. He wore a white apron tied tightly around his waist; a visor over his brown hair shaded his brown eyes. The process is mesmerizing to watch but impossible to follow—to break down into discrete, comprehensible, imitable steps. All I could make out was a blur of dexterous fingers that looked as if they were swaddling an endless succession of infants at warp speed.

While he shaped loaves, we talked. I asked Chad about his starter. I had brought along mine in a Tupperware container, hoping to pick up some pointers on care and feeding—and, secretly, perhaps some good microbes as well, since I figured the bakery must be crawling with them.

"When I was starting out I was superstitious about my starter," Chad told me, as he swiftly cut and weighed lumps of dough. "I would take it on vacation because I didn't trust anyone with it. Once, I took it to the movies with me, so I could feed it exactly on time. But now that I've lost the culture and had to start it over a few times, I'm more relaxed about it. I now tend to think it's less about nature than nurture." Meaning, roughly, that the requisite bugs are everywhere, but can be selected and trained by the baker to perform as he wants them to.

Chad showed me his culture, taking down from a high, warm shelf a metal bowl half filled with an animated white soup. It was wetter and warmer than mine, and smelled less sour. He told a story about the night one of his apprentices, cleaning the bakery at the end of her shift, accidentally threw out the bowl of starter.

"I cried. I thought I was finished as a baker. But then I found I was able to start a new culture that within a couple of days smelled exactly like the old one." Chad judges a starter by its aroma, which in his view should be more fruity than vinegary; in fact, he doesn't like his sourdough to be very sour at all. ("Sour is easy to achieve: Just don't feed the starter as often. But it's one dimensional.") Chad figures that by now the "right" yeasts and bacteria are all over his bakery and easy enough to capture. Though he also recently had experiences starting new cultures while in France and Mexico that soon came to smell and perform much like his culture in San Francisco. This has led him to the conclusion that the feeding schedule and the ambient temperature are the most important factors determining the character of a sourdough culture. But it could also be that by now Chad Robertson carries some really good bugs on his person. Which is why, before I left the bakery that evening, I opened my Tupperware to the Tartine air and asked him to pronounce on the quality of my culture. Chad raised the container to his nose, sniffed, and nodded in mild approval.

Chad Robertson can name the very day that bread baking first captivated him: the spring afternoon in 1992 when his class at the Culinary Institute of America, in Hyde Park, New York, went on a field trip to the Berkshire Mountain Bakery in Housatonic, Massachusetts. This was the day he met Richard Bourdon, a thirty-five-year-old "radical baker" from Quebec whose whole-grain sesame boule and soaring, sexy spiel about the wonders of sourdough fermentation set Robertson on his course in life.

This was not the first right-angled turn in Chad's twenty-one-year-old life, however. Growing up in West Texas, on rectangles of sliced Oroweat bread, he had never given much thought to cooking as a career, much less baking. (His father had, like his father and grandfather before him, worked in the family business, making custom cowboy boots.) Chad recalls being "an obsessive kid, the type who would keep daily charts of the weather." As a teenager, he planned to become an architect, but when the one and only school he applied to—Rice University, in Houston—rejected him, he abruptly changed course and decided to go to culinary school. "I figured if I could cook I could always get work in a restaurant."

For Chad the two most important things that happened in culinary school were meeting his future wife and partner, Elisabeth Prueitt, a pastry chef, and going on that fateful field trip to Housatonic. Over lunch one afternoon during one of the shifts I worked at Tartine, he recounted the story while the bulk fermentation bubbled along back in the bakery.

"It was weird, because in the van on the way up there I had already decided that this was going to be it. I had this fantasy of apprenticing myself to Richard Bourdon and becoming a baker. It made no sense whatsoever; I had never met him or given much thought to bread. But I loved the idea of this underground baker out there in the middle of nowhere, working through the night in perfect solitude." A restaurant kitchen is a hectic, loud, chaotic place, and Chad had already begun to question whether it was the right place for him. A bakery is a monastery by comparison.

Bourdon and his bread lived up to expectations. "It was exactly what I had been imagining. I loved the atmosphere of his bakery, this big, old, dimly lit brick barn on the bank of a river. The whole bakery had the sweet smell of natural leaven. It was a new aroma and a new flavor for me. I had never seen bread that wasn't rectangular. And his bread was incredible. It had a contrast between crust and crumb I had never experienced before, and this moist, glistening interior. And then there was Bourdon himself, the radical baker! He had an intense, sexual way of talking about fermentation, the invisible orgy of microbes he was orchestrating. He wanted to take everything to the absolute limit: the super-wet doughs, the long fermentation, the hard, dark bake. I loved the idea of this underground baker pushing his doughs just as far as they could go. He was a guru."

A few months later, I traveled to the Berkshires to meet the bread guru. Richard Bourdon is now approaching sixty, and though the passage of time had clearly mellowed him a bit (he's relented, slightly, on the subject of white flour), the man was still possessed by a Dionysian fervor about bread, and fermentation, and wheat, which he mills himself fresh every day. Bourdon has an ungovernable mop of gray curls and an open, expressive face that appears to have been lined more by laughter than worry. He somewhat resembles Harpo Marx, and, like Harpo, can get across anything he wants solely by means of his facial expressions and dancing eyes. Unlike Harpo, however, Bourdon can also, in his faintly Frenchified English, talk a blue streak, giving him a doubly powerful presence. In fact, the man would probably be hard to take if he were not so charming and charismatic.

I filled several notebooks with Bourdon's soaring disquisitions on fermentation, a subject about which he has developed a great many theories, some of them more susceptible to scientific proof than others. A central one is that "souring" grains—fermenting them—"is not a cultural but a natural, instinctual process. We humans did not discover it. All indigenous peoples sour their grains, but so do many animals." This particular treatise took him all the way from Ghana to Greenland and then looped back around to his front yard and ended back in his bakery.

"What do you think the squirrel is doing when he buries acorns in my yard? He is not just hiding them! No, he's souring them, because if he didn't do that the nut would be indigestible. Birds? They don't just swallow seeds fresh. No! First they sprout them in their craw so the enzymes can start to free the minerals. Animals instinctively sour, sprout, ferment foods to extract the maximum nourishment from them while expending as little of their own body's energy as possible. That's the iron law of economy: Take the most you can from nature with the least amount of effort. So, instead of doing all the work of digestion ourselves, we let the bacteria do it for us." What he was describing sounded a lot like cooking.

"Now let us look at bread. It is the same principle but even more clever. It starts with the flour mill, this big stone tooth that chews the seed for us so we don't need to break our teeth on it. Then the sourdough culture breaks down the phytic acid in the flour, so the bacteria can get at those minerals. (Because bacteria want all the same things we do, food and sex and babies!) But bread is the most intelligent system for processing food, because it has everything. It even makes its own pot! Put dough in a hot oven and the first thing that happens is, a crust forms to trap the steam. The loaf becomes its own pressure cooker! That's what cooks the starches."

For Bourdon, the problem with most bread is that it is essentially undercooked, and therefore more difficult to digest than it should be. This is why he favors long fermentations and unusually wet doughs. Wet dough was the norm before the mechanization of baking. Human hands can't handle dry doughs very well (even if they are easier to shape, they are much harder to mix and knead), and machines can't handle wet ones at all. But they make much better breads. Bourdon is fond of saying, "You would never cook a cup of rice in half a cup of water." Even more than flavor or beauty, Bourdon is after the perfect nourishment that only the most thorough cooking can ensure. He came out of the macrobiotic movement, and is something of a poet of human digestion. Which, he explains, begins in the mouth the moment you bite into a bread.

"This is why the acids in sourdough are so important! They make your mouth water, so the enzymes in your saliva can begin to digest the starches. That's how you can tell good bread from bad: Roll a little ball of it and put it in your mouth. What happens? Does your mouth feel dry, like you want a sip of water, or is it nice and wet?" The baker is the conductor of an intricate symphony of transformation that takes in everything from the grass seed to the millstone, the microbial fermentation to the pressure-cooking, and culminates in the salivation that a well-baked bread inspires in the mouth.

It was easy to see how a twenty-one-year-old might come away from a few hours in Richard Bourdon's presence convinced that baking bread was the most important thing you could do with your life. The work put you in direct, bodily contact with some of the deeper currents of the natural world, as well as some of the oldest traditions of human community. Bread, as something "made" by microbial action and human hands working in concert, falls somewhere between nature and culture, which in Bourdon's worldview exist not in opposition to each other but on one glorious, Rabelaisian continuum, reaching all the way from "the mindless fucking and farting" of bacteria to the sprouting of acorns by squirrels to the civilized pleasures of breaking bread at the table.

Before the group left Bourdon's bakery that afternoon, Chad summoned the nerve to ask him about an apprenticeship. So began five months of a brutal but life-altering internship, with Chad making the long drive up to Housatonic every night after classes, working in the bakery from four until nine in the morning, and then driving back down to Hyde Park for another day of classes. After graduation, Bourdon wanted to hire Robertson, but had no openings. So Chad worked for nothing but room and board, until a spot opened up. Chad ended up spending two years in Housatonic, absorbing Richard's passions and methods and ways with the wet dough.

Richard recalls, "Chad was good at everything, but he had a perfectionist streak. He would bake only three loaves wide, so that each bread had plenty of personal space in the oven. And if the loaves didn't spring up nice and big, he'd be upset. Would call it a shitty bake. I'd say to him, 'Chad, don't worry, it's all good food!' But that was never enough for him. The bread had to be beautiful, too."

After two years, Richard told Chad that it was time for him to move on, that he had learned all he had to teach him. Richard no longer remembers the conversation, but it seems possible that Chad's perfectionism was getting under Richard's skin. That was certainly the case at Chad's next job, working for a former Bourdon apprentice named Dave Miller, at a bakery Miller had taken over in Chico, in northern California. "Chad had very specific ideas of what he wanted in a bread," Dave told me, choosing his words with care. "And I was trying to run a business."

After a year that both describe as uncomfortable, Chad and Dave parted amicably. Chad and Liz headed to southwestern France to work with Richard Bourdon's own mentor, a baker named Patrick LePort, whom both Richard and Chad described as an avatar of wet doughs and whole grains and also something of a mystic. Chad recalls that Patrick would take naps alongside his mixer, because it stood on the precise spot where he had determined that the meridians of universal energy intersected. After a year in France, Chad decided he was ready to strike out on his own. In a house on Main Street in Point Reyes Station, in West Marin County, California, he and Liz opened the Bay Village Bakers; they lived in back. Chad baked in a wood-fired masonry oven built by Alan Scott, a legendary local mason and baker, and over the course of six years in Point Reyes, he worked assiduously, even obsessively, to develop what would become his signature bread— what he describes in his book as "a certain loaf with an old soul."

The first few chapters of Chad's bread autobiography had taken up the entire lunch. Afterward, we strolled back to the bakery to shape loaves. We had mixed the dough before noon, one big batch in a Bongard mixer that can hold and, by rotating its giant steel screw, slowly knead 350 pounds of willful dough at a time. That morning I had helped Chad's young assistant bakers, Lori Oyamada and Nathan Yanko, empty fifty-pound bags of flour into the mixer. Both bakers were a few years older than Chad had been when he worked for Richard Bourdon, and both, it seemed to me, shared certain attributes with Chad. They looked more like athletes than bakers, with muscled arms (elaborately tattooed, in the case of Nate and Chad) and bodies sleek as cats.

I quickly came to understand exactly how Lori and Nate developed such well-muscled arms. After the dough was mixed and given some time to rest in the Bongard's big stainless-steel bowl, it had to be lifted out, an armful of dough at a time, and transferred to the five-gallon buckets in which it would ferment. This involved rolling up your sleeves, wetting your hands and forearms, and then plunging them deep into the pool of warm dough. By now the gluten was sufficiently well developed to form gigantic, muscular sinews that would stretch but not break no matter how hard you pulled them; after losing a tug of war with one of them, I was forced to conclude that gluten is considerably stronger than I am. Lori showed me how to pinch off a manageable length by squeezing my fist closed way down at the bottom of the bowl. That made it possible to lift out a thick, ropy length of the dough, thirty or forty pounds of the stuff per armful, minus the pound or so that adamantly clung to the hairs on my arms. It took two or three armloads to fill a bucket.

The bulk fermentation was complete by the time Chad and I returned from lunch, so, while Chad picked up the thread of his country loaf's biography, we got to work turning the bubbling white pools of dough out onto the butcher-block counter for cutting and shaping. Using a dough scraper, Chad cut two-pound chunks from the mass, weighed them on an old-time balance scale, and then deftly rotated them with both hands against the floured wood surface until they tightened into nice rounds. To keep them from getting chilled, he gently pressed each shaped round against its neighbor, eventually forming a rolling landscape of powdery white buttocks.

It was during the years in Point Reyes that Chad perfected his country loaf, the flavor first, and then the structure. He took from Richard Bourdon the idea of a very wet dough, but he left behind, at least for the time being, Richard's devotion to whole-grain flours and to nutrition as the baker's foremost concern. Compared with Richard (or for that matter Dave Miller), Chad was very much the aesthete, chasing after flavor and beauty rather than nourishment and health. The "loaf with an old soul" that Chad was after was definitely a white bread—he had glimpsed it not just in his mind's eye, but in a specific painting by Émile Friant, the late-nineteenth-century French painter.

The painting, which is reproduced in Chad's book, depicts a group of weekend boaters sitting down to a summertime lunch al fresco. One of them is pouring wine while another is holding a gigantic, thickly crusted wheel of bread, from which he's sawing off big white chunks for his friends. At the time, Chad explained, each worker in France was allotted two pounds of bread every day. Bread was elemental food, yet it was also the stuff of ceremony and community—the giant loaves were made for sharing. And for enjoying: In Friant's tender, scrupulous depiction, this looked like a bread you very much wanted to eat.

Chad worked night and day to get the flavor he imagined that bread had. With such a tiny number of ingredients in play, this becomes mostly a matter of manipulating time and temperature. But, as with so much in baking, an iron law of compensation is at work. Any move the baker makes in one direction is liable to produce an undesirable effect in another direction, making trade-offs difficult to avoid. So a longer fermentation might give you deeper flavors, for example, but if the extra time tires out the yeasts, oven spring will suffer. Chad found that if he "retarded" fermentation, by cooling the loaves while they proofed, he could slow down the yeasts while encouraging the bacteria that contribute most to the flavor. He couldn't afford a retarder, however, so most nights he stacked his two hundred baskets of shaped dough into the back of his delivery van, a yellow 1953 Chevrolet, and opened all the windows. But though this move gave him the flavor he was after, the loaves came out of the oven flatter than he wanted. A warmer final proof would add air and volume, yet that risked souring the flavor.

The breakthrough came when Chad turned his attention to his starter. "I realized that I needed a younger culture. So I began using smaller and smaller amounts of starter in my leaven, and then less leaven in my dough." He experimented with his feeding schedule, using less starter to inoculate more flour more frequently, so that at each step in the process—starter, leaven, dough—he managed to build a fresher, sweeter, younger culture. In effect, he was resetting the fermentation clock, and the results were immediately apparent.

"I could smell the difference: Instead of being vinegary, like most leavens, mine became fruity, sweet, and floral." These qualities carried over into the flavor of the bread, and the vibrant young yeasts ensured a terrific oven spring. Chad had figured out a way to maximize both flavor and air in his bread, defying, or at least outwitting, the iron law of sourdough compensation.

After the globes of dough had their rest, Chad invited me to try my hand at shaping. My eye-hand coordination is challenged, and I struggled to follow, much less mimic, Chad's lightning-quick manipulations of the dough. I felt like I did the first few times I attempted to diaper Isaac as an infant—clumsy. But Chad was patient, kept feeding me new rounds of dough, and eventually I managed to shape what I, at least, deemed to be some respectable-looking papooses. I did notice, however, that Chad, ever the perfectionist, carefully segregated my loaves from his batch, putting mine into round, rather than rectangular, baskets. I got the feeling that, when and if my loaves were baked, they would not go on sale with the rest.

My time in the bakery had a salutary effect on my baking at home. I felt more fluent in the ways of dough, more comfortable not just ma-nipulating it, but judging its development—and that of my starter—by smell and touch and appearance. Shaping was no longer slapstick. My starter was livelier than ever, some days even exuberant, probably because I fed it more frequently, or perhaps because it had picked up some good bugs from Chad's bakery. My time in the bakery also helped me see that baking by the book—*any* book—can take you only so far toward a decent loaf, and that that's okay. As I've often heard bakers (and also cooks) put it, *the recipe is not the recipe*. It never is. It would take a great many more pages than Chad's twenty-seven to capture everything that goes into making a great loaf of bread.

While at lunch, I had shown Chad a crumb shot of my first Tartin-ian loaf on my phone, the loaf with the sorry case of cavitation. It may not be possible to judge a loaf of bread by its crust, but Chad believes he *can* judge it by its crumb shot.

"I can see how a bread will taste," he explained matter-of-factly, as if this were normal. But apparently, to the expert eye, the pattern of alveolation and the sheen of its cells tell of the extent of its fermenta-tion and, by extension, its flavor. In my case, the cavitation indicated that my gluten was probably too weak to contain the gases in their cells as they expanded in the heat. The bread was rising faster than the gluten could stretch, so the gas was busting out, then pooling beneath the hard roof of crust. A few more folds might help to strengthen the gluten, he suggested, as would a longer, slower fermentation. Chad thought I should try overnighting my dough in the refrigerator before baking.

This gave me my breakthrough. The very first loaf I retarded overnight in the refrigerator emerged from the oven a thing of beauty. The loaf had achieved an oven spring just this side of spectacular, and its crust, which in all my previous efforts had been a tentative, wan shade of brown, was now deeply colored, forming a dark, weather-beaten hide rent across the top by a sharply turned and blackened ear. This crust had conviction. As for the crumb, I had to wait an hour for it to cool, but when I finally sawed off a slice, I exposed a cross section of evenly distributed holes in various sizes, their stretched walls glistening just slightly. True, my crumb was somewhat tighter than Tartine's, the alveolation not nearly so shiny or wild, but this looked like a fine loaf of bread, and I felt an upwelling of pride the force of which took me by surprise. This was immediately followed by the sagging realization that my proud achievement, the product of so many weeks of work and study, would soon get eaten and be forever lost to history.

So I took its picture. I briefly considered posting it to TheFreshloaf .com, thinking I could impress the bread geeks with it, but the impulse soon passed. Too peacocky. I did text it to Chad, however. "Nice loaf," he texted back, a little more laconically than I had perhaps hoped—I felt like I had been patted on the head—but I didn't mind. The bread was delicious: sweet, a little nutty, with just the slightest acid tang. Judith and Isaac, at least, were suitably impressed, and together we worked through the great white loaf, first at dinner that night, then at breakfast the following morning, when it made some exemplary toast.

I have spent some time trying to parse the almost absurd pride I felt about this loaf and various others I've baked since. I mean, a loaf of bread, big deal. And yet it did feel big. I couldn't imagine feeling quite this way about a great stew or braise, much less taking its picture and texting it to someone or posting it online.

The only thing I've cooked that prompted the same impulse to show off is a whole barbecued hog, whose appeal, especially to the male ego (large beast killed; food enough to feed a village), is all too obvious. But what is it about a loaf of bread, something that is much smaller and yet in some ways even more impressive?

Part of it is aesthetic—the satisfaction of making something, something beautiful that didn't exist before. A good-looking loaf of bread declares itself as an artifact, an original, man-made, freestanding object, something that cannot be said of too many other foods. Most foods, even the whole hog, are altered versions of nature's already existing animals and plants, which more or less retain their form after cooking. But a loaf of bread is something new added to the world, an edged object wrested from the flux of nature—and specifically from the living, shifting, Dionysian swamp that is dough. Bread is the Apollonian food. Which might explain some of its appeal to the male ego, as might the miraculous fact that it rises.

Yet the pride I felt wasn't only aesthetic or, for that matter, necessarily masculine. It had more to do, I think, with the sense of personal competence my success conferred. Or at least that's how it felt to me. Bread is such a fundamental necessity and comfort of everyday life, as it has been in the West for at least six thousand years. And yet in our time the ability to make this necessary thing has passed out of our hands and into those of specialists. Whether artisans or corporations, it makes little difference: The only way for most of us to obtain it is to trade our professional labor for theirs. I doubt baking bread is something I am ever going to do more than every once in a while. Yet the fact that doing so is now solidly within the orbit of my competence, that my hands now know how to transform a pile of cheap flour and free water (free microbes, too!) into something that will not only nourish but also give so much pleasure to my family, changes everything. Or at least changes me. I am a little less dependent, and a little more self-reliant, than I used to be.

And then there is the matter of the air itself. (Or is it the antimatter?)

To compare a loaf of bread with a bowl of porridge is to realize how much of bread's power, sensory as well as symbolic, resides precisely in those empty cells of spaces. Some 80 percent of a loaf of bread consists of nothing more than air. But air is not nothing.

In bread, it is where much of the flavor resides, and is the reason bread is so much more aromatic than porridge. The air trapped in the alveoli conducts bread's aromas—the two hundred or so volatile compounds that have been identified in a well-baked sourdough—to the back of the mouth, where they then drift up into the nasal passages and, by means of retronasal olfaction, reach the brain.

"Retronasal olfaction" is the technical term for our ability to smell food that is already in our mouth. Whereas the nose's olfactory sense—"orthonasal olfaction"—identifies smells when we sniff in, retronasal olfaction identifies smells when we breathe out, as the molecules released from our food rise from the back of the mouth up into our nasal passages. Orthonasal olfaction allows us to identify smells from the outside world, including smells from foods we are deciding whether to ingest. The purpose of retronasal olfaction is different, as is the range of compounds it detects and the regions of the brain to which it reports. The signals from retronasal smell are interpreted at the highest cognitive levels of our cerebral cortex as well as in regions involved in memory and emotion. This has led some scientists to hypothesize that the function of retronasal smell may be primarily analytical, helping us to archive the vast catalog of food flavors and record them in memory for future use.

Perhaps this helps explain the keen pleasure we seem to take in all kinds of aerated foods and beverages: the sparkling wines and sodas, the soufflés and whipped cream, the lofted breads and ethereal croissants and weightless meringues, and the laminated pastries with their 128 layers of air. Bakers and chefs labor mightily to work sweet nothings into their creations, striving to deliver the most flavorful airs deep into our mouths. The palate of taste is limited to the five or six primary colors that the tongue can recognize; olfaction, by comparison, is seemingly limitless in the shadings and combinations it can register and archive—and retronasal olfaction can perceive aromas to which even the nose is blind.

Symbolically, too, air is not nothing. Air elevates our food, in every sense, raises it from the earthbound subsistence of gruel to something so fundamentally transformed as to hint at human and even divine transcendence. Air lifts food up out of the mud and so lifts us, dignifying both the food and its eaters. Surely it is no accident that Christ turned to bread to demonstrate his divinity; bread is partially inspired already, an everyday proof of the possibility of transcendence.[*]

---

[*]Milton has a beautiful passage in *Paradise Lost* in which he describes humankind's inexorable progress toward ever more ethereal types of nourishment, culminating in the bread of Christ:

> So from the root
> Springs lighter the green stalk, from thence the leaves
> More airy, last the bright consummate flow'r
> Spirits odorous breathes: flow'rs and their fruit.
> Man's nourishment, by gradual scale sublimed,
> To vital spirits aspire . . .
> Time may come when men
> With angels may participate, and find
> No inconvenient diet, nor too light fare;
> And from these corporal nutriments perhaps
> Your bodies may at last turn all to spirit. . . .

What other food could do all this symbolic work and yet still reliably fill human bellies? No wonder long stretches of European history can be told as the story of bread, or, rather, its two stories: a fight for access to bread on the part of Europe's peasantry and working class, and a fight over the meaning of bread on the part of its elite. For what was the Reformation if not an extended, centuries-long argument over the proper interpretation of bread? Was it merely the symbol of Christ or his actual body?

Around the time I felt like I could reliably bake a voluminous white loaf, I hatched the idea of preparing an entire dinner on the theme of air, and one Saturday Samin and I got together at my house to cook it. In addition to a couple of nicely lofted loaves of Tartinian bread that I'd baked, we made two soufflés, a savory green-garlic one to serve with dinner, and a rose-and-ginger one for dessert. For the main course we served (what else?) a bird, albeit a flightless one: chicken. I broke out a bottle of vintage champagne. And Samin made honeycomb candy, a hard yet weirdly effervescent brittle made by stirring a spoonful of baking soda into a bubbling pot of caramelizing sugar.

The evening was a spree of retronasal olfaction, but what made the most lasting impression was the ginger-and-rose soufflé. There was actually not a speck of ginger or rose in it, just a few drops of essential oil, one distilled from ginger root and the other from the petals of roses. The recipe came from an eccentric cookbook titled, simply, *Aroma*, the collaboration of a chef, Daniel Patterson, and a perfumer, Mandy Aftel. It called for a tremendous number of egg whites whipped to an airy froth. The albumen proteins in the whites of eggs can hold air much like gluten does, allowing the cells of gas whipped into it to expand dramatically when heated. For the base, instead of calling for an equivalent number of yolks to carry the flavor, or cream, the recipe called for yogurt, which made for a soufflé (the word of course means "blown") even more dematerialized than usual. Its flavor was powerful yet largely illusory, the result of the way the essential oils played on the human brain's difficulty in distinguishing between information obtained by the sense of taste and that provided by the sense of smell. Each weightless bite amounted to a little poem of synesthesia—a confusion of the senses that delighted. It made for a fitting end to an effervescent evening.

By now you will not be surprised to learn that Gaston Bachelard had a few things to say about the element of air. In a book called *Air and Dreams*, he points out that we categorize many of our emotions by their relative weight; they make us feel heavier or lighter. Perhaps because uprightness is the human quality, we imagine human emotions arranged on a vertical scale from ground to sky. So sadness is weighed down and earthbound, joy is aerial, and the sensation of freedom defies the bonds of gravity. "Air," Bachelard writes, "is the very substance of our freedom, the substance of superhuman joy."

Elation, effervescence, elevation, levity, inspiration: air words all, alveolated with vowels, leavening the dough of everyday life.

II.

THINKING LIKE A SEED

Not that I *want* to puncture my own balloon now that it is finally aloft, but I'm afraid I have no choice. As mentioned, the loaf that I mastered, or nearly so, is a loaf of white bread, and white bread is . . . well, problematic. I came to see that I had been bewitched by the aesthetics of bread, completely losing sight of certain other desirable qualities in a food, such as nutrition. (Oh, that!) Eating white bread is a *little* better than eating pure starch, which is itself a *little* better than eating pure sugar, but not by much. I have been dwelling here on the wonders of gluten, but of course those proteins represent only a fraction of the calories in white flour—at most maybe 15 percent. The rest, I'm afraid, is starch, which, beginning on the tongue, our enzymes swiftly translate into glucose—sugar. Americans obtain a fifth of their calories from wheat—and 95 percent of that is in the form of nutritionally nearly worthless white flour. I say "nearly" because, ever since the nutritional vacuousness of white flour became impossible to ignore, early in the twentieth century, governments have required that millers add back in a handful of the nutrients (B vitamins, mainly) that they have gone to such great lengths to take out.

Stand back far enough, and the absurdity of this enterprise makes you wonder about the sanity of our species. But consider: When millers mill wheat, they scrupulously sheer off the most nutritious parts of the seed—the coat of bran and the embryo, or germ, that it protects—and sell that off, retaining the least nourishing part to feed us. In effect, they're throwing away the best 25 percent of the seed: The vitamins and antioxidants, most of the minerals, and the healthy oils all go to factory farms to feed animals, or to the pharmaceutical industry, which recovers some of the vitamins from the germ and then sells them back to us—to help remedy nutritional deficiencies created at least in part by white flour. A terrific business model, perhaps, but terrible biology.

Surely this qualifies as maladaptive behavior on our part, and yet humankind has been intent on whitening wheat flour almost as long as we have been eating bread. But we didn't get really good at it till the nineteenth century, with the advent of roller mills that could cleanly scalp *all* the germ and bran from the seed, and the subsequent discovery that, by exposing milled flour to gusts of chlorine gas, we could whiten it still further by expunging the last remaining nutrient from it: the beta-carotene that tinted flour just slightly yellow. What a triumph!

Before these dubious achievements, the best millers could do to whiten flour was to sift, or "bolt," wheat that had first been crushed on a stone wheel. But the millstone usually smushed the germ into the endosperm, so people couldn't avoid eating those nutrients, and bolting could only catch and remove the biggest, chunkiest bits of the bran, leaving behind a fair amount of fiber. The result was an off-white flour that was nourishing enough to keep alive all those people for whom wheat made up the bulk of their diet—which until the last century or so was most of the population of Europe. Though it looks white, the bread "with the old soul" in the painting by Émile Friant that inspired Chad Robertson was almost certainly made with this kind of flour.

The quest for an ever-whiter shade of bread, which goes all the way back to the Greeks and Romans, is a parable about the folly of human ingenuity—about how our species can sometimes be too smart for its own good. After figuring out an ingenious system for transforming an all but nutritionally worthless grass into a wholesome food, humanity pushed on intrepidly until it had figured out a way to make that food all but nutritionally worthless yet again!

Here in miniature, I realized, is the whole checkered history of "food processing." Our species' discovery and development of cooking (in the broadest sense of the word) gave us a handful of ingenious technologies for rendering plants and animals more nutritious and unlocking calories unavailable to other creatures. But there eventually came a moment when, propelled by the logic of human desire and technological progress, we began to overprocess certain foods in such a way as to actually render them detrimental to our health and well-being. What had been a highly adaptive set of techniques that contributed substantially to our success as a species turned into a maladaptive

one—contributing to disease and general ill health and now actually
threatening to shorten human lives. When and where did we pass
over, from processing food to make it healthier to making it less so?
To what might be thought of as "overcooking"? There are a couple of
places we could reasonably draw that line. The refining of pure sugar
from cane or beets would certainly be one. But perhaps the sharpest
and clearest line would be the advent of pure white flour (and the
bread made from it) in the second half of the nineteenth century.

The prestige of white flour is ancient and has several sources, some
practical, others sentimental. Whiteness has always symbolized clean-
ness, and especially at times when disease has been rife and food
frequently contaminated, the whiteness of flour symbolized its purity.
I say "symbolized" because for most of history it was no guarantee:
Unscrupulous millers routinely whitened their flour by adulterating it
with everything from alum and chalk to pulverized bone. (For centuries both millers and bakers have been regarded with suspicion,
often with good reason. It has always been hard to determine what
exactly is in a bag of flour or a loaf of bread, and easy to pass off ingredients that are cheaper and less wholesome than wheat flour. This
is why, during periods of hunger and political ferment, millers and
bakers were frequent targets of popular wrath, occasionally put in the
stocks and pelted with bad bread.)

Adulterated or not, however, white (or whitish) flour was generally regarded as healthier than whole grain well into the nineteenth
century. "Coarse flour"—wheat that had simply been ground on a
stone and never sifted—was coarse indeed, and gradually ground
down the teeth of the people who had no choice but to eat the dark
bread made from it. Sifted flour was also thought to be easier and

swifter to digest, and certainly for people struggling to obtain enough calories, white bread was a superior source of quick energy. It was also easier to chew, no small thing before modern dentistry.

So the rich demanded the whitest possible flour, and the poor were left to eat "kaka," as the French sometimes called brown bread. Going back to ancient Rome, the shade of the bread you could afford precisely indicated your social standing; to know one's place, Juvenal wrote, is "to know the color of one's bread." Some historians and anthropologists have suggested that the prestige of white flour might also have had a racist tint to it. Maybe. And yet white rice has enjoyed a similar prestige in Asia, among nonwhites, so maybe not.

Whitish flour, which before roller mills could only be obtained by sifting flour through progressively finer meshes of cloth, had a lot to recommend it. Bran tends to be bitter, so the whiter the flour the sweeter the bread. White flour also made for a much airier loaf; even the microscopic shards of milled bran are sharp, and, like millions of tiny knives, they can pierce the strands of gluten in dough, impairing its ability to hold air and rise. (On the same principle, some gardeners kill slugs by spreading wheat bran in their path.) Those tiny bran knives are relatively heavy, too, making it more difficult to leaven a whole-grain loaf. Even at its best, it will never achieve the exaltation of a loaf made with white flour.

As a solution to these problems, sifting coarse flour was less than ideal. The multistep process was time consuming and expensive. It also failed to address what is perhaps the most serious rap against whole-grain flours: their relatively short shelf life. Whole-grain flour tends to go "off" within several weeks of being milled, releasing an unmistakable odor of rancidity. Part of what makes the germ so nutritious—its unsaturated omega-3 fats—also makes it unstable, and prone to oxidization. Sifting might whiten stone-ground flour, but it could not remove the perishable germ, which meant that flour had to be milled frequently and locally. This is why every town used to have its own mill.

The advent of roller milling in the middle of the nineteenth century made white flour cheap, stable, and whiter than it had ever been. For a revolutionary technology, roller milling seems almost obvious, and benign. The new mills replaced the old millstones with a sequence of steel or porcelain drums arranged in pairs, each subsequent pair calibrated to have a narrower space between them than the previous set, in order to grind the flour ever more finely. To begin, the seed is dropped between a pair of corrugated drums rotating in opposite directions. During the "first break," the bran and germ are sheared from the endosperm. Those parts are sifted out before the now naked endosperm moves on to the next pair of slightly more closely spaced rollers, and so on, until the starch (or "farina") has been pulverized to the desired degree of fineness.

The new technology was greeted as a boon to humankind, and so at first it seemed. Bread became whiter and airier and cheaper than ever. Commercial yeast performed particularly well with the new flour, vastly speeding and simplifying the work of baking. The shelf life of flour, now that the unstable embryo had been eliminated, became indefinite, allowing the milling industry to consolidate. Thousands of local stone mills closed, since big industrial operations could now supply whole nations. Cheap, stable, transportable white flour made it possible to export flour around the world and to feed swelling urban populations during the industrial revolution. According to one history of bread,* the advantages of white bread were something on

---

*John Marchant, Bryan Reuben, and Joan Alcock, *Bread: A Slice of History* (Charleston, SC: History Press, 2009).

which both workers and employers could agree: Brown breads high in fiber "meant that workers had to leave their machines frequently to go to the lavatory, and this disrupted production."

Indeed, in many ways, white flour not only gratified human desires but also meshed especially well with the logic of industrial capitalism. No longer a living, perishable thing, flour now became a stable, predictable, and flexible commodity, making not only the production of bread faster and more efficient, but also its consumption. In effect, roller mills "sped up" wheat as a food, making it possible for the human body to absorb its energy much more readily than before. Flour, and bread in turn, became more like fuel and, at least calorically, more efficient. In the jargon of modern nutrition science, bread became more "energy dense," which, along with extended shelf life, is one of the most common outcomes of modern food processing. Not surprisingly, white flour proved enormously popular with a species hardwired by natural selection to favor sweet foods. The taste of sweetness, which signals a particularly rich source of energy, had always been rare and hard to find in nature (ripe fruit, honey), but with the industrial refining of certain cultivated grasses (wheat, cane, corn), it now became cheap and ubiquitous, with what would turn out to be unfortunate consequences for human health.

More than just a new food product, white flour helped usher in a new food system, one that would extend all the way from the field to the loaf of presliced and fortified white bread, which now could be manufactured on an assembly line in three or four hours without ever being touched by human hands. The wheat plant changed, too. The new roller mills worked best with hard-kerneled red wheat; the big, tough bran coat on this type of wheat could be sheared cleanly and completely from the endosperm, whereas softer white wheat left infinitesimal specks of bran in the flour. So, over time, breeding changed the plant to better suit the new machine. But because hard wheat has tougher, bitterer bran, it made whole-grain flour even coarser and bitterer than it had been before—one of several ways that the triumph of white flour made whole wheat less good. Even today, breeders continue to select for ever-harder wheats with ever-whiter— and therefore less nutritious—endosperms. As Steve Jones, the former wheat breeder for the State of Washington, told me, "Wheat breeders are selecting against health."

Ah yes, health. Here was the fly in the ointment. The compelling industrial logic of white flour meshed beautifully with everything except human biology. Not long after roller mills became widespread in the 1880s, alarming rates of nutritional deficiency and chronic disease began cropping up in populations that relied on the new white flour. Around the turn of the century, a group of French and British doctors and medical experts began searching for the causes of what they dubbed "the Western diseases" (heart disease, stroke, diabetes, and several disorders of the digestive tract, including cancer), so called because they were virtually unheard of in places where people hadn't switched to modern diets containing large amounts of refined sugar and white flour. These medical men, many of them posted to Britain's colonies in Asia and Africa, had observed that, soon after white flour and sugar arrived in places where previously what one of them (Robert McCarrison) called "the unsophisticated foods of Nature" had been the norm, the Western diseases would predictably appear. Some of these doctors blamed the lack of fiber in the Western diet, others the surfeit of refined carbohydrates, and still others the lack of vitamins. But whatever the culprit nutrient or the precise mechanism by which it operated, these men were convinced of a link between processed white flour and sugar and the panoply of new chronic diseases. A large body of contemporary research suggests they were right.

What to do? Certainly not return to the "unsophisticated foods of Nature"—no one wanted to do that! And yet, by the end of the nineteenth century, several voices were raised in support of just such a course, including a return to whole-grain flour. "The true staff of life is wholemeal bread," declared Thomas Allinson, a prominent English physician, and one of the first to link refined carbohydrates to disease. To counter the scourge of white flour, in 1892 he bought a stone grinding mill and began baking and selling whole-grain bread under the slogan "health without medicine." (He was also involved in a group called the Bread and Food Reform League.) Earlier in the century, the American minister and nutritional reformer Sylvester Graham, eponym of the whole-grain cracker, had published an influential *Treatise on Bread and Bread-Making* that blamed white flour for many, if not quite all, of the ills of modern life, including constipation (a nineteenth-century scourge), and fervently extolled the virtues of coarse dark breads high in fiber. To remove the precious health-giving fraction of bran from wheat was to "put asunder what God had joined together"—a fall from dietary grace for which modern man was paying with his troubled, sluggish digestion.

By the early decades of the twentieth century, public health authorities in England and the United States could no longer ignore the links between refined white flour and widespread nutritional deficiencies, including beriberi, as well as increases in the rates of both heart disease and diabetes. (It was noted that during both world wars, when the British government had mandated a higher fiber content in flour as part of food rationing, people's health improved and rates of type 2 diabetes declined.) But by now the White Flour Industrial Complex was so well entrenched that a shift back to whole-grain flour was never seriously contemplated.

Instead, the milling industry and government came up with a clever technological fix: A handful of the vitamins that modern milling had removed from bread would now be put back in. So in the early 1940s, in what was called "the quiet miracle," the U.S. government worked with baking companies—including the Continental Baking Company, makers of Wonder Bread—to develop and promote a white bread fortified with a handful of B vitamins. Here was a classic capitalist "solution." Rather than go back to address a problem at its source—the processing of key nutrients out of wheat—the industry set about processing the product even *more*. This was sheer brilliance: The milling industry could now sell the problem *and* the solution in one neat package.

But fortifying white flour with the missing vitamins represents only a partial, reductionist solution to what turns out to be a much more complex problem. By now the nutritional superiority of whole grains over even fortified white flour is universally acknowledged—yet still only imperfectly understood. People who eat lots of whole-grain foods significantly reduce their risk of all chronic diseases; they also weigh less and live longer than people who don't. This much we know from the epidemiology.* But why, exactly? Is it, as Sylvester Graham believed, the benefits of dietary fiber? And if so, is it the fiber itself, or the various phytochemicals that typically accompany fiber? Or maybe it's the vitamins, not all of which are put back when flour is fortified. It could also be the minerals in the bran. Or the omega-3 fatty acids in the germ. Or it could be the antioxidants found in the "aleurone layer," the innermost layer of the bran. Scientists still can't say for sure.

But here is the most curious fact: People whose diets contain adequate amounts of all these good nutrients from sources other than

---

*The epidemiologists correct for the fact that, today, people who eat more whole grains also tend to be more affluent and better educated and more health conscious in general.

whole grains (from supplements, say, or other foods) aren't nearly as healthy as people who simply eat lots of whole grains. According to a 2003 study by David Jacobs and Lyn Steffen,* epidemiologists at the University of Minnesota, the health benefits of whole grains cannot be completely explained in terms of the nutrients we know those grains contain: the dietary fiber, vitamin E, folic acid, phytic acid, iron, zinc, manganese, and magnesium. Either there are synergies at work among these nutrients, or there is some X-factor in whole grains that scientists have yet to identify. We are talking, after all, about a seed: a package that contains everything needed to create a new life. Such a recipe still exceeds science's powers of comprehension and technology's powers of creation.

The fact that a whole food might actually be more than the sum of its nutrient parts, such that those parts are probably best not "put asunder," poses a stiff challenge to food processors. They have always assumed they understood biology well enough to improve on the "unsophisticated foods of Nature," by taking them apart and then putting them back together again. The industry would be more than happy to sell us bread fortified with any one (or twelve or one hundred) of these nutrients if science could just tell it which ones to focus on. But, so far at least, science can't reduce this complexity to a simple answer.

This has been good news for the food itself: Whole-grain bread has been enjoying something of a renaissance. Actually, that renaissance got a first, false start during the 1960s, when the counterculture, steeped in romantic ideas about "natural food," seized on white bread as a symbol of all that was wrong with modern civilization. Brown bread, being less processed than white, was clearly what na-

---

*Jacobs, David R., and Lyn M. Steffen, "Nutrients, Foods, and Dietary Patterns as Exposures in Research: A Framework for Food Synergy," *American Journal of Clinical Nutrition* 78 suppl. (2003): 508S–13S.

ture intended us to eat. They probably should have stopped there, but did not, alas. Baking and eating brown bread also became a political act: a way to express one's solidarity with the world's brown peoples (seriously), and to protest the "white bread" values of one's parents, who likely served Wonder Bread at home. These ideals resulted in the production of some uncompromising and notably bricklike loaves of dark, seedy bread, which probably set back the revival of whole-grain baking a generation. "That hippie texture" is a cross that whole-grain bakers still bear today, along with the widespread belief that whole-grain bread promises rather more nutritional and ideological rigor than eating pleasure.

But whole-grain bread seems to be recovering from its sixties revival and is currently enjoying a reversal of fortune, or at least prestige, with white bread, in a sort of carnival of traditional bread values. Now it is the well-to-do who want brown bread, while white bread is becoming déclassé. The public has gotten the news about the health benefits of whole grain. The government's latest nutritional guidelines recommend that at least half of one's daily calories from grain come in the form of whole grains. When you consider that even today only 5 percent of wheat is milled into whole-grain flour, this becomes a challenging recommendation to follow.

America's expanding tribe of artisanal bakers, who started out in the 1990s as Francophiles devoted to the white-flour baguette, has begun to take a strong interest in baking with whole grains. Chad Robertson's next book will take up whole-grain baking, and much of his energies are now devoted to research and development of whole-grain recipes. Craig Ponsford, the former chairman of the board of directors for the Bread Bakers Guild of America and the first American ever to win a first prize in the Coupe du Monde de la Boulangerie baking competition in France, now bakes exclusively with whole-grain flours, and is outspoken about their benefits. (He told me he could never have promoted whole grains at the Guild without offending its milling- and yeast-industry sponsors, so after his conversion he chose to step down.) The supermarket shelves are stuffed with breads and other products making whole-grain claims, some of them more meaningful than others.*

Even Hostess, the company that, until its recent bankruptcy, manufactured Wonder Bread, has responded to the public's demand for more wholesome and nutritious bread. It developed exotic new formulations that contained not just added vitamins and minerals and fiber, but quantities of the actual foodstuff itself: whole-grain flour. Well, actually, in most cases they were offering something more like the aura of whole grain, which is not quite the same thing. For example, they sold a "Smart White" bread offering "the fiber of 100% whole wheat," said fiber derived not from wheat or any other cereal grain but from cottonseed, cellulose (aka trees), and soybeans. (The wheat itself was actually white flour.) Then they offered a "Whole Grain White" that you had to get really close to to read the small-print prefix "made with"; it turned out the first ingredient here was still white flour. These products strike me as borderline fraudulent. But Wonder Bread did then come up with one real whole-wheat bread that sounds like a breakthrough in modern food science: "Soft 100% Whole Wheat."

Whole-wheat Wonder Bread! This has all the makings of a happy ending, in which the human quest for softer, sweeter, whiter, and airier bread is married to the nutritional benefits of whole grain. But things are seldom that simple in the food industry. The White Flour Industrial Complex is not about to go quietly into the dark-bread night. How could it, when its mills have been expressly designed to produce

---

*Many products that call themselves "whole grain" turn out to have white flour as their first (and therefore biggest) ingredient. A product may use the Whole Grain Council stamp even if it contains as much as 49 percent white flour. A bread, like Wonder Bread's Soft 100% Whole Wheat is not 100 percent whole wheat—only the part of it that is wheat is, and much of it consists of other ingredients. The idea of whole grain is evidently much more appealing to industry than the reality.

the whitest possible flour, splitting off the germ and embryo at the first break? When milling white flour and selling off the nutrients is more profitable than selling flour whole? To leave the germ in the flour would literally gum up the works, I was told by an experienced miller by the name of Joe Vanderliet. This is why it is always removed at the beginning of the milling process, even when making "whole" wheat flour.

"The engineering and the nutrition are pulling in opposite directions," Vanderliet explained. Most commercial whole-wheat flour is actually white flour to which the bran and germ have been added back in. Whether such reconstituted flour is as good, or good for you, as flour from wheat milled whole on a stone is questionable, but the industry can't do it any other way.

Adapting the reductive logic of industrial bread baking to the complexities of whole grain can't be easy. What do you do about the volatility of the germ? Vanderliet claims that many large mills, including ones he used to work for, simply leave the germ out of their "whole-grain" flour "because it's just too much trouble"—a serious charge, but a difficult one to prove. (So here we are again, not quite certain what is really in a sack of flour.) And what to do about the bitterness of the bran in modern wheat varieties? (Most commercial whole-grain breads cover it up with sweeteners.) Or the difficulty of leavening whole-grain dough with commercial yeast? This last problem was (literally) the downfall of a great many hippie loaves; without a sourdough culture to promote gluten development, 100-percent whole-grain breads tend to rise lethargically and crumble in the toaster. Yet it is hard to imagine the bakers at Hostess taking on the care and feeding of a temperamental culture of unidentified wild bacteria and yeast.

By now I was curious to find out exactly how Wonder Bread solved the riddle of baking a whole-wheat white bread. Was it actually pos-

sible to modify the logic of an industrial system based on white flour
to produce a genuine and appealing whole-grain loaf? So before the
company went belly-up I put in a call to the Texas headquarters of
Hostess Brands, managed to get through to the public-affairs office,
and asked the young man who answered the phone if I might visit
one of their factories to learn how whole-wheat Wonder Bread was
made. It was his first day on the job, but he promised to get back to me.
I was pleasantly surprised when, a week later, I received an e-mail in-
forming me that a visit to the Hostess bakery in Sacramento had been
approved. When I studied the map, I saw that the Hostess plant was
only an hour or so south of Dave Miller's bakery—the artisanal whole-
grain baker for whom Chad Robertson had worked—so I decided I
would pay a visit to his bakery after my tour at the Hostess plant. Dave
Miller mills his own grain and bakes 400, 100 percent whole-grain
loaves a week for sale at the farmers' market. The Hostess plant produced up to 155,000 loaves a day for sale at supermarkets across the
western United States. It promised to be a day of extremes.

The Hostess plant occupies a sprawling, one-story industrial building
on the outskirts of Sacramento. The smell of bread hits you in the
parking lot, pleasant at first, but soon oddly cloying. Before the plant
manager escorted me onto the factory floor, he handed me earplugs
to muffle the din. A single waist-high production line snakes through
the dim, cavernous space, vaguely reminiscent of a wildly ambitious
model train set, with loaves of bread in metal pans taking the place of
train cars. The line traveled all the way from the silos that store flour
out back to the mixing drums, through the dough cutters and shapers,
into the proofing chamber, beneath the scoring machine (where a
thin jet of water neatly scores each loaf), into the tunnel-like oven,

then onto the slicing and bagging machine, and finally the twist-tie-er, which puts exactly four twists into every tie. The same line can produce Classic Wonder Bread, or Made with Whole Grain White or Soft 100% Whole Wheat as well as Nature's Pride, a new line of "all-natural"—i.e., no chemical additives—whole-grain and -grainish breads, in roughly the same amount of time: four hours, from flour dump to cooled, sliced, packaged, and twist-tied loaf.

The genius of the food scientists at Hostess has been to alter the ingredient formulas (type of flour, amount of yeast, source of fiber) without otherwise disturbing a mechanized system designed to bake white bread quickly. From the point of view of the bakers running the line, bread is pretty much bread, whether white, whole grain, whole grainish, no-high-fructose-corn-syrup, ton-o'-fiber, or whatever the currently compelling health claim dictates. Though the bakers did complain, cheerfully, about the challenge of getting air into breads that had to contain so much added fiber and minerals—"raising all that garbage," one called it. Many of the company's "healthier" brands are fortified with calcium, a mineral not ordinarily associated with wheat, but these days a compelling health claim.

"You're basically breaking up rock and throwing it in your dough," the head baker explained. He was talking about the challenge of adding prodigious amounts of calcium to bread, and his candor was disarming. "It takes a helluva lot of yeast to lift all that rock." That's when it clicked that the cloying odor—now upgraded to slightly nauseating—was the smell of yeast, lots and lots of it.

Having by now spent time in bakeries, and done a fair amount of baking at home, I was struck by how similar and yet at once how very different the industrial version of bread baking is. I watched flour and water being mixed into the familiar cement-colored slurry—and yet what are all those other ingredients getting added to the mix? The fifty-pound bags labeled simply "dough conditioner"? The ethoxylated mono- and diglycerides? The four types of sugar (high-fructose corn syrup, molasses, barley-malt extract, and corn syrup solids)? The wheat gluten and ammonium chloride and calcium propionate and sodium stearoyl lactylate and "yeast nutrients"? And why would yeasts living in such sweet dough need more nutrients, anyway? To balance their sugary diet?

The bakers in charge couldn't tell me the function of the thirty-one ingredients listed on a package of Soft 100% Whole Wheat; they suggested I ask the food scientists at headquarters. But HQ wouldn't let me to talk to their food scientists, ostensibly for fear they would inadvertently disclose proprietary baking secrets. Eventually I was able to ascertain from other food scientists the specific functions of the thirty-one ingredients, most of which fell into one or more of these categories: to back up a health claim; to "condition" the dough so it doesn't stick to and thereby slow the machines; to get as much air into the dough as rapidly as possible; to give the bread the cottony texture and moist cakey crumb consumers expect from the Wonder brand; to protect the bread from staling or molding; and, last but far from least, to sweeten the bread and thereby cover up the bitterness of bran and, even more important, the chemical taste of all the other additives.

Once upon a time not so long ago, most of those chemical additives would have been deemed "adulterants" by the Food and Drug Administration. But after an all-out campaign of lobbying by the baking industry in the 1950s, the FDA liberalized its "standard of identity" for bread, permitting bakeries to add dozens of new additives to what had previously been a simple two- or three-ingredient food. Earlier in the twentieth century, a group of experts convened by the International Congress for the Suppression of Fraud (quaint idea!) proposed a legal definition of bread that the loaves I was watching being baked would not have met. "The word bread, without any qualifier, is exclusively reserved for the product resulting from cooking dough made with a mixture of wheat flour, sourdough culture or yeast (made from beer or grain), drinking water, and salt." How far this thing called bread has come!

And yet even after all these novel ingredients have been mixed into the dough, the process still sort of resembles the baking of bread. At one point early in the tour I stepped into the sponge room, where big hoppers filled with wet dough are bubbling and rising like sofa cushions as they undergo bulk fermentation. The only difference from a bulk fermentation in my kitchen or at Tartine is how quickly it happens here. By putting vast quantities of yeast to work—as much as 10 percent by weight—Hostess can get the great big belch of CO_2 needed to raise a whole-grain or super-high-fiber dough in just an hour or two.

Indeed, much of the innovation in industrial baking has gone into speeding up what has traditionally and perhaps necessarily been a slow process. But time is money. So the dough is inoculated with legions of fast-acting yeast to speed its rise; it then gets one set of conditioners so it can withstand rapid handling by machines, and another to speed up (or replace) gluten development, and then it is heavily sweetened, so that even a 100 percent whole-grain loaf will deliver that quick hit of sugar on the tongue the consumer has come to expect from white bread. In the end, what has been removed from industrial bread by the addition of so many chemical additives is the ingredient of time.

Yet there are problems with speeding up whole-grain bread, and they begin with the flour. Many if not most of the new whole-grain white breads on the market are made with a new variety of hard white wheat developed by ConAgra. This is why the bread doesn't look like whole wheat: the specks of bran are white, or whitish. They are also microscopic: The wheat is milled by ConAgra using a patented process called Ultrafine that attains a degree of fineness never before achieved in a whole-grain flour. This resulting flour, called Ultragrain, makes for a softer, whiter whole-grain bread, but at a price. It is metabolized almost as fast as white flour, obviating one of the most important health advantages of whole grains: that our bodies absorb and metabolize them slowly, and so avoid the insulin spikes that typically accompany refined carbohydrates. A common measure of the speed by which a food raises glucose levels in the blood (and therefore insulin, an important risk factor for many chronic diseases) is the glycemic index. The glycemic index of a whole-grain Wonder Bread (around 71) is essentially the same as that of Classic Wonderbread (73). (By comparison, the glycemic index of whole-grain bread made with stone-ground flour is only 52.) So perhaps we really have gotten too smart for our own good.

Using commercial yeast to leaven whole-grain flour so rapidly may present another problem for our health. All whole grains contain phytic acid, which locks up minerals not only in the bread but, if you eat enough of it, in the body of the bread eater as well. One of the advantages of a long sourdough fermentation, as we've seen, is that it breaks down the phytic acid, freeing up those minerals. It also makes the gluten proteins more digestible and slows the body's absorption of starch. That's why a sourdough white bread actually has a lower glycemic index than a commercially yeasted whole-grain bread.

There is a second paradox here: Wonder Bread would seem to be a much more highly processed product than the bread I bake at home, with its dozens of additional ingredients and high-speed production methods. And yet, since the wheat in it never undergoes a true fermentation, Wonder Bread is in some respects less processed—less completely cooked—than the bread I bake at home. At least when it comes to processing wheat, sometimes less is more and more turns out to be less.

At the conclusion of my tour the Hostess bakers gave me a few loaves, and on the drive up to Dave Miller's I sampled three types of neo–Wonder Bread. The Soft 100% Whole Wheat smelled strongly of yeast and molasses and was a shade darker than the white–as–Wonder Bread "Made with Whole Grain" loaf. The two loaves tasted equally sweet, which is to say very, and though the 100 percent whole wheat was not quite as cottony soft, I'm not sure I could have told them apart with my eyes closed. (Since I was driving, I decided to postpone that particular test.) My least favorite loaf was the Smart White, the one with the fiber equivalent of (but not the actual fiber from) 100 percent whole wheat. After an initial impression of sweetness, I registered several distinctly off flavors, probably from the cottonseed, wood pulp, and other nonwheat fibers and the minerals added to it—all the fibrous and rocky "garbage" that Hostess had baked into it.

After a while, all the neo–Wonder Breads began to seem the same, and less like bread than nutrient delivery systems. Yet it isn't at all clear that such a reductive approach to nutrition—in which wheat seeds are broken down into their component parts and then reassembled along with other processed plant parts, some minerals, an additive or two derived from petroleum, and a ton of yeast to loft the whole deal—actually yields a healthy or even a healthier loaf of bread. These breads were really nutritional conceits, clever ways to work the words "whole grain" or "whole wheat" onto a package, now that those magic words constitute an implied health claim. But the idea of whole grain in these products clearly counted for more than the reality, which Hostess treated as something to overcome, disguise, or merely allude to. These were notional breads, and eventually they turned to cotton in my mouth. I was reminded of Richard Bourdon's

saliva test for good bread: Did a wad of it make your mouth water?
These three flunked.

◉

I had heard from Chad that Dave Miller had once owned a bakery
called Wunder Brot, so when I showed up at the door to his bakery—
basically a suite of rooms attached to his house, which was tucked
into a lovely remote hillside in the Sierra Foothills, south and east of
Chico—I presented him with a couple of loaves of late-model Wonder Bread. He looked slightly horrified, but managed a smile. A slender man in his late forties with a trim goatee, Dave was dressed in a
crisp white pocket T-shirt and clogs. I wondered if this was the first
plastic-bagged loaf of sliced bread ever to cross his threshold.

Miller's Bake House is a one-man show. It was a Thursday, and
Dave was grinding wheat and mixing dough for his weekly bake the
next morning. He kept one eye on the mill, a stone wheel encased in
a handsomely crafted wooden cabinet made in Austria, and the other
on his Artofex mixer, an old-timey, pink-painted contraption from
Switzerland. A pair of steel arms moved lazily up and down through
the bowl of wet flour, convincingly simulating the action of human
hands kneading dough.

Dave Miller is an uncompromising baker, as fiercely devoted to
whole grains and wet doughs and natural leavens as Richard Bourdon.
(If not more so: Only one of his breads contains any white flour.) But
compared with his voluble, flamboyant mentor, Miller comes across
as very much the Protestant baker, spare with his pronouncements
and something of an ascetic. Though he used to own bakeries and
manage employees (including Chad Robertson), for the past seven
years he has stripped his vocation down to its Thoreauvian essentials:
one man, some sacks of wheat, a couple of machines, and an oven.

Miller's Bake House is almost completely off the grid: Solar panels power the mill and the cold room where he retards his loaves, and the Italian deck oven is fired with wood that he chops himself. I asked if the wood imparted flavor to the bread. "It's not about the flavor. It's that I would rather not be a party to wars for oil."

The afternoon I visited, Miller was agonizing over whether to add a pinch of ascorbic acid—often used to strengthen low-protein flours—to his Kamut dough. Dave disdained additives on principle, but the crop of Kamut (an ancient variety of durum wheat) that a farmer had grown for him had come in weak—low in protein—this year, and the loaves were somewhat depressed as a result. The ascorbic acid promised to help the dough hold a bit more air, but adding it meant veering ever so slightly from "the right path," as the Miller's Bake House Web site describes his approach. Short of landing at a bakery on Alpha Centauri, I could not have traveled farther from the Hostess plant, where ascorbic acid is one of the more natural ingredients in use. "I have met the bread monk," I jotted in my notebook.

Dave took me into the back room to see his mill. It was a tall wooden contraption with a hopper on top that held fifty pounds of wheat at a time, feeding it gradually through an aperture that opened onto the sandwich of revolving stones inside. Though "gradually" does not do justice to the glacial pace of this machine. The kernels of wheat entered the aperture virtually in single file, as if passing between a thumb and an index finger. To mill any faster risked overheating the stone, which in turn risked damaging the flour. In this fact, Dave explained, lies the origin of the phrase "nose to the grindstone": a scrupulous miller leans in frequently to smell his grindstone for signs of flour beginning to overheat. (So the saying does not signify hard work as much as attentiveness.) A wooden spout at the bottom of the mill emitted a gentle breeze of warm, tan flour that slowly accumulated in a white cloth bag. I leaned in close for a whiff. Freshly milled whole-grain flour is powerfully fragrant, redolent of hazelnuts and flowers. For the first time I appreciated what I'd read about the etymology of the word "flour"—that it is the flower, or best part, of the wheat seed. Indeed. White flour has little aroma to speak of; this flour smelled delicious.

That whiff of fresh flour delivered a little epiphany. Up to now, I had been more or less indifferent to whole wheat. I liked it okay, probably more than most, but I ate it mainly because it was better for me than white bread, not because it tasted better. So you might say that I, too, liked the idea of whole grain more than the actual experience, just like the bakers and food scientists at Hostess. Though I didn't mind the coarseness, or the density, even the best whole-grain breads usually tasted as though they were being stingy with their flavor, holding something back. I hadn't yet tried Dave's bread, but the fragrance of his flour made me think I had probably never really experienced the full potential of whole-grain wheat, something I now suddenly very much wanted to do.

Dave milled his own grain because that was the only way he could buy wheat directly from farmers and guarantee the freshness of his flour. "The moment the seed is opened up is the moment of its greatest potential. As soon as it's milled, it begins to oxidize, losing the energy that could be nourishing us. That's also the moment of maximum flavor before it begins to fade."

Dave's foremost concern as a baker has always been with health. His own "eureka moment" came in the early eighties at a bakery in Minneapolis, with a taste of a 100 percent whole-grain bread. "One bite of that bread and I could feel my whole body respond. It just felt so right." Extracting the full nutritional value from wheat dictates every step of his baking process, yet Dave sees no trade-off between health and flavor, and in fact believes that the flavor of bread is a good indicator of its nutritional quality. In this, grains are a little like fruit, the fragrant ripeness of which signifies they have arrived at their nutritional peak. But, unlike fruit, grains also need to be processed with care—properly fermented and baked—in order to achieve peak taste and nutrition. For Dave that means a wet dough to thoroughly cook the grain, a long, slow fermentation, and a thorough bake in a hot oven.

Dave invited me to spend the night so I could watch the whole twenty-four-hour process unfold from start to finish. When I dragged myself from bed the following morning at five, he had already been at it for a couple of hours, firing up the oven and shaping loaves that had risen in the walk-in cooler overnight. Dave's doughs were by far the wettest I'd seen (up to 104 percent hydration*), and he handled them as gently as newborns, turning them in their buckets even less frequently than Chad did. Dave was long accustomed to working by himself ("I like baking alone; it's such an intense sensory thing"), but by the second day he was willing to let me handle his babies, showing me how to shape the bâtards and pan breads. Some of these doughs were so wet that to keep them from sticking you dipped your hands in water rather than flour. It was monastically quiet in the bakery as we worked, still dark outside, and the smells were captivating: malty and floral and, as soon as Dave began feeding loaves into the oven, irresistible.

But Dave wouldn't let me taste any bread until it had properly cooled and "set," so I couldn't have a taste until I was already on the road home. The warm loaves filled the car with the aroma I had smelled in the mill room. Don't tell Dave, but I was able to hold off only as long as it took to steer my car out of his driveway.

The bread was a revelation. I felt as though I was tasting wheat for

---

*In so-called baker's math, every ingredient in a recipe is expressed as a percentage of the weight of the flour, which is always expressed as 100 percent. Thus 104 percent hydration means that the dough contains slightly more water by weight than flour—a lot.

the very first time. The flavor held nothing back; it was rich, nutty, completely obliging in its sweetness. The crumb was moist and glossy. I ate a whole loaf before I got to the highway.

But the bread was not perfect. There could have been much more contrast between crumb and crust, which wasn't crisp at all, and the loaves were broad and low-slung. "You're always fighting gravity with whole grain," Dave had said earlier that morning, as he withdrew from the oven a wooden peel laden with loaves that looked a tad depressed. "But I don't mind a dense loaf if it's moist." Dave had accepted the trade-off: flavor and nutrition for volume. A sacrifice of air.

Dave Miller's bread was delicious, but not everything I'd dreamed of in a whole-grain loaf. Yet what I tasted and smelled in his bakery made me determined to bake with whole grains from now on—to see if I couldn't get some of those flavors in my bread, but with a tougher crust and a lot more air. Baking white bread suddenly seemed boring. I'd had a glimpse, a taste, of what was possible, and it was so much more than I'd ever imagined. A good whole-grain loaf became my grail, and I spent the next few months baking 100 percent whole-wheat loaves one after another.

That first month, a great many worthy brown bricks came out of my oven, loaves decidedly more virtuous than tasty. The G-forces at work in my oven had never seemed so oppressive, as if I were suddenly baking on another, much larger planet. I struggled for weeks with sourness. The whole-grain flour seemed to overstimulate my sourdough culture, inspiring prodigious outpourings of acid from the bacteria while quickly tuckering out the yeasts. I wasn't sure if I should attribute the anemic oven spring I was experiencing to exhausted yeasts or to the sharp bran knives slashing my gluten to ribbons.

I was still using Chad Robertson's basic recipe, substituting whole-grain flour for white, and soon realized I needed to make some adjustments. I read that since bran softens as it absorbs water, those little knives could be somewhat dulled with a wetter dough and a longer rest before mixing. So I stepped up to a 90 percent hydration and extended the autolyse to an hour. The wetter mix seemed to soften the bran, yet left me with me a dough that proved trickier to shape and build tension into—yet another cause of lousy oven spring. Dave Miller's words—"You're always fighting gravity with whole grains"—rang in my ears after every one of those disappointing bakes. Yet I wasn't quite prepared to give up on air.

Even as I struggled, though, I began to suspect that the conventional view that there is an inevitable trade-off between whole grains and great bread—a view accepted by everyone from the food scientists at Hostess to any number of gifted artisanal bakers—might not necessarily be true. More likely, we'd come to regard the trade-off as inevitable simply because it was so much easier to bake good white bread than whole grain. From any bag of white flour and packet of yeast in the supermarket it was possible to bake a sweet and impressively airy loaf of bread. This was the whole point and promise of white flour and commercial yeast: They were standardized commodities that behaved in predictable ways. But try to make whole-grain bread in a system that has been organized around white flour—using reconstituted whole-grain flour, fast-acting yeasts, white-flour recipes, dry doughs, etc.—and the bread will reliably disappoint: earthbound, crumbling, stingy with flavor. Yet another advertisement for white bread.

To bake a truly great whole-grain loaf would take more than a good recipe. It would mean getting out from under the whole white-flour regime, as Dave Miller had done when he began working directly with farmers and milling their grain fresh. It would mean recognizing that whole-grain bread has a system of its own, or at least it once did, before the advent of the roller mill and commercial yeast and mechanized baking. That system was built around stone mills to grind wheat whole, access to fresh flour, natural leavens, tons of time, and a human culture, or body of knowledge, that understood how to manage the whole process and its numberless contingencies.

If this already seems like too much to hope for, I could think of more. Ideally, a whole-grain regimen would offer varieties of wheat that had been bred for something other than a giant super-white endosperm and a hard coat of bran. And, also ideally, this wheat would figure in a much shorter food chain, one where local mills bought directly from nearby farmers so that bakers could get flour that has been freshly milled from the most desirable varieties of wheat.

To view the problem this way is to despair of ever baking a truly great whole-grain bread. The white flour industrial complex so completely dominates the food landscape (including even the artisanal corner of that landscape) that to wish for anything substantially different seems, well, wishful and nostalgic. To bake the bread I wanted, I didn't just need a better recipe. I needed a whole different civilization.

But a couple of stray facts gave me just enough hope to keep on baking. The first came when I noticed that the price of Soft 100% Whole Wheat Wonder Bread at my local Safeway was $4.59—not cheap. How was it that Dave Miller could sell his incomparably more delicious and nourishing organic, freshly milled, long-fermented loaves at the farmers' market for $5.00, only 41 cents more than Hostess charged? Perhaps the industrial bread system might not be as indomitable as it appears, at least when it came to meeting the demand for whole-grain bread. In the middle of an economy organized around white flour, whole-grain flour and all the technology required to make it acceptable to the consumer is expensive. The second encouraging fact was that several of the most gifted bakers in the Bay Area, including Chad Robertson at Tartine, Steve Sullivan at Acme, Craig Ponsford, and Mike Zakowski, were at work developing new whole-grain breads, many of them 100 percent whole grain. So something was in the air—the first stirrings, perhaps, of a cultural revival. Even the newsletter of the Bread Bakers Guild of America, which for years had been openly hostile to whole grain, was beginning to question the white-flour orthodoxy and to shine a flattering light on bakers, like Ponsford, who had rejected it.

The last encouraging fact was scattered evidence that a local whole-grain economy might also be stirring here and there. New grain farmers and millers were popping up in New England and the Pacific Northwest and even in my own backyard, part of the national movement to supply a growing demand for local food. I talked to a wheat breeder in Washington State who was working to develop varieties better suited to whole-grain milling and baking. He mentioned that he had been in touch with new local grain projects all over the country.

And then I heard about a new enterprise called Community Grains, based near me in Oakland, that had started selling stone-ground whole-wheat flour grown in California. I didn't even know you could grow wheat in California. But it had apparently been an important crop in the nineteenth century, before the big irrigation projects, because it can be planted in the fall and then watered by the winter rains. Community Grains was selling wheat that was being grown by a group of farmers in the Sacramento Valley and milled in Woodland at a small company called Certified Foods.

As soon as I heard about Community Grains, I knew there was one more field trip in my baking education. As a baker of white bread, I had had no need to make the acquaintance of a miller, much less a wheat farmer. Indeed, that was the great virtue of the white-flour economy: a baker could focus on bread and pretty much ignore the long and largely invisible food chain that delivered the white powder to his door. But to bake a great, or even a decent, loaf of whole-grain bread, I needed to know a little more about wheat and milling. And unless I was going to buy my own mill, I needed a source of good, fresh whole-wheat flour. So I made plans to travel to Woodland, to meet my wheat.

I would not have guessed that Joe Vanderliet, the proprietor of Certified Foods and the miller for Community Grains, is in his eighties, he is so robust. Six feet three and unbent, he has a full head of gray hair, piercing blue eyes, and a sly sidelong twinkle about him. Joe grew up in the Netherlands, and recalls several hungry years as a boy during the war. He bears a trace of a Dutch accent, as well as a courtly Old World manner that leavens, slightly, his forceful personality. In the 1950s, Joe landed in Minnesota, and went to work as a grain buyer for Archer Daniels Midland. In the 1960s he worked for Montana Flour Mills Company, which was later absorbed by ConAgra during the consolidation of the milling industry during the sixties and seventies. Joe Vanderliet is very much a product of the white flour industrial complex.

But in the 1980s he had his own conversion experience, a story that he has by now milled to a high degree of refinement. A miller from Australia visited the plant he ran for Montana Flour Mills Company in Oakland, a high-tech mill of which Vanderliet could not have been more proud. "We had it all, a pneumatic system for moving the flour, state of the art everything. But this fellow looked me straight in the eye and said, 'Have you ever thought about the nutritional value of this white flour you're milling?'" Vanderliet hadn't, but from that moment, "I could never leave the question alone."

"Personally, you understand, I was doing very well. I was happy. I had the most beautiful mill in the world. I was an officer of the company. I had the credit cards and the Brooks Brothers suits. But no one in the industry ever talked about nutrition. We were throwing the most nutritious part of our product in the garbage! The mill run [the discarded bran and germ] was going to the feedlot.

"I came home at night to my wife and said, 'What in God's name are we selling? We are not selling nutrition. Just endosperm. If you could only see what we're doing to the wheat. We're selling garbage! This has got to stop.'

"Well, that was thirty years ago. I've been milling whole grains ever since."

In 1992, Vanderliet gave up his comfortable perch in the milling industry to launch a start-up that would focus exclusively on whole grains. Today, Certified Foods operates one of the larger whole-grain mills in the country, in a sprawling warehouse building alongside the railroad tracks in Woodland. It took months of journalistic courtship before he would consent to let me visit; in fact, Certified's mill proved harder to get into than the Wonder Bread factory. But eventually Joe relented, on the condition I agree to some "ground rules," which he never actually specified. Vanderliet is extremely secretive about his milling methods and worried, or at least professed to be, that I would somehow spill the proprietary beans to the competition.

He need not have worried. Only another miller could have toured his plant and understood the first thing about what was going on deep inside all those freshly painted tan steel contraptions. Since the millstones and rollers are encased in steel and the flour moves between them in sealed pneumatic tubes, just about every step in the milling process takes place out of sight. What seemed distinctive about Vanderliet's operation is that the grain went through a multistep milling process that partakes of both traditional and modern technologies. So, after being milled whole on stone, the grain is passed through a roller mill and a hammer mill. (This is a chamber in which the grain is thrown against a rough surface to further refine it.) These extra steps allow Certified to produce a more finely granulated whole-grain flour than a stone mill alone could produce without overheating it. The extra steps may also increase the shelf life of the flour by sealing the volatile germ within a coat of starch—but this is only a theory. As we walked through the plant, Vanderliet explained over the pounding din what was in his view the most important feature of his milling: "We keep the whole seed intact throughout the entire process.

"You cannot fractionate the seed without ruining the flour. As soon as you separate the bran from the germ, that's it, it's all over: The germ will turn rancid. Its nutrition will be lost. What you have to understand—write this down!—is that nature made a perfect package when it made the seed, all the parts working together in a living system. So, for example, there are antioxidant compounds in the bran that protect the oils in the germ from oxidizing. But only if they are kept together! Once you break apart the seed, you can never put Humpty Dumpty back together again." He pointed at my notebook. "Write that down."

This was the key to good whole-grain flour. And this, according to Vanderliet, is the reason that the big mills can never produce it, since their roller mills separate the seed into its component parts at the first break. Yet as soon as the germ is separated from its antioxidant protector, it begins to deteriorate. That's why, according to Vanderliet, most big millers routinely leave out the germ when they reconstitute whole-grain flours. When I asked for proof of this claim—which if true means that most of what is sold as whole wheat is actually nothing of the kind—he brought me into the mill's control room to meet

Roger Bane, his chief engineer. Joe hired Roger away from General Mills, which until recently operated a mill in Vallejo. Roger confirmed Vanderliet's claim: "The germ is too troublesome to deal with, so we just got rid of it." That troublesome germ may constitute only a tiny fraction of the wheat seed, but happens to contain a whole suite of valuable nutrients—omega-3s, vitamin E, folic acid, and more—along with most of the flavor and aroma of wheat. (When I contacted General Mills for comment, I received an unsigned e-mail stating that "by law, whole wheat flour must contain all three parts of the wheat berry" and that while "it is true that the germ portion shortens the shelf life of the flour . . . it must be included, as it is in ours.")

I left Certified Foods with two sacks of flour and some new ideas about how to bake a better loaf of whole-grain bread. For Vanderliet, everything came back to the seed—that "perfect package." To mill good whole-grain flour, the miller had to understand what was going on in that package, not just the parts—the germ, bran, and endosperm—but the intricate relationship between them, and the biological system at work. The function of that system was to protect the embryo of a new wheat plant until the time came for it to germinate, and then to supply all the nutrients the new plant needed to get its start in life. This much is obvious, but the implications for milling, and in turn for baking bread, are not.

During my tour I had asked Joe if he wetted, or tempered, his grain before milling it, something commercial mills routinely do in order to loosen the bran coat so that it will more easily slip off the seed. "Never!" he barked. Wetting the seed, he explained, ruins whole-grain flour. As soon as the bran coat absorbs water, the seed receives a signal to germinate, setting off a cascade of chemical events in the germ and bran that would destabilize any flour that still contained them. (Since the bran and germ are removed when milling white flour, tempering in that case is not a problem.) Enzymes are activated. Some of them begin to break open the polymers of starch and protein, while others liberate the sequestered minerals—all to nourish the nascent plant. The miller's job is to keep the seed in dormant mode rather than throw it into germination mode.

"So, to mill whole-grain flour well," I had said to Joe, "you really have to be able to think like a seed, don't you?" He smiled.

"You're a very good student."

That's when it dawned on me: The same holds true for the baker. He, too, needs to think like a seed in order to bake a whole-grain loaf full of flavor and air. Except that his seed thoughts are a little different from the miller's. The baker *wants* to set off that cascade of chemical events. He wants the amylase enzymes to break up those tasteless balls of starch, creating simple sugars to flavor his bread and feed his hungry yeasts. (The baker needs to think like yeast and bacteria, too, which is a lot of thinking.) The baker wants the proteases to begin breaking the wheat proteins into amino acids and the phytase to unlock the minerals, not to nourish the plant but to nourish us. And water was the key.

I had read about techniques for "presoaking" flours—part of the traditional culture of whole-grain baking that we have lost—and now I understood the logic behind them: to trick the crushed seed into thinking it was time to germinate. So I embarked on a set of experiments to kick-start the enzymatic activity in my dough even before fermentation got under way. I began mixing my flour and water in the evening, at the same time I started my leaven. Not until the next morning, however, would I introduce the one to the other. By the time the sourdough culture began to work on the presoaked flour, it would find all the nutrients it could want: plenty of sugars, amino acids, and minerals. This was a fact I could taste: The flour sweetened dramatically overnight. And the results out of the oven were encouraging. I started getting loaves that were generous with their flavors, had crispier and more handsome crusts (probably because more sugars and amino acids were available for browning reactions), and markedly more air.

But not quite as much air as I hoped for, not yet. The bran was still undermining the gluten, either by puncturing the gas bubbles or by weighing them down, giving me a too-tight crumb. I hit on a slightly wacky idea: I would remove the bran from the inside of the bread and put it on the outside, where it could do no damage to the gluten. So, before mixing my flour and water, I sifted the chunkiest bran out of the flour, maybe 10 percent of the total volume.

In effect, I was making white (or whitish) flour circa 1850, pre–roller mill, the kind of flour in the painting by Émile Friant that had inspired Chad Robertson. It still had the germ, but only those particles of bran small enough to slip through an ordinary sieve. However, I reserved the sifted bran in a bowl, and after shaping the loaves, I rolled them in the stuff, making sure that every last shard of bran was taken up by the wet skin of the dough.

It worked: The trick allowed me to bake an airy and delicious loaf with a toasty, particulate crust—all the while preserving my claim to a "100 percent whole-grain" bread. Does this seem like cheating? I don't think so: Every last bit of the whole grain was somewhere in this triumphantly voluminous loaf. I felt like I had broken whole grain's Gordian knot.

Though on reflection I seriously doubt this solution is original with me. In the age-old quest to bake the airiest possible loaf from whole-grain flour, a great many other bakers would surely have hit on the same trick. Like presoaking flours, it is too good an adaptation not to have been tried before. In all likelihood, "my" technique or one like it is part of the traditional culture of whole-grain baking that got crushed by the roller mills late in the nineteenth century.

In the weeks and months since, I've loosened up considerably in my baking. I still mostly use whole-grain flours, but I no longer obsess about percentages or purity. I don't always roll my loaves in bran— sometimes I use it in the garden instead, to thwart slugs and snails. I've also found a commercial version of the kind of flour I was making by sifting whole grains. Called "high extraction" flours, these are milled whole and then partially sifted. This strikes me as a reasonable compromise between 100 percent whole-grain and white flour, between nutrition and aesthetics. (After all, even 100-percent whole-grain flour is 75-percent endosperm.) But even when I bake with these flours, I add a variety of other whole grains to deepen and complicate the bread's flavor: some pumpernickel that I got from Joe Vanderliet, some purple rye that Chad Robertson gave me, even lately some Kernza, an experimental flour milled (whole) from a new strain of perennial grain being developed by the Land Institute in Salina, Kansas. A perennial wheat field that could be mowed like a lawn rather than planted each year from seed would have tremendous benefits for both the land and the farmer, but it is probably still some ways off. Kernza has an interesting flavor but, as yet, not enough gluten to raise a loaf of bread on its own.

Everything that I've learned about wheat and milling, fermentation and baking has definitely complicated my understanding of what "good bread" is, but that hasn't dimmed my ardor for the stuff. When I buy whole-grain bread I look for words like "stone milled" and "whole grain"* and I check the ingredients to make sure whole grain is listed first. And, white or brown, I look for breads that have been

---

*Not that these terms are ironclad guarantees: "Stone milled" is not a government-backed claim, and whole grain, if it's not stone milled, may or may not contain the germ.

fermented with a sourdough culture; the word "levain" indicates as much. And I stay away from any bread containing any ingredient that isn't the name of a grain or salt.

But I try to bake my own when I can, and I can see that I've gotten fairly improvisational in my baking. I never look at recipes anymore. Instead, I look at dough, and feel it, taste it, and smell it, almost continuously. I also check in every morning with my starter, gauging by eye and nose its happiness before feeding it a few tablespoons of fresh flour and water. When I started baking a few months ago, I could never have imagined the work would become such an intuitive and sensory process—or such an obsession—but there it is. Actually, baking has begun to feel a lot like gardening, a pastime, or practice, I've been working at much longer.

In my experience, gardening successfully depends on two different but related faculties, both highly relevant to baking. The first is the green thumb's ability to notice and absorb everything going on in his garden, from the precise tint of the leaves to the aroma of the soil. The data of your senses have more to tell you about the work than anything you can read in a book. The second is the green thumb's knack for imagining what his plants and soil want in order to be maximally happy and thrive. Same with baking bread: It helps to be able to think like a grass seed and, at the same time, like the community of yeasts and bacteria living in your sourdough culture. Control you can just forget about: There are too many interests and variables in play. (The dream of control is seductive, but it leads straight to monoculture in the field and fortified white bread in the supermarket.) Behind a great loaf of bread is a deft orchestration, not only of time and temperature, but also of a great many diverse species and interests, our own—for something nourishing and delicious to eat— included. I am no maestro, no white thumb yet, but my bread is getting tastier, and airier, all the time.

III.

CODA: MEET YOUR WHEAT

The morning before I toured the mill in Woodland, I paid a visit to one of the growers that supply wheat to Community Grains. The Rominger family plants a dozen or so different crops, and runs sheep, on seven thousand acres of rich, dark bottomland a few miles down the road from Woodland, near the town of Winters. They use wheat as a rotational crop, planting it in November, before the winter rains, and harvesting it in the scorching heat of July.

I had never set foot in a wheat field before. Yet the sight of one is so iconic that the landscape feels immediately familiar, weirdly so. Standing in a field of wheat, it is impossible not to think about Flemish painters like Brueghel or van Ruisdael, or van Gogh. The wheat itself has changed—modern breeders have made the plant shorter in stature and its seed head fatter—but from a distance the overwhelming impression of ripe golden bounty, of nature's grace and sufficiency, remains indelible. The Romingers' wheat crop was still a few weeks away from harvest, almost but yet not completely dried to gold in the sun. If you looked closely at the leaves, there were still streaks of grassy green.

I picked a stalk of wheat. A wooden stake planted on the edge of the field said it was a variety called Red Wing. This, it would turn out, was the variety in the sack of flour I got from Joe Vanderliet. Up close, a wheat plant looks like a particularly buff and muscular grass, handsome, but perhaps just a little over the top, like a bodybuilder. The spike formed an intricate ladder of seeds arranged around the stem in a stepped, herringbone pattern, each with its own elegant golden needle reaching for the sky. I rubbed the seed head between my palms. The light jacket of chaff came free from the kernels and blew away, leaving a small handful of seeds. I bit into one of the fresh kernels. It was still slightly soft, and though not quite ripe it already tasted wheaty and sweet. The complexities and possibilities contained within this inconspicuous speck, this seed, were hard to imagine, but there they were: everything needed to produce a wheat plant. And much more than that. With enough of these seeds, and the knowledge of how to process them into bread, you had most of what is needed to grow a person. Or for that matter a civilization.

From where I stood, the field stretched west to the bluish ridge of the Coast Range, a shimmering blond avenue of lawn. If you stand in a wheat field at this time of year, a few weeks from harvest, it's not hard to imagine you're looking at something out of mythology: all this golden sunlight brought down to earth, captured in kernels of gold, and rendered fit for mortals to eat. But of course this is no myth at all, just the plain miraculous fact.

PART IV

EARTH

FERMENTATION'S COLD FIRE

"God made yeast, as well as dough, and loves
fermentation just as dearly as he loves
vegetation."

—*Ralph Waldo Emerson*

"The taste for partial spoilage can become a
passion, an embrace of the earthy side of life
that expresses itself best in paradoxes."

—*Harold McGee*

"No poems can please long or live that are
written by water drinkers."

—*Horace*

FERMENT I.

VEGETABLE

Consider, just for a moment, the everyday proximity of death. No, not the swerve of the oncoming car or the bomb in the baby carriage. I'm thinking more of the bloom of yeast on the ripe fruit, patiently waiting for a breach in its skin so that it might invade and decompose its sweet flesh. Or the lactobacillus loitering on the cabbage leaf for the same purpose. We, too, carry around invisible microbial shadows: the Brevibacterium breeding in the saline damp between our toes, or the enterococci lurking in the coiled dark of the intestine. Everything that lives, it seems, must play host to the germ of its own dissolution. Whether a fungus or a bacterium, these invisibles come wielding precisely the right kit of enzymes to take apart, molecule by molecule, life's most intricate structures, reducing them, ourselves included, to simple foods for themselves and other living and incipient beings.

Plants stave off decomposition with sturdy cell walls constructed of cellulose or lignin, carbohydrates too complex for most microbes to penetrate. We humans rely on our various membranes: our skin, of course, and then an even larger interior membrane made up of epithelial cells that, at least when we are well, can hold most of the bugs at bay. This second, gastrointestinal skin lines our digestive tract and is painted with a protective layer of mucus made from carbohydrate-rich glycoproteins that the microbial mob cannot easily breach. If you could spread out the lining of just the small intestine, it would completely cover a tennis court. These thin, tenuous membranes are all that stand between us and the microbes' ultimate objective: to ferment us.

Not terribly appetizing, I know, especially in a book about food. You probably don't want to identify too closely with the cabbage when making sauerkraut, but sometimes you can't help it. Here, deliciousness is the by-product of decay, as the funky scent will occasionally remind us. As one of the primary processes by which nature breaks down living things so that their energies and atoms might be reused by other living things, fermentation puts us in touch with the ever-present tug, in life, of death.

◉

Now I am terrified at the Earth, it is that calm and patient,
It grows such sweet things out of such corruptions,
It turns harmless and stainless on its axis, with such endless
    successions of diseas'd corpses . . .
It gives such divine materials to men, and accepts such leavings from
    them at last.

It is the earth—the earth as understood here by Walt Whitman in "This Compost"—that breeds and shadows every fermentation. Earth into grapevines into wine, barley seeds into beer, cabbage into kraut or kimchi, milk into cheese (or yogurt or kefir), soybeans into miso (or soy sauce or natto or tempeh), rice into sake, pig into prosciutto, vegetable into pickle: All these transformations depend on the fermenter's careful management of rot, on taking the decomposition of those seeds and fruits and fleshes just so far and no further. For, left to its own devices, the stain of corruption would continue and dilate and deepen until the life form in question—the "fermentation substrate"—had been broken down completely and returned to earth, an increment of humus. Most of our fermentations are instances of rot interrupted, dust-to-dust delayed. And in fact some of the microbes that do this work for us, the bacilli and fungi, are denizens of the soil, on temporary loan to the aboveground world. They splash onto leaves, find their way into milk, drift onto seeds and flesh, but ultimately they are on a mission from the soil, venturing out into the macrocosm—the visible world of plants and animals we inhabit—to scavenge food for the microbial wilderness beneath our feet.

All cooking is transformation and, rightly viewed, miraculous, but fermentation has always struck people as particularly mysterious. For one thing, the transformations are so dramatic: fruit juice into wine?!—a liquid with the power to change minds? For another, it has only been 155 years since Louis Pasteur figured out what was actually going on in a barrel of crushed grapes when it starts to seethe. To ferment is to "boil," people would say confidently ("to boil" is what the word "ferment" means), but they could not begin to say how the process started or why this particular boil wasn't hot to the touch. Most other kinds of cooking rely on outside energy—the application of heat, mainly—to transform foodstuffs; the laws of physics and chemistry rule the process, which operates on the only formerly alive.

Fermentation is different. In fermentation the laws of biology have primary jurisdiction and are required to explain how a ferment generates its own energy from within. It not only seems alive, it is alive. And most of this living takes place at a scale inaccessible to us without a microscope. No wonder so many cultures have had their

fermentation gods—how else to explain this cold fire that can cook
so many marvelous things?

◉

Now, any true fermento would say that, by dwelling on the links
between fermentation and death, I'm being way too hard on these
microbes, most of which they count as benign friends and partners.
I'm trapped in a hygienic, Pasteurian perspective, they would say, in
which the microbial world is regarded foremost as a mortal threat.
Actually, Louis Pasteur himself held a more nuanced view of the microbes he discovered, but his legacy is a century-long war on bacteria,
a war in which most of us have volunteered or been enlisted. We
deploy our antibiotics and hand sanitizers and deodorants and boiling water and "pasteurization" and federal regulations to hold off the
molds and bacteria and so, we hope, hold off disease and death.

I grew up on that field of battle. My mother instilled a deep fear of
molds, trichinosis, botulism, and countless other unnamed germs
possibly lurking in our food. She maintained an under-the-sink and
in-the-medicine-cabinet antimicrobial arsenal stocked with Lysol,
Clorox, Listerine, and Bactine. A touch of white on a wedge of cheese
was enough to condemn it. The slightest dent in a can of food con-
signed it to the trash, no matter that the dent came from being
dropped on the floor. You never know; could be botulism; better safe
than sorry.

The molds and bacteria now have a small but growing tribe of
human defenders. These post-Pasteurians,* as they sometimes call
themselves, form one of the more curious subcultures in America. It

---

*I first encountered the term in a fascinating article on the debate over raw-milk cheeses by MIT
anthropologist Heather Paxson: "Post-Pasteurian Cultures: The Microbiopolitics of Raw-Milk
Cheese in the United States," *Cultural Anthropology* 23 No. 1 (2008): 15–47.

is sometimes called the fermentation underground, a word that seems fitting, given the fierceness of their devotion to microbes and their willingness to break the law to consume them. These are people who will fight for the right to drink unpasteurized milk and eat unpasteurized cheeses, who ferment all manner of foods and beverages using "wild cultures" exclusively, and who generally believe the time has come for humanity to renegotiate the terms of its relationship with "the microcosmos"—the biologist Lynn Margulis's term for the unseen universe of microbes all around and within us. Much more than a way to prepare and preserve food, fermentation for these people becomes a political and ecological act, a way to engage with the bacteria and fungi, honor our coevolutionary interdependence, and get over our self-destructive germophobia. It seems there's a lot more going on in a crock of homemade sauerkraut than a handful of lactobacilli species diligently fermenting the sugars in a cabbage; at stake in that crock is our whole relationship to nature.

The man who first taught me how to make sauerkraut is a leader of this underground and possibly the most famous fermento in America. Sandor Katz is the Johnny Appleseed of fermentation, a fiftyish writer, advocate, and itinerant teacher with a suitably retro appearance. Six feet tall and loose limbed, he has electrified muttonchops that drift together and link chops above his lips to form a bushy mustache that would not have been out of place in nineteenth-century America; Katz could easily pass for a Civil War veteran. Yet Katz grew up on the Upper West Side of Manhattan, eating sour dills from Zabar's, studied history at Brown, and learned the arts of fermentation while living on "a fairy commune" in rural Tennessee; he had to figure out something to do with all the surplus produce from the garden. Katz has been HIV-positive since 1991, and partly credits a diet rich in "live culture" foods—i.e., ones teeming with living bacteria—for his continued vigor and good health.

Since his first book, Wild Fermentation, was published in 2003, Katz has traveled the country teaching people how to make kraut and kimchi, pickled vegetables of every kind, mead and beer and wine, miso, natto, tempeh, kvass, smreka, sourdough bread, ogi, kefir, cheese, yogurt, labneh, tej, shrub, kishk, and dozens of other obscure fermentations I had never heard of. But, like John Chapman, whose offer of apple trees was really just a way to get his foot in the door so that he might expound his Swedenborgian gospel, Sandor Katz's sauerkraut teachings open onto an evangelism, too—a microbial gospel. Both characters would have us turn our attention to an invisible realm, both plied their message along a frontier, and both bid us to see the natural world around us in a striking new light.

But first the kraut. I caught up with Sandor at a health-food store in Alameda, California, where he was conducting a workshop. He was in town on a two-week tour of the Bay Area, offering classes, visiting pickle makers, participating in panels and "culture swaps" and "skill shares," leading a bicycle tour–cum–tasting of home brews in the East Bay (only a few minor accidents were reported), and giving the keynote address at the third annual Fermentation Festival up in Freestone. (About which more later.) Here in Alameda, on a weekday afternoon, twenty aspiring fermenters had gathered with their notebooks around the café tables in the store's sunny window to watch Sandor make sauerkraut and expound on "cultural revival."

"So really there's not much to it. Chop or grate the cabbage, fine or rough, however you like it. Chopper's choice, I always say." I was immediately struck by Sandor's anticharismatic mode of address. He is utterly unpretentious, refusing to mystify his expertise in any way. If anything, he makes what he does sound rather ho-hum. Sandor also refuses to be categorical about anything. His answer to every other question is "Well, it is and it isn't," or "Yes and no," or "It really depends," or "Every fermentation is different." His shrug gets a good workout, too.

I came to see that his diffidence reflects both a practical and a philosophical stance. There is no "right" way to ferment anything, no hard and fast rules. And, given how little we understand about the microbial world, one where bacteria can trade genes and their exact identities are often up for grabs, it would be hubris to pretend to certainty. As I realized when I was learning to bake bread, for a human to have a good working relationship with bacteria and fungi, it helps to possess a healthy degree of negative capability. These are cultures you can nudge, perhaps even manage, but never entirely control, or even comprehend. "Nature imperfectly mastered," a phrase I heard from a cheese maker, stands as a pretty good definition of this work, which has much in common with gardening. Every ferment retains a certain element of unknowable wildness.

While Sandor walked us through the nuts and bolts of pickling—a term serious fermenters apply to all vegetable ferments, not just cucumbers—he occasionally wandered off the how-to trail, saunter-ing into the political, ecological, and philosophical implications of fermentation. He regards his work as a form of "cultural revival"—by which he has in mind both meanings of the word "culture," the mi-crobial and the human. The revival of these food cultures depends on reviving the microbial cultures that create them, and the reverse is true as well. The word "ferment," too, had a double meaning: "When people get excited about ideas, they get bubbly. I want to leave you with thoughts of social and political ferment, too." The DIY skills he was imparting held within them an implicit politics. They would help people take back control of their diet from the corporations, whose "dead food" was damaging our health and "homogenizing" our experience. Mastery of the fermentation arts could also help us break the dependency of consumerism, rebuild local food systems (since fermented foods allow us to eat locally all year long), and rediscover the "pleasures and wonders of transformation."

"As a culture we need to rehabilitate the image of bacteria. They are our ancestors and our allies. Did you know you have more bacterial cells in your body than human cells? By a factor of ten! Most of the DNA we're carrying around is microbial DNA, not human. Which raises an interesting question: Who exactly are we?" Katz suggested that a visitor from another planet would be forced to conclude who we are is a superorganism, a symbiotic community of several hundred species, with Homo sapiens serving as unwitting front man and ambulatory device. "We need them and they need us."

Okay, but what about microbial disease? "To declare war on ninety-nine percent of bacteria when less than one percent of them threaten our health makes no sense. Many of the bacteria we're killing are our protectors." In fact, the twentieth-century war on bacteria—with its profligate use of antibiotics, and routine sterilization of food—has undermined our health by wrecking the ecology of our gut. "For the first time in human history, it has become important to consciously replenish our microflora." Hence the urgency of cultural revival. And it all begins with sauerkraut, the "gateway ferment" he had come here to empower us to make ourselves.

In modern civilization's war on bacteria, Sandor Katz is a conscientious objector—a pacifist. He has a remarkably relaxed attitude toward all microbes, the ones you want in your food as well as the ones you don't. He's notably relaxed about sanitation, too. "I clean my bowls, crocks, and utensils with soapy water, but you really don't need to sterilize them. These practices all developed in a nonsterile world, after all. The lactic acid will take care of it."

He explained how this worked. The bacteria responsible for the fermentation were wild strains of lactic acid bacteria* already present on the raw vegetables, including Leuconostoc mesenteroides, Lactobacillus brevis, and Lactobacillus plantarum. These bugs are halophilic (salt-tolerant) anaerobes, so thrive in the airless saline niche the pickler has created for them in the brine. They get right to work eating the sugars in the vegetables, multiplying furiously, and releasing copious amounts of lactic acid—which they produce for the purpose of poisoning their competitors.

Katz likened a sauerkraut to a forest ecosystem, in which one type of bacteria succeeds another, each species transforming the environment in such a way as to prepare the ground for the next. In a vegetable ferment, each succeeding species is more acid tolerant than the last, until the environment arrives at a climax stage dominated by L. plantarum—the great acid-loving oak of the pickle ecosystem. All that lactic acid gives the ferment its tang as well as its keeping qualities, since few other microbes can survive in such a low pH environment. The idea that the safety of a food is guaranteed by the bacteria still alive in it is a hard one for us Pasteurians to stomach. I seriously doubted I could ever sell it to my mother.

Sandor emphasized that oxygen is the enemy of a vegetable ferment, but should the uppermost layer of cabbage begin to rot, it is no cause for alarm. Though it should be removed, he advised, lest the molds send their filaments down into the kraut and reduce it to mush with their pectin- and cellulose-destroying enzymes. Katz described digging "perfectly good" sauerkraut out from under a layer of moldy

---

*Lactobacillus is a genus of common bacteria that convert sugars—including lactose—into lactic acid. A "lactofermentation" is fermentation conducted primarily by this type of bacteria.

slime, and "off odors" that sometimes developed during the course of fermentation, but these were nothing to get upset about. But what if things in there got seriously funky? someone wanted to know. Began to smell like a dead animal, say? Sandor shrugged. "You have to trust your senses." As he passed around little plastic cups filled with a radish kraut he had kept in a barrel in his basement since the previous summer, I thought about my mother, vigilantly tossing out her dented cans on suspicion of botulism. The strong, just-this-side-of-funky smell of Sandor's radish kraut wafted through the store. But the kraut tasted good: still crunchy, with a bracing sour tang.

Before there were cans, before there were freezers and refrigerators, fermentation was the main way people preserved food from spoiling. The very earliest fermentations were done in pits dug into the earth, lined with leaves, and filled with various foodstuffs: vegetables, meat, fish, grain, tubers, fruits, whatever. The earth kept the temperature low and steady and perhaps also contributed some helpful microbes. Under these conditions a lactofermentation (that is, a fermentation conducted by lactobacilli) would commence within days, and eventually produce enough lactic acid to preserve the food for months, sometimes even years. In the 1980s an abandoned fermentation pit estimated to be three hundred years old was discovered in Fiji. The breadfruit in it had been reduced to a sour mush, but it was reported to be "still in edible condition." (You first.)

Pit fermentation is still practiced here and there around the world. I've seen whole cabbages fermenting in dirt trenches in China, a practice also common in certain parts of Austria and Poland. The Inuit still bury fish in the Arctic tundra, and in the South Pacific, starchy root vegetables like cassava and taro are buried in pits lined with banana leaves. In Iceland not long ago, I had the dubious privilege of tasting hákarl: shark that has been buried underground for several months, until it develops the texture and blinding ammonia stink of an exceptionally strong cheese. What began as a practical necessity—to get through the winter without starving—has become a cherished delicacy, at least among Icelanders. Whenever I read that "rotten" is a culturally constructed concept, as anthropologists tell us, I think back on my hákarl and nod in assent.

Nowadays, pit fermentation strikes most of us as primitive, strange, and unsanitary, yet we think nothing of aging cheeses underground, in caves, which is not so very different. And how different is a pit fermentation, really, from fermenting food in a crock? "Earthenware," as it's called, is really just earth once removed, cleaner and more portable perhaps, but otherwise the same basic idea. Even today, Koreans bury their child-sized crocks of kimchi in the backyard, in order to maintain the even, cool conditions that the lactobacilli prefer. The earthenware crock is a good reminder that *every* ferment is food and drink stolen, or borrowed, from the earth, by temporarily diverting its microbial-gravitational pull to our own ends. Everyone knows who stole the power of fire from the gods for the benefit of humankind, but who is the Prometheus of pickling? If mythology lacks for one, it is only because fermenting a heap of vegetables or grain seems a less heroic mode of engaging with nature than putting a large animal onto a fire. (There's much less to look at, too.) But the argument can be made (and has been, by Sandor Katz, among others) that humankind's mastery of fermentation rivals the control of fire in its importance to our success as a species.

If there is a culture that does not practice some fermentation of food or drink, anthropologists have yet to discover it. Fermentation would appear to be a cultural universal, and remains one of the most important ways that food is processed. Even today, as much as a third of the food in the world's diet is produced in a process involving fermentation. Many of these foods and drinks happen to be among the most cherished, though in many cases the role of fermentation in creating them is not widely understood. But coffee, chocolate, vanilla, bread, cheese, wine and beer, yogurt, ketchup and most other condiments, vinegar, soy sauce, miso, certain teas, corned beef and pastrami, prosciutto and salami—all depend on fermentation.

Basically, it's all the really good stuff.

I suspect people in other cultures feel much the same way about their fermented foods, rotten shark included. Fermented foods are typically both strongly flavored and strongly prized in their cultures. This suggests that there may be a microbiology of desire at work in these foods, the bacteria and fungi having been selected over time for their ability to produce the flavors people find most compelling. Put another way, the microbes that could induce us to care for their cultures, as in a long-maintained sourdough starter or cheese culture, were the ones that prospered and survived. They travel with us through history, in a dance of biocultural symbiosis. As with L. *sanfranciscensis*, the bacteria found exclusively in sourdough cultures, some of the microbial strains found in fermented foods appear to live nowhere else—those foods have become their exclusive ecological niche. The microbes depend for their survival on a continuing human desire for the flavors they produce—one kind of culture upholding the other.

Ten years ago, a retired Cornell microbiologist and fermentation expert by the name of K. H. Steinkraus conducted a global survey of fermented food products, organized by type. Here is a very small sample of what he found:

LACTIC-ACID FERMENTS: sauerkraut, olives, pickled vegetables, Chinese hum choy, Malaysian tempoyak, Korean kimchi, Russian kefir, Indian dahi, Middle Eastern yogurts, Egyptian laban rayeb and laban zeer, Malaysian tairu, Western cheeses, Egyptian kishk, Greek trahanas and Turkish tarhanas, Mexican pozole, Ghanaian kenkey, Nigerian gari, Philippine balao balao and burong dalag, sourdough bread, Sri Lankan hoppers, Indian idli, dhokla, and khaman, Ethiopian injera, Sudanese kisra, Philippine puto, Western sausages, and Thai nham.

ALKALINE FERMENTS: Nigerian dawadawa, Ivory Coast soumbara, African iru, ogiri, Indian kenima, Japanese natto, Thai thua nao . . .

On and on it goes, through the savory amino-acid ferments (soy sauce, fish sauce, ketchup); the fermented vegetable proteins (tempeh and ontjom); the acetic-acid ferments (vinegar, kombucha, nata de coco); and of course the numberless alcoholic ferments practiced in almost every culture, including South American Indian chicha, Egyptian bouza, Ethiopian tej, Kenyan busaa, Chinese lao-chao, and Japanese rice wine. To read Steinkraus's vast exotic catalog is to begin to appreciate the deep links between human and microbial cultural diversity, and how through history each has fed and so sustained the other. To read him is also to worry about the survival of this biocultural diversity, since the industrialization of the world's food strongly favors both homogenization and sterilization.

Important as fermentation has been to human culture, we can't take credit for inventing it. It is, like fire, a natural process, nature's primary way of breaking down organic matter and recycling energy. Without it, as Steinkraus points out, "the earth would be a gigantic, permanent waste dump"—the dead would pile up and there would be no food for the living. Humans are also not the only animal that has learned to exploit fermentation for its own purposes: Think of the squirrel burying acorns (a kind of pit fermentation) or the bird souring seeds in its craw. Some animals also enjoy one of the most important by-products of fermentation: alcohol. And though few animals can be said to actually make alcohol (though it's been reported that monkeys in eastern China will hoard flowers and fruits and patiently wait days for the cocktail to ferment before imbibing), some have it prepared for them by plants. The pen-tailed tree shrew (Ptilocercus lowii) of Malaysia enjoys a daily nip, drinking from a reservoir of alcohol prepared for its enjoyment by the bertram palm (Eugeissona tristis) in "specialized flower buds that harbor a fermenting yeast community." The palm serves wine to the shrew that, in exchange for this kindness, pollinates the palm in the course of his barhopping through the jungle. Plant, animal, and yeast all benefit from this clever coevolutionary arrangement.

As the example of alcohol suggests, the uses of fermentation extend well beyond preservation, though it seems likely that preservation was humanity's original impetus for mastering the process. (Alcohol—a strong antiseptic—is itself an important preservative.) Archaeologists believe that, until there were reliable methods to preserve food, humanity could not have moved from hunting and gathering to a more settled, agricultural pattern of life. Fermentation (along with other preservation techniques, such as salting, smoking, and drying) provided a critical measure of food security, allowing agriculturists to survive the long months between harvests and to withstand the inevitable crop failures. Though, as I would discover when I started to brew beer (because brewers can always be counted on to mention it), there is a school of archaeological thought that contends that the reason humanity turned to agriculture was to secure a more reliable supply of alcohol, not food. Either way, the mastery of fermentation and the advent of agriculture (and civilization in turn) appear to go hand in hand.

As so often happens, the original purpose of an invention or adaptation doesn't turn out to be the ultimate or even highest use to which it is put. Humans soon recognized that fermenting various foodstuffs did a lot more than extend their shelf life, important as that was. Fermenting the juices of fruit not only sterilized the beverage, but also turned it into a powerful intoxicant. A great many foodstuffs become significantly more nutritious after fermentation. In some cases, the process creates entirely new nutrients—several B vitamins are synthesized in the fermentation of beer, soy sauce, and various grains. Natto, the slimy odiferous ferment of soybeans beloved by the Japanese, produces a unique therapeutic compound called nattokinase. Many grain ferments yield important amino acids, such as lysine. Sauerkraut contains breakdown products believed to fight cancer, including isothiocyanates such as sulforaphane. (It also contains goodly amounts of vitamin C: Captain Cook kept his crew free from scurvy during a twenty-seven-month journey by forcing them to eat sauerkraut.) As I learned when I was baking bread, the fermentation process renders grain more nutritious by breaking down chemical compounds that interfere with nutrient absorption, such as phytate. Fermentation also breaks down toxic compounds in certain plants. That shark I tasted in Iceland? It would have sickened me (well, even more than it did) had it not been fermented. This particular species of shark has no kidneys, so toxic levels of uric acid accumulate in its flesh; the fermentation renders it harmless. Oxalic acid, another antinutrient, found in certain vegetables, is also broken down during fermentation.

To ferment food is to predigest it, in effect, breaking long chains of proteins, fats, and carbohydrates our bodies might not be able to make good use of into simpler, safer compounds that they can. Think of the kraut crock as a burbling auxiliary stomach, doing much of the work of digestion before your body has to. As with cooking, it offers your body an energy savings. Unlike cooking, however, the energy required to ferment food does not need to come from burning wood or fossil fuel. It is self-generated, by the metabolism of microbes breaking down the substrate. Fermentation can easily be done off the grid, a quality that commends it to the enviros, anarchists, and peak-oil types who help make up the subculture. "The historical bubble of refrigeration may not last," Katz likes to point out. When that particular bubble bursts, you're going to want to know people like Sandor Katz and microbes like L. plantarum.

Fermenting foods also intensifies their flavors, a particular boon to agricultural humans. The advent of agriculture dramatically narrowed the human diet, in many cases down to a small handful of bland staples, most of them carbohydrates. All the year long, fermented foods allowed people to enliven a monotonous diet with strong flavors, while supplementing it with vitamins, minerals, and phytochemicals that staple foods often lack.

People tend to feel very strongly about the flavors of fermentation, one way or the other. "Between fresh and rotten," Katz has written, "there is a creative space in which some of the most compelling flavors arise." In the same way that the process of ripening fruits imbues them with deeper, richer flavors and scents, many other foods acquire powerful new sensory qualities just as they begin to decompose. Why should this be? Perhaps for the same reason that our taste buds respond more strongly to simple sugars than to complex carbohydrates, or to amino acids rather than long protein chains. We've evolved specific taste receptors for these basic molecular building blocks (umami) and simple packets of energy (sweetness), so respond favorably to foods that have been broken down to those indispensable elements, whether by cooking or fermentation.

Yet many of the flavor molecules created by fermentation are not so simple or universal in their appeal. Could it be that, like ripening fruits, the microbes that decompose foods produce powerfully aromatic compounds for their own purposes? The reason fruits produce strong scents and flavors when ripe is to attract animals that can transport their seeds. The microbes that rot fruit or other foods also emit signaling chemicals. Some are designed to repel competitors. But others are attractants. Like the seeds of plants, fermentation microbes sometimes need help with transportation, especially after they've exhausted a food source. Some scientists believe that bacteria and fungi produce their own taxi-hailing scent compounds, in order to attract the insects and other animals they need to transport them to the next feast of putrefaction.

What's curious is how culturally specific so many of the flavors of fermentation turn out to be. Unlike sweetness or umami, these are not the kinds of simple flavors humans are hardwired to like. To the contrary, these are "acquired tastes," by which we mean that to enjoy them we often must overcome a hardwired aversion, something it usually takes the force of culture, and probably repeated exposure as a child, to achieve. The most common term children and adults alike will use to describe the fermented foods of another culture is some variation on the word "rotten." A wrinkle of the nose is how we react to both rottenness and foreignness. Many of these foods occupy a biological frontier—on the edge of decomposition—that turns out to be a well-patrolled cultural frontier as well.

Considered as a method, or set of methods, for food processing—for turning the stuff of nature into safe, nutritious, durable, and delicious things to eat—the ancient arts of fermentation have yet to be improved on. For what has modern food science given us that can compare? Vacuum-sealed cans. Frozen foods. Microwavable entrées. Mock meats made from soy. Baby formula. Irradiated food. Vitamin-fortified breakfast cereal in colors. Energy bars. Powdered Jell-O.

Marshmallow fluff. Cryovacking. Freeze-drying. Artificial sweeteners. Artificial sweeteners with fiber. Margarine. High-fructose corn syrup. Low-fat and no-fat cheese. Quorn. Cake mix. Frozen peanut butter and jelly sandwiches. The countless simulations of real foods and real flavors that line the center aisles of the supermarket. Stack any of these inventions up against such achievements as wine or beer, against cheese, against chocolate, soy sauce, coffee, yogurt, cured olives, vinegar, pickled vegetables of all kinds, cured meats, and the conclusion is inescapable: Thousands of years on, we still haven't discovered techniques for processing food as powerful, versatile, safe, or nutritious as microbial fermentation.

And yet these latter-day industrial methods of food preservation and processing have pushed most live-culture foods out of our diet. Yogurt is the exception that proves the rule, which is that very few of our foods any longer contain living bacteria or fungi. Vegetables are far more likely to be canned or frozen (or eaten fresh) than pickled. Meats are cured with chemicals rather than microbes and salt. Bread is still leavened with yeast, but seldom with a wild culture. Even the sauerkraut and kimchi are now pasteurized and vacuum packed— their cultures killed off long before the jar hits the supermarket shelf. These days most pickles are no longer truly pickled: They're soured with pasteurized vinegar, no lactobacilli involved. Open virtually any modern recipe book for putting up or pickling food and you will be hard pressed to find a recipe for lactofermentation: What once was pickling has been reduced to marinating in vinegar. And though it's true that vinegar is itself the product of fermentation, it is frequently pasteurized, a finished, lifeless product, and far too acidic to support most live cultures.

The modern food industry has a problem with bacteria, which it works assiduously to expunge from everything it sells, except for the yogurt. Wild fermentation is probably a little too wild for the supermarket, which has become yet another sterile battlefield in the war on bacteria. Worries about food safety are very real, of course, which is why it's probably easier for the industry to stand staunchly behind Pasteur than to try to tell a more nuanced story about good and bad bugs in your food. With the result that live-culture foods, which used to make up a large part of the human diet, have been relegated to the handful of artisanal producers and do-it-yourselfers signing up for Sandor Katz's "cultural revival."

This might not matter to much of anyone but a confirmed Slow Foodie, eager to save and sample endangered food traditions, except for one notable fact: Medical researchers are coming around to the startling conclusion that, in order to be healthy, people need *more* exposure to microbes, not less; and that one of the problems with the so-called Western diet—besides all the refined carbohydrates and fats and novel chemicals in it—is the absence from it of live-culture foods. The theory is that these foods have a crucial role to play in nourishing the vast community of microbes living inside us, which in turn plays a much larger role in our overall health and well-being than we ever realized. Bacteria-free food may be making us sick.

My first solo expedition into the wilds of the post-Pasteurian world came last summer, when I tested a few of Sandor Katz's pickling recipes at home. I decided to begin my education with vegetable ferments because they seemed the easiest and, which is important, the safest. No less an authority than Steinkraus had written that the safety record of fermented vegetables was very good even when "the foods are manufactured by people without training in microbiology or chemistry in unhygienic, contaminated environments." (That would be me.) One USDA scientist went so far as to claim that there has never been a documented case of food-borne illness from eating fermented vegetables.

Suitably reassured, I bought a case of quart-sized Mason jars at the hardware store. I did not sterilize them, just rinsed them out with some hot tap water. I also ordered online a 7.5-liter German sauerkraut crock. The perimeter of this ceramic crock has a deep circular well into which the lid fits; filling this moat with an inch or two of water creates an airlock that prevents oxygen from getting in while allowing the carbon dioxide emitted during fermentation to bubble out. Note: I discovered when it arrived that 7.5 liters is a much bigger crock than anyone needs, unless you're planning to feed a small German village. It took no fewer than six large heads of cabbage to fill my crock. That represents easily a few years' worth of sauerkraut in my house.

Fermentation vessels at the ready, I paid a visit to the farmers' market and bought a bunch of pickle-able vegetables: cabbages of course (both Napa and regular), cucumbers, carrots, cauliflower, sweet and hot peppers, beets, radishes, turnips, etc. At the supermarket, I loaded up on bulbs of garlic, ginger roots, and various pickling spices—juniper berries; dill, coriander, and caraway seeds; star anise; and black pepper—and a big box of sea salt.

According to Katz, there are two basic approaches to fermenting vegetables: leafy ones, like cabbage, are best fermented in their own juices, whereas others require the addition of a brine to keep them fully submerged in liquid. The saltiness of the brine is a matter of personal preference, but several of the sources I consulted recommended 5 percent, so I started with that. I dissolved the salt in a pot of hot water (roughly an ounce of salt for every three cups of water), to which I added various combinations of spices.* While the mixture cooled on the stovetop, I packed the vegetables into a Mason jar (usually with cloves of garlic, sometimes with sliced ginger as well) and then poured the brine over them. Katz had said the vegetables should be completely submerged, but invariably some insist on floating to the top, exposing themselves to oxygen—and the possibility of rot. I tried a variety of tricks to force them back underwater, including a saucer, some Ping-Pong balls, a plastic bag filled with pebbles, and some weighted grape leaves. I had read that grape leaves, which contain tannins, help keep the vegetables crisp by suppressing certain fungi. (Oak, cherry, or horseradish leaves, do the same thing.)

The procedure for making sauerkraut is slightly more involved. After quartering the cabbages and cutting out their hard cores, you can either shred the resulting chunks on a mandoline or cut them with a knife. I found shredding made life easier and produced more liquid more quickly than cutting with a sharp knife, probably because the knife doesn't leave as much surface area for the salt to go to work on. Put the shredded cabbage in the biggest bowl you own, sprinkling as you go with salt, and then, with all your fingers, press and squeeze and generally bruise the cabbage leaves without mercy until your hands begin to cramp. Now put something heavy on top of the heap to force the water from the leaves—a second bowl full of rocks will work, or use the crock itself. Within twenty minutes or so, the shredded cabbage will be awash in cabbage juice, magically beckoned out of the leaves by the salt.

Pack handfuls of shredded cabbage, with its liquid, into the crock

---

*There are no rules here, but I more or less tried to honor the classic "flavor principles": an Asian mix of ginger, garlic, coriander, and star anise for the turnips and beets; Indian spices like turmeric, cinnamon, and cardamom for the cauliflower and carrots; garlic, dill, and peppercorns for the cucumbers and green tomatoes.

as tightly as you can, a layer at a time. Add garlic and spices (for my first batch I used juniper berries, dill, and coriander) after each layer, pushing the mixture down and squeezing out air as you work. If you're using a sauerkraut crock, it probably came with a heavy inner lid made from fired clay or brick. Place this on top of the kraut and force it down until liquid rises high enough to cover everything. Then fit the outer lid into the lip and fill with water to create the seal. Keep the crock in the kitchen, where you can watch (and listen to) it for the first few days.

The procedure for making kimchi is either only slightly different, according to Sandor Katz and other American fermentos I consulted, or substantially different, according to actual Korean people. Aware of, but unperturbed by, the authenticity issue, Sandor calls his version "kraut-chi," and that's what I tried to make first. With a sharp knife, I cut heads of Napa cabbage into one-inch rounds. In addition to the salt, I added enough red chili powder to turn the cabbage red, along with as much garlic and ginger as I could stand to grate, and some fresh hot peppers. I also added slices of daikon radish and apple, as well as a bunch of spring onions. You can pack this into a kraut crock or an ordinary glass jar, making sure there's some way for gases to escape. But I found that an airlock is not critical when making kim-chi, probably because the peppers and garlic, both vigorously antimi-crobial, keep fungi from getting established. (In Korea, as I would learn, kimchi is made by soaking Napa cabbage in a brine overnight; the heads are then rinsed before the leaves are individually rubbed with a paste of ground-up red peppers, garlic, and ginger.)

Within a few days, and straight through that fall, my kitchen counters were lined with an assortment of jars, bowls, bottles, and crocks of various fermenting vegetables. In addition to the sauerkraut and kimchi, I pickled cauliflower, carrots, cucumbers, chard stems, beets, ramp bulbs, garlic cloves, turnips, and radishes. As the colors of the vegetables grew more vivid in their brines, and the brines themselves took on the pigments of the vegetables, the jars and bottles grew more exotically beautiful. I was reminded of tanks of tropical fish. And just like fish tanks, some of the crocks bubbled. Three days after filling it, the big crock of kraut began to stir, every few minutes emitting a bubble of gas with a resonant cartoony-sounding baritone burble. Fermentation had begun, which meant it was time to move the crock to a cooler location in the basement, so that it wouldn't proceed too fast.

So what was going on in there, deep within those thick brown ceramic walls? This sort of microbial cooking is invisible and gradual—not much drama to observe, apart from the occasional bubble or bulging of lids on the Mason jars. Yet there was a kind of drama unfolding in these containers, a microscaled drama I had set in motion simply by shredding and salting some dead plant parts. In doing so, I had created a very particular environment—an ecological niche that was in the process of being colonized by new life. (In this respect, too, the crock resembled a fish tank—only this was a microbe tank.) But what was uncanny was how the niche had populated itself—spontaneously. I had done nothing to inoculate it,[*] and yet on the evidence of the increasingly insistent bubbling, the kraut was now very much alive. The necessary bacteria had been there from the start, dormant but lurking on the cabbage leaves, waiting patiently for conditions to be exactly right—wet, airless, saline, the leaves too badly

---

[*]Though you can inoculate it if you want to: Some old-school pickling recipes call for adding some whey to the brine, a liquid teeming with lactobacilli; I tried it once, adding a spoonful of the clear liquid from the top of a yogurt container, and it did seem to speed the process. But what's the rush?

wounded to keep them out—to set about their methodical work of destruction and creation.

As to the precise identity of the microbes at work in my crock, it was hard to know for certain; temperature, place, and chance play a role in selecting them. But according to the microbiologists I consulted, my first fermenters were probably Enterobacteriaceae, a ubiquitous and rather cosmopolitan family of bacteria that can survive in a great many different environments, including in the soil and on plants. I was alarmed to learn that one of the environments in which Enterobacteriaceae do well is (as the name suggests) the gut of animals, and some of them (like salmonella and E. coli) are pathogens. This seemed a good argument for not sampling my sauerkraut too soon.

The Enterobacteriaceae, which begin the process of acidification, are soon succeeded by Leuconostoc mesenteroides, the first of several lactobacilli that will dominate the natural history of my sauerkraut. Like the weedy species that initially colonize a disturbed patch of land, the L. mesenteroides thrive under a wide range of conditions, including the salty, sugary, partially aerobic, low-acid conditions typically present at the beginning of a fermentation. Like many lactobacilli, these characters turn sugars into lactic acid, acetic acid, and carbon dioxide—the gas bubbling out from my crock. The CO_2 flushes any remaining oxygen from the ecosystem, preparing the ground for the strict anaerobes, as well as preventing the plant matter from getting mushy and preserving its color.

The objective of all these bugs is to render the environment safe for themselves and inhospitable to competitors. In the case of the lactobacilli, this is accomplished by producing copious amounts of acid, rapidly lowering the pH of the environment. But the L. mesenteroides eventually go overboard, acidifying the environment to the point where they have, in effect, fouled their own nest. (Remind you of anyone?) Yet what is foul to one microbial fermenter is fair to another: the L. *mesenteroides* inadvertently create the perfect conditions for another, hardier lactobacillus to succeed them, a more acid-tolerant species such as *Lactobacillus plantarum*.

I'm not sure exactly which of these characters were ascendant when, after three weeks, I first opened my crock to assess the progress of my kraut, but the scent that wafted up from the fermenting pinkish mass put me back on my heels. It was nasty. "Note of septic tank" would be a generous descriptor. In view of the off-putting scent, I wasn't sure whether sampling the sauerkraut was a good idea, but, trying my best to channel Sandor Katz's nonchalance, I held my nose and tasted. It wasn't terrible and I didn't get sick. That was a relief, but . . . well, this seemed kind of a low bar for a food. Judith compounded my disappointment by requesting that I get the crock out of the house as soon as possible. I wondered if I should throw out the whole batch and start over.

But before doing anything rash, I decided to check in with Sandor Katz. He advised me to stick with my kraut a little longer. He explained that some ferments seem to go through "a funky period," during which certain unpleasant-smelling microbes temporarily predominate. Some of the bacteria that show up to ferment vegetables are "sulfate reducers": they obtain their energy by turning sulfur into hydrogen sulfide—the odor of rotten eggs. I definitely had a few of those bugs. But my sulfate reducers would eventually be succeeded by other, more benign microbes, he suggested. In all likelihood my ferment was just going through an awkward stage.

Sandor was right. A month later, when I dared to open the crock again, the stink was gone. Whichever the bad bug had been, by now it had been supplanted by the acid-loving climax species that ultimately dominates nearly all vegetable ferments, L. *plantarum*. When

L. *plantarum* arrives on the scene, you're out of the woods. The ferment is sufficiently acidic to kill off any pathological or otherwise undesirable microbes. L. *plantarum* establishes a bacteriological regime so stable and low in pH that it can endure more or less unchanged for months, even years.

Yet, truth be told, the sauerkraut wasn't very good. The septic stench may have left, but a disconcerting beard of gray mold had sprouted along the perimeter of the cabbage. I heeded Sandor's advice, carefully shaving it off while trying to override the visceral, possibly instinctual, disgust rising in me. But the mold had obviously been there for while, because my kraut had lost most of its crunchiness. Some filamentous fungus had sent its fine tendrils deep into the kraut, dispatching enzymes to decompose the plant cell walls, turning them nearly to mush. I had been warned that summer sauerkrauts often suffered this fate, which is why Germans traditionally make kraut from cabbages harvested late in the fall.

I had much better luck with my kimchi, or kraut-chi, which after a month of fermentation was still crunchy, its spiciness bright with acid and ginger. As for the dill pickles, the cucumbers tasted just right but had a slightly grayish cast and suboptimal crunch. The carrots and cauliflower pickled with Indian spices were excellent, the carrots marred only slightly by a thin, barely noticeable slime coat. (Probably a bloom of yeast, another challenge of fermenting in warm weather.) But by far my favorite pickle was the chard stems, which after two weeks were crunchy and a brilliant ruby red, lightly inflected with coriander and juniper. They were delicious, particularly with eggs.

As a mode of cooking, pickling plants was at once remarkably straightforward—*cut, salt, and season vegetables, then wait a few weeks*—and yet borderline magical: the way these common microbes just show up and utterly transform the vegetables, creating whole new flavors and qualities. And yet it wasn't so easy to pickle really well. To an extent you can guide or manage the microbes, by adjusting the temperature and salinity of their environment, but in the end you can't control them. That's why most of the serious picklers I talked to agreed this was not a craft for the control freak or obsessive.

"You do your best preparing the ferment, but finally you have to be able to let go," Alex Hozven, a local artisanal pickler, told me, "and let the microbes do their thing." The fermenters I met cultivated a relaxed and genuinely humble attitude to their work, which they regarded as a collaboration between species. It helped to have the kind of temperament that could tolerate mystery, doubt, and uncertainty without reaching for rule or reason. Instead of the pH meter, they trusted their senses. And they were willing, with a shrug and a rueful smile, to throw out a bad batch every now and then.

The phrase "live-culture foods" is of course a euphemism: for fermented foods teeming with living bacteria and fungi. "Live-culture" sounds a lot more appetizing than, say, "bacteria" for breakfast, in the same way that calling a cheese "washed rind" goes down more easily than "coated with a biofilm of bacteria and mold," which is what a washed-rind cheese is. Enjoying my "live-culture" pickles and kimchi, I gave some thought to the billions of microbes I was ingesting along with the vegetables, wondering what in the world they might be doing down there. But somewhere deep in the coils of my intestines one community of microbes was presumably encountering another. I hoped for the best. At the time, I had no idea what that best might be.

I began to get some strong and surprising hints when I accom-

panied Sandor Katz to the third annual Fermentation Festival, in Freestone, California. Held over the course of a sparkling spring weekend,
on the grounds of an elementary school that had temporarily sprouted
tents and stages and booths, a thousand or so people had gathered to
celebrate the tastes, wonders, and putative health benefits of fermentation. In this crowd, which had more than its share of hippies both
old and young, Sandor Katz was a major celebrity, unable to cross
a room or field without stopping to sign an autograph or pose for a
picture. This was the place to be if you wanted to buy a "kombucha
mother"—the slimy mass of fungi and bacteria used to ferment this
ancient Chinese tea soda—or the cultures to make your own tempeh,
natto, kvass, or kefir, all of which were available for sampling. Never
before had I knowingly ingested so many different kinds of fungi and
bacteria. And except for the natto, a filamentous soybean-and-mucus
treat that gave off a nauseating whiff of putrefaction, it all went down
the hatch without a hitch.

While cruising the book tables, I spotted and purchased a thick
self-published volume titled, refreshingly noneuphemistically, Bacteria
for Breakfast: Probiotics for Good Health. The author, a pharmacist living in
Pennsylvania, patiently laid out the case for the myriad health benefits
of fermented foods and "probiotics"—the beneficial bacteria, most of
them lactobacilli, often found in those foods. These "good bugs" and
their by-products were credited with all kinds of good works, from
improving digestion, reducing inflammation, and "educating" the
immune system, to preventing cancers of the gastrointestinal tract.

It turns out there is a substantial body of peer-reviewed science to
back up all these claims, and more generally give credence to the age-
old belief, shared by many cultures, that fermented foods confer special benefits on our health. (The Romans treated various ailments
with live-culture foods, and Confucius insisted the key to long life

and good health was to eat a fermented condiment, called a *jiang*, with every meal.) Yet some hard-core fermentos go much, much further, claiming live-culture foods as a panacea for a range of ailments that would seem to have nothing whatever to do with "gut health," from AIDS and diabetes to various disorders of the mind. At the Festival I talked to a woman who claimed to have cured her child's autism with raw milk and sauerkraut. I learned about the GAPS (gut and psychology syndrome) Diet, recommended for everything from autism to attention deficit disorder, and took in a lecture about "leaky gut syndrome," a condition caused by the "overgrowth" of bad bugs in the colon that undermines the integrity of the epithelial barrier, allowing various toxins to seep into the bloodstream and wreak all kinds of havoc. Talking to these people, and listening to their fervent monologues, I was reminded of Dr. Casaubon, the character in *Middlemarch* who is convinced he has discovered "the key to all mythologies." Here among the fermentos, the key to all health, in body as well as mind, was a lactofermented pickle.

At first I figured I had wandered into a hothouse of pseudoscientific quackery that could be easily dismissed. Sandor Katz himself is careful to distance himself from the more extreme claims of the fermentation underground. "I don't believe kombucha can cure diabetes," he told the audience at one point. After he wrote in *Wild Fermentation*, his first book, that a diet rich in fermented foods was an important part of his self-treatment for HIV, so many patients took his prescription to heart that he felt compelled to add a disclaimer in his new book, *The Art of Fermentation*: "While I wish it were so, live-culture foods are not a cure for AIDS." But Katz also urged me to look into the rapidly growing body of scientific research on the role of fermented foods in gut health, and in turn the role of a healthy gut in our well-being overall. "I think you'll be surprised."

I did, and I was. Following up on some leads from Sandor, I began reading around in the subject, and speaking to scientists who study the "gut microbiota"* or "microflora"—basically, the vast community of organisms (bacteria, fungi, archaea, viruses, and protozoa) that reside in our intestines and exert far more influence on our lives than was recognized until very recently. Sometimes the scientists working in a particular field come across as just plain more *excited* than scientists working in another area. Radical hypotheses and incipient breakthroughs and Nobel Prizes are in the professional air, creating a bracing ozone of possibility. The scientists working today on "microbial ecology" are as excited as any I've ever interviewed, convinced, as one of them put it, that they "stand on the verge of a paradigm shift in our understanding of health as well as our relationship to other species." And fermentation—as it unfolds both inside and outside the body—is at the heart of this new understanding.

In the decades since Louis Pasteur founded microbiology, medical research has focused mainly on bacteria's role in causing disease. The bacteria that reside in and on our bodies were generally regarded as either harmless "commensals"—freeloaders, basically—or pathogens to be defended against. Scientists tended to study these bugs one at a time, rather than as communities. This was partly a deeply ingrained habit of reductive science, and partly a function of the available tools. Scientists naturally focused their attention on the bacteria they could see, which meant the handful of individual bugs that could be cultured in a petri dish. There, they found some good guys and some

---

*Biologists use the term "microbiota" to refer to a community of microbes, and "microbiome" to refer to the collective genome of those microbes.

bad guys. But the general stance toward the bacteria we had discovered all around us was shaped by metaphors of war, and in that war, antibiotics became the weapons of choice.

But it turns out that the overwhelming majority of bacteria residing in the gut simply refuse to grow on a petri dish—a phenomenon now known among researchers as "the great plate anomaly." Without realizing it, they were practicing what is sometimes called parking-lot science—named for the human tendency to search for lost keys under the streetlights not because that's where we lost them but because that is where we can best see. The petri dish was a streetlight. But when, in the early 2000s, researchers developed genetic "batch" sequencing techniques allowing them to catalog *all* the DNA in a sample of soil, say, or seawater or feces, science suddenly acquired a broad and powerful beam of light that could illuminate the entire parking lot. When it did, we discovered hundreds of new species in the human gut doing all sorts of unexpected things.

To their surprise, microbiologists discovered that nine of every ten cells in our bodies belong not to us, but to these microbial species (most of them residents of our gut), and that 99 percent of the DNA we're carrying around belongs to those microbes. Some scientists, trained in evolutionary biology, began looking at the human individual in a humbling new light: as a kind of superorganism, a community of several hundred coevolved and interdependent species. War metaphors no longer made much sense. So the microbiologists began borrowing new metaphors from the ecologists.

It's important to keep in mind that, despite the powerful new exploratory tools, the microbial world within our body remains very much a terra incognita—its age of exploration has only just begun. But already scientists have established that the microbiota of the human gut is in fact an ecosystem, a complex community of species doing a whole lot more than just hanging out or helping us break down foods or making us sick.

So what exactly *are* the five hundred or so distinct species and countless different strains of those species that make up the kilogram or so of microbes in our gut doing there? Evolutionary theory supplied the first big clue. For most of these microbes, their survival depends on our own, and so they do all sorts of things to keep their host—us— alive and well. Indeed, even speaking of "us" and "them" may soon seem quaint; as a group of microbiologists recently wrote in *Microbiology and Molecular Biology Reviews*,* we need to begin thinking of health "as a collective property of the human-associated microbiota"—that is, as a function of the community, not the individual.

Perhaps the most important function of the microbes in our gut is to maintain the health of the gut wall, or epithelium. This is the tennis-court-sized membrane that, like our skin or respiratory system, mediates our relationship to the world outside our bodies. In the course of a lifetime, sixty tons of food pass through the gastrointestinal tract, an exposure to the world that is fraught with risk. It appears that much of that risk is managed, most of the time brilliantly, by the gut microbiota. So, for example, the microbial fermenters living in the colon break down the indigestible carbohydrates in our food— that is, the fiber—into the organic acids that are the most important source of nourishment for the gut wall. (Unlike most other tissues, which obtain nutrients from the bloodstream, the gut wall gets most of its nutrients from the by-products of fermentation in the colon.) Some of these organic acids, like butyrate, are such a good fuel for the cells of the intestines that they are believed to help prevent cancers of the digestive tract.

---

*Robinson, Courtney J., et al., "From Structure to Function."

Meanwhile, other gut bacteria have evolved the ability to adhere to the inner surface of the epithelium, where they crowd out pathogenic strains of such microbes as E. *coli* and salmonella, and keep them from breaching the gut wall. Many such pathogens can be found within the gut but don't make us sick unless they manage to get out and into the bloodstream. The reason some people are more susceptible to food poisoning than others may owe less to their ingestion of bad bugs than to the failure of their epithelium to keep those bugs from escaping (as well as to the overall health of their immune system). Helping to maintain the health and integrity of the gut wall is one of the most valuable services gut bacteria provide.

As a more or less stable ecological community, the microbes in the gut share our interest in resisting invasion and colonizations by microbial interlopers. Some of them produce antibiotic compounds for this purpose, whereas others help manage and train our body's immune system, by dispatching chemical signals that activate or calm various defenses. Though to speak of "our" immune system or self-interest no longer makes much sense. Taken as a whole, the microbiota constitutes the largest and one of the human body's most important organs of defense.*

An interesting question is why the body would enlist bacteria in all these critical functions, rather than evolve its own systems to do this work. One theory is that, because microbes can evolve so much more rapidly than the "higher animals," they can respond with much greater speed and agility to changes in the environment—to threats as well as opportunities. Exquisitely reactive and fungible, bacteria

---

*This is equally true for the somewhat different bacterial communities found in other locations on the body—the mouth, the skin, the nasal passages, and the vagina. In the vagina, for example, dozens of species of *Lactobacillus* ferment glycogen, a sugar secreted by the vaginal lining. The lactic acid produced by these bacteria helps maintain a pH low enough to protect the vagina against pathogens.

can swap genes and pieces of DNA among themselves, picking them up and dropping them almost as if they were tools. This capability is especially handy when a new toxin or food source appears in the environment. The microbiota can swiftly find precisely the right gene needed to fight it—or eat it.

One intriguing recent study, done by Jan-Hendrik Hehemann from the University of Victoria in British Columbia, reported that a bacterium commonly found in the gut of Japanese people produces a rare enzyme capable of digesting seaweed, a trait seldom found in the same bacteria in other populations. The researchers demonstrated that the gene coding for this enzyme originally came from a marine bacterium commonly found on seaweed—*Zobellia galactanivorans*. The resident gut bacteria, called *Bacteroides plebeius*, had apparently picked up this useful gene from seaweed in the diet and incorporated it in its genome, where it has been preserved ever since, allowing most Japanese to make good use of the seaweed in their diet.* No doubt scientists will soon find other examples of our microbiota mediating our relationship to the rest of nature, speeding our ability to adapt. In effect, the microbiome vastly extends our genome, giving us access to a tremendous bag of tricks we did not need to evolve ourselves.

So it made very good sense, evolutionarily speaking, for us to join forces with the microbes, which are simply more skilled than we are at all the ways of biochemically contending. During the two billion years of natural selection that bacteria have undergone before more complex multicellular creatures arrived on the scene, they managed to invent virtually every important metabolic trick known to evolu-

---

*Hehemann, Jan-Henrik, et al., "Transfer of Carbohydrate-Active Enzymes from Marine Bacteria to Japanese Gut Microbiota," *Nature* 464 (2010): 908–12.

tion, from fermentation to photosynthesis. (According to Lynn Margulis, who until her death in 2011 was the microbiome's most eloquent human advocate, the only important biochemical innovations to come along in the billion years since then are snake venom, plant hallucinogens, and—this is a big one—cerebral cortices.) And one of bacteria's greatest tricks of all is to combine forces with other creatures, taking up residence in or on their bodies, possibly even their cells, trading various metabolic services for their upkeep.*

◎

Researchers have identified several, but surely not all, of the services that resident gut microbes supply to their hosts. Though we've tended to think of bacteria as agents of destruction, they are, like other fermenters, invaluable creators as well. In addition to producing organic acids, the gut bugs manufacture essential vitamins (including vitamin K as well as several B vitamins), enzymes necessary to digestion, and a great many other bioactive compounds scientists are only just beginning to recognize. Some of these compounds act on the central nervous system, moderating our appetite and the mechanisms that determine how we store fat.

Indeed, the microbiota may play an important role in regulating our weight. It has long been known that feeding antibiotics to livestock makes them gain more weight on the same amount of feed, and though the mechanism has not been identified, intriguing new clues are emerging. A group of researchers at Washington University in St.

---

*Margulis theorized that both photosynthesis and cellular metabolism in animals began when bacteria took up residence in the evolutionary ancestors of plant and animal cells, contributing their metabolic expertise; eventually these invaders became the chloroplasts in plant cells and the mitochondria in the cells of animals.

Louis discovered that the types of bacteria dominant in the gut of obese individuals (in both mice and humans) are very different from those found in slender people, and that the different species of gut bacteria metabolize food more or less efficiently. This suggests that the amount of energy we obtain from a given amount of food may vary depending on the kinds of microbes living in our gut. So might changing the composition of our gut bacteria in turn change our weight? Possibly: The researchers found that when they transferred bacteria from the gut of fat mice into germ-free mice, the germ-free mice gained nearly twice as much weight as when they received gut bacteria from skinny mice.* Other research has found that specific gut microbes, such as Helicobacter pylori, play a role in regulating the hormones that control appetite.

Could it be possible that the microbiota also affects mental function and mood, as some of the fermentos I met in Freestone claimed? The idea no longer seems preposterous. A recent study performed in Ireland found that introducing a certain probiotic species found in some fermented foods (Lactobacillus rhamnosus JB-1) to the diet of mice had a measurable effect on their stress levels and mood, altering the levels of certain neurotransmitters in the brain.† Precisely how the presence of a certain bacterium in the gut might affect mental function is unclear, yet the researchers found they could block the effect by severing the vagus nerve that links the gut to the brain. Studies like this one make you wonder if it might someday be possi-

---

*Turnbaugh, Peter J., et al., "An Obesity-Associated Gut Microbiome with Increased Capacity for Energy Harvest," Nature 444 (2006): 1027–31; Turnbaugh, P. J., et al., "A Core Gut Microbiome in Obese and Lean Twins," Nature 457 (2009): 480–84; Turnbaugh, Peter J., et al., "The Human Microbiome Project," Nature 449 (2007): 804–10.

†This particular probiotic is found in some kinds of yogurt. (Bravo, J. A., et al., "Ingestion of Lactobacillus Strain Regulates Emotional Behavior and Central GABA Receptor Expression in a Mouse via the Vagus Nerve," Proceedings of the National Academy of Sciences 108 No. 38 [2011]: 16050–55).

ble to cultivate, or garden, our microbiota, altering its makeup to improve our physical and possibly also our mental well-being.[*]

◉

Right now, of course, and for the last several decades at least, we have been assiduously doing exactly the opposite: disordering the community of microbes in our bodies without even realizing it, much less with any sense of what might be at stake. Under the pressures of broad-spectrum antibiotics, a Pasteurian regime of "good sanitation," and a modern diet notably hostile to bacteria, the human microbiota has probably changed more in the last hundred years than in the previous ten thousand, when the shift to agriculture altered our diet and lifestyle. We are only just beginning to recognize the implications of these changes for our health.

For some of us, the deleterious changes to our gut microflora begin at birth, the moment when we are first inoculated with the microbes that will accompany us through life. In utero, our bodies

---

[*]It has long been recognized that people with autism and schizophrenia often suffer from gastrointestinal disorders, and some recent work suggests there may be anomalies in their microflora. It's important to remember that correlation is not causation, and if there is causation, we don't know which way it goes. But evidence is accumulating that certain microbes in our bodies can affect our behavior and do so for their own purposes. *Toxoplasma gondii*, a parasite found in more than one billion people worldwide, has been shown to inspire neurotic self-destructive behavior in rats. The protozoa's reproductive cycle depends on infecting cats, which it does by getting them to eat the rats and mice in whose brains the parasite commonly resides. When the parasite infects a rat or mouse, it increases dopamine levels in its host, inspiring it to wander around recklessly in a way more likely to attract the attention of cats; the mice and rats also become attracted to the smell of cat urine, an odor that, under normal circumstances, causes them to flee or freeze. "Fatal feline attraction" is the name for this phenomenon. In people, the presence of *Toxoplasma gondii* has been linked to schizophrenia, obsessive compulsive disorder, poor attention and reaction times, and a greater likelihood of car accidents. (House, Patrick K., et al., "Predator Cat Odors Activate Sexual Arousal Pathways in Brains of *Toxoplasma gondii*-Infected Rats," *PLoS ONE* 6 No. 8 (August 2011): e23277 and Benson, Alicia, et al., "Gut Commensal Bacteria Direct a Protective Immune Response Against the Human Pathogen *Toxoplasma Gondii*," *Cell Host & Microbe* 6 No. 2 [2009]: 187–96.)

are sterile, but the microbially messy process of vaginal birth exposes the baby to a set of bacteria that immediately begin to colonize its body. Children born by Cesarean section, a far more hygienic process, take much longer to populate their intestinal tract, and never acquire quite the same assortment of bugs. Some researchers believe this could help explain the higher rates of allergies, asthma, and obesity observed in children born by Cesarean.

The sanitized environment in which we try to surround our children is probably also taking its toll on their microbiota. Now widely accepted, the "hygiene hypothesis" holds that children need to be exposed to more bacteria, not fewer, in order to properly develop their immune system, so that it can learn to accurately distinguish between good and bad microbes. Without that training, the theory goes, the body is apt to mistake benign proteins, such as those in certain foods, for mortal threats, and react accordingly. The hypothesis explains escalating rates of allergy, asthma, and autoimmune disease in the developed world, as well as the curious fact that children reared in the microbially rich—some would say perilous—environment of a farm have fewer allergies and generally more robust immune systems.*

---

*The PARSIFAL (Prevention of Allergy–Risk Factors for Sensitization Related to Farming and Anthroposophic Lifestyle) study, conducted with nearly fifteen thousand children in five European countries between 2000 and 2002, compared rates of asthma, allergies, and eczema in children attending Rudolf Steiner Waldorf schools, children living on farms, and control groups. The children living on farms (where they were regularly exposed to dirt, microorganisms, and livestock) and the children in Waldorf schools (who ate more fermented vegetables and who received fewer antibiotics and fever-reducing medications) had lower rates of allergic diseases. Douwes, J., et al., "Farm Exposure in Utero May Protect Against Asthma," European Respiratory Journal 32 (2008): 603–11; Ege, M. J., et al., "Prenatal Farm Exposure Is Related to the Expression of Receptors of the Innate Immunity and to Atopic Sensitization in School-Age Children," Journal of Allergy and Clinical Immunology 117 (2006): 817–23. Alfvén, T., et al., "Allergic Diseases and Atopic Sensitization in Children Related to Farming and Anthroposophic Lifestyle—the PARSIFAL Study," Allergy 61 (2006): 414–21. Perkin, Michael R., and David P. Strachan, "Which Aspects of the Farming Lifestyle Explain the Inverse Association with Childhood Allergy?," Journal of Allergy and Clinical Immunology 117 (2006): 1374–81. (Flöistrup, H., et al., "Allergic Disease and Sensitization in Steiner School Children," Journal of Allergy and Clinical Immunology 117 [2006]: 59–66.)

The average child in the developed world has also received between ten and twenty courses of antibiotics before his or her eighteenth birthday, an assault on the microflora the implications of which
researchers are just beginning to reckon.[*] Like the pesticides applied
to a farm field, antibiotics "work," at least in the short term. Yet as
soon as you widen the lens from a narrow focus on the "enemy species," you see that that such blunt weapons inflict collateral damage to
the larger environment, including, in the case of pesticides, the microbial community of the soil. Resistant bugs and various other health
problems soon emerge; the soil's ability to nourish plants and help
them withstand disease is also compromised, because the toxins have
reduced the community's biodiversity and thereby compromised its
resilience. As in the soil, so in the gut. The drive for control and order
ends up leading to more disorder.[†]

And then of course there is the diet, perhaps the most important
factor in first establishing and then maintaining the microbial community in our gut. The process begins with nursing, which shapes the
gut flora in some unexpected ways. A mother's nipple harbors a community of lactobacilli, and it was recently discovered that the milk
itself contains bacteria that may play a role in colonizing the baby's
gut. But the most important contribution of mother's milk to the infant microbiota may be in encouraging the "right" kinds of bacteria to
dominate it from the start. For years nutritionists were mystified by

---

[*]Blaser, Martin,. "Antibiotic Overuse: Stop the Killing of Beneficial Bacteria," *Nature* 476 (2011): 393–94.
[†]Consider the saga of the once-common stomach bacteria *Helicobacter pylori*. Long considered the pathogen responsible for causing peptic ulcers, the bacterium was routinely attacked with antibi-otics, and as a result has become rare—today, less than 10 percent of American children test positive for *H. pylori*. Only recently have researchers discovered it also plays a positive role in our health: *H. pylori* helps regulate both stomach acid and ghrelin, one of the key hormones involved in appetite. People who have been treated with antibiotics to eradicate the bacterium gain weight, possibly because the *H. pylori* is not acting to regulate their appetite. See Blaser, Martin J., "Who Are We? Indigenous Microbes and the Ecology of Human Disease," *EMBO Reports* 7 No. 10 (2006): 956–60.

the presence in mother's milk of certain complex carbohydrates, called oligosaccharides, which the infant lacked the necessary enzymes to digest. Evolutionary theory argues that *every* component of mother's milk should have some value to the developing baby, or else natural selection would be likely to discard it as a poor use of the mother's precious resources. So why would she produce nutrients her baby can't metabolize? It turns out the oligosaccharides are there to feed not the baby but certain of its intestinal microbes: Their presence in the diet ensures that certain optimal species of bacteria, and specifically *Bifidobacterium infantis*, proliferate and get established before less savory characters gain a toehold.*

As nature's most perfect food—having been shaped entirely by natural selection—mother's milk has much to teach us, and not least these two crucial facts: that bacteria is good food, and that feeding the bacteria is as important as feeding the baby. Put in a more scientific way, the diet should include both "probiotics"—beneficial bacteria—and "prebiotics"—something good for those bacteria to eat. But for most of the last century, those of us living in the developed world have heeded neither of these principles.

To the contrary: We are, literally, "anti-biotic." We've worked hard to eliminate bacteria from the diet, by sterilizing our food, and, by processing it, we've removed much of the fiber—precisely that component of the diet of greatest value to the microbiota. With the exception of yogurt, live-culture foods have all but vanished from our plates. To take just one example, *L. plantarum*, the bacterium found in such abundance in most vegetable ferments, has been ubiquitous in the human diet since prehistoric times, along with all the vegetables it typically accompanied. But the so-called Western diet, with its refined

---

*Zivkovic, Angela M., J. Bruce German, et al., "Human Milk Glycobiome and Its Impact on the Infant Gastrointestinal Microbiota," *Proceedings of the National Academy of Sciences* 107 No. suppl 1 (2011): 4653–58.

carbohydrates, highly processed foods, and dearth of fresh vegetables, is downright hostile to fermentation: It preserves foods by killing bacteria rather than cultivating them, and then deprives our gut bacteria of much of anything good for it to ferment.

"The big problem with the Western diet," Stephen O'Keefe, a gastroenterologist at the University of Pittsburgh, told me, "is that it doesn't feed the gut, only the upper GI [gastrointestinal tract]. All the food has been processed to be readily absorbed, leaving nothing for the lower GI. But it turns out that one of the keys to health is fermentation in the large intestine." A diet as rich in fats and refined carbohydrates as ours may supply our bodies with plenty of energy, but the lack of fiber in the diet is, in effect, starving our gut and its microbial residents. O'Keefe and many others are convinced that the myriad intestinal disorders that have become common among people eating a Western diet can be traced to this imbalance. We have changed the human diet in such a way that it no longer feeds the whole superorganism, as it were, only our human selves. We're eating for one, when we need to be eating for, oh, a few trillion.

But intestinal problems may be the least of it. For more than a century now, medicine has recognized a link between this Western diet and the historically novel set of chronic diseases that now kill most of us in the West: heart disease and stroke, obesity, cancer, and type 2 diabetes. Populations that eat a Western diet consistently develop high rates of these diseases. What remains subject to debate is exactly *what* about this diet makes it so lethal: Is it the presence in it of some "bad" nutrient, such as saturated fat or refined carbohydrates or cholesterol? Or is it the absence from it of some essential "good" nutrient, like fiber or omega-3 fatty acids?

Any one of these nutrients, present or absent, might be the dietary culprit responsible for this or that chronic disease. But lately some researchers are beginning to suspect that the problem with the Western diet may be both less direct and more systemic, and that most if not all the important chronic diseases may have a similar etiology. Though none has yet dared use such an ambitious term, several scientists across several disciplines appear to be working toward what looks very much like a Grand Unified Theory of Diet and Chronic Disease. The theory turns on the concept of inflammation, something in which the human microbiota may turn out to play a crucial role.

A growing number of medical researchers are coming around to the idea that the common denominator of many, if not most, of the chronic diseases is inflammation—a persistent and heightened immune response by the body to a real or perceived threat. For example, the buildup of plaque in the arteries, once thought to be the result of saturated fat and cholesterol in the diet, now appears to be an inflammatory response, the arteries' attempt to heal themselves. Various markers for inflammation are common in people with "metabolic syndrome," the complex of abnormalities that predisposes people to cardiovascular disease, type 2 diabetes, and cancer, and which now afflicts 44 percent of Americans over the age of fifty. So what might be the source of these inflammatory responses, across so many organs and systems and people? One theory—and so far it is just a theory—is that the problem begins in the gut, with a disorder of the microbiota, and specifically of the gut wall. For when the integrity of the epithelium has been compromised, various bacteria, endotoxins, and proteins can slip into the bloodstream, causing the body's immune system to mount a response. It is the resulting inflammation, which affects the entire organism and may never subside, that over time can lead to any number of the chronic diseases that have been linked to diet.

That, at least, is the theory. It no longer sounds even the least bit crazy to me, but, then, maybe I've been spending too much time among the fermentos, people who believe that the cure for diabetes and whatever else that ails you is kombucha. It obviously can't be that simple. And yet the case for getting more live-culture foods in the diet (especially of our children) is already compelling and growing more so. Consider the research that has come out in just the past decade or so. Probiotics—beneficial bacteria ingested either in fermented foods or in supplements—have been shown to: calm the immune system and reduce inflammation;[1] shorten the duration and severity of colds in children;[2] relieve diarrhea[3] and irritable bowel syndrome;[4] reduce allergic responses, including asthma;[5] stimulate the immune response;[6] possibly reduce the risk of certain cancers;[7] reduce anxiety;[8] prevent bacterial vaginosis;[9] diminish levels of E. coli 0157:H7 in cattle[10] and salmonella in chickens;[11] and improve the health and function of the gut epithelium.[12]

Much about the microbiota and fermented foods remains to be explored. Scientists still don't understand exactly how the probiotics in

1. Isolauri, E., et al., "Probiotics: A Role in the Treatment of Intestinal Infection and Inflammation?," Gut 50 Suppl 3 (2002): iii54–iii59.
2. Leyer, Gregory J., et al., "Probiotic Effects on Cold and Influenza-like Symptom Incidence and Duration in Children," Pediatrics 124 No. 2 (2009): e172–79.
3. Vrese, Michael de, and Philippe R. Marteau, "Probiotics and Prebiotics: Effects on Diarrhea," Journal of Nutrition 137 No. 3 (2007): 803S–11s.
4. Quigley, E. M., "The Efficacy of Probiotics in IBS," Journal of Clinical Gastroenterology 42 No. Suppl 2 (2008): S85–90.
5. Michail, Sonia, "The Role of Probiotics in Allergic Diseases," Allergy, Asthma, and Clinical Immunology: Official Journal of the Canadian Society of Allergy and Clinical Immunology 5 No. 1 (2009): 5.
6. Pagnini, Cristiano, et al., "Probiotics Promote Gut Health Through Stimulation of Epithelial Innate Immunity," Proceedings of the National Academy of Sciences 107 No. 1 (2010): 454–59.
7. Saikali, Joumana, et al., "Fermented Milks, Probiotic Cultures, and Colon Cancer," Nutrition and Cancer 49 No. 1 (2004): 14–24.
8. Messaoudi, Michaël, et al., "Beneficial Psychological Effects of a Probiotic Formulation (Lactobacillus helveticus R0052 and Bifidobacterium longum R0175) in Healthy Human Volunteers," Gut Microbes 2 No. 4 (2011): 256–61.
9. Falagas, M. E., et al., "Probiotics for the Treatment of Women with Bacterial Vaginosis," Clinical Microbiology and Infection 13 No. 7 (2007): 657–64.
10. Brashears, M. M., et al., "Prevalence of Escherichia Coli O157:H7 and Performance by Beef Feedlot Cattle Given Lactobacillus Direct-Fed Microbials," Journal of Food Protection 66 No. 5 (2003): 748–54.
11. Coillie, E. Van, et al., "Identification of Lactobacilli Isolated from the Cloaca and Vagina of Laying Hens and Characterization for Potential Use as Probiotics to Control Salmonella Enteritidis," Journal of Applied Microbiology 102 No. 4 (2007): 1095–106.
12. Corridoni, Daniele, et al., "Probiotic Bacteria Regulate Intestinal Epithelial Permeability in Experimental Ileitis by a TNF-Dependent Mechanism," PloS One 7 No. 7 (2012): e42067.

fermented foods achieve their effects. Only occasionally do they actually take up permanent residence in the gut. Some of them, notably L. plantarum, move in and adhere to the epithelium, helping to crowd out various pathogens and strengthen the gut wall. But other probiotic species appear to be only transient members of the microbial community. And yet, like visitors often do, they seem to leave their mark, contributing things of value—a useful gene or plasmid, a bioactive chemical, some "news" of the microbial environment out there—to the biota. Somehow, they seem to stimulate the local residents to better resist invasion by pathogens. A series of recent papers has demonstrated that even bacteria that are just passing through can alter the genetic expression, and sometimes the genome, of resident gut bacteria, teaching them some new metabolic tricks.[*]

Taken together, the microflora may function as a kind of sensory organ, bringing the body the latest information from the environment, as well as the new tools needed to deal with it. "The bacteria in your gut are continually reading the environment and responding," says Joel Kimmons, a nutrition scientist and epidemiologist at the Centers for Disease Control and Prevention, in Atlanta. "They're a molecular mirror of the changing world. And because they can evolve so quickly, they help our bodies respond to changes in our environment."

Mysteries remain, obviously, but the case for eating live-culture foods seems strong, and perhaps strongest for fermented vegetables.[†] For in addition to bringing large numbers of probiotic guests to the party (including such impressive characters as L. plantarum), the vege-

---

[*]Smillie, Chris S., et al., "Ecology Drives a Global Network of Gene Exchange Connecting the Human Microbiome," Nature 480 (2011): 241–44. Arias, Maria Cecilia, et al., "Eukaryote to Gut Bacteria Transfer of a Glycoside Hydrolase Gene Essential for Starch Breakdown in Plants," Mobile Genetic Elements 2 No. 2 (2012): 81–87.

[†]And possibly for fermenting your own vegetables at home, according to the CDC's Kimmons: "Ideally, you want to grow your own bacteria at home, since [these local strains] will best reflect the world you live in."

tables themselves also supply plenty of prebiotics—nourishment for the bacteria already there. So you won't be surprised to learn I have been busy at my pickling, working to perfect my sauerkraut and kim-chi. Since they have been in the human diet for thousands of years, it makes sense that these fermented foods would by now have become tightly woven into our biology. We have coevolved with them, not just the plants, but the microbial species these ferments contain in such abundance, especially ones such as L. *plantarum*, which for all we know might be one of the unsung heroes of human health.

And yet it's not at all hard to see why it would take this long to recognize and appreciate the complexity of these foods and these relationships—because that complexity is, literally, so hard to see. As with the microbiota of the soil, another fermenting universe of bio-logical complexity that it closely resembles, the complexity of the gut microbiota is supremely difficult to comprehend. So much more than the sum of its unprepossessing parts, it has been, until very recently, invisible to the reductive lens of Western science, which has always been better at understanding individuals (pathogens, variables, ele-ments, whatever) than communities. And then there is the fact that it utterly fails to conform to our ideas—including our aesthetic ideas—of what a system or an organ should look like. Let's face it, the kilo-gram mass of microbes living in our gut don't look like much. It doesn't help that we also find it disgusting.

FERMENT II.

ANIMAL

A dairyman I know from Wales, a man who with his son produces a remarkable cheddar, once told me that "everything" affects the quality and flavor of his cheeses, up to and including "the mood of the milker." This struck me as a nice romantic conceit, until I pressed him to explain how that might actually be so. "Well, it's really quite simple. If the milker is calm, the cow is calm. And a calm cow doesn't shit as much in the milking parlor, which means her milk will likely be cleaner. This is why the milk is always better when women do the milking."

Several things about this little story came as news to me, not least the disturbing fact that there might be any shit in milk, ever. The cheddar my friend makes is an organic raw-milk cheese, and I was a little alarmed by what seemed like his cavalier attitude toward sanitation. Yes, you wanted as little manure in the milk as possible, he was suggesting, but the reality of a dairy farm is such that milk will never be perfectly sterile—and that isn't necessarily a wholly desirable outcome in any case. One of the reasons cheese makers swear by the superiority of raw-milk cheeses is the complex flavors contributed by the richly diverse bacterial cultures living in them. Where in the world did I think those came from?

In the intensifying struggle between the Pasteurians and post-Pasteurians, raw-milk cheese has emerged as perhaps the single most fiercely contested terrain. I have not given my friend's name here because his candor on the subject of shit-in-milk would probably bring the full force of the health authorities down on his little dairy

farm. Live-culture sauerkraut and kimchi makers have not had reason to fear predawn raids from the Pasteurian police, but, rightly or
wrongly, people selling raw milk and raw-milk cheese now do—they
are bearing the full brunt of the war on bacteria. Raw-milk cheese
makers *are* subject to predawn raids by the FDA, with SWAT teams
brandishing guns showing up on farms unannounced, pouring cans
of fresh milk out onto the ground.

Milk was the first important food to be subject to "pasteurization"
by law, beginning in Chicago in 1908. So perhaps it shouldn't surprise
us that milk and cheese would become ground zero in the clash of
worldviews between the public-health authorities—whose authority
was founded on Pasteur's discovery of an invisible realm of disease-
causing microbes—and those who would seek to renegotiate our relationship to the microcosmos.

In fact, both sides in this struggle have a compelling case to make,
yet at the same time both sides seem blind to serious defects in their
own arguments. As Pasteurians are quick to point out, the reason we
first began pasteurizing milk (that is, heating it to 145°F for thirty
minutes, or 161°F for fifteen seconds, in order to kill bacteria) is very
simple: Raw milk was killing lots of people. Rich in sugars (such as
lactose) and proteins (such as casein), milk is a perfect breeding
ground for bacteria, and in the nineteenth century it became one of
the principal vectors for the transmission of tuberculosis and typhoid.
Pasteurization has saved thousands of lives.

Ah, but that was then, the post-Pasteurians reply. It is not at all
surprising that milk was so badly contaminated in the nineteenth-
century metropolis. In the days before refrigerated storage and transportation, fresh milk typically came not from cows in the countryside
but from cows brought into the city. Here, they were confined to
dark, dank cellars, where they were fed on brewery wastes and milked
by wretchedly poor people carrying infectious diseases. No wonder

raw milk could be lethal! Pasteurization is an industrial Band-Aid applied to an industrial problem. As long as cows are given a proper diet and good husbandry, it is unnecessary.

Yet even today, the Pasteurians respond, when most cows once again live on farms, their milk can be contaminated with pathogenic microbes, including such deadly (and novel) ones as E. coli 0157:H7 and Listeria monocytogenes. The fact is that raw milk, and the cheeses made from it, continue to kill a handful of people every year, and sicken a great many more. So why take chances when we have a proven technology to ensure the safety of our milk?

Reply the post-Pasteurians: People are also sickened by cheese and other milk products that have been pasteurized, a process that offers no guarantee of safety. Milk and cheese can be contaminated after pasteurization, and often are. Also, the cleanliness of dairying has only gotten worse under the regime of pasteurization; since dairy farmers know their milk will be sterilized after it leaves the farm and gets mixed with milk from countless other farms, they have less incentive to be scrupulous about hygiene.

Nowadays, the post-Pasteurians can cite in their support the hygiene hypothesis. This is perhaps their most devastating argument, though it, too, has unacknowledged weaknesses. According to the argument, the problem is not so much with the bacteria in the milk, which they're prepared to concede, but with the compromised immune systems of us milk drinkers—compromised (need it be said?) by years of misrule by the Pasteurians themselves, with their antibiotics, sterilized food, and sanitized child-rearing regimes. The Pasteurian drive for absolute control of the microbial realm has led to new vulnerabilities, reflected in antibiotic-resistant microbes and lethal new pathogens.

Instead of technology, the post-Pasteurians want us to put our faith in the microbes themselves and in striking a healthier, more tolerant relationship with them. They cite studies demonstrating that children who grow up drinking raw milk are measurably healthier than other children, with markedly lower rates of allergy and asthma.* Some of these children live in environments teeming with deadly pathogens, including E. *coli* and listeria, yet they don't get sick from them. The post-Pasteurians further point out that the best protection against bad bugs in milk or cheese is not the heavy hand of pasteurization but, rather, the countervailing influence of various "good" bugs, which pasteurization indiscriminately kills off. Milk and cheese are complex ecological systems that can, at least to some extent, defend and police themselves.

This proposition, I was about to learn, is by no means crazy. Sister Noëlla Marcellino is a cheese maker and microbiologist who would probably describe herself as a post-Pasteurian (though with an important caveat I will get to). In fact, one of the reasons she went back to school to become a microbiologist (she was in her thirties at the time and already an accomplished cheese maker) was so that she could scientifically test that very proposition.

The cheese nun, as she is inevitably called in the numerous profiles about her that have been published and broadcast, has been making a Connecticut version of a Saint-Nectaire since the late 1970s. Named Bethlehem, for the rural Litchfield County town that is home to Regina Laudis, her Benedictine abbey, Sister Noëlla's cheese is a raw-milk, semihard, fungal-ripened cheese made strictly according to ancient techniques that have been practiced in the Auvergne region of France since at least the seventeenth century. Sister Noëlla learned the

---

*Perkin and Strachan, "Which Aspects of the Farming Lifestyle."

techniques, which are usually closely held family or village secrets, from Lydie Zawislak, a third-generation French cheese maker who visited the abbey in 1977 at the invitation of the Abbess. Sister Noëlla had been attempting to make cheese from the abbey's surplus of milk, but found cheese making was a craft you couldn't learn very well from a book.

"So I began praying for an old French lady to come teach me," she recalled. Her prayers were answered when Lydie came to visit. (Lydie wasn't old, however.) Monasteries have historically been places where traditional food-making techniques, many of them involving fermentation, have been scrupulously perfected and preserved; Lydie was willing to entrust her family's Saint-Nectaire recipe to Sister Noëlla and the abbey.

Several things about that centuries-old recipe were guaranteed to give an American health inspector conniptions; indeed, the raw milk may have been the least of it. No, what gave the health inspector fits was the old wooden barrel in which the milk is curdled, and the wooden paddle used to stir the curds, which was carved (with two cutouts in the shape of a cross) from beech wood by a craftsman in the Auvergne. Cheese in America is *always* made in stainless-steel vats with stainless-steel tools. Easy to clean and disinfect, stainless steel is the Pasteurian's material of choice. Once scrubbed, its perfectly smooth, machine-tooled surface gleams, offering an objective correlative of good hygiene. Wood on the other hand bears all the imperfections of a natural material, with grooves and nicks and pocks where bacteria can easily hide. And indeed the inside of Sister Noëlla's cheese-making barrel wears a permanent cloak of white—a biofilm of milk solids and bacteria. You could not completely sterilize it if you tried, and part of the recipe for Saint-Nectaire involves not trying: Lydie told Noëlla that between batches the barrel should only be lightly rinsed with water.

So it happened that in 1985, after raw-milk cheese was implicated in the deaths of twenty-nine people in California, the state health inspector demanded that Sister Noëlla get rid of her wooden barrel and replace it with stainless steel.

Sister Noëlla regarded her wooden barrel and paddle not merely as quaint antiques, but as essential elements of the traditional cheese-making process. The fact that the wood harbored bacteria was actually a good thing. She preferred to think of them not as contaminants but "more like a sourdough culture." So Sister Noëlla designed an experiment for the benefit of the health inspector. From the same raw milk, she made two batches of cheese, one in the wooden barrel, and the other in a stainless-steel vat. She deliberately inoculated both batches with *E. coli*.

What happened next was, at least to a Pasteurian, utterly baffling: The cheese that had been started in the sterile vat had high levels of *E. coli*, and the cheese made in the wooden barrel had next to none. Just as Sister Noëlla had expected, the "good bacteria" living in the barrel—most of them lactobacilli—had outcompeted the *E. coli*, creating an environment in which it couldn't survive. As had happened in my sauerkraut, the good bugs, and the acids they produced, had driven out the bad. The community of microbes in the raw-milk cheese was, in effect, policing itself.

Sister Noëlla had eloquently made her point: The traditional makers of something like Saint-Nectaire have, without realizing it, been practicing a kind of folk microbiology, developed over generations by trial and error, and it works to help keep them safe. Wood, and the bacteria wood harbored, formed an indispensable part of this process, and, ironically enough, introducing a more hygienic material only made the process *less* hygienic.

Presented with the results of this elegant little experiment, the health inspector relented, allowing Sister Noëlla to keep her wooden barrel. More than a quarter century later, she is still making cheese in it.

Sister Noëlla has become something of a hero to the post-Pasteurians. A nun's habit and a Ph.D. in microbiology—the abbey sent her to the University of Connecticut so that she might better be able to defend her cheese, both from pathogens and from public health authorities—are an unbeatable combination, and, so far at least, the FDA has thought better than to mess with Sister Noëlla, even as the agency has come down hard on many other raw-milk cheese makers. Yet when I visited her at the abbey recently, hoping to learn from her how to make cheese, she was more equivocal on the subject of raw milk than I expected.

"I'm not quite the champion of raw milk that people think I am," she explained, as she showed me how to use the notorious wooden paddle to gently corral pearly white curds into a mass. "People say, Raw milk was fine for our grandfathers so why not for us? Because you are not your grandfather, and those are not your grandfather's microbes. Some of them have gotten much nastier. We're dealing with a different reality. So we can't say a raw-milk cheese is automatically safe. It has to be made with care."

What Sister Noëlla was suggesting was that many of the post-Pasteurians were in fact pre-Pasteurian in their assumptions, harking back to a biologically more innocent time, when people were hardier and the bugs more benign. We have no choice but to take account of history—including the impact of the Pasteurian regimen on our immune systems and on the microcosmos.* The techniques of traditional cheese making still offer a measure of protection, but America's

---

*There are additional reasons that may explain why people have become more vulnerable to pathogens over time: The population is older; also, a substantial number of people have had their immune systems compromised by chemotherapy and immune-suppressant drugs.

cheese culture is fairly young, and not everyone making cheese has mastered them.

Sister Noëlla and I were working together in the cheese room, which sounds grander than it is: a low-ceilinged kitchen with a few extra work sinks and a bulk tank for milk, in the back of a clapboard house on the grounds of the abbey. In the fenced pasture behind it, the abbey's Dutch Belted cows were lounging on the ground, looking very much like exceptionally fat Oreo cookies. I had spent the night at the abbey, sleeping, or trying to, on a microscopic sliver of bed in a microscopic cell upstairs in the stoplight-red converted barn that houses the tiny number of men in residence—altar boys, interns, and guests. Except when the nuns were at work—in the garden tending vegetables, in the barn caring for the cattle, in the shop working wood or leather or iron, or in the dairy making cheese—they were supposed to have no contact with men. I had spotted Noëlla earlier that morning at mass, where she and the sisters were singing some of the most hauntingly ethereal music I'd ever heard, from behind the grille of bars that symbolizes their detachment from men and the outside world.

But although life at the abbey was as hushed, solemn, and regimented as you might expect, Sister Noëlla herself exhibited none of those qualities. To the contrary: She enjoys nothing more than making people laugh, and the powerful beam of her smile is infectious. There was a lot of joking around in the cheese room, some of it fairly crude. Apart from her habit and wimple (and while at work the sisters can wear a special habit made from blue denim), there was little to remind you she was a nun.

Noëlla grew up in a big Italian family outside Boston (her older brother cofounded the fifties nostalgia band Sha Na Na), and after a difficult year at Sarah Lawrence—she enrolled in 1969, at the height of the messy ferment of the sixties counterculture—she embarked on a quest to find a more sympathetic, and more structured, environment. She visited Regina Laudis at the suggestion of a friend in 1970, and three years later she entered the abbey as a postulant—the first step on the long road to becoming a nun.

My first impression of Sister Noëlla was of a woman decidedly more earthy than spiritual. But I soon came to see that, for her, the miracles of Christ were many, and could be witnessed in the unlikeliest of places, including in a barrel of milk or under a microscope. Several of Christ's miracles rather famously involve fermentation, as she pointed out to me with a twinkle. Like bread and wine, cheese is the transformation of ordinary matter into something extraordinary, a process suggestive of transcendence.

"I never did understand why cheese wasn't included in the Eucharist," she told me at one point. At first I thought she was joking, but she turned serious. As a sacrament, Sister Noëlla suggested, cheese would actually offer something that wine or bread cannot. "Cheese forces you to contemplate death, and confronting our mortality is a necessary part of spiritual growth."

I knew enough to know Sister Noëlla wasn't referring to the mortal risk of food poisoning, but what exactly she *was* referring to with this comment, clearly heartfelt, it would take me some time in the cheese-making room, and the cave, to figure out.

◉

Learning how to make cheese from Sister Noëlla, rather than another of America's rapidly growing tribe of artisanal cheese makers, has its advantages and disadvantages. On the positive side, her method and approach are so Old World that they reveal the process at its most stripped down and elemental. Not only does Sister Noëlla have no use

for pasteurization or stainless steel, but she relies exclusively on naturally occurring bacteria and fungi—she adds no commercial cultures,
which is virtually unheard of in modern cheese making. That brings
me to one of the disadvantages of learning from Sister Noëlla: Her
approach is so far outside of the mainstream that it is in no way rep-
resentative of how most cheese is made today, even artisanal cheese.
Yet there is one other, crucial advantage: Whereas most of the cheese
makers I visited and interviewed would only let me watch them work,
and then only after walking through a vale of disinfectant and don-
ning a virtual hazmat suit, Sister Noëlla was perfectly happy to let me
get my hands wet and to handle the curd.

The work of making cheese at the abbey is carefully stitched into
the daily rhythms of the place, which revolve around worship, seven
times a day and once in the middle of the night. After Lauds at 6:00
a.m., the abbey's five cows are milked, and the milk is carried, still
warm, to the cheese room, where it is poured into the wooden barrel. Right before eight o'clock mass, Sister Noëlla adds two tiny vials
of rennet to initiate the coagulation of the milk. While she and her
sisters are at mass, singing Gregorian chants and taking communion,
a complex biochemical alchemy begins to unfold in the big barrel.

Lactobacilli present in the raw milk and the surface of the wooden
barrel begin furiously to reproduce, gobbling up lactose and convert-
ing it into lactic acid. The pH of the milk gradually falls, and as it
does, the milk becomes inhospitable to undesirable strains of bacteria, including any E. coli that may have found their way into it. The
acidifying environment also promotes the action of the rennet, which
begins magically to transform the fluid milk into a silky white gel.
Returning from mass at ten-thirty, Sister Noëlla ran her index finger
through the surface, cleaving open a little canyon where, just an hour
or two before, there had been only liquid. It looked like a soft tofu,

but it gleamed. For most of the cheese makers I've met, Sister Noëlla included, this is the moment of magic.

Rennet, the catalyst of this alchemy, is stuff so strange as to be almost mythological. *Ripped from the belly of a baby animal:* And so it is, literally. Rennet comes from the lining of the first stomach of a calf, lamb, or baby goat. It contains an enzyme called chymosin, the function of which in a baby's stomach is to curdle mother's milk, thereby slowing its absorption and rearranging the milk proteins in such ways as to aid the baby's digestion. Anyone who has ever burped a baby and been spit up on for his troubles, has observed the action of chymosin on milk.

Presumably some herder discovered the process several thousand years ago, when he or she slaughtered a young ruminant, opened up its stomach, and found some lumpy curds of milk. Or perhaps the ancient herder used the stomach of a young animal as a vessel in which to store or carry milk. Exposed to the rennet in the stomach lining, the milk would have turned to something much like cheese. Whatever its taste, the advantages of this "processed" milk over fresh would have been immediately apparent, particularly to a nomadic people in a time before refrigeration. Since curdling removes most of the water from the milk, it renders the food much more portable, and the curds, having been acidified in the animal's stomach, would remain edible much longer than fresh milk.

What this suggests is that cheese was not so much an invention as a discovery. Like other fermentations, cheese making is a form of "biomimicry"—a technology modeled on a naturally occurring biological process. Certainly there was plenty of room for improving on stomach-curdled milk, including its taste and appearance and longevity. But, like other fermentations, cheese was from the beginning a boon to humankind: a perishable foodstuff that has been processed in such a way as to render it more digestible, more nutritious, more durable, and more flavorful than the original.

Rennet, which, remarkably, still often comes from the stomach linings of baby animals,* requires an acidic environment in order to best perform its magic of coagulation. In cheese making, the acid is supplied by bacterial fermentation rather than stomach acids. As in pickles and sauerkraut, the necessary bacteria are ubiquitous in the environment and on the "substrate"—in this case, the raw milk. But pasteurizing milk creates a biologically blank slate, into which cultures of lactobacilli must be reintroduced after pasteurization in order to acidify the milk and begin to build flavors. Starting with a clean slate has its advantages: The cheese maker can decide precisely which bacteria to introduce, and there will be few surprises—or "*accidents de fromages*," as the French call their cheese-making disasters. That's why such blank-slate ferments are now the rule, and not only in cheesemaking. Most brewers and winemakers work the same way, killing off the native bacteria and yeasts and then reintroducing only the ones they want. Yet the gain in control of the process comes at the price of a loss in complexity that, according to proponents of rawmilk cheeses and other wild fermentations, you can taste.

One of the things you can taste in a raw-milk cheese is the taste of a particular place. For her dissertation research, Sister Noëlla drove around the French countryside, collecting samples of the microbes living on the rinds of various raw-milk cheeses. She focused her attention on *Geotrichum candidum*, a fungus I had never heard of but, it turns out, I have been eating large quantities of all my life: It is the mold that forms the downy white jacket on fungal-ripened cheeses

---

*Many cheese makers today use "vegetable rennets"—chymosin produced by a genetically engineered bacterium, mold, or a yeast.

like Camembert and Brie. (The French call it the *jolie robe*—"pretty dress.") Using genetic-sequencing techniques to compare her samples, Sister Noëlla found "an enormous diversity" among strains of geotrichum. She also discovered that different strains of the same mold feasted on different nutrients in the milk, producing different chemical by-products that contribute different flavors to a cheese. She concluded that at least some part of the astounding diversity of French cheeses—"How can anyone be expected to govern a country with 246 cheeses?" Charles de Gaulle once famously asked—owes to the wide diversity of its microbes.

What this suggests is that *terroir*—the French term for the taste of place—is influenced not just by the local climate or soil but also by differences in the local bacteria and fungi. Sister Noëlla has come to think of this microbial biodiversity as part of a nation's patrimony. "People understand the importance of preserving an endangered white rhino," she told me. "But a strain of fungus no one has ever seen or even heard of is a tougher sell"—yet in her view no less important. As Italo Calvino wrote in *Palomar*:

> Behind every cheese there is a pasture of a different green under a different sky: meadows encrusted with salt that the tides of Normandy deposit every evening; meadows perfumed with aromas in the windy sunlight of Provence; there are different herds, with their shelters and their movements across the countryside; there are secret methods handed down over the centuries. This [cheese] shop is a museum: . . . behind every displayed object the presence of the civilization that gave it form and takes form from it.

Later that afternoon, in her little laboratory on the abbey grounds, Sister Noëlla elaborated on the elusive concept of *terroir*. The particular taste of a place, as she conceives it, owes to a tight weave of natural and cultural threads that cannot readily be teased apart. Clearly the qualities of the milk (What breed were the cows? What plants grew in the pasture they grazed? What was the weather like?*) influence the flavor of a cheese, but so does even the tiniest detail in the technique of the cheese maker. And though we would tend to regard such details as artifacts of human culture rather than nature, their influence on the flavor of a cheese is mediated by microbes—that is, by nature. So, for example, the temperature in the vat; the time between steps; the tools used to cut the curd; the geometry of the molds into which they were pressed; how hard they are pressed; how much salt is introduced; the humidity in the cave; even the type of straw on which the cheeses rest as they age—all these details help to determine precisely which microbes will predominate, and these in turn help determine the sensory qualities of the finished cheese. (The rye straw? Sister Noëlla explained that rye grass favors the growth of Trichothecium roseum, "the flower of the molds"—lending a pinkish cast to the rind that is prized by the French.)

"A cheese is an ecological system," Sister Noëlla explained, "and the cheese maker's techniques operate like forces of natural selection to determine which species will succeed"—thereby creating the specific flavors and aromas and texture of a Saint-Nectaire rather than, say, a Mont d'Or or Reblochon. In this, a cheese is much like a sourdough bread culture, except that its microbial community is even more complex and long-lived. Indeed, it is still living when we eat it, whereas the culture in a bread dies in the oven.

When Lydie returned to the abbey two years after teaching Sister Noëlla to make cheese, she was astonished to find that the rind of a Connecticut Saint-Nectaire had developed the very same fungi as a

---

*When the weather is cold, another cheese maker told me, calves need more energy to keep themselves warm, so on those days the proportion of fat in their mother's milk increases.

Saint-Nectaire ripened in the Auvergne—up to and including the Trichothecium roseum. So was it possible Lydie had unwittingly carried those French microbes on her person during her first visit? Not likely, according to Sister Noëlla.

"Everything is everywhere," she explains, referring to the numberless species of fungi and bacteria ubiquitous in the environment, "and then our technology selects" which among them will thrive. But wouldn't this selection-by-culture argue against the idea of terroir? Only if your concept of terroir is limited to the local expression of nature. Yet a place is much more than a patch of earth; it is also the people who live in it and the traditions they follow, and so in turn the microbes they unconsciously favor—and which in turn have favored them, with desirable flavors and aromas. These highly particular qualities (which seem to be found in fermented foods especially[*]) owe at least partly to the reciprocal relationship of microbe and man—nature and culture together, as expressed through fermentation. So along with all the other elements contributing to the particular taste of a place—soil, climate, flora, tradition, technique, story—we need to add one more: the microbiology of human desire.

◉

After Sister Noëlla had satisfied herself that the milk was sufficiently coagulated, she invited me to run my fingers through the pristine white Jell-O, gently breaking it up into tinier and tinier curds. I worked alongside the abbey's newest postulant, Stephanie Cassidy. A willowy thirty-year-old with big brown eyes, Stephanie took care of the abbey's cows and had recently begun helping out with the

---

[*]Perhaps this explains why so many of the foods thought to best express terroir—such as wine and cheese—are products of fermentation.

cheese making. Bending over the barrel from opposite sides, we ran our hands through the warm curd, carefully subdividing it into little white peas. The recipe specifies that the curd be kept at the same temperature as the cow's body, so from time to time Sister Noëlla poured a little hot water along the inside edges of the barrel to keep it from cooling. When Stephanie judged the curds uniformly tiny enough, she took the wooden paddle from its nail and, running it slowly along the side of the barrel, began to herd the little curds together.

They seemed to like one another's company. That's because the chymosin in the rennet had snipped off a specific bit of one of the casein proteins that, in fresh milk, functions like a bumper to keep the particles bouncing off one another and so dispersed in solution. The milk coagulates when the now bumperless casein proteins bond to form a kind of mesh that traps fat and water. The goal in handling the curds is to gently expel the water from them while losing as little of the fat as possible.

The curds tasted sweet and clean but bland, more like fresh warm milk than cheese. But their blandness gave no hint of the frenzy of activity going on deep within them, as the curds formed and re-formed. Virtually all of the microbial DNA necessary to create a mature cheese was now present and accounted for and beginning to do its fermentative work. The lactobacilli were proliferating wildly in the warm milk, turning the lactose into lactic acid, contributing flavors, and lowering the pH, a souring process I could faintly smell. The acidification would continue in the cheese for several weeks before reversing course, as the fungi—also already present in the milk, as spores—took over, inaugurating a second fermentation in the rind. But I'm getting ahead of myself and the microbes. . . .

Once the wooden paddle had persuaded the curdlets to come together in a casual mass, Stephanie began removing the whey from the barrel with a flat-bottomed pan. Then, with the palms of her hands, she began pushing the mass of curd down toward the bottom of the barrel. I joined her, leaning over the barrel and pressing the curd down as slowly and gently as I possibly could, so as not to disturb the precious butterfat.

"*Restez là,*" Sister Noëlla implored us as we worked, explaining that that is what Lydie's mother used to tell her whenever she had her hands on the curd. "Stay there"—move your hands as little and as gently as possible. Impatience would be ruinous; by forcing out the fat, it would make the paste—the interior of the cheese—rubbery. (Thus does the mood of the cheese maker find its way into a cheese.) The muscles in my wrists and lower back had begun to howl, but I kept at it, pressing down as slowly and deliberately as I could bear to. After decades of doing this kind of work several times a week, Sister Noëlla has had to have several surgeries to repair the carpal tunnel in her wrists.

At last Sister Noëlla pronounced herself satisfied with the curd. It now formed a three-inch-thick layer at the bottom of the barrel, snowy white beneath a few remaining inches of yellowish, sour whey. Standing up straight had never felt so wonderful. Alas, it was not to be for long. The time had come to cut the curd, and Stephanie handed me a long knife. She had me cut it in thirds, first top to bottom and then side to side. Then, with our hands, we scooped up the white bricks and piled them into the molds. Cylindrical containers the size of deep pie tins, the molds are made of wood or white plastic with a pattern of holes drilled into their bottoms. Now came more urgings to "*restez là*" as I slowly pressed the blocks of curd into the molds, turning them over from time to time. A thin trickle of whey wept from the holes. The curds were now tightly knit into something that looked and felt like a cheese, except that it was completely white and tasteless. We sprinkled some salt on the exposed side.

The term for these fresh discs is a "green cheese" and, incredibly, we had made only three of them from nearly fifty gallons of milk.

Now, stacked one on top of another, the cheeses went into the press, an old wooden contraption with a big steel screw that could be manually tightened to gradually build pressure, squeezing still more water from the cheeses. We were done. The green cheeses would spend the night in the press, weeping their last few tears of whey, before being rinsed and moved into the "cave" the following morning. Here, they would spend the next two months, growing old.

Cheese is milk that has grown up. . . . It is preeminently the food of man—the older it grows the more manly it becomes, and in the last stages of senility it almost requires a room to itself. —Edward Bunyard (1878–1939), *The Epicure's Companion*

Compared with other fermentations—of vegetables, grains, or grapes—the fermentation of fresh milk into a mature cheese depends on a remarkably complex dance of taxonomically far-flung species, including mammals, bacteria, and fungi. Or perhaps I should say *fermentations*, plural, because what takes place in the aging room is so different from what happens in the milk vat as to constitute a whole other order of transformation.

Most of the activity in the vat involves anaerobic bacteria turning lactose into lactic acids; that process continues in the paste—the airless interior of the cheese—with some elaborations, as enzymes produced by the bacteria break down fats, proteins, and sugars into simpler and generally more flavorful molecules. But as soon as the cheese maker forms the curds into, well, forms, she has created something new: an inside, the paste, and an outside, the incipient rind. Biologically, the rind comprises a new environment—airy and moist, but no longer wet—which selects for a new set of microbes: the aerobes. The spores of these aerobic microbes are already present (*everything is everywhere*) in the milk, in the air, clinging to the stone walls and earthen floor of the cave. And so, within hours, this new cast of microbial characters, beginning with a group of acid- and air-loving fungi, begins to colonize the wide-open frontier of the cheese rind.

Standing in the abbey's "cave," it is possible to observe this succession of species as if in time lapse. The cave is really just a ten-foot-square corner of a cellar, walled off and air-conditioned to maintain cavelike temperatures and levels of humidity all year long. Lining the walls are tall wooden cabinets faced with screen doors. Their shelves hold two months' production of cheeses, arranged according to seniority. Written on the side of each cheese in blue ink is the date on which it was made and the initials of its maker. Starting with the fat white discs made yesterday, I could follow the cheeses' progression from callow youth to venerable age, as the bloomy white rinds gradually take on some gray, then slowly mottle and shrink, until you arrive at the wrinkled and stinky gray-brown visage of a Saint-Nectaire that, after two months, is fully ripe and ready to eat.

What takes place in the rind over the course of these eight weeks is a more or less orderly form of rot. As successive rounds of decomposition unfold, one species dines on the waste products of another, in the process creating the conditions, and often the food, for the next. Most of these fungi you know well and have had reason to despise in the past: They are the same molds that turn white bread blue, that establish furry white beachheads on a ripe tomato or draw a dilating brown target on a pear. The cheese maker has learned, at least to an extent, how to manage or guide these familiar wild species, getting them to behave in more or less predictable ways.

Sister Noëlla walked me through the stages of fungal life and death unfolding in her cave. By the second day, a fine lawn of yeasts—primarily *Debaryomyces* and *Torulopsis*—has spread across the fresh cheese, though it is only visible through a microscope. There are also invisible colonies of bacteria, such as *Streptococcus cremoris*, working to turn the lactose in the milk into lactic acid—food for future fungi. By the sixth day, the cheese has grown a fine white beard of hyphae from a fungus called *Mucor*. This particular fungus, which the French sometimes call the *bête noire*, is considered a catastrophe when it appears in a Brie or Camembert, but is warmly welcomed in a Saint-Nectaire or Tomme de Savoie. When on day nine the *Mucor* sporulates, a field of what (under the microscope) looks like black daisy seed heads colonizes the rind, transforming its pristine white to a grayish brown. By now the cheese looks as though it has lost its youthful innocence and acquired a few unsightly scars of experience. It has also visibly shrunk, as the water in it continues to evaporate.

In the shade of those blackish *Mucor* hyphae, strains of *Geotrichum candidum*, Sister Noëlla's favorite fungus, are feasting on lactic acid and growing their own hyphae, though they are not yet visible to the naked eye. "Geo," as some American cheese makers call it for short, is responsible for the downy white coat—the *jolie robe*—found on a Saint-Marcellin. The fungus introduces a set of powerful enzymes that break down various fats and proteins, in the process helping to develop the cheese's flavor and releasing several strongly aromatic compounds, including the faint whiff of ammonia that filled the cave. Sister Noëlla has ultimate respect for *Geotrichum*, which was the subject of her dissertation. She mentioned that its enzymes have been known to bore holes through plastic. Some strains of *Geo* also seem to make it more difficult for Listeria to survive in a cheese.

By breaking down lactic acid and producing ammonia, *Geotrichum* neutralizes the pH of the rind, changing the environment in such a way as to make it hospitable to subsequent waves of bacteria and fungi. By sending its filamentous hyphae down into the paste, the fungus in effect "tills" the rind of the cheese, digging microscopic channels that allow other aerobic microbes, like *Penicillium*, to move deeper into the cheese, contributing new flavors and aromas. These penetrations gradually thicken the rind and multiply its population of microbes, both in number and in kind. Soon the rind accumulates a grayish dust of "fungal debris"—spores and the bodies of dead fungi—that gives off the musty odor of a dank, neglected cellar. By day thirteen pinkish patches of *Trichothecium roseum* have begun to powder the rind, giving a violet cast to the Saint-Nectaire. By now the pH of the rind has been neutralized, creating a happy habitat for coryneform bacteria such as *Brevibacterium*, which eventually will contribute powerful aromas to the ripening cheese.

And so it goes for the two months it takes a Saint-Nectaire to ripen, each species altering the rind environs in such a way as to pave the way for the next, in a predictable ecological succession that Sister Noëlla carefully documented in her dissertation. Along the way, each species releases its own set of enzymes, each one a customized molecular tool for breaking down a specific fat or sugar or protein into an amino acid or peptide or ester that contributes a specific flavor or aroma to the ripening cheese. Within a few weeks, the process of ecological succession has culminated in the establishment of a fairly stable community of fungi and bacteria. Much about this microbial community remains a wilderness to science. But Sister Noëlla is in touch with a group of microbiologists who are actively exploring the cheese-rind ecosystem, hoping to learn how the various species compete and cooperate, and how they may communicate with one another to defend their turf (and in turn the cheese beneath it) from invasion, in a process known as "quorum sensing."

Listening to Sister Noëlla exalt this leprous skin of decomposed milk as a vibrant ecological community is to appreciate just what a weird and wonderful achievement cheese is: how our ancestors figured out how to guide the decomposition of milk so that it might be arrested and then defended, using a jujitsu move that deftly deploys rot against rot, fungus against fungus, to suspend milk's inexorable slide into putrefaction just long enough for us to enjoy a tasty cheese. Other ferments operate on the same general principle, earth to earth deferred, but, unlike wine or beer or a pickled beet, the aroma of a ripened cheese won't ever let us forget the role rot has played in its creation.

◉

Over time, the fungi living and dying in a cheese rind work to neutralize their environment, a development that hastens the ripening of the cheese in two important ways. First, the difference in pH between the paste and the rind creates a "gradient," or imbalance, that serves to draw the strong-smelling compounds produced on the rind deep into the paste; ripening from the outside in, the cheese is bland no longer. At the same time, the rising pH of the rind creates conditions much to the liking of a notorious microbe called Brevibacterium linens, the appearance of which, beginning around week three, is marked by a distinct reddish-orange cast creeping over the rind. But you don't need to see B. linens to know it has arrived: B. linens is the bacterium responsible for much of the stink in a stinky cheese. Along with a few other members of its bacterial family, the coryneforms, B. linens is the reason certain ripe cheeses need a room of their own.

Saint-Nectaire is home to a healthy population of B. linens that, when the cheese is fully ripe, gives it its distinctive barnyard smell. But it is in the washed-rind cheeses—Époisse, Limburger, Taleggio, and, in America, newer ones like Red Hawk or Winnimere—where B. linens is actively encouraged to flourish, imbuing these cheeses with their powerful and occasionally room-clearing aromas. Washing the rind, usually with salty water (sometimes with wine or beer), creates an environment maximally hospitable to B. linens, which in turn can single-handedly create an environment that is either much more or much less hospitable to members of our species. Some people love the smell of B. linens, or learn to; others find it revolting. And still others are repelled and attracted to it at the same time, captivated by what might be called the erotics of disgust.

"Oh, I really like that term," Sister Noëlla said, when I raised, as delicately as I could, the issue of rankness in her cheese. The subject of disgust is not something I've found many cheese makers eager to discuss, at least not in the company of journalists. But Sister Noëlla is happy to talk about the earthier dimension of her work, at least up to a point.

"Cheese is all about the dark side of life," she said one afternoon as we were strolling up the hill to her lab. She told me about a French cheese maker of her acquaintance, a monk by the name of Frère Nathanaël, who makes a strong cheese called Tamié at his monastery in the Haute-Savoie. She once asked him how he determined when a Tamié is ripe. You turn it over and sniff the bottom, Frère Nathaniaël told her. "Ça sent la vache." It's ready when it smells like the cow. And then, in case that wasn't quite clear enough, he added, "The back end of the cow!"

It suddenly dawned on me that "barnyardy"—a term cheese mongers use in praise of certain stinky cheeses—is a euphemism for manure. (Duh!) Certainly the manure of some farm animals, such as cows, is not unappealing, at least when they've been out grazing on pasture. Yet some cheeses make even less socially acceptable allusions, if that's the right word. The various aromas of washed-rind cheeses are often likened to those of the human body in its various parts. A French poet famously referred to the aroma of certain cheeses as the "pieds de Dieu"—the feet of god. Just to be clear: foot odor of a particularly exalted quality, but still—foot odor.

Sister Noëlla told me about another cheese-maker friend of hers, James Stillwaggon, an American living in France, who holds unusually frank views on the subject of cheese olfaction. She had recently quoted him at the end of the draft of an article on the microbiology of cheese rinds, though she wasn't sure if his remarks would survive editing. The quote came from an exchange the two had had on the question of why the vocabulary used to describe wine is so much richer and more nuanced than the vocabulary used to describe cheese. Wine talk is full of vivid metaphor—comparing wines to specific fruits and flowers, for example—whereas, as Stillwaggon pointed out, the flavors of cheese usually elicit only vague, generalized comments "like 'Mmmm, good!' 'Interesting!' 'Fantastic!'

"If we address frankly what is evoked by cheese, I think it becomes clear why so little is said. So what does cheese evoke? Damp dark cellars, molds, mildews and mushrooms galore, dirty laundry and high school locker rooms, digestive processes and visceral fermentations, he-goats which do not remind of Chanel . . . In sum, cheese reminds of dubious, even unsavory places, both in nature and in our own organisms. And yet we love it."

In its very suggestiveness, cheese is both like and unlike many of the other foods humans cook or ferment. Whether by fire or water or the action of microbes, one of the ways humans transform the edible stuff of nature is in the direction of greater allusiveness—in taste or smell or appearance. Just as we take pleasure in enriching our language with layers of metaphor and allusion, we apparently like to trope what we eat and drink, too, extracting from it not only more nourishment but more meaning as well—more psychic nourishment, if you will. It just so happens that the more vivid, odiferous tropes that cheese makers have teased out of milk can verge on the indecent, taking us places polite society doesn't like to go.

But the question arises: Why would we want to go there in the first place? Why don't cheese makers stop with the sweet, freshly showered scent of mozzarella, rather than press on to the ripe raw-milk Camembert with its suggestions of, well, negligent hygiene?

Compared with some other mammals, we humans have long been alienated from our sense of smell. From the moment we began to walk upright, the eye took precedence over the nose. This, at least, is Sigmund Freud's theory for why humans have repressed so much of the sensory data supplied by the nose, and why our vocabulary for describing smells is comparatively so thin and generalized. (*Mmmm, good!*) The smells we are repressing are of course those of the lower body and the earth, which walking upright allows us to transcend, or at least overlook, in humanity's age-old top-priority project of putting space between itself and all the other animals. But that project has a cost. The reason those smells so transfix mammals that still walk on four legs is that they contain deeply compelling information, information the high-minded biped is missing. Freud never said this, but Stillwaggon conceivably might: A strong cheese puts us back on all fours.

Metaphorically speaking, of course. Or maybe not. Because one of the most curious things I learned about the bacteria that give cheese their aromas is that they are, at least in some cases, closely related to the bacteria that give us our aromas. *Brevibacterium?* It not only lives in the salty damp of a washed-rind cheese, but is equally at home in the salty damp under human arms or between human toes. (I give you "the feet of god.") Sweat by itself has no discernible odor; what you think you smell when you smell sweat are the metabolic byproducts of *brevibacteria*, as they busily go about fermenting, well, *you*. And your toes and armpits are not the only bodily zones where such fermentations are taking place, either.* So it may well be that the allusiveness of a funky cheese to the human body is actually more lit-

---

*See the footnote on page 325 describing the process of fermentation in the human vagina.

eral than metaphoric, a matter not so much *this stands for that* as *this is that, too*, in food form. What's going on in certain cheeses doesn't just remind us of the body; in some sense it *is* the body, or at least the fermentations unfolding thereon and -in.

As you might expect, the French are much more comfortable with these ideas, and these cheeses, than Americans seem to be. In fact, some Frenchmen regard America's uneasiness with raw-milk cheeses (which tend to be more odiferous than cheeses made from pasteurized milk) as further proof of our puritanism in carnal matters. Pierre Boisard, a French sociologist, celebrates a raw-milk Camembert as "a living substance produced by an animal organism, [that] constantly reminds us of the body, of sensual pleasure, of sexual fulfillment, and of all that is forbidden in it." Only "hidden Puritanism re-entering through the backdoor [of] alimentary hygiene"—and *not* the threat from listeria, say, or salmonella—could possibly explain the American government's ban on raw-milk Camembert.[*]

No, I never did float this theory to Sister Noëlla. Didn't get the chance. . . . Okay, actually I could never figure out quite how to broach it. How *do* you ask a nun whether she believes the government's crackdown on raw-milk cheese is rooted in sexual repression?

Though I did ask her, before leaving the abbey, if she could put me in touch with her friend Jim Stillwaggon, or refer me to any of his writings. She had described him as a philosopher as well as a cheese maker. Had he published any of his reflections on sex and death in cheese? Did he have a Web site, perhaps?

"No, and it's probably just as well. I'm just not sure the world is ready for Jim."

---

[*]Under current regulations, only raw-milk cheeses that have been aged a minimum of sixty days may be sold in the United States, and you would not want to eat a Camembert quite that old—it would presumably have liquefied by then and begun to stink beyond approach. The theory behind this rule is that the aging process should render the cheese safer, but it now appears there is little scientific basis for this belief.

On my drive home, a fragrant chunk of Sister's Noëlla's ripe Saint-Nectaire warming on the seat beside me, I wondered if the French might be right, and if the disgust we sometimes register at the smell of a strong cheese is the product of sexual repression—a taboo at work. It does seem to be the case that the smells of cheese are ripe with the smells of the body, human or animal. Yet not all of those smells are necessarily sexual in nature. When we consider "the body," certainly there is sex to consider, but isn't there also death? I also wondered if maybe, on the theory (contra Freud) that sometimes a cigar is just a cigar, disgust is sometimes just disgust.

When I got home I began to dig around in the literature of disgust, which in the last several decades has attracted a handful of interesting thinkers from a wide range of disciplines, including psychology (Paul Rozin), philosophy (Aurel Kolnai), even law (William Ian Miller). Disgust, I learned, is one of the primary human emotions; it appears on even the shortest list of human emotions, and in fact is unique to our species. (Though you do have to wonder, how can we be so sure?) Darwin, who wrote about disgust in his 1872 book, *The Expression of the Emotions in Man and Animals*, described it as a reaction to something that offends our sense of taste (the word comes from the Middle French *desgouster*, or "distaste"), rooted in the biological imperative to reject foods that might be dangerous.

Building on Darwin, Paul Rozin writes that the emotion of disgust originates in "the revulsion at the prospect of oral incorporation of an offensive object." Disgust is thus a crucial tool for an omnivore at constant risk of ingesting toxic substances. But the emotion of disgust has since been co-opted by other, higher human faculties, such as morality, so that we are disgusted by certain kinds of morally offensive behavior. Rozin writes, "A mechanism for avoiding harm to the body became a mechanism for avoiding harm to the soul."

Disgust, as an emotion exclusive to humans, also helps put distance between us and the rest of nature. It is a crucial component of the civilizing process. Rozin points out that anything that reminds us that we are in fact still animals can elicit feelings of disgust. This includes bodily secretions,* sexuality, and death. But for Rozin it is the third term here that is the most important.

"The prototypical odor of disgust is the odor of decay," he points out, "which is the odor of death." Thus disgust can be understood as a defense against our fear of death, another emotion that happens to be unique to our species.† Rozin says that people who score high on psychological tests for "disgust sensitivity" also score high on tests measuring the fear of death.

Putrefaction is repulsive to us because it reminds us of our ultimate fate, which is to have the noble and intricate form of our bodies disintegrate into a suppurating, stinking puddle of formlessness, then to be returned to the earth as food for the worms. This work of decomposition will be performed by bacteria and fungi, and the method they will deploy will be fermentation. Oddly, it is this process of decomposition that disgusts us, not the final result of that process: Rotting flesh is disgusting, but skeletons are not.

So why should we ever be attracted to the very processes and products that, for the very good reasons Rozin gives, repulse us? Surely this is perverse. Yet if disgust is in fact one of the ways humans draw a line between themselves and the other animals, then to deliberately put ourselves in situations that elicit disgust may allow us to

---

*The exception that proves the rule is tears, which only humans produce, and which do not disgust.

†Of course, there is also an adaptive value in being repulsed by putrefying matter, corpses, and feces: These things often harbor pathogens.

underscore and enforce that distinction. Perhaps we "enjoy" the experience of disgust for the flattering things the reaction implies about us—the wrinkling of the nose a visible index of our superiority and refinement.

I became curious to know what Stillwaggon would have to say on the subject, and in the middle of my journey through the literature of disgust, I went looking for him online. Something had raised my antennae—didn't smell quite right—when Sister Noëlla told me he hadn't published. Stillwaggon didn't sound like a man who could keep his views under a bushel basket even if he tried. When I searched his name, I found no books or Web sites, but I did find a Facebook page, and there on its wall a URL. Bingo: In large type the words "Cheese, Sex, Death and Madness" popped up on my screen, above a photo of an aproned man stirring a copper vat of milk, next to a photo of a particularly hideous cheese oozing yellow from its broken crust.[*]

The Web site, half in French and half in English, was itself an aromatic ferment of truly wild ideas about, well, sex and death and cheese, which Stillwaggon defined as "nature imperfectly mastered." This struck me as a pretty good definition for fermentation in general. (If not for the entire human enterprise.) He went on to describe cheese as "an incarnate Passion Play, unfolding in its lifetime (briefer, in general, than our own) all the characteristics of the newborn, of juvenility and adolescence, of maturity and of decrepitude." Cheese was flesh, heir to all its glories and mortifications. On the home page I clicked on "Attraction & Repulsion" and found this soaring, over-ripe, and ungrammatical flight of cheesy exegesis:

"Cheese shares the same ambiguity of attraction/repulsion which marks and characterizes our genital and anal zones as passage from

---

[*]When I tried to revisit Stillwaggon's Web site in August 2012, the link no longer worked.

the scrubbed and well-aired exterior toward the organic, unsurveyed and uncontrolled interior: infernal microcosm fermenting, composting, the seething haven of impersonal microbiota. . . .

"In both domains—the cheese and the sex—we are drawn to the limits of our comfort zone. Both zones of experience therefore invite us to exceed our limits, to test, to uncover, to abandon our reserve, to relativize our notions and principles—of limit, of desirable, of good & bad, of attractiveness and hideousness. The direction of this discovery is from pure and simple toward impure and complex, from a formal, cared-for aesthetic toward a formlessness, an aesthetic of abandon and degradation."

Whew . . .

Stillwaggon had single-handedly yanked Dionysus out of the world of wine, where he had been comfortably ensconced for thirty-five hundred years, and brought him into the world of cheese. (Where, surprisingly enough, he seemed very much at home.) Stillwaggon and Sister Noëlla shared large ambitions for the significance of cheese in human affairs, though I could certainly see why she might not think the world was ready for his writings. Stillwaggon's mad Web site achieved a kind of perverse brilliance, accompanied by a handful of louche cheese photos and the occasional clipping from the French press. (Including one about a French study of human odor that found that men, when ripe, smell more like washed-rind cheese than women, who smell more like sauvignon blanc.) But I found the "Cheese, Sex, Death and Madness" so rhetorically moist and overheated that I soon clicked out of it. And made my way back to Freud, who had never before seemed quite so moderate and sane.

True, Freud had nothing specific to say about cheese, but his thoughts on disgust were illuminating even so. For Freud, disgust is a "reaction formation" designed to keep us from indulging desires our civilization has sought to repress. We are drawn to what disgusts because it is a cover for precisely what most attracts. Freud points out that children are not in the least disgusted by feces; to the contrary, they're fascinated by them. But they learn to be disgusted as part of their socialization. Disgust thus operates as a kind of deeply internalized taboo against desires civilization needs to repress.

But taboos are always ripe for breaking, especially when they can be broken without doing serious harm, to either the individual or society. A cheese that stinks—of manure, of sex—offers a relatively safe way for us to flirt with forbidden desires. And even a cheese that stinks of death—one that, like a ripe Vacherin, has completely disintegrated into a formless ooze—may offer a perverse sort of pleasure. For, if the final fermentation that awaits us all is too horrible to contemplate, perhaps a little preview of putrefaction on a cheese plate can, like a gothic tale or horror movie, give us the little frisson of pleasure that comes from rehearsing precisely what we most fear.

Freud was surely right to suggest that disgust is a learned response, mediated by culture. Anthropologists have amply documented the fact that, although the emotion of disgust is a human universal, the specific things that elicit disgust in one culture don't necessarily disgust people in another. Cheese is the perfect example. Until very recently, most Americans found strong French cheeses repulsive. When Red Hawk was introduced a decade or so ago, there was only a handful of washed-rind cheeses made in America. Claude Lévi-Strauss writes that, after the American troops landed in Normandy in 1944, they destroyed several of the dairies where Camembert was made because they reeked—of what the troops assumed had to be corpses. Oops.

Many Asians regard cheese of any kind as repulsive, and stinky cheeses so disgusting as to be utterly incomprehensible as food. Lest you conclude that people in Asia have more delicate noses than do we in the West, consider a few of the East's own stinking delicacies. The Japanese prize natto, the stringy, mucilaginous ferment of soybeans that is strongly redolent of garbage. Fish sauce, used to flavor foods in many Southeast Asian nations, is the liquid secreted by dead fish that have been allowed to rot under the equatorial sun until they lose any hint of form and stink magnificently. The Chinese love their "stinky tofu," which is made by steeping blocks of tofu in a very old, black ooze of putrefying vegetable matter. Being far too odiferous to bring indoors, stinky tofu is usually eaten as a street food, though even out in the open air it can stink up an entire city block.

I recently had the opportunity to sample stinky tofu in Shanghai. The stink is unmistakably the stink of putrefaction, and, at least to this nose, is more disgusting than any cheese I've ever encountered. But, then, I am not Asian. (Surprisingly, it tasted pretty good once you got it safely past the nostrils, and I'm convinced the rich menagerie of local bacteria did much to settle a stomach discombobulated by travel.) Asians who have tasted a strong cheese like Roquefort will swear that rotted milk is much more disgusting than rotted soybeans, because the animal fats in the cheese coat the mouth, causing the flavors to linger. What makes stinky tofu superior, in their view, is that the taste, which they claim is "cleaner," doesn't last long. But what kind of selling point is that, for a food whose taste you supposedly like?

Arguing over which culture has the more disgusting delicacy is never going to be very productive. What's interesting here is that so many cultures seem to have one powerful, smelly food that they prize with as much fervor as other cultures despise it. In some places, that culturally defining food is notable for its pungency rather than its odor—think of hot chilis in Mexico or India. But many, if not most, of these iconic foods—natto, stinky tofu, cheese, fish sauce, sauerkraut, kimchi—get their power from fermentation. And, just as curiously, the devotees of these strong ferments (or spicy foods) frequently take pleasure in the fact that people from other cultures can't easily choke them down. One of the things a food can do for people is to help define them as a group—*we are the people who* like *to eat rotted shark*. It could be that the success of this self-definition depends on other people finding the very same food inedible or disgusting. In the same way that disgust can be used to draw lines between humans and other animals, it can also help draw lines between cultures.

Certainly it can take the full force of culture to overcome people's resistance to the odor of rotting plants or the back end of animals in something you're supposed to eat. This is what is meant by an acquired taste. If culture is capable of inspiring disgust, it can also help us overcome it when doing so suits its purposes. Culture is nothing if not powerful, especially when it comes to defining or defending itself.

In South Korea recently, I watched classes of kindergarteners marched through a kimchi museum in Seoul, one of two in that city and many more in that country. There were dioramas of women rubbing spice into cabbage leaves, and displays of kimchi urns. The schoolchildren were being gently indoctrinated in the culture of the national dish, learning its history and trying their hand at making it. As a docent explained to me, "Children are not born loving kimchi." That is, it is something they have to learn. Why? To become fully Korean. A sweet red strawberry just wouldn't have done the trick. If a food is going to help forge cultural identity, it must be an acquired taste, not a universal one. Surely that explains why fermented foods have so often and so reliably played this role.

The taste of fermented foods is the taste of us, and them.

During my first visit to the Abbey of Regina Laudis, Sister Noëlla invited me to attend the morning mass. Mass takes place on a wooded hillside above the abbey in a building that, from the outside, looks like a plain old New England barn, but inside reveals itself as a soaring wooden cathedral, flooded with light. I took a seat way in the back. I could see Sister Noëlla and Stephanie with the other nuns behind the grille of black bars behind the altar, where a lanky young priest was presiding. Two by two, the nuns in their flowing black habits floated up to a little teller's window in the grille to take communion from Father Ian, taking first the wafer on their tongue and then a sip of wine from his cup.

By now, I subscribed wholeheartedly to Sister Noëlla's possibly heretical notion that cheese deserved a place alongside wine and bread in the Eucharist. Cheese seemed easily as good a symbol of the body as bread, maybe better: Certainly it offered a sharper, more poignant reminder of the flesh's mortality. "Everything about cheese reminds us of death," she had told me. "The caves in which they age are like crypts; then there are the smells of decomposition." Though you could also see why the early church fathers might have rejected cheese, as perhaps a little too reminiscent of the flesh in a ritual that was, after all, not just about transformation and death but transcendence too.

As it happened, Father Ian's sermon that morning was on the subject of fermentation. The day's text was the exchange between Jesus and the Pharisees. What was Jesus's attitude to the covenant of the Old Testament? He did not seek simply to reject it, Father Ian said. "No one who has been drinking old wine desires new," Jesus tells the Pharisees. Tradition, like an old wine, is too precious to throw out. And yet Christ's gospel did introduce something new and transformative, the result of a process Father Ian likened to fermentation. In the same way that "fermentation releases energy in the process of breaking down the wheat, grape juice or curds; so Jesus is saying that his interpretation and revelation of the covenant is a life-giving and transformative mediation of the covenant. . . ."

I wasn't sure how hard Father Ian wanted to push the analogy of Jesus as a fungus breaking down the Old Testament in order to create the New. And if the Old Testament was already such a fine old wine, then why ferment it again? Yet to figure spiritual faith as a kind of fermentation—a transformation of the substrate of nature or everyday life into something infinitely more powerful, meaningful, and symbolic—well, that seemed to me exactly right. It offered us a way, as Father Ian said in closing, "to transform what is old in us, the fruit of the earth and the work of human hands, into something new." Just barely, I could make out the silhouette of Sister Noëlla in the pews beyond him, her wimple nodding slowly up and down.

FERMENT III.

ALCOHOL

But if by some chance the Pope were ever actually to heed Sister Noëlla's suggestion, and revised the Catholic liturgy to make a place in it for a nice, stinky cheese, I do hope it doesn't come at the expense of the wine. The fermentation that gives us alcohol, by transforming plant sugars into a liquid with the power to alter our experience of consciousness, is just the sort of miracle on which whole faiths can rest. And indeed wine—or beer or mead—figured prominently in religious ritual for centuries before Christ made use of its magic to convince his followers of his divinity.* The belief that alcohol gives people access to a divine realm—whether of gods or ancestors—is shared by a great many cultures, and it's not hard to see why. In the absence of a scientific explanation, how else could such a miraculous transformation be explained if not as a gift from the gods? And what else could these altered perceptions and visions signify if not the astounding fact that a glimpse of another world, one infinitely more vivid and interesting, had somehow sailed into view?

Of all humankind's fermentations, alcohol is the oldest and by far the most popular, consumed in all but a small handful of cultures for all of recorded history and no doubt for a long time before that. If milk and vegetable ferments divide one culture from another, fermentations of fruit juice or honey or grain unite them. A single, shimmering single-celled blue-brown yeast by the name of *Saccharomyces cerevisiae* is responsible for all these ferments, producing some twenty billion liters of wine, beer, or distilled spirits every year, which comes to about three liters for every man, woman, and child on earth. Can you name another species that has given us quite so much? And this tally doesn't include the alcohol fermented for fuel and other industrial purposes (usually going by the name of ethanol) or, for that matter, all the chance spontaneous fermentations that *S. cerevisiae* performs on fallen or split fruit, wet seeds, and tree sap, ferments that redound mainly to the benefit of animals.

Many of whom, it turns out, enjoy alcohol nearly as much as we

---

*"Jesus saith unto them, Fill the waterpots with water. And they filled them up to the brim. And he saith unto them, Draw out now, and bear unto the governor of the feast. And they bare [it]. When the ruler of the feast had tasted the water that was made wine, and knew not whence it was: (but the servants which drew the water knew) the governor of the feast called the bridegroom, And saith unto him, Every man at the beginning doth set forth good wine; and when men have well drunk, then that which is worse: [but] thou hast kept the good wine until now.
"This beginning of miracles did Jesus in Cana of Galilee, and manifested forth his glory; and his disciples believed on him." (John 2:7–11)

do. According to Ronald Siegel, the UCLA psychopharmacologist who wrote Intoxication: The Universal Drive for Mind-Altering Substances, insects like to get tipsy on fermented fruit and sap;* birds and bats do, too, sometimes at considerable risk to their safety. Some have been known to drop dead-drunk out of the sky. Tree shrews sip fermented nectar from flower cups held out by palms. When, in the jungles of Malaysia, a durian fruit falls to the forest floor and promptly rots, "a menagerie of jungle beasts," including wild pigs, deer, tapirs, tigers, rhinos (and people), will swiftly converge on its alcoholic custard, fighting over it if need be. Elephants will deploy their considerable intelligence to secure the large quantities of alcohol they require in order to get drunk, whether by gorging themselves on fermented fruit (whence "they start swaying in a lethargic manner"), or simply by busting into buildings suspected of housing a still or stash of booze, as has been reported in India.

In laboratory experiments, some animals will drink to excess, sometimes even death. Chimps faced with an open bar will maintain themselves in a permanent state of drunkenness. But some other species will judiciously moderate their intake. Rats presented with an unlimited supply of alcohol will drink much as many people do: gathering for a cocktail before dinner, taking a nightcap before sleep, and then, every three or four days, holding a raucous, drunken party. Social rather than solitary drinking seems to be the rule, among not only rats but several other species as well, and for good reason: Drunkenness makes an animal more vulnerable to predation, and there is safety in numbers.

A biologist named Robert Dudley has proposed "the drunken

*One species of fruit fly—Drosophila melanogaster—consumes alcohol as a way to medicate itself; the alcohol poisons a tiny parasitic wasp in its gut that otherwise would kill the fly. The alcohol kills the wasp by causing its internal organs to shoot out of its anus. Milan, Neil F., et al., "Alcohol Consumption as Self-Medication Against Blood-Borne Parasites in the Fruit Fly," Current Biology 22 No. 6 (2012): 488–93.

monkey hypothesis" to explain why we might have evolved such a strong fondness for alcohol. Fruit formed a large part of the diet of the primates from whom we are descended. When ripe fruit is bruised, the yeasts on its skin begin to ferment the sugars in its flesh, producing ethyl alcohol in the process. These volatile molecules are light enough to float some distance on the air, and animals with a strong attraction to their odor are at a distinct advantage for locating fruit at the peak of its nutritional quality. According to the hypothesis, animals that like the smell and taste of alcohol ended up with more food, and therefore more offspring, than those that didn't.

Alcohol happens to be a toxin, however. The reason the yeasts produce it in the first place is to keep other creatures from competing for their food. Since most microbes can't tolerate nearly as much alcohol as saccharomyces can, by producing lots of it, the yeast in effect is cleverly contaminating the local food supply, much like the child who licks all the cookies on a plate so he doesn't have to share. Yet this toxin also happens to be a rich source of energy—it can fuel your car, after all—and nature won't allow any source of energy to go unexploited for very long. Species with the ability to detoxify and metabolize alcohol were bound to come along eventually, and so they did: Most vertebrates possess the metabolic equipment needed to detoxify ethyl alcohol and burn it for fuel. A tenth of the enzymes in the human liver are dedicated to metabolizing ethyl alcohol.

All this naturally occurring alcohol suggests that, as in the case of bread and cheese, humans didn't so much invent alcoholic fermentation as bump into it. A beehive falls or drips honey into a hollow in a tree, rainwater collects in the hollow, and the diluted honey ferments: You've got mead. Or a gruel of mashed grass seeds—the wild ancestors of barley or wheat—begin to ferment: You've got beer. The "new and enticing sensations" (in the words of one archaeologist of alcohol) that these novelties produced in the mind of anyone who dared to drink them would have brought them back for more, and inspired them to apply their intellectual gifts to mastering the process. But though it is remarkably easy to make alcohol, I discovered that it is much harder to make it well.

The first time I ever tried to ferment alcohol, I was only ten. My motive was not to obtain wine to drink; like most kids, I didn't like the taste of wine, though it had occurred to me that my parents, who did, might appreciate my efforts. But my principal motivation was the alchemist's: I was from an early age obsessed with metamorphosis, and this was not the first time I had tried to turn some common form of dross into something that might in some way glow. Actually, my first stab at alchemy had come several years earlier, soon after learning the astounding fact that, given enough heat and pressure and time, a lowly lump of coal would eventually turn into a diamond. Imagine: a recipe for diamonds!

Back then, in the early 1960s, some ships were still powered by coal-fired boilers, and at the beach I would occasionally find shiny black lumps of anthracite. Surely there had to be some way to speed up the transformation process. By my reckoning, the single most powerful energy source in our house was a Tensor lamp. It looked totally high tech and gave off an unusually strong, focused beam of light. So I put a lump of coal directly in its beam and left the light on 24/7, checking each morning to see if the facets of my incipient diamond had gotten any shinier or less black.

I had somewhat more success turning grape juice into wine. It was September, and the wild grapevines around our house were weighed down with a bumper crop of dark-purple berries, hanging in dense, downy clusters. I picked several bunches of the ripest grapes and put them in the red plastic container my mother used to mix up frozen orange juice concentrate; it had a matching red plastic screw top. I crushed the grapes right in the container, using a potato masher—skins, seeds, and all. My plan was to make red wine. I don't recall whether I added any yeast; I doubt it. But I did screw the top on nice and tight and put the container on a coffee table in the living room, where I could keep an eye on it.

Not a very eagle-y eye, apparently. Because I have no recollection of the plastic container beginning to bulge, slightly at first, and then cartoonishly, as the carbon dioxide built up inside it. What I do remember, with a pained clarity a half century later, is coming home with my parents late one evening and flicking on the lights to find the white walls and ceiling of our living room evenly spattered with splotches of dark purple. Some were just smears of purple pigment; others drooled jagged slivers of grape skin like wet confetti. Ecstatic fruit flies were everywhere, and the living room had acquired an unmistakable new smell. It smelled like wine!

"Plenty were drunk with nectar," Plato writes, referring to mead, or fermented honey, "for wine was not yet invented." Wine made from honey was probably the first alcoholic beverage humans fermented on purpose. (And when we read of the ancients' fondness for nectar, we can safely assume they're talking about fermented nectar.) Alcoholic fermentation depends on sugar, and, at least before the advent of agriculture, the sweet nectar that bees concentrate into honey was the richest and most readily accessible source of sugars in nature. In the hive, however, honey is so completely saturated with sugar that nothing can live in it, yeasts included. The hydrostatic pressure will promptly suck the water out of any microbe that falls into it. This of course is exactly what the bees want. But I read (in Sandor Katz's book) that as soon as honey is diluted with water it will spontaneously begin to ferment.

I was curious to find out if making mead was really that simple, and, if it was, to sample what the very earliest alcoholic beverage might have tasted like. I happen to be blessed, or cursed, with a ready supply of honey: My friend Will Rogers keeps bees in a neighboring town, and I seldom visit him without coming away with yet another pint jar of the stuff. By now I had an entire shelf of honey jars in the pantry. It's a delicious, cosmopolitan sort of honey, a distillation of the diverse riot of flowering plants that, here in the East Bay, are in bloom every month of the year.

So I diluted a pound or so of Will's honey in a gallon jug of water, one part honey to four parts water, and fitted the jug with an airlock. This is a cork attached to a curvaceous piece of plastic piping with a little reservoir of water at the bottom of a bend that keeps oxygen from getting in but allows carbon dioxide to escape. Every day I checked in on my jug, examining it for fizz or escaping gas bubbles, but the pale-gold liquid gave no sign of life. It might as well have been a lump of coal under a Tensor lamp.

I was tempted to add some yeast to get things going. That's what Will had suggested, as had the fermentos down at the Oak Barrel, the local home-brewing supply store where I purchased the airlock. But after spending time with Sandor Katz, I was attached to the idea of a wild fermentation using local yeasts. So I e-mailed Sandor for advice.

"What I would have recommended that you do differently," he wrote back, "is to leave the diluted honey in an open vessel for a few days and stir frequently until bubbling becomes evident, and only then move to an airlock." It seems that the aeration stimulates the yeast, the spores of which might be in the air or in the honey itself.

His advice was based on an unusual fact about the particular yeast

I was trying to entice. *Saccharomyces cerevisiae* is a microbe that can operate equally well aerobically and anaerobically, employing a completely different metabolic pathway depending on the conditions in which it finds itself. In evolutionary terms, this dual metabolism is a newish development for *S. cerevesiae*. Before the advent of the flowering plants (and their fruit) some eighty million years ago, the yeast's ancestors relied strictly on an aerobic mode of metabolism to generate energy. This system was highly efficient, and, among yeasts, nothing out of the ordinary. After the angiosperms arrived on the scene, however, *S cerevesiae* acquired a new bag of metabolic tricks that gave it a tremendous edge over its competition: the ability to survive in the airless conditions deep within a fruit or nectar, and, once there, to transform sugars into alcohol. This new metabolic pathway is a less efficient way to generate energy—the alcohol produced by it still has plenty left to burn—yet it has the considerable advantage of expanding the yeast's habitat and poisoning its competition—not to mention endearing itself to some of the higher animals, notably including ourselves.[*]

Because aerobic metabolism gives the yeast the maximum amount of energy from its food, oxygenating the liquid in question is a good way to kick-start a fermentation. So I started a new batch of mead, diluting the honey with four parts water and leaving it out on the kitchen counter for several days, uncovered. I had read that mead was often flavored with various herbs and spices, in order to contribute a bit of acidity, some tannins, and nutrients for the yeasts, so I added a bay leaf, some cardamom seeds, a star anise, and a few tablespoons of black tea. (Mead to which such herbs and spices are added used to be called "metheglin.") And just in case I lacked for wild yeasts, I dropped

---

[*]After it runs out of sugars to ferment, *S. cerevisiae* can switch on an enzyme that allows it to live off the ethanol it has produced, yet another neat trick.

in an overripe, split fig from the garden that I figured must be crawling with them.

Every time I passed the bowl of honey water, I gave it a vigorous stir with a wooden spoon, working a little more air into it. After about a week, I noticed a fizz of tiny bubbles on the surface. Day by day, the bubbles got a little bigger and more vigorous. When I thought I could detect the faintest smell of alcohol, I poured the liquid into the jug and plugged it with the airlock. The very next day I had the satisfaction of watching a nice fat bubble of carbon dioxide shoulder its way through the pocket of water in the airlock. Fermentation!

The jug perked along for a week or so, rhythmically emitting a bubble every several minutes, and then seemed to grow quiet. A shake of the jug would enliven things for a few hours, but after a while the fermentation had subsided for good. It was time for a taste. So I pulled out the airlock and poured some of the liquid into a wine glass. It was golden but cloudy, like a pale, unfiltered cider.

I could smell the alcohol and the sweet spices. The mead had a light fizz on the tongue and tasted like a mulled wine, sweet and a bit heavy. So this was metheglin. It wasn't half bad, I decided. Definitely interesting. But perhaps a little too sweet to drink in any quantity. Clearly the wild yeast had thrown in the towel before completely fermenting all the sugars in the honey.

Apparently this is often the case with wild yeasts. They will ferment a sugary liquid only up to about 5 percent alcohol, at which point they "crap out," as Kel Alcala, the young guy behind the counter at the Oak Barrel put it. It seems that 5 percent alcohol—or ten proof—is fairly standard for a fermented beverage in nature. This could explain why alcoholism doesn't appear to be much of a problem in the animal world. Also, honey presents special challenges to yeast, since it contains various antimicrobial compounds to prevent it from spoiling; from a bee's perspective, fermented honey is spoiled honey. Kel recommended that, for my next batch, I try some champagne yeast, and he sold me a packet. "I call it the killer yeast," he said. "It'll ferment anything you throw it at, until it's pretty much bone dry."

I was curious to try it. But, honestly, I was impressed with what my local wild yeasts had accomplished on their own, completely free and voluntary. They had made me a jug of mead after all, Beowulf's drink of choice. It was low proof, true, but an alcoholic beverage just the same. By the time I finished the glass of mead, I felt a pleasant buzz in my brain, a mild and agreeable lightness. This mead might not impress the boys at the Oak Barrel yet, but as my first home brew (not counting the living-room-ceiling cuvée of my childhood) it felt to me like an achievement.

Figuring out how to make something like my mead was a development of inestimable value to our ancestors. Leaving aside for a moment the blessings of intoxication—which were mixed, it's true, but on balance a boon—fermented drinks offered a great many other benefits to early humans. Mead and beer and wine were safer to drink than water, since the alcohol in these drinks (and the fact that some of them, like beer, had been boiled) killed off any pathogens in the water. As in the case of so many other fermentations, the process itself rendered the original food or drink more nutritious, less perishable, and more interesting than it had previously been. The yeasts that fermented my honey water also contributed vitamins (B-complex), minerals (selenium, chromium, copper), and protein (the multiplying yeasts themselves). Some anthropologists believe that beer making, which began in earnest around the same time that farming did, helped the early agriculturists compensate for the decline in the nutritional quality of their diet as they turned from hunting and gathering a great many different foods to a monotonous diet of grains and tubers. The B vitamins and minerals in beer, for example, helped compensate for the loss of meat from their diet.

The alcohol itself probably contributed to the health, as well as the happiness, of ancient people. Alcohol is a rich source of calories as well as nutrients. People who drink in moderation (which a 5-percent mead pretty much guarantees) live longer and endure lower rates of many diseases than both people who don't drink at all and people who drink to excess. The exact mechanisms for these effects have yet to be identified, but the scientific consensus today is that drinking alcohol (of any kind) in moderation protects against heart attack, stroke, type 2 diabetes, arthritis, dementia, and several types of cancer. The teetotaler is at greater risk for disease and early death than the drinker.

Alcohol is a powerful and versatile drug, and for most of human history was the most important drug in the pharmacopeia—a panacea, literally. It reduces stress. It also muffles pain, and for most of history served as humankind's principal analgesic and anesthetic. (Opium probably wasn't cultivated until 3400 B.C.) Also, many of the plant drugs, like opium, require alcohol as a solvent to unlock their powerful chemistries and make them available to us. In fact, it was once common practice to add various psychoactive plants (including opium and wormwood) to beer and wine; the addition of hops flowers to beer is all that remains of that venerable tradition.*

We humans owe a large debt to S. cerevisiae. Were it a creature that people could see, they might well decide this yeast has a stronger

---

*Some brewers today regard the fifteenth-century German beer laws that mandated hops as the only permissible additive as a regrettable victory in an earlier war on drugs. Compared with some of the other psychoactive plants that once were added to beer, hops, which is a sedative distantly related to cannabis, is fairly mild.

claim to the title of man's best friend than the dog. Some evolutionary biologists contend that it was the world's very first domesticated species. Using DNA analysis, they've constructed an evolutionary tree for *S. cerevisiae* demonstrating that, more than ten thousand years ago, it diverged from a few, and possibly just one, wild ancestor into several distinct strains under the pressure of human selection. When humans began making mead and wine, brewing beer and sake, and baking bread, the yeast evolved and diversified to take maximum advantage of the rich new opportunities, or niches, humans presented it— whether a mash of grain, or diluted honey, or pressed grapes. Several thousand years later, the various strains of *S. cerevisiae* exhibit substantially different qualities, levels of alcohol production (and tolerance), and flavors. The process of "artificial selection" that shaped these yeasts is much like the one that transformed the wild wolf into a variety of different dogs, except that in the case of *S. cerevisiae*, the selection came earlier and was entirely unconscious.

In some cases, *S. cerevisiae* appears to have hybridized with other yeast species to acquire the genes it needed to make the most of a human fermentation opportunity. Consider lager, the class of light, effervescent beers made by fermenting a mash of grain under cold conditions. Most strains of *S. cerevisiae* go dormant at temperatures below 55°F. But when people in Bavaria began trying to ferment beers in caves during the winter, a novel strain of yeast that could thrive under those conditions soon appeared. (We now know it as *Saccharomyces pastorianus*.) New tools of genetic analysis indicate that this hearty lager strain contains genes from a distantly related species of *Saccharomyces*, called *Saccharomyces eubayanus*, that has been traced to Patagonia, where it is found on the bark of certain trees.* Researchers

---

*Libkind, Diego, et al., "Microbe Domestication and the Identification of the Wild Genetic Stock of Lager-Brewing Yeast," *Proceedings of the National Academy of Sciences* 108 No. 35 (2011): 14539–44.

hypothesize that, shortly after Columbus's voyages, this cold-tolerant yeast found its way to Europe, perhaps in a shipment of lumber, or in a barrel that was then used to brew beer. So it appears that lager, like the tomato and the potato and the chili pepper, is yet another gift from the New World to the Old, tendered as part of the Columbian Exchange.

S. cerevisiae has demonstrated remarkable ingenuity in exploiting the human desire for alcohol, particularly in finding ways to transport itself from one batch of the stuff to another. Some strains get themselves passed on by colonizing the vessels in which alcohol is fermented, or the wooden tools used to stir the pot. "Brewing sticks" are prized possessions in parts of Africa, believed to inaugurate the miracle of fermentation when used to stir a mash—and so they do, much like Sister Noëlla's wooden paddle. Other yeasts, like the ones that give us ale, evolved the trick of floating to the top of a fermented liquid, where they are much more likely to hitch a ride to the next sugary feast. That's because brewers typically scoop yeasts from the top of one batch to start the next. The most successful yeasts were the ones that learned to clump together and then float to the surface by attaching themselves to the rising bubbles of carbon dioxide—a conveyance that they of course created.

But surely the greatest evolutionary trick of all came when S. cerevisiae first figured out—unconsciously, of course—that the very same molecule it had originally devised to poison its enemies was also capable of making it a coevolutionary partner as powerful, ingenious, and well traveled as Homo sapiens. The human desire for alcohol has been a tremendous boon to Saccharomyces cerevisiae. To supply it with endless rivers of liquid substrate to ferment, we have reconfigured vast swaths of the earth's surface, planting tens of millions of acres of grain and fruit, in the process creating a paradise of fermentable sugars to sustain this supremely enterprising family of fungi.

In the 1980s, an anthropologist at the University of Pennsylvania by the name of Solomon Katz put forth the arresting theory that it was the human desire for a steady supply of alcohol, not food, that drove the shift from hunting and gathering to agriculture and settlement. Beer, in other words, came before bread, and as soon as people got a taste of it, Katz reasoned, they would have wanted more than could be produced by gathering seeds or fruits or honey. The hypothesis is difficult to prove, but plausible. It would certainly help explain why early humans would ever have traded the comparatively easy lifestyle of the hunter-gatherer, who typically devotes far less time and effort to obtaining food than the farmer, for the toil and inferior diet of the early agriculturist. A reliable supply of food is much easier to secure in the wild than fermentable sugars, which tend to be rare and hard to find. There is only so much honey in the forest, and what there is, is well defended by bees. The only way to guarantee an adequate year-round supply of fermentable sugars would be to take up agriculture. Analysis of yeast DNA indicates that the domesticated strains go back at least as far as the domestication of grain, and perhaps further.

One suggestive new piece of evidence for the beer-before-bread hypothesis comes from the analysis of the carbon isotopes in the skeletons of ancient people in South America. Though corn had been domesticated by 6000 B.C., bones from the period immediately following give no evidence of corn proteins in the diet. This suggests that people were consuming the corn they were growing not as solid food but as an alcoholic beverage, since alcohol made from corn would contain little protein, hence leave little trace of it in bone. So it appears likely that Native Americans were drinking corn before they began eating it.

Yet it isn't at all self-evident how one would go about turning a pile of corn, or any other grain, into alcohol. To learn how to make beer is to marvel at the ingenuity of the people who first figured it out. The process is much more complicated, and involves many more steps, than making mead, or for that matter wine. Charlie Bamforth, the Anheuser-Busch Endowed Professor of Brewing Science at the University of California, Davis, likes to begin his lectures with a little joke. "Do you know why Jesus performed the miracle of turning water into wine? Because it's so much easier than making beer!"

Corn kernels, like the seeds of many other grasses, contain plenty of sugars, but they are not in a form that S. cerevisiae can make use of. The sugars are tightly bound together in long carbohydrate chains that the tiny yeasts can't break apart. This well serves the seed, which has an interest in keeping its precious cargo of sugars intact and safe from microbial attack until the germinating plant needs them. But certain enzymes can cleave those carbohydrate chains into simple, fermentable sugars, and, as the earliest beer makers discovered, one of those enzymes—ptyalin—is present in human saliva. The first beers were made by chewing kernels of corn and other seeds, mixing them with saliva, and then spitting the resulting slurry into a vessel, where it would readily begin to ferment. (The desire for an alcoholic drink must have been keen indeed.) To this day, there are indigenous groups in South America that rely on the chewing method to make an alcoholic beverage called chicha—a corn-and-saliva beer.

Surely there had to be a better way, and eventually it was discovered. Instead of chewing the grain to release its sugars, our ancestors figured out that if they briefly germinated the seeds before mashing them in water, the mash would become sweet enough to ferment. Malting, as this process is called, is essentially a way to trick the seed into releasing its own diastatic enzymes, to break down its carbohydrates into sugars to nourish the (supposed) new plant. In beer making, seeds of grain, most often barley (which contain high levels of both fermentable sugars and enzymes), are moistened and allowed to germinate for a few days before being dried in a kiln. The heat kills the embryonic barley plant, but not before the enzymes have been released and begun breaking down the seed's stash of carbohydrates.

In time, maltsters, as they were called, figured out that, by adjusting the cooking time and temperature in the kiln, they could take advantage of the browning reactions—Maillard and caramelization—to manipulate the flavor, aroma, and color of their beers. At the Oak Barrel, the long central aisle is lined with wooden bins with glass windows displaying more than a dozen different malts—cooked seeds of barley in colors ranging from pale gold to ebony, and giving off aromas as various and wonderful as raisin, coffee, chocolate, fresh bread, dark toast, biscuit, toffee, smoked peat, and caramel. It's a remarkably rich palette of flavors and aromas—sense metaphors, really—to tease out of a simple, and all but tasteless, seed of grass simply by cooking it.

But as I was about to discover, the choice of malt is only one of the daunting number of variables in brewing beer; there is also the type of hops that, depending on the strain, can impart completely different flavors (spicy, fruity, herbal, grassy, earthy, floral, citrus, or evergreen). Then there is the yeast, which helps determine exactly how sweet, bitter, fruity, or spicy your beer will be. Finally, there is the fermentation temperature and time, which can yield a crisp, light, bubbly lager at 45°F (in forty-five days) or a softer, richer ale at room temperature (in fourteen days). The first time I set foot in the Oak Barrel, I was so daunted by the sheer number of decisions that went into brewing a beer—a beer!— that I turned around and left without buying a thing.

The second time, I bought one of the Oak Barrel's beer-brewing kits and, with the help of Isaac, brewed my first batch of beer. We opted for an English Pale Ale. The kit makes all the hard decisions, in effect, and contains everything you need: the malt (an English type called Crystal in our case), the hops (Magnum, Sterling, and Cascade), some flavoring grains (malted Carawheat), and a bag of priming sugars we would need when it came time to bottle. But when you buy a kit, the malted grain comes in the form of a liquid extract (made by grinding the malted barley, soaking it in hot water, and then evaporating the resulting "wort" down to a sweet, black syrup), and the hops come in little pale-green pellets. As Kel packed up our purchases, I wondered, were we somehow cheating by using a kit?

Brewing beer, even from a kit, turned out to be an enjoyable way for Isaac and me to spend a Saturday afternoon together. Being an eighteen-year-old, Isaac had an acute interest in beer, and he approached the making of it in a spirit of high seriousness. It probably didn't hurt that fermenting alcohol was a grown-up enterprise that I knew no more about than he did, and which carried a faint whiff of outlawry. His mother wasn't entirely sure about the advisability of this particular father-son project, which also counted in its favor. The work itself called for four hands and at least one strong back (for lifting and pouring five-gallon kettles and heavy glass carboys), all of which combined to make for an agreeable collaboration of equals. Working side by side is always a good recipe for easy conversation with a teenager, and I learned more than I probably wanted to about various other beer exploits, involving consumption rather than production.

Following the Oak Barrel recipe, we began by boiling tap water in a five-gallon pot, poured in the malt extract, and then added the Magnum hops, a type used to bitter the beer. With a rolling pin, Isaac cracked the grains, which came in a muslin bag, and then suspended the bag in the rapidly boiling wort like a big tea bag. At the thirty-minute mark, we added the Sterling hops. After an hour, we took the kettle off the heat and added yet a third type of hops, Cascade, which is meant to contribute aroma. We cooled the liquid to room temperature, poured it through a strainer into a five-gallon glass carboy, and then "pitched" the yeast into it. The whole operation, which took slightly more than two hours from start to finish, felt a little like working from a cake mix, frankly. It might produce a decent cake, but would you be justified in calling the final product, however tasty, "homemade"?

And yet the following morning, when Isaac and I went down to the basement to check on our carboy, we got pretty excited. Overnight, the big jug of honey-colored liquid had leapt dramatically to life. A thick layer of creamy foam had formed on the surface, like a great frothy head on a beer, and through the glass walls of the carboy we could see thick currents of brown wort circulating like powerful weather systems in time lapse. The little reservoir of water in the airlock was bubbling like crazy, releasing a damp, yeasty gas that smelled, agreeably, like an English pub. By now I knew all about yeasts and their appetite for sugars, but it was hard not to feel there was some serious magic under way down here in our basement.

After a few days, the fermentation settled into a less hectic rhythm, the bubbles now infrequent enough to count as they formed and, one by one, slid through the airlock to perfume the room. The currents in the wort slowed, too, and a whitish-gray mass of yeast and other detritus, called "trub," formed at the bottom of the carboy. (Only centuries of British devotion to beer making could produce such a superbly earthy vocabulary of Anglo-Saxon brewing terms: "trub," "wort," "pitch," "malt," "mash tun," and, my favorite, "sparge.") The instructions said we could bottle after two weeks, so, on a Saturday morning, Isaac and I together hoisted the carboy out onto the back porch, and carefully siphoned the fermented liquid into bottles, which we then sealed with metal caps. We had already added the bag of priming sugar to the beer to stimulate a last climactic bout of fermentation in the bottles; trapped under the bottle cap, the carbon dioxide produced by the yeasts would disperse in the beer as bubbles. Two weeks later, it would be ready to drink.

Our English ale was pretty good, too. I mean, it tasted just like beer, which, at this point in my education, was good enough for me. Isaac was somewhat more discriminating. "The bubbles could definitely be livelier," he declared, "and I could do with less hoppiness." Befitting the English style, our ale was fairly bitter, with a pronounced hops flavor and aroma. We had brewed two whole cases of the stuff, and I wondered if we would ever get through it all. But as the weeks went by, the beer got better and better, as the hops mellowed and the warm, malty flavors came to the fore. After a month of "conditioning" in the bottle, I felt good enough about Pollan's Pale Ale to bring a cold bottle down to Kel Alcala, at the Oak Barrel, for his professional evaluation. Kel, who is an earnest young brewer with a long blond ponytail and thick forearms tattooed with Goth-pagan imagery, poured himself a glass. He sniffed; he held it up to the light; he sipped. And then he stared at the beer for what seemed a very long time.

"For a first effort?" Kel's voice is a friendly growl. "I'd say this is really not bad at all." He brought the glass of beer to his nose a second time, inhaling deeply. "But I'm getting a slight off note in the finish. Do you get that? Fresh Band-Aid. Yep, that's it." I took a sip and had to admit he was right. There was a faint chemical scent reminiscent of first aid. "That comes from a compound called chlorophenol. I'm guessing your fermentation was a little warmer than you probably want. Even just a few degrees can do it."

It's funny how a well-chosen metaphor can, for better or worse, completely change the flavor of something. Never again could I drink Pollan's Pale without thinking about Band-Aids. Johnson & Johnson's Pale Ale would probably have been a better name for our first brew. But I was not discouraged. I wrote off the flaw to the fact that we had made this first batch in August; a second batch brewed over the winter turned out much better, with not even the slightest hint of hospital. Yet the Betty Crocker question still nagged at me, and when an opportunity presented itself to help brew a batch of beer truly from scratch, I grabbed it.

I had heard that a friend I hadn't seen in a few years, a psychiatrist whose son had gone to middle school with Isaac, had fallen deep into home brewing. I knew Shane MacKay to be an inveterate, if not obsessive, tinkerer and gear head (a serious guitarist, he also built his own amps and speakers from junkyard parts), and when I heard he had transformed part of his backyard into a brewery, I immediately gave him a call to see if I might assist on his next batch. I was certain Shane MacKay would not be using any kit.

There was the unmistakable hint of the mad scientist about Shane as he proudly showed me around his backyard setup early on a Sunday morning, his white thatch uncombed, his steel-blue eyes lit up by this latest DIY fire. Shane's teenage boys having long since lost interest in Dad's brewing project, the alchemist seemed delighted to have an eager new apprentice. In the shade of a lean-to he'd built behind the house, Shane had erected a tall structure of steel shelving to hold, at different heights, various kettles and kegs, each atop a propane burner, and all of them linked together by clear plastic tubing that passed through various valves and spigots. Thermometers, hydrometers, jars of sanitizing chemicals, pumps, filters, funnels, carboys, bottles, air-locks, and propane tanks completed the scene. It occurred to me that, by learning to brew beer, Shane had found the perfect way to combine his engineering gifts with his professional interest in brain chemistry and how it might profitably be altered.

With the help of some incomprehensibly elaborate brewing software, Shane had concocted a recipe for a beer modeled on a traditional Irish ale; he was calling it, for obscure reasons, "Humboldt Spingo." As he typed into his laptop various parameters—types of malt, hops, and yeasts; temperatures and times—the software showed him exactly where the finished beer would fall along several different spectrums, including maltiness, sweetness, bitterness (measured in IBUs, or International Bittering Units), original and final "gravity" (dissolved solids), and alcohol level. Shane's whole approach—the software, the metrics, the scrupulous sanitation—was a world away from Sandor Katz's. Wild fermentation was the last thing Shane wanted going on in his carboys.

Shane had picked up the ingredients at the Oak Barrel the day before: a blend of malts, dominated by an English type called Maris Otter and supplemented with smaller amounts of Victory, Biscuit, Cara Red (for color), and a few ounces of roasted (i.e., unmalted) barley. For hops (which Shane proudly showed me he had planted along his back fence), we would use U.S. Golding to supply the bitterness (but not very much—the Irish ale style is considerably less bitter than the English) and Willamette for aroma. As for yeast, we were going to divide the batch in half and pitch two different strains: an English yeast and a Scottish. Shane proposed that I take one of the carboys home to ferment in my basement, and later we could compare the effects on the beer of the different yeasts. A controlled experiment, or close to one.

Brewing from scratch, or "all-grain" brewing, begins with the soaking of the malt in hot (but not boiling) water. Before we added the crushed grain to the water, I sampled a few of the seeds. They tasted surprisingly good, sweet and nutty, but full of cellulose, like a ridiculously high-fiber breakfast cereal. The hour-long soak allowed the enzymes in the barley to break down the grain's carbohydrates into fermentable sugars. As we stood around the mash tun—a steel kettle with a screen at the bottom—watching the hot cereal steep, Shane asked about my brewing experiences to date. Being both a psychiatrist and a Canadian, he did a magnificent job politely masking his disdain for my Duncan Hines approach to beer making; he had started out the same way.

But though it added a couple of hours to the brewing process, steeping the grain seemed well within my capabilities. So did the next step, which was to sparge the cooked mash. After Shane opened a valve at the bottom of the mash tun to drain the sweet brown steep water into a second kettle, he directed a stream of boiling water from a third kettle overhead down onto the mash, in order to leach, or sparge, any remaining sugars from the nearly spent grains. After this water passed through the mash, it emerged from the spigot below golden brown, warm, and fragrant. I tasted the grains again. They had been completely bleached of flavor.

Now we had our wort—thirteen gallons of sugary brown liquid. Shane poured a few ounces of it into a glass test tube into which he floated what looked like a big fat thermometer. In fact it was a hydrometer, which measures the density, or "gravity," of the wort: the amount of dissolved sugars in the liquid, which gives the brewer a good idea of just how much alcohol the final beer will contain. The scale on the side of the hydrometer indicated the wort had an "original gravity" of 10.50—precisely what the software had predicted.

(When it dropped to 10.14, the software said, the fermentation would be complete.) Shane pronounced himself pleased. Now he rigged up a system to cool the wort as quickly as possible by submerging a spiral of copper tubing that he then connected to a cold-water line. You want to cool the wort as rapidly as possible to minimize the risk of bacterial contamination. (The addition of hops, which contains anti-microbial compounds, also helps prevent contamination.)

Between steps, brewing beer consists mainly of hanging around watching pots boil, so there's plenty of time for talk. (Drinking, too, though, this being a Sunday morning, we stuck mainly to coffee.) Shane and I covered many bases, catching up on family and work and other fermentation projects. He asked about this book. I told him the premise, how the four elements corresponded to the principal methods humans have devised for transforming the stuff of nature into things good to eat and drink.

"So where does beer fit into your scheme?" Earth, I explained, since fermentation draws on the same microbial processes of destruction and creation at work in the soil. But then it occurred to me that, in fact, all four elements were represented in the beer-making process. The barley is first cooked over a fire; the grain is then boiled in water; and the beer, after fermentation, is carbonated with air. Beer is the complete four-element food. Which, I realized, is exactly the sort of insight you would expect beer to sponsor.

When, after forty-five minutes, the temperature of the wort had fallen to our target of 70°F, we divided the liquid between two carboys and pitched the yeast, the English in one and the Scottish in the other. To aerate the yeasts, we vigorously shook and rolled the carboys till the wort began to froth. Then we plugged them with air-locks. Nearly five hours after putting the grain in to soak, we were done. Shane helped me hoist the carboy out to my car.

On the drive home, one hand on the steering wheel and the other steadying the neck of my carboy, I thought about *S. cerevisiae*, the invisible single-celled creature that had been the recipient of the morning's sustained and scrupulous attentions. "Man's best friend": By now, I had heard several brewers use the same phrase to describe it. But after devoting five hours of our weekend to the building of an idyllic environment for this species—a carboy full of sweet brown wort—it seemed to me it would be just as accurate to call Shane and me and all the other fermenters "Saccharomyces' best friend."

"Coevolution" is a strong term, implying that both partners have been changed by their relationship. It's not hard to demonstrate how the human desire for alcohol (bread, too) helped to redirect the evolutionary path of this particular fungus, as our species selected yeasts for their ability to ferment various substrates and produce varying amounts of alcohol or carbon dioxide. But for our relationship to this yeast to qualify as coevolution, the changes must be reciprocal. So can we make a case that *S. cerevisiae* changed us, too?

I think we can. While we were altering the genome of *S. cerevisiae*, it was altering ours: Our ancestors evolved the metabolic pathways to detoxify ethyl alcohol in order to make use of its prodigious energy (and, conceivably, some of its other benefits). Even today, not all humans possess the required genes, and some ethnic groups, lacking the ability to produce the necessary enzymes in their liver, have more trouble metabolizing alcohol than others. For them, alcohol remains more toxin than intoxicant. Yet the proportion of the human population that carries the genes to metabolize alcohol has almost certainly increased in the time since our species has been seriously drinking, in much the same way that the number of humans who can digest lactose as adults increased in places, such as Northern Europe, where cow's milk was widely available. In both instances, those who carried the genes needed to take advantage of the new food source produced more offspring than those who didn't.

Yet the changes that alcohol wrought in our species have not been confined to the human genome or the human liver. *S. cerevisiae* exerted what may be an even more profound, if somewhat harder to pinpoint, effect on the plane of human culture. Precisely where genes leave off and culture begins (or vice versa) is never an easy line to draw, since eventually useful cultural practices and values influence reproductive success, and so leave their mark on our genes. And though we don't yet know everything we would need to in order to write a comprehensive natural history of such important human traits as sociality, or religiosity, or the poetic imagination, when we do, there seems little doubt that *S. cerevisiae* (along with a few of the other species that produce important human intoxicants) will play a starring role. This little yeast has helped to make us who we are.

Alcohol is probably the most social drug we humans have. It takes cooperation to produce it, and it is commonly consumed in the company of others. In ancient Sumerian depictions of beer drinking, groups of people are shown sipping from the same gourd through straws. (Early beers would have been covered with a thick layer of dead yeast, foam, and floating debris, so were commonly sipped through straws.) In most cultures, anthropologists tell us, drinking alcohol has been a social ritual, and, much like hunting large animals and cooking them over fires, the practice helped foster social cohesion.

True, drunkenness can also lead to aggression and antisocial behavior, which is why drinking in many cultures is carefully regulated. But as paradoxical as this might sound, the very fact that alcohol inspired the need for such rules is another way in which it has contributed to our socialization.

This paradox points to one of the challenges of generalizing about alcohol's effect on us and our species: Almost anything you can say about it is true, and so is its opposite. This same molecule can make people violent or docile; amorous or indifferent; loquacious or silent; euphoric or depressed; stimulated or sedated; eloquent or idiotic.* Perhaps because it affects so many different neural pathways, alcohol is remarkably plastic in its effects, person to person, group to group, even culture to culture. As Griffith Edwards, the English author of *Alcohol: The World's Favorite Drug*, puts it, "Cultures can differ profoundly in their modes of drunken comportment." (A delicious phrase!)

Edwards suggests that this plasticity could explain why alcohol is so widely accepted as a recreational drug: "Intoxication with this particular substance is remarkably susceptible to cultural prescriptions and proscriptions, all the way from Bolivia to Tahiti." When you compare alcohol with other drugs—think of LSD or crack cocaine— it becomes clear that societies are better able to channel and regulate the response of individuals to alcohol, making the drug more socially useful and less threatening than some others.

◉

So a natural history of human sociality would have to take account of the influence of alcohol in all its complexity. As would, I believe, a natural history of religion. "Wherever we look in the ancient or modern world," archaeologist Patrick McGovern has written, "we see that the principal way to communicate with the gods or the ancestors in-

---

*Horace got at this plasticity in the following lines he addressed to a forty-year-old cask of wine (dating from the year of his birth): "Whether you bear in yourself complaints or laughter, or whether you contain strife and mad love or friendly sleep, O faithful cask."

volves an alcoholic beverage, whether it is the wine of the Eucharist, the beer presented to the Sumerian goddess Ninkasi, the mead of the Vikings, or the elixir of an Amazonian or African tribe." Alcohol has served religion as a proof of gods' existence, a means of access to sacred realms, and a mode of observance, whether solemn (as in the Eucharist) or ecstatic (as in the worship of Dionysus or, in Judaism, the celebration of Purim). The decidedly peculiar belief that, behind or above or within the physical world available to our senses, there exists a second world of spirits, surely must owe at least a partial debt to the experience of intoxication. Even today, when we raise and clink glasses in a toast, what are we really doing if not invoking a supernatural power? That's why a glass of water or milk just doesn't do the trick.

In *The Varieties of Religious Experience*, William James placed alcohol at the very center of the religious experience. "The sway of alcohol over mankind is unquestionably due to its power to stimulate the mystical faculties of human nature," he writes, which are "usually crushed to earth by the cold facts and dry criticisms of the sober hour. Sobriety diminishes, discriminates, and says no; drunkenness expands, unites, and says yes. It is in fact the great exciter of the *Yes* function in man."

James is being perhaps a bit too unambiguously sunny here about alcohol, playing down the drug's potential for destructiveness. The ancient Greeks worshipped the wine god Dionysus, but always in the full knowledge of alcohol's paradoxical nature, how the same drug could make angels of us or beasts, confer blessings or bring down a curse. Indeed, that paradox goes to the very heart of the cult of Dionysus.* Wine "enters the world as a miracle," the classicist Walter Otto wrote in *Dionysus*, but the drunken worship of Dionysus devolves

---

*Though best known as the bringer of wine to humankind, Dionysus was also credited with giving us beer and honey.

into a kind of madness that is itself paradoxical. For it holds within it at the same time (here he quotes Nietzsche) "the power to generate and the power to destroy."

Otto's own sentences eventually fall under the Dionysian spell: "All earthly powers are united in the god: the generating, nourishing, intoxicating rapture; the life giving inexhaustibility; and the tearing pain, the deathly pallor, the speechless night of having been." (You'll recall that the Dionysian rapture ends badly, with the drunken revelers finally turning on the god to tear him limb from limb and then feast on his flesh.) "He is the mad ecstasy which hovers over every conception and birth and whose wildness is always ready to move on to destruction and death."

Have another?

To drink the wine of Dionysus is to dissolve the clear sunlit distinctions of Apollonian sobriety, muddying the bright lines between destruction and creation, matter and spirit, life and death—in fact, smearing the very idea of distinction itself. Commanding "the powers of earth," Dionysus' gravitational force pulls us back down into the primal mud. And yet: It is precisely here in the mud that creation begins, breeding the beauty of flowers—forms!—out of the dead ground, new life from death's rot.

"Just like fermentation," I scribble madly in the margins of my Otto. The Greeks had no scientific understanding of the process— that would await Louis Pasteur and the discovery of the responsible microbes—but it seems to me they deeply understood fermentation just the same. They had crushed grapes and watched great urns of blackish must begin to seethe and breathe and come to life, under the influence of a transformational power they ascribed to Dionysus. And they had felt what that same force did to their minds and bodies when they drank its creation, the way the liquid seemed to ferment them: shifting the mind's attention from the physical to the spiritual, italicizing everyday experience, proposing fresh ways of seeing the most familiar things—new metaphors. The Dionysian magic of fermentation was at once a property of nature and of the human soul, and one could unlock the other.

"Nature overpowering mind" is how Nietzsche described Dionysian intoxication, but for him, as for the Greeks, intoxication is no mere trifle or indulgence. Rather, it is the wellspring of a certain kind of creativity. Which brings me to the third natural history in which S. *cerevisiae* will surely loom large: the natural history of poetry.

That alcohol can inspire metaphor is something the poets themselves have been trying to tell us for centuries. "No poems can please long or live that are written by water drinkers," as Horace wrote two thousand years ago. So why don't we take the poets at their word on this? Perhaps because, as the heirs of Descartes, we're troubled by the idea that a molecule manufactured by a single-celled yeast could have anything to do with something as exalted as human consciousness and art. Matter should stay put over here; spirit over there.

"For art to exist," Nietzsche wrote, "for any sort of aesthetic activity or perception to exist, a certain physiological precondition is indispensable: intoxication." One could argue that he's speaking metaphorically here, that intoxication is a mental state that doesn't necessarily depend on a molecule. Let's grant that there are other, non-chemical ways to achieve an altered state of consciousness.* But, then, why is it we always use *that* particular metaphor—intoxication—to describe it? Probably because it is the model for the state of altered consciousness, or one of them. (Dreams would be another.) And because the fastest, most direct route to altered consciousness is an in-

---

*Or at least *nonexternal* chemical ways, because who knows how meditation, fasting, risk, or extreme physical exertion work their effects on consciousness?

toxicant, the most widely available one for most of human history being the molecule manufactured by S. cerevisiae.

The poet, wrote Ralph Waldo Emerson, speaks "not with intellect alone, but with the intellect inebriated with nectar." Put another way, new perceptions and metaphors arise when the spirit of Dionysus breaks Apollo's tight grip on the rational mind. "As the traveller who has lost his way throws the reins on his horse's neck and trusts to the instincts of the animal to find his road, so must we do with the divine animal who carries us through this world." Reins are useful, even necessary—like poetic meter—but the poet doesn't get very far without the animal instinct. "If in any manner we can stimulate this instinct, new passages are opened for us into nature. . . . This is the reason why bards love wine, mead, narcotics, coffee, tea, opium, the fumes of sandalwood and tobacco, or whatever other procurers of animal exhilaration." To the poet endeavoring to trope the prose of everyday life, a molecule like ethyl alcohol offers a powerful tool.

Samuel Taylor Coleridge, a hero of the young Emerson's with a notorious drug habit, described a mental operation he called "secondary imagination" that he believed was the wellspring of a certain type of poetic creation. Secondary imagination, Coleridge wrote, is the faculty that "dissolves, diffuses, dissipates, in order to re-create." This notion of imaginatively transforming the givens of ordinary perception through a process of mental distortion is an idea that would go on to shape Romanticism in all the arts, from abstract painting to improvisational jazz. Can Coleridge's transforming imagination really be understood without reference to the experience of intoxication?*

---

*For more on the Romantic imagination and intoxication, see David Lenson's important book, On Drugs (Minneapolis: University of Minnesota, 1995), and also his Hess Family Lecture, "The High Imagination," at the University of Virginia, April 29, 1999. See also my discussion on plant drugs and the arts in the marijuana section of The Botany of Desire (New York: Random House, 2001).

Whether by means of a flowering plant or a microbe invisible to the naked eye, letting nature overpower us is a way to break down stale perspectives and open up fresh ones, or so the poets have always believed. We may not be able to tally it with any precision, but can there be much doubt that the poetic imagination owes a sizable debt to this yeast?

All this talk of intoxication was getting me in the mood to sample one of my home brews. But my Irish ale was still fermenting in the basement, and when I checked its gravity (10.18) I knew it needed a few more days before it would be ready. (Heroic patience is a critical component of successful brewing.) What I did have on hand and ready to drink was my jug of wild mead. The week before, I had restarted its fermentation, in the hopes of diminishing its sweetness and elevating its alcohol. Champagne yeast is a strain of *S. cerevisiae* selected over the years for its exceptional vigor, alcohol tolerance, and prodigious output of carbon dioxide—important in making champagne. Kel had warned me to put the mead in a heavy swing-top or champagne bottle, since the yeast was liable to blow the cap off an ordinary beer bottle.

I had already had one explosion in my basement. In the middle of the second night of the Irish ale's fermentation, I was awakened by an extremely loud clap. I didn't think much of it—this is a city that percolates at night with all sorts of obscure sounds, not to mention the occasional earthquake. But when I went down to the basement to check on the carboy the next morning, it had literally blown its top. The airlock was gone; the clap I'd heard must have been the report of it hitting the ceiling. A cascade of oatmeal-colored foam was erupting in slow motion from the neck of the bottle, and the white ceiling directly above had been splattered by rude blotches of brown wort. I made a mental note to tell my parents how very little has changed.

It had been two weeks since I pitched my low-proof wild mead with the killer yeast. There was no way to tell if anything was happening in the bottles, since the fermentation was now taking place in a sealed environment—no bubbles to watch squeezing their way through an airlock. But I figured whatever was going to happen had happened by now, so I chilled a bottle of the mead, and popped open the swing top. The bottle gave a satisfying *pop!* and emitted a tiny puff of cold steam before the mead began to bubble over its lip. When I poured the mead into a wineglass, I could tell immediately that the champagne yeast had done its job: The mead had become several degrees paler in color and considerably livelier. Measuring the final gravity, I calculated the alcohol was up over 13 percent.

The mead was almost completely dry and exuberantly effervescent. It actually tasted a little like champagne, though it was obviously something very different: There were strong hints of honey, as well as figs and sweet spices and something I hadn't noticed before, the unmistakable scent of flowers. It was not only unusual but really good. And it was strong. By the time I got down to the bottom of the glass, where a pale powdery remnant of champagne yeast had collected, I could feel the warm, suffusing glow of alcohol wash over me. There's really nothing quite like that first soft spring breeze of intoxication. Keep drinking all you want, but you will never get it back.

Nothing has really changed, you're the same guy sitting at the same kitchen table, and yet everything feels just a little different: Several degrees less literal. Leavened. And whether or not this angle of mental refreshment offers anything of genuine value, anything worth saving for the consideration of more ordinary hours, it does seem to open up, however briefly, a slightly less earthbound and more generous perspective on life.

I found myself turning that Coleridge quote over in my mind, thinking about imagination as a kind of mental algorithm that "dissolves, diffuses, dissipates, in order to re-create." Okay, it seemed completely obvious that Coleridge had to be talking about getting high. But what was less obvious, and what now struck me with some force, was the correspondence between Coleridge's notion of the imagination and (can you see it coming?) the process of fermentation. For what is fermentation but a *biological* faculty for doing the same thing: transforming the ordinary stuff of nature by "dissolving, diffusing, and dissipating" whatever is given, as the necessary prelude to creating something new? Fermentation is the secondary imagination of nature.

Hey, I told you I'd been drinking. Yet even now, in a more sober hour, I wonder if there might not be something here, a metaphor worth stretching and bending to see what it can do for us. Try this: In the same way that yeasts break down a substrate of simple plant sugars to create something infinitely more powerful—more complex and richly allusive—so Coleridge's secondary imagination breaks down the substrate of ordinary experience or consciousness in order to create something that is likewise less literal and more metaphorical: the strong wine of poetry where before there was only the ordinary juice of prose. And yet these two phenomena are not just analogies, existing in parallel. No, they cross, literally, since alcohol figures in both: as the final product of biological fermentation, and as a primary catalyst of imaginative fermentation. As yeast goes to work on sugars to produce alcohol, alcohol goes to work on ordinary consciousness. It ferments us. (So says the drunk: *I'm pickled.*) To produce . . . what? Well, all sorts of things, most of them stupid and mistaken and forgettable, but every now and again that alcohol-inspired mental ferment will throw off the bubble of a useful idea or metaphor.

I like to think of the one in the last paragraph as exhibit A.

AFTERWORD

HAND TASTE

I.

Two weeks later, on another Sunday morning, the carboy and I made the trip back to Shane's house so he and I could bottle our ten gallons of Humboldt Spingo. Shane had gone so far as to find a Victorian English beer label on the Internet, and then used some graphics software to swap out the letters for the original brewer's name with those of our home brew, a pixel at a time.

As we carefully siphoned the fresh beer into bottles and capped them, I couldn't help but wonder about the sanity of the whole project. Two grown men with a great many other, more pressing things to do had blown a big hole in two weekends to make something they could just as easily have bought for a few dollars. (It's not like you can't buy excellent "craft" beer these days, even in the supermarket.) So why had we gone to the considerable trouble of making something that in all likelihood would never surpass the commercial product?

To justify brewing your own beer—or baking your own bread, or fermenting your own sauerkraut or yogurt—on purely practical grounds is not easy. To save money? Maybe in the case of the bread, and surely in the case of everyday home cooking, but brewing beer requires an investment in equipment it would take an awful lot of drinking to recoup. So why do we do it? Just to see if we can, is one answer, I suppose, though that doesn't take you much past your first acceptable batch. If you do get that far, however, there does come the deeper satisfaction of finding yourself in a position to give a very personal kind of gift—the bottle of home brew (or jar of pickles, or loaf of bread) being a convenient and concrete expression of the generosity that is behind every act of cooking.

There is, too, the pleasure of learning how a certain everyday something gets made, a process that seldom turns out to be as simple as you imagined, or as complicated. True, I could have read all about brewing, or taken a tour of a brewery and watched the process. Yet there is a deeper kind of learning that can only be had by doing the work yourself, acquainting all your senses with the ins and outs and how-tos and wherefores of an intricate making. What you end up with is a first-person, physical kind of knowledge that is the precise opposite of abstract or academic. I think of it as embodied knowledge, as when your nose or your fingertips can tell you that the dough needs another turn or is ready to be baked. Knowing how to bake bread or brew beer with your own two hands is to more deeply appreciate a really good beer or loaf of bread—the sheer wonder of it!—when you're lucky enough to come across one. You won't take it for granted, and you won't stand for the synthetic.

But even better, I found, is the satisfaction that comes from temporarily breaking free of one's accustomed role as the producer of one thing—whatever it is we sell into the market for a living—and the passive consumer of everything else. Especially when what we produce for a living is something as abstract as words and ideas and "services," the opportunity to produce something material and use-ful, something that contributes directly to the support of your own body (and that of your family and friends), is a gratifying way to spend a little time—or a lot. I doubt it's a coincidence that interest in all kinds of DIY pursuits has intensified at the precise historical mo-ment when we find ourselves spending most of our waking hours in front of screens—senseless, or nearly so. At a time when four of our five senses and the whole right side of our brains must be feeling sorely underemployed, these kinds of projects offer the best kind of respite. They're antidotes to our abstraction.

To join the makers of the world is always to feel at least a little more self-reliant, a little more omnicompetent. For everyone to bake his own bread or brew her own beer is, we're told, inefficient, and by the usual measures it probably is. Specialization has much to recom-mend it; it is what allows Chad Robertson to make a living baking bread and me to make one writing books. But though it is certainly cheaper and easier to rely on untold, unseen others to provide for our everyday needs, to live that way comes at a price, not least to our sense of competence and independence. We prize these virtues, and yet they have absolutely nothing to do with the efficiencies of mod-ern consumer capitalism. Except perhaps to suggest that there might be some problems with modern consumer capitalism.

Of all the roles the economist ascribes to us, "consumer" is surely the least ennobling. It suggests a taking rather than a giving. It as-sumes dependence and, in a global economy, a measure of ignorance about the origins of everything that we consume. Who makes this stuff? Where in the world does it come from? What's in it and how was it made? The economic and ecological lines that connect us to the distant others we now rely on for our sustenance have grown so long and attenuated as to render both the products and their connections to us and the world utterly opaque. You would be forgiven for thinking—indeed, you are encouraged to think!—there is nothing more behind a bottle of beer than a corporation and a factory, somewhere. It is simply a "product."

To brew beer, to make cheese, to bake a loaf of bread, to braise a pork shoulder, is to be forcibly reminded that all these things are not just products, in fact are not even really "things." Most of what presents itself to us in the marketplace as a product is in truth a web of relationships, between people, yes, but also between ourselves and all the other species on which we still depend. Eating and drinking especially implicate us in the natural world in ways that the industrial economy, with its long and illegible supply chains, would have us forget. The beer in that bottle, I'm reminded as soon as I brew it myself, ultimately comes not from a factory but from nature—from a field of barley snapping in the wind, from a hops vine clambering over a trellis, from a host of invisible microbes feasting on sugars. It took the carefully orchestrated collaboration of three far-flung taxonomic kingdoms—plants, animals, and fungi—to produce that ale. To make it yourself once in a while, to handle the barley and inhale the aroma of hops and yeast, becomes, among other things, a form of observance, a weekend ritual of remembrance.

The world becomes literally more wonderful (and wonderfully more literal) as soon as we are reminded of these relationships. They unfold over the span of evolutionary time but also over the course of a few hours on a Sunday in a neighbor's backyard. I'm thinking of the relationship of the barley grass (Hordeum vulgare) and the brewer (Homo sapiens) and the remarkable fungus (Sacccharomyces cerevisiae), working together to create all these interesting new molecules—the intoxicating one, of course, but also all those other magic chemical compounds that fermentation teases out of a grass seed so that, when the ale washes over our tongue, we're made to think of a great many other unexpected things: fresh bread and chocolate and nuts, biscuits and raisins. (And, occasionally, Band-Aids.) Fermentation, like all the other transformations we call cooking, is a way of inflecting nature, of bringing forth from it, above and beyond our sustenance, some precious increment of meaning.

II.

In the year or so since I completed the quasi-formal part of my education in the kitchen, several of the transformations I've not yet quite mastered have found their way into the weave of everyday life, and others have fallen away or been relegated to special occasions. It's curious what sticks and what doesn't—what turns out to suit your temperament and the rhythm of your days. To try your hand at doing something new is to find out a few new things about yourself, too. Which is yet another good reason for coming into the kitchen.

For me, of all the transformations, braising has proved to be the most sustainable and most sustaining. Improving my knife skills (and mental attitude toward chopping onions), and learning how to slow cook in a pot just about anything in the market, has changed the way we eat, especially in the cooler months of the year. What not so long ago had seemed insurmountably daunting has become an agreeable way to spend half a Sunday: finely dicing my way through piles of onions, carrots, and celery, slowly simmering those while browning a cheap cut of meat, and then braising it all in wine or stock or water for a few unattended hours. Not only do we get a couple of weeknight meals out of it, but the meals are infinitely more delicious and interesting (and inexpensive) than anything we ever used to have on a Tuesday or Wednesday night.

I must say my time with the pit masters has definitely made me a more confident and accomplished griller. (I try not to misuse the hallowed term "barbecue.") Some nights I even cook with wood, taking the time to burn the logs down to bright cinders before putting on the meat or fish. In general, I cook much more slowly and carefully with fire than I used to, and the results are well worth it, in both tenderness and flavor. Though on many weeknights, when time is tight, I still crank up the gas grill and quickly sear some kind of filet.

But the most surprising legacy of my time in North Carolina is the annual pig roast we throw every fall. Before meeting Ed Mitchell and the Joneses, I was definitely not the sort of person who would ever think to cook a whole animal in the front yard, much less have any idea how to go about it. Now I guess I am. Though it's very much a team effort, with Judith and Isaac and Samin and my old friend (and amateur pit master) Jack Hitt playing key roles, along with a crew of volunteers who come by to tend the fire through the long night of slow cooking. Early in November, I arrange for a pig from Mark Pasternak, a farmer in Nicasio, and drive out there with Jack or Samin to pick it up on a Friday morning. That afternoon, once we've seasoned it and built a wood fire, Jack and I hoist the pig onto the pit for its twenty-hour or so cook.

The fire pit has gotten a few upgrades, including a sturdy cast-iron grate to hold the pig, and a hemispheric steel frame (contributed by my brother-in-law, Chuck Adams, even though he keeps kosher) that we wrap with heavy-duty foil and painter's tarps to create a sealed oven. The contraption still looks like a redneck spaceship landed in the garden, but it holds the heat so well that the pig can go hours before we have to add new wood coals. (Or charcoals: We're not averse to using a little Kingsford during the night if it'll buy us a few more hours of sleep.) We deploy a half dozen probes wired to oven thermometers in order to monitor the temperature both in the pit and in the pig itself, and try to keep the oven no hotter than 200°F.

All day Saturday, while we work on the side dishes (coleslaw, rice and beans, cornbread), friends and neighbors drift in and out of the yard, drawn by the smoke and its captivating aromas.

When the thermometers inform us the internal temperature of the meat is approaching 190°F, the pig is done—usually early Saturday evening, shortly after the guests arrive. Everyone gathers around as we lift the cover off the pit to reveal a considerably smaller but now handsomely lacquered and fragrant pig. Now it's showtime. Jack pulls the meat from the bones, chopping and seasoning it on a big wooden plank, while I use Ed Mitchell's technique to crisp the skin on the gas grill, flipping rubbery flaps of pigskin this way and that until the magic moment when they suddenly turn into blistered brown glass: crackling! We mix it all together, the steaming meat and the precious crackling, and let people build their own sandwiches. Memorable sandwiches.

The whole event is a ridiculously ambitious undertaking, and every year we vow this is the last one, but that hasn't happened yet and probably won't. What was an experiment has become a tradition, and traditions have a way of gathering momentum around them over time. People start asking about the date of the next pig roast before the end of the summer; they've come to count on it. Judith will tell you the best part of the pig roast happens long before the first guest arrives: For her, it's all about the team working together to create a special occasion. For me, the pig roast is also an opportunity to reconnect with a wider circle of friends, as well as with Jack and the rest of the pit crew, the farmer who supplies the pig, and then with the whole culture of barbecue.

Any time you cook a whole animal in public is going to feel like a ritual, will have that ceremonial weight. Maybe it's the presence of the animal itself, providing such a vivid reminder of what's involved whenever we eat meat—those echoes of sacrifice. Or maybe it's the

sight of fifty or sixty people sharing the same pig, enjoying their barbecue. Is there a sweeter proof of the power of cooking to bring
people together—to create a community, even if only for a night?
"There's something very powerful about that dish," as Ed Mitchell
told me that afternoon in Wilson, "just don't ask me what it is."

For next year, Isaac and I have been talking about brewing a special beer for the pig roast, and maybe we'll get it together in time.
But, honestly, I'm not sure brewing will ever be more than a very
occasional activity, something he and I might do when he's home
visiting from college. Though we are getting better at it, I realized
the other day, when I opened the fridge and reached for a Pollan's
Pale Ale rather than a Sierra Nevada. (Though the Humboldt Spingo
proved something of a disappointment—not enough hops, Shane and
I decided, to balance out the heaviness of the malt.) But even if I don't
brew more than once or twice a year, I already have a much better
understanding of what is going on in a really good ale, and as a result
enjoy drinking them much more than I used to.

I would never have expected bread baking to take up permanent
residence in my life, but apparently it has—not every day, but a couple of times a month, and always with satisfaction. I've found the
work is easy to fold into the rhythms of a writing day at home; it gets
me up from my chair every forty-five minutes to turn (and smell and
taste) the dough. I'll bake a couple of loaves on a Saturday when we
have friends coming to dinner, or as a treat for the family—baking
never fails to improve the mood of a household. For a long time, I
was feeling a little trapped by a sense of responsibility to the sourdough starter—the need to care for and feed it every day, like a pet.
But recently I learned how to safely put it into hibernation for weeks
at a time. I'll feed it well, wait an hour or two, then add enough additional flour to form a dry ball, and simply lose the container in the
back of the refrigerator. A few days before I want to bake again, I dig

the starter out and wake it up, by feeding and stirring it twice daily. Every time I take it out of the fridge, the gray clay seems so inert and lifeless and sour that I'm sure the culture has finally died. But after a couple of days of attention it starts throwing bubbles and smelling like apples again, and I'm back in business as a baker. It's been a lesson to me, in the continuing possibility of "cultural revival," to borrow Sandor Katz's nice term. Meanwhile, the bread gets better and better, and I find that a really good oven spring can still make my day.

III.

Each of the different methods I learned for turning the stuff of nature into tasty creations of culture implies a different way of engaging with the world, and some are more sympathetic than others. The pit master performs his mastery of animal and fire on a public stage. The cook marries the flavors of aromatic plants in her pot at home. Both of these ways of cooking have found their places in my life, the first one on special occasions, and the second more routinely. Yet I would have to say that of all the transformations, fermentation has proved to be the one that has engaged me most deeply.

Maybe it's because fermenting has so much in common with gardening, work that has always suited me temperamentally. Like a gardener, the brewer and the baker, the pickler and the cheese maker all find themselves engaging in a lively conversation with nature. All work with living creatures that come to the table with their own interests, interests that must be understood and respected if we are to succeed. And we succeed precisely to the extent we manage to align our interests with theirs. As I learned from Sandor Katz and Sister Noëlla and Chad Robertson and all the other fermentos I met, mastery is never more than partial or temporary. "Dude, I don't make this beer," a brewer in Oakland once told me after I had complimented him on his black lager. "The yeasts make the beer. My job is just to feed them really well. If I do that, they'll do all the rest."

But the work of fermentation is collaborative in another sense as well. It brought me into contact with a whole subculture of fermentos, many more in fact than I've mentioned here by name. I'm thinking of all the brewers and cheese makers, the picklers and bakers, who seemed to come out of the woodwork, like so many wild yeasts and lactobacilli, as soon as I resolved to learn their crafts. (Everything is everywhere.) Each of the various fermentation arts depends on not one but two subcultures, a microbial culture and a human culture. I would have thought that the industrialization (and pasteurization) of the modern food chain would have long since put both these cultures to rout. But in fact they are still very much alive and all around us, hidden in plain sight, awaiting just the right conditions, or questions, to reappear and revive.

This, it seems to me, is one of the greatest pleasures of doing this wholly unnecessary work: the spontaneous communities that spring up and gather around it. Fermentos, I found, are uncommonly generous with their knowledge and recipes and starter cultures, perhaps because the microbes have taught them modesty, or because they understand that cultures of every kind depend for their survival on getting passed on, one hand to the next, down through time. Maybe, too, there is the sense of solidarity that comes from feeling yourself in the minority, as these post-Pasteurians surely do in this era of mass-produced and industrially sanitized food.

To ferment your own food is to lodge a small but eloquent protest—on behalf of the senses and the microbes—against the homogenization of flavors and food experiences now rolling like a great, undifferentiated lawn across the globe. It is also a declaration of independence from an economy that would much prefer we remain passive consumers of its standardized commodities, rather than creators of idiosyncratic products expressive of ourselves and of the places where we live, because your pale ale or sourdough bread or kimchi is going to taste nothing like mine or anyone else's.

But surely the most important of all the relationships sponsored by this work is the one between those of us who elect to do it and the people it gives us the opportunity to feed and nourish and, when all goes well, delight. Cooking is all about connection, I've learned, between us and other species, other times, other cultures (human and microbial both), but, most important, other people. Cooking is one of the more beautiful forms that human generosity takes; that much I sort of knew. But the very best cooking, I discovered, is also a form of intimacy.

One of the most memorable cooking teachers I met in the course of my education was Hyeon Hee Lee, a Korean woman I visited in a town outside Seoul hoping to learn how to make traditional kimchi. It was a fairly brief encounter, no more than a few hours, but in retrospect it did as much as any other to help me find myself in the kitchen. Before we began, Hyeon Hee made sure, through our translator, that I understood that there are a hundred different ways of making kimchi; what she was going to teach me was just one way, the way of her mother and her grandmother before that.

Hyeon Hee had done most of the prep before I arrived, brining the Napa cabbages overnight and pounding the red peppers, garlic, and ginger into a thick paste. What remained was for us to carefully rub the brilliant red paste into the leaves of the cabbages, which are kept intact, one leaf at a time. You had to make sure that every internal and external square inch of every head of cabbage received its own spice massage. Then you folded the leaves back on themselves and wrapped them around so that the whole thing vaguely resembled a pretzel, before gently placing the bright-scarlet knot at the bottom of an urn. Once the urn was full, it would be buried in the earth, beneath a little lean-to in the backyard.

While we worked together that wintry November afternoon, kneeling side by side on straw mats, Hyeon Hee mentioned that Koreans traditionally make a distinction between the "tongue taste" and the "hand taste" of a food. *Hand taste?* I was beginning to have my doubts about the translator. But as Hyeon Hee elaborated on the distinction, while the two of us gently and methodically massaged spice into leaf, the notion began to come into a rough focus.

Tongue taste is the straightforward chemical phenomenon that takes place whenever molecules make contact with taste buds, something that happens with any food as a matter of course. Tongue taste is the kind of easy, accessible flavor that any food scientist or manufacturer can reliably produce in order to make food appealing. "McDonald's has tongue taste," Hyeon Hee explained.

Hand taste, however, involves something greater than mere flavor. It is the infinitely more complex experience of a food that bears the unmistakable signature of the individual who made it—the care and thought and idiosyncrasy that that person has put into the work of preparing it. Hand taste cannot be faked, Hyeon Hee insisted, and hand taste is the reason we go to all this trouble, massaging the individual leaves of each cabbage and then folding them and packing them in the urn just so. What hand taste is, I understood all at once, is the taste of love.

APPENDIX I:

FOUR RECIPES

Below are four basic recipes, one based on each of the four transformations: a pork shoulder slow cooked over a fire, a sugo (or Bolognese sauce) cooked in a pot, a whole-grain bread, and a sauerkraut. In some cases, the recipe comes from the cook who taught it to me; in others, I have adapted it from what I was taught. A word of caution that is at the same time a word of encouragement: As I learned in the course of my education in the kitchen, "the recipe is never the recipe." It might look comprehensive and legally binding, but in fact these recipes should be treated as a set of sketches or notes. Each of them has been tested by a professional recipe tester, so faithfulness to details and procedures will be rewarded on your first attempt. But after that you should feel free to adjust and improvise—these are templates that can be varied endlessly with little risk and much potential reward. I cook these dishes, or variations on them, regularly, only seldom looking at the text. That way, they continue to mutate and evolve, as recipes should. Eventually they become your own.

1. FIRE

PORK SHOULDER BARBECUE

Active Time: 40 minutes

Total Time: 4–6 hours (once the meat has been seasoned)

FOR THE PORK

- 2 tablespoons kosher salt
- 2 tablespoons granulated sugar
- One 5- to 6-pound pork shoulder, preferably with bone in and skin on (ask for a "Boston butt")
- 2 handfuls hickory chips (other types of wood chips can be substituted)
- 1 disposable aluminum foil shallow pan
- 1 smoker box (see note)

FOR THE VINEGAR-BBQ SAUCE

- 2 cups apple cider vinegar
- 1 cup water
- ¼ cup packed brown sugar
- 2¾ teaspoons fine sea salt
- 4 teaspoons hot pepper flakes
- 1 teaspoon freshly ground black pepper

PREPARE THE PORK

In a small bowl, mix the salt and sugar until combined. One to three days before you plan to grill, generously sprinkle the salt-sugar rub over the entire pork shoulder, covering every surface. You may not need the full ¼ cup of rub. (A good rule of thumb is 2 teaspoons per pound of meat.) If you're lucky enough to have a shoulder with skin on it, score the skin in a crosshatch pattern, leaving an inch or so between the lines. Try to work some of the rub into the scorings. Refrigerate the pork shoulder uncovered. Bring to room temperature before you put it on the grill.

Prepare a gas grill for smoking. Soak the wood chips in water for about 30 minutes; set aside. On a section of the grill that won't receive direct heat, place a disposable pan or tray beneath the cooking grate and directly on the flavorizer bars or lava rocks (whichever your grill has). Fill the pan about halfway with water; this will catch drippings and keep the inside of the grill moist. Set the cooking grate back on the grill. Adjust the burners so the temperature in the grill is somewhere between 200°F and 300°F. Keep the burners under the drip pan off, and those not under it on. Drain the wood chips and place them in a smoker box. A few minutes before putting the meat on the grill, set the smoker box directly over the heat source. (Smoke works best early in the cooking process.) Place the shoulder on the grill above the drip pan, skin or fat side up.

Cover the grill and roast the pork shoulder for 4 to 6 hours. The time it takes will vary depending on your piece of meat, the grill, and the cooking temperature. Lower temperature is better but takes much longer to cook. Whichever temperature you choose, check occasionally to make sure it does not exceed

300°F or fall below 200°F. When the temperature of the interior of the meat is 195°F, it should be done. Don't be alarmed if the temperature of the pork shoulder rises quickly and then stays at 150°F for a long time (sometimes for several hours). This is called the "stall." Be patient and wait for it to reach 195°F. Check to see if the meat feels relaxed to the touch or if you can pull it apart with a fork. If it resists, give it another 30 minutes.

The meat should by now be a deep brown color. If the outside of the shoulder doesn't have some dark, crispy areas (i.e., bark or, if you started with skin, crackling), crank up the temperature to 500°F for a few minutes. (Keep a close eye on it so it doesn't burn.) Remove the meat from the grill and let it rest for at least 20 to 30 minutes.

MAKE THE VINEGAR-BBQ SAUCE

Combine the vinegar, water, sugar, salt, hot pepper flakes, and black pepper in a medium-size bowl and stir until the sugar and salt have dissolved; set aside.

Either pull the pork shoulder apart with a fork or roughly chop with a cleaver, incorporating crispy bits of crackling (if you have it) or bark. Mix in a generous splash of the vinegar BBQ sauce; adjust the seasoning, making sure there's enough acid (vinegar) and salt. Put the remainder of the sauce in a pitcher on the table. Serve with soft rolls. Coleslaw and beans and rice make good accompaniments.

NOTE: If you don't have a smoker box, you can make one by piercing holes all over a shallow and narrow foil-covered aluminum pan.

VARIATION: With a few small changes, the same pork shoulder can be prepared in an Asian manner. This variation is loosely adapted from a David Chang recipe; the dashi recipe is adapted from Sylvan Brackett's. Cook the shoulder as above but omit the vinegar BBQ sauce. Instead, serve it with this dashi-based ginger-and-scallion dipping sauce. Make the sauce several hours before using so that the flavors have time to meld.

ASIAN DIPPING SAUCE

FOR THE DASHI

½ ounce (three 7-inch pieces) kombu seaweed, available at Japanese markets

6 cups cool water

1 ounce shaved katsuobushi (bonito flakes), available at Japanese markets

1 dried shiitake mushroom, optional

FOR THE SAUCE

2 cups cooled dashi, from recipe below

¼ cup thinly sliced scallions

¼ cup roughly chopped cilantro

¼ cup rice vinegar (cider vinegar or ume plum vinegar can be used instead)

3 tablespoons soy sauce

2 tablespoons minced ginger (from a 2-inch piece)

2 tablespoons mirin

½ teaspoon toasted sesame oil

Pinch hot pepper flakes or togarashi, optional

MAKE THE DASHI

In a medium saucepan, soak the kombu in the water for 1 to
2 hours.

Set the saucepan of kombu on the stove and turn the heat up to
high. When the water begins to throw bubbles but before it reaches
a rolling boil, remove the kombu with tongs and discard. Stir the
katsuobushi into the broth, and return to a boil. Reduce the heat
and simmer for 1 minute. Remove from the heat and let sit for
10 minutes.

Strain through a cheesecloth-lined strainer set over a large bowl,
then press as much liquid out of the katsuobushi as you can. Reserve
the liquid. Discard the katsuobushi. You can add a dried shiitake
mushroom to the liquid as it cools. Dashi keeps in the refrigerator
for 1 week, or until it starts to cloud.

MAKE THE SAUCE

Combine the dashi, scallions, cilantro, vinegar, soy sauce, ginger,
mirin, sesame oil, and hot pepper flakes in a medium bowl. Season
to taste with more vinegar, soy, and red pepper flakes. Give the
sauce a few hours to meld before serving.

Serve the pork shoulder shredded or chopped, along with rice
and leaves of bibb (or other) lettuce. Let guests use the lettuce leaves
to make rolls filled with pork and rice and dipped in the sauce.

2. WATER

MEAT SUGO AND PASTA

Here is Samin Nosrat's recipe for sugo, the classic Italian meat sauce that, depending on the region, is also known as Bolognese or ragù. This might not at first seem like a braise—there's no featured chunk of animal protein—but the principles are the same: a dice of onions, carrots, and celery; browned meat; a long, slow simmer in liquid. Making this recipe takes a few hours, so I usually prepare a big batch and freeze some of it in containers. Samin's recipe calls for pork and beef, but it can be made with any kind of meat, including chicken, duck, rabbit, or game.

Active Time: about 3 hours
Total Time: between 5 and 7 hours

FOR THE SPICE SACHET
    3 whole cloves
    One 1-inch piece cinnamon stick
    1 teaspoon black peppercorns
    1 teaspoon juniper berries
    ½ teaspoon whole allspice
    ¼ teaspoon freshly grated nutmeg

FOR THE SUGO
    2 cups pure olive oil (not extra-virgin)
    3 pounds boneless pork shoulder (ask butcher to coarsely grind
        the meat through a ⅜-inch die, if possible)

3 pounds beef, veal, or a combination, coarsely ground (any
  braising cut, such as chuck or round, is fine)

1 (750 ml) bottle dry red wine

4 medium red onions (about 2 pounds), peeled

3 medium carrots (about 12 ounces), peeled

3 medium ribs celery (about 8 ounces), rinsed

1 cup tomato paste

Parmesan rinds, optional

4 bay leaves

One 3-inch strip orange peel

One 3-inch strip lemon peel

3 to 4 cups beef, veal, or chicken stock, preferably homemade

Salt to taste

3 to 4 cups whole milk

FOR SERVING

Cooked pasta

Butter

Parmesan

MAKE THE SACHET

Combine the cloves, cinnamon, peppercorns, juniper berries,
allspice, and nutmeg in a cheesecloth and tie with string; set aside.

MAKE THE SUGO

Set a large, wide rondeau or sauté pan over high heat and add
enough olive oil to just coat. (In general the bigger the pan, the
better.) Cook the pork in batches, adding a third to a half at a time,
so that there is space in the pan. (If it's too crowded it will steam
instead of sear.) Cook, stirring and breaking up the meat with a
wooden spoon, until it sizzles and turns golden brown. (Do not

season the meat—salt draws out water and prevents browning.)
Using a slotted spoon, transfer the pork to a large bowl, leaving the
rendered fat in the pan.

Add more oil to coat the pan, as needed, and continue cooking
the remaining pork and beef in the same way. (If browned bits start
to burn on the bottom of the pan, deglaze it between batches with a
little red wine, scraping with a wooden spoon as the wine simmers
to pull up the tasty bits. Transfer the deglazing liquids to the bowl
of meats, wipe the pan dry, add more oil, and continue browning
the meats.)

While the meats are browning, make a soffritto. Use a knife or a
food processor to mince the onions, carrots, and celery separately
until all are very fine. You don't want to be able to identify any of
the ingredients in the soffritto once the dish is cooked. (If you
choose to use a food processor, pulse the machine frequently,
stopping often to scrape down the sides of the bowl to ensure the
vegetables are evenly cut. The celery and onion will release a lot of
water, so make sure to drain or pat them dry before cooking.)

When the last of the beef has finished cooking, add enough oil
to the pan to rise about ¼ inch deep. (There should be what you
might consider a scary amount of olive oil in the pot, about
1½ cups, as soffritto means "subfried.") Add the minced soffritto
vegetables and reduce the flame to medium. Cook, stirring often to
prevent burning, until the vegetables are brown and tender
throughout, about 50 minutes. The vegetables will steam at first
and then sizzle. If they start to burn, add some salt or a ladleful of
water or stock, and turn down the heat.

Once you are satisfied with the soffritto (don't rush it!), add the
bottle of wine to deglaze the pan. As the wine simmers, use the
wooden spoon to scrape up the delicious brown bits on the bottom
of the pan. Once the wine has reduced a bit and its alcohol has

burned off, add the browned meats, along with the sachet, tomato paste, Parmesan rinds (if using), bay leaves, orange and lemon peels, and about 3 cups of the stock. Season with salt. Bring to a boil, and then add enough milk to just cover the meat, about 3 cups. Let simmer. Once the milk breaks down and the color starts to look appetizing, after 30 to 40 minutes, start tasting the mixture and adjusting salt, acid, sweetness, richness, and body. If the mixture needs more acid, add wine. If it seems bland, add tomato paste to bring it to life and make it a bit more acidic and sweet. If it needs to be richer or the meat seems dry, add a splash of milk. If it needs more body, add stock.

Simmer over the lowest possible heat, skimming off the fat from time to time, and stirring often, until both the pork and beef are tender and the flavors have melded, anywhere from 2 to 4 hours total. Add more of the remaining milk, stock, or water to ensure that the meat always stays just barely immersed. (But don't drown the meat in liquid.) Continue to taste as you go but stop adding ingredients at least 30 minutes before the sugo is done so they have time to cook into the sauce.

When you are satisfied that the sugo is done, use a spoon or ladle to skim off the fat that has risen to the surface and remove the spice sachet, Parmesan rinds, bay leaves, and orange and lemon peels. Taste and adjust the salt again.

TO SERVE

Serve with pasta cooked al dente and tossed with a few tablespoons of butter. Top with lots of grated Parmesan cheese. This recipe makes a lot, but for this much work, you deserve leftovers!

3. AIR

WHOLE-WHEAT COUNTRY LOAF

This recipe is adapted from Chad Robertson's country loaf, in *Tartine Bread*. Simply replacing white flour with whole grain in his recipe will create a decent loaf of bread, but it won't be as airy or flavorful as it will be if you follow this revised version of the recipe. This recipe calls for 75 percent of the flour to be whole grain; you can adjust the percentage of whole-grain flour higher or lower as you prefer. In keeping with the custom for bread recipes, quantities here are given by weight rather than volume; you will need a digital scale, calibrated in grams, to follow this recipe. Note: Be sure to build your starter at least a week before you plan to bake. Make two loaves.

Active Time: about 70 minutes
Total Time: between 5 and 10 days

FOR THE STARTER
  50 grams stone-ground whole-grain flour, plus more as needed
    to feed the starter (at least 150 grams more)
  50 grams unbleached all-purpose flour, plus more as needed to
    feed the starter (at least 150 grams more)
  100 grams warm tap water, plus more as needed to feed the starter

FOR THE LEAVEN
  100 grams stone-ground whole-grain flour
  100 grams unbleached all-purpose flour

200 grams warm tap water

30–35 grams starter (recipe from above)

FOR THE BREAD

600 grams stone-ground whole-grain flour

250 grams unbleached all-purpose flour (higher protein
bread flour is okay), plus extra for dusting work surface

150 grams rye or pumpernickel flour

900 grams warm (roughly 80°F) tap water

3½ grams or 1⅛ teaspoons instant or rapid-rise yeast
(or half of a ¼-ounce packet) mixed with 50 grams
warm tap water, optional

25 grams kosher or fine sea salt

Rice flour, for dusting proofing bowl, optional

MAKE THE STARTER

In a small glass or plastic container (a clear container allows you to
watch microbial activity), mix 50 grams each of the whole-grain
and all-purpose flours until combined. Add the water and stir
until the consistency of a smooth batter. Leave the mixture open to
the air, stirring vigorously for about 30 seconds at least once a day
or whenever you think of it. If the mixture dries out, add a
bit of warm water to bring it back to the consistency of a batter.
The wild yeast and bacteria in the air, on the flour, and on your
hands will eventually start to eat the sugars in the flour and
ferment.

As soon as you observe signs of microbial activity (e.g., lumps on
the top, bubbles within the batter, or the smell of beer or yeast or
ripe fruit)—which can take as long as a week—feed the starter daily:
Discard approximately 80 percent of it and replace with fresh flour

and water in equal amounts (about 50 grams of whole-wheat flour, 50 grams of all-purpose flour, and 100 grams warm water). Stir until smooth. Once it has become active again (i.e., bubbling), keep the starter covered at a warm room temperature. If you won't be baking for a while, you can refrigerate or freeze your starter. To do so, feed it, let it sit for a couple of hours at room temperature, then add enough additional flour (the 50/50 mixture) to dry it out in a ball; freeze or refrigerate. A few days before you want to use it again, wake up the starter by bringing it to room temperature; feed it with the same amount of water and flour as above twice daily, discarding 80 percent of it each time, until it's lively again.

MAKE THE LEAVEN
The night before baking the bread, make a leaven. In a glass bowl, combine the whole-wheat and all-purpose flours with the water. Add 2 tablespoons of the starter and mix thoroughly. Cover with a towel and leave out overnight in a draft-free spot.

MAKE THE BREAD
The night before baking the bread, "soak" the whole-grain, all-purpose, and rye flours: In a large bowl, combine the whole-grain, all-purpose, and rye flours with 850 grams of the water, mixing with a spatula or by hand until there are no lumps or patches of dry flour remaining. (A recommended extra step: In the case of the whole-grain flour and the rye flour, pass them through a flour sifter to remove the larger bits of bran; reserve the larger bits in a small bowl for use later.) Cover the bowl with plastic wrap and leave out overnight in a draft-free spot. The reason for this step is to thoroughly moisten the whole-grain flours before the fermentation begins; this softens the bran (making for a more voluminous loaf)

and begins the breakdown of the starches into sugars (deepening flavors and color).

In the morning, test your leaven by dropping a tablespoon of it in warm water. If it floats, you're all set. If not, you'll probably want to add some yeast to the leaven as an insurance policy—mix 3½ grams (1⅛ teaspoons) of fast-acting yeast into 50 grams of warm water. After a few minutes, add to the bowl of leaven. It will seem alarmingly wet—the consistency of a thick batter. Don't worry.

Add about half of the leaven to the bowl with the wet dough; reserve the rest of the leaven as your starter going forward. (If you use commercial yeast, put aside half the leaven before adding it.) Mix the dough thoroughly and let rest for at least 20 and up to 45 minutes.

Meanwhile, in a cup, mix the salt in the remaining 50 grams of the warm tap water. After the dough mixture has rested, add the salty water and work it in thoroughly by hand.

BULK FERMENTING THE DOUGH

This takes 4 to 5 hours, depending on the ambient temperature and the vigor of your starter. Every 45 to 60 minutes, give the dough a turn in the bowl—wet your dominant hand, work it down the side of the bowl, and bring up the mass of dough from the bottom, stretching it upward and then folding it over the top. Give the bowl a quarter turn, and repeat this action until you've completed at least one revolution of the bowl. These stretches will strengthen the gluten and fold air into the dough. Watch for the formation of air bubbles; smell and taste along the way. The dough is ready to be divided and shaped when it feels billowy and cohesive—it wants to stick to itself more than the bowl. It should smell mildly yeasty and slightly sour. If it smells distinctly sour, end bulk fermentation and proceed to the next step.

DIVIDING THE DOUGH

When you're ready to shape, sprinkle a work surface with flour. Spill the dough out on the surface. Using a plastic dough scraper, divide the mass into 2 more or less equal halves. Shape these into globes, using your floured hands together with the scraper to rotate the dough against the work surface until it forms a ball with some surface tension. Cover the 2 globes with a towel and let them rest for 20 minutes.

SHAPING THE DOUGH

Using the scraper, flip one of the globes, which will have flattened somewhat, onto its back. Grab the edge of dough farthest from you with all your fingers, stretch it away from you, and then fold it back over the top. Do the same to the edge of dough closest to you, and then to each of the sides. You should have before you a rough rectangle of dough. Next, take each of the corners in turn, stretching and folding over the top. Now, cup your hands around the package of dough and roll it away from you until you have a short, taut cylinder, with the seams on the bottom.

If you sifted the whole-grain flour, spread the reserved bran on a plate or baking sheet and gently roll the dough in it to cover. Sprinkle either rice flour or any remaining bran into the bottom of a large bowl and then place the round of dough in the bowl, top side down. (Use a proofing basket instead if you have one.) Do the same with the second loaf, giving it its own bowl.

PROOFING

This is the second fermentation. Cover the bowls with towels and let them rest in a warm spot for 2 to 3 hours, till the dough gets puffy again. (Alternatively, put the shaped loaves in the refrigerator for several hours or overnight; this will retard fermentation while continuing to build flavor. It's not necessary to proof it again after refrigeration, but give it an hour or so at room temperature before baking.)

BAKING

Place the top and bottom of a Dutch oven (or a large ceramic casserole or combo cooker) on the center rack in the oven and preheat to 500°F.

With kitchen mitts, carefully remove the bottom of the pot from the oven and set it on the stovetop. Turn the bowl (or basket) over the pot to drop the proofed loaf into it. Don't worry if it doesn't land squarely; it will straighten out. Now, take a single-edge razor blade (or a lame) and score the top of the loaf, in any pattern you like. But be decisive! Now take the top of the pot from the oven and place it over the pot to seal, then move the whole thing into the oven. Lower the temperature to 450°F and set a timer for 20 minutes.

After 20 minutes, remove the top of the pot. The loaf will have doubled in volume and acquired a pale brown or tan color. Close the oven and give it another 23 to 25 minutes to bake with the top off. The loaf should now be a dark mahogany with a bit of blackening here and there, especially where it was scored. Remove the pot from the oven and the bread from the pot, using an oven mitt and a spatula. Tap it on the bottom, which should be very dark. A hollow percussive sound means the bread is properly cooked. If the bottom is pale and the sound is not percussive, return it to the oven for 5 more minutes.

Set it on a rack to cool for a few hours. Whole-grain bread is usually at its best on day two and remains good for several days after that, kept in a paper (not plastic) bag.

4. EARTH

SAUERKRAUT

Active Time: 1 hour
Total Time: 1 to 2 weeks, or longer

This recipe is based on Sandor Katz's version of sauerkraut, or
"kraut-chi," though it is more like a template for cabbage-based
ferments than a formal recipe. For spices, you can add juniper
berries, caraway seeds, and coriander for a more Old World kraut,
or add ginger, garlic, and hot peppers for something more like
kimchi. But do use some spice—they inhibit mold from forming.

   4 pounds cabbage (or a mixture of mostly cabbage, plus fruits
      and vegetables, such as apples, onions, daikon radish, carrots)
   6–8 teaspoons fine sea salt
   Spices (1½ teaspoons juniper berries, 1 tablespoon coriander
      seeds, or 1 tablespoon caraway seeds for Old World kraut, or
      whatever spices and quantities you like)
   One (½- to 1-gallon) wide-mouthed glass or ceramic container
      fitted with a lid, or two to three 1-quart containers, or a
      sauerkraut crock

Thinly chop or shred the cabbage into roughly ¼-inch thick slices
and place in a very large bowl or tub. Shredding the cabbage on a
mandoline gives the best result. If using other fruits and vegetables,
slice them to about the same thickness as the cabbage and add to the

bowl. For odd-shaped vegetables like carrots, using a thick box grater is easiest. The rougher the cut, the better as more surface area is exposed to the salt.

Add the salt (1½ to 2 teaspoons per pound of cabbage mixture) to the cabbage mixture, mixing it into the shredded leaves with your hands, squeezing the cabbage and pounding on the mixture as you go. (It's best to start by adding 1 teaspoon of fine sea salt per pound and then add another half or whole teaspoon extra per pound if needed.) Within several minutes, the salt will begin drawing water from the cabbage leaves. Continue to squeeze, bruise, or pound the cabbage to speed up the process. You can also place a weight on the mixture to drive out liquid. Wait until the vegetables are dripping wet, like a sopping sponge. Taste the cabbage. It should taste salted but not salty. If it's too salty, add more shredded cabbage or briefly rinse with water to remove. If it's not salty enough, or not wet enough, add a little more salt. Add the spices, if using, and toss.

Pack the mixture tightly in a glass jar or crock fitted with a lid that can hold at least 8 cups, making sure all the air is squeezed out and the vegetables are completely submerged in their liquid. (If you don't have a large container, use two or three smaller containers, about 1 quart each in volume.) There should be at least 3 inches between the packed cabbage and the top of the jar. Push the vegetables down tightly using your fist. They should be covered in their liquid. Before sealing the jar, either weight the vegetables down with a small ceramic or glass jar or insert something nonreactive between the lid and the vegetables to keep them submerged in the liquid: a plastic bag filled with stones or Ping-Pong balls works well or lay a large cabbage, fig, or grape leaf over the shredded cabbage and weight that down with clean stones or other heavy nonreactive objects. There should be enough liquid to cover, but if not add a little water. (Cabbages can lose cell water depending on growing and storage conditions.) Any vegetables exposed to the air will rot. If surface molds form, scrape them away and remove discolored sauerkraut. The kraut may smell funky, like a gym locker, but it shouldn't smell rotten. For the first few days, store at room temperature, ideally between 65°F and 75°F, then move to a cooler location, such as a basement. That's it: The mixture will ferment on its own; the necessary microbes are already present on the leaves.

If you're making kraut in a sealed glass container, make sure to release the pressure every few days, especially the first couple of days, when bubbling will be most active. In a mason jar, you'll know pressure is building when the metal top begins to bulge; open just enough to release the gas and reseal. Those old-timey glass crocks with the hinged tops held in place by a metal clasp work well since they will release pressure along their rubber gasket. Easiest of all is a ceramic crock designed for making sauerkraut. Available online in various sizes, these crocks have a water lock that releases bubbles of gas while keeping air out. If at any point water seeps out of the jar during fermentation and the cabbage mixture is not fully submerged in liquid, dissolve ½ teaspoon of fine sea salt in a cup of water. Add enough brine to keep the sauerkraut submerged in liquid.

How long before the kraut is ready? It depends—on the ambient temperature, the amount of salt used, and the local population of microbes. Taste it after a week, then two weeks, and then weekly after that. When the level of sourness and crunchiness is to your liking, move your kraut to the refrigerator to put the breaks on the fermentation.

VARIATION: To make a version of kimchi, replace the cabbage with Napa cabbage and Daikon radish; the cabbage can be sliced into half-inch rounds, and the daikon into quarter-inch rounds. Replace the sauerkraut spice mixture with:

4 cloves minced or crushed garlic (or more, to taste)
4-inch piece fresh ginger, sliced (or more, to taste)
2 tablespoons powdered red pepper (or more, to taste)
2 tablespoons coriander seeds (or half a bunch of fresh cilantro, roughly chopped)
4 green onions

The rest of the process is the same as for sauerkraut.

APPENDIX II:

A SHORT SHELF OF BOOKS ON COOKING

These are the cookbooks and books on cooking I've found indispensable and to which I return again and again for explanation and inspiration.

COOKING IN GENERAL

The *Art of Simple Food*, by Alice Waters

The *Cambridge World History of Food*, edited by Kenneth F. Kiple and Kriemhild Coneè Ornelas

Catching Fire: How Cooking Made Us Human, by Richard Wrangham

The *Essence of Cookery*, by Karl Friedrich von Rumohr

An Everlasting Meal: Cooking with Economy and Grace, by Tamar Adler

A History of Cooks and Cooking, by Michael Symons

How to Cook Everything, by Mark Bittman

On Food and Cooking: The Science and Lore of the Kitchen, by Harold McGee

FIRE

The Barbecue! Bible, by Steven Raichlen

The Magic of Fire: Hearth Cooking, by William Rubel

Seven Fires: Grilling the Argentine Way, by Francis Mallmann

Smokestack Lightning: Adventures in the Heart of Barbecue Country, by Lolis Eric
Elie; photographs by Frank Stewart

WATER

Braise: A Journey Through International Cuisine, by Daniel Boulud

Mediterranean Clay Pot Cooking, by Paula Wolfert

A Platter of Figs and Other Recipes, by David Tanis

Soffritto: Tradition and Innovation in Tuscan Cooking, by Benedetta Vitali

Something from the Oven: Reinventing Dinner in 1950s America, by Laura Shapiro

The Taste for Civilization: Food, Politics, and Civil Society, by Janet A. Flammang

AIR

The Bread Baker's Apprentice: Mastering the Art of Extraordinary Bread, by Peter
Reinhart

The Bread Builders: Hearth Loaves and Masonry Ovens, by Daniel Wing and
Alan Scott

English Bread and Yeast Cookery, by Elizabeth David

Peter Reinhart's Whole Grain Breads, by Peter Reinhart

Tartine Bread, by Chad Robertson

EARTH

The Art of Fermentation, by Sandor Katz

Brewing Classic Styles: 80 Winning Recipes Anyone Can Brew, by John J. Palmer
and Jamil Zainasheff

How to Brew: Everything You Need to Know to Brew Beer Right the First Time,
by John J. Palmer

Microcosmos: Four Billion Years of Microbial Evolution, by Lynn Margulis and
Dorion Sagan

Uncorking the Past: The Quest for Wine, Beer, and Other Alcoholic Beverages,
by Patrick E. McGovern

Wild Fermentation, by Sandor Katz

ACKNOWLEDGMENTS

Cooked is the story of my education, so I want first to thank all my extraordinary teachers, for their generosity and patience as much as for their knowledge.

In the arts of cooking with fire, I was privileged to learn from a great pit master, Ed Mitchell. But I had tutorials with several other masters of smoke and want to thank Francis Mallmann for several inspiring sessions in Texas, Alice Waters for sharing her passion for the grill (and her restless flipping technique), and Bittor Arguinonez for admitting me into the sanctuary of his kitchen. I also learned a lot about grilling from Jack Hitt, Mike Emmanuel, and Chuck Adams. Thanks too to Lisa Abend, for her guidance, translation, and good company in Spain, and to Dan Barber for encouraging me to go there in the first place. John T. Edge, at the Southern Foodways Alliance, could not have been more generous with his knowledge and contacts in the barbecue world. Thanks also to Joe Nick Patoski for a memorable introduction to the cuisine that Texans call barbecue, to Greg Hatem for his hospitality in North Carolina, Peter Kaminsky for his insights into both barbecue and pigs, and to "Kitchen Sister" Davia Nelson, for her leads and generosity.

Not only this chapter, but the entire book owes a tremendous debt to Richard Wrangham, for his pathbreaking writings on how cooking made us human, which I've drawn on throughout, and for taking the time to educate me about the "cooking hypothesis."

In learning about cooking in pots (which is to say "cooking," as the term is generally understood), I could not have done better than to apprentice myself to Samin Nosrat, who, besides being a great cook, turns out to be a brilliant teacher as well. Her contribution to this project extends far beyond the dishes and lessons she taught me; she also introduced me to grillers and bakers and fermenters, and was a continual source of timely advice, good company, and general inspiration. Amaryll Schwertner also welcomed me into her kitchen at Boulette's Larder and gave me a valuable lesson on braising, as well as the importance of even the most minor ingredient. Sylvan Mishima Brackett generously taught me how to make the magic water known as dashi. A bit further from the stove, Harry Balzer at the market research firm NPD gave me a graduate education in how Americans eat and think about food. Mark Kurlansky deepened my appreciation for salt, Jerry Bertrand for flavor, Richard Wilk for ritual. My exchanges with, and readings of, Joan Dye Gussow and Janet Flammang proved crucial as I navigated the treacherous waters of gender in the kitchen.

Getting to know Chad Robertson and learning how to bake even a pale imitation of a Tartine loaf was one of the highlights of this project. His stance toward the craft of baking—focused, uncompromising, never complacent—became an example to me, and not only in the kitchen. Lori Oyamada and Nathan Yanko, bakers at Tartine, could not have been more hospitable or generous or fun to work with. Keith Giusto and Joseph Vanderliet shared some of the secrets of milling (and millers are a secretive bunch) as well as their superb flours.

Thanks also to Richard Bourdon and Dave Miller for welcoming me into their bakeries, as well as to Steve Sullivan at Acme in Berkeley, Craig Ponsford at Ponsford's Place in San Rafael, Kathleen Weber at Della Fattoria in Petaluma, and Mike Zakowski, "the Bejkr" at the Sonoma farmers' market. Bob Klein at Community Grains (and Oliveto) admitted me into his "Grain Trust" and invited me to my first "wheat tasting." Monica Spiller, David R. Jacobs, and Steve Jones shared their deep knowledge about whole-grain milling and nutrition. Cereal scientists David Killilea and Russell Jones taught me all about the seed itself; Glenn Roberts, Jon Faubion, R. Carl Hoseney, and Peter Reinhart shared their expertise. Emily Buehler answered myriad queries about sourdough fermentation. I learned much about wheat and other grasses from the work of Richard Manning and Evan Eisenberg. And the Rominger family not only welcomed me to their farm, but had the questionable judgment to let me take the wheel of their combine and harvest a few rows of their wheat. Thanks to biologist Michael Eisen, my colleague at Berkeley, for generously offering to sequence the genome of my sourdough starter in his lab; I only wish I could have made more sense of the results. Chef Daniel Patterson, perfumer Mandy Aftel, and neuroscientist Gordon M. Shepherd tutored me in olfaction and inspired some helpful experiments.

I'm in debt to all the many fermentos who guided me through so many personally uncharted territories, but especially to Sandor Katz, to cheese maker Sister Noëlla, and to the brewers, amateur and pro alike: Shane MacKay, Will Rogers, Adam Lamoreaux, and Kel Alcala. Though I didn't end up writing about them, several other cheese makers gave freely of their time and knowledge and so left their mark on these pages: Soyoung Scanlan of Andante, Marcia Barinaga of Barinaga Ranch, and Sue Conley at Cowgirl Creamery. Thank you, Alex Hozven, for sharing your story and letting me work at the Cultured Pickle—my time there vastly improved my pickling, in theory as well as practice. In Korea, I had a wonderful guide to traditional ferments in farmer and Slow Food leader Kim Byung Soo, and got a priceless lesson in the making of kimchi and the meaning of "hand taste" from Hyeon Hee Lee. While researching fermentation, a generous and deeply knowledgeable group of academic fermentos gave me a crash course in microbiology and food science: Bruce German, who opened my eyes over and over again; Patrick Brown, friend of the fungi; Maria Marco, my guide to the kingdom of lactobacillus; and Rachel Dutton, pioneer of the cheese-rind ecosystem. Thanks also to Momofuko fermentos David Chang and Daniel Felder. I don't personally know Burkhard Bilger, but he must be a closet fermento; I learned much from his writings on the subject in the *New Yorker*. Joel Kimmons at the CDC was an inspiring guide to the microbiome and so much more.

One more teacher turned out to be absolutely indispensable to the entire project: Harold McGee. As any chef will tell you, Harold is the go-to guy for all questions of kitchen science, and I went to him more than I care to admit. But whether the question stumping me involved chemistry or physics or microbiology, he had the answer at his fingertips or could soon find it, and just as important, express it in terms I could follow. I don't know how anyone wrote about the science of cooking before the publication of *On Food and Cooking*, which was always within reach.

When I decided to include four recipes in an appendix, I had no idea how hard a recipe is to write and get right. Jill Santopietro tested them all, over and again, and edited the recipes for clarity, gracefully indulging and repairing my ignorance. They should all work now, which was not the case before she got hold of them.

Back in Berkeley, I was blessed to have the extraordinary research assistance of Malia Wollan. A gifted reporter and writer, Malia brought the full range of her journalistic wiles to the project and never failed to track down the study or statistic or source I needed, no matter how sketchy my requests. She also fact-checked the manuscript, saving me from countless errors and embarrassments, and gracefully fixed all sorts of problems in the text. Her dedication and good humor made the hard work of getting all the science right as agreeable as it could possibly be. I'm grateful also for the research contributed by Elisa Colombani and my student-assistants at the School of Journalism, Teresa Chin and Michelle Konstantinovsky. Thanks to the School of Journalism for being understanding about all the time off, and to the John S. and James L. Knight Foundation for supporting my research over the past decade. I'm also ever grateful to Steven Barclay for his wise counsel and support, and to his amazing team in Petaluma, for making the speaking part of the writing life so agreeable.

Cooked is my seventh book, published twenty-two years after Second Nature, my first, and looking back at the acknowledgments in that book, I'm gratified to see several names that belong in this one too, colleagues, friends, and loved ones who have had a hand in my writing from the beginning. The only book editor I have ever worked with is Ann Godoff; maybe there's a better editor out there—more acute, more supportive, more wise—but I can't imagine it. She is quite simply the best, and by now a dear friend as well. Happily I can say the same of Amanda Urban, my agent this whole career; her judgment on all matters large and small is not something you ever want to mess with. I owe them both what success I have had in the book business. And heartfelt thanks to the A team in their respective offices: Tracy Locke, Sarah Hutson, Lindsay Whalen, Ben Platt, and Ryan Chapman at Penguin; Liz Farrell, Molly Atlas, and Maggie Southard at ICM.

My longtime friends Mark Edmundson and Gerry Marzorati have discussed, read, and improved every one of my books—what a gift to have readers as perceptive as Mark and Gerry, and friends as steadfast and true. My old friend Michael Schwarz served once again as a valued counselor, and Mark Danner offered the perfect sounding board during our long walks at Inspiration Point, entertaining my ideas long before they had been baked into a book.

But my very first and best reader—the one who alone decides when a manuscript is ready to leave the house—is Judith Belzer. In addition to being my cherished partner in life, she is my indispensable editor, adviser, consoler, and kitchen collaborator. Our respective lines of work—my writing, her painting—have grown so entwined that I can no longer imagine what the books would be like—indeed, if they would be at all—if we had not met and joined forces way back when.

For my conviction that cooking matters I have my mom, Corky Pollan, to thank. Preparing dinner every night for four kids (three of them vegetarians), and now as often as she can for us and our spouses and her eleven grandchildren, she continually reminds us of the unparalleled satisfaction that comes from preparing a beautiful meal and enjoying it at the table together. She is a constant inspiration.

Lastly there is Isaac, who came into our lives very soon after my first book was published. Ever since, he has left his mark on all my books, but never more deeply than on this one. Isaac's evolution as an eater and a cook has taught me more about food, and cooking, than he probably realizes. The period of our lives that Cooked covers happened to coincide with Isaac's leaving home for college, and so with the end of our regular family dinner. If I have romanticized that institution in these pages, it is because it has been so very sweet in our lives, not always, but certainly in the last few years, when the three of us could share the work in the kitchen and then reap the pleasure at the table. Thanks for every one of those meals.

—Berkeley

SELECTED SOURCES

Listed below, by chapter, are the principal works referred to in the text, as well as others that supplied me with facts or influenced my thinking. Web site URLs are current as of September 2012. Any articles of mine cited here are available at michaelpollan.com.

INTRODUCTION: WHY COOK?

I explored the "Cooking Paradox" in a 2009 essay for the *New York Times Magazine*:
Pollan, Michael. "Out of the Kitchen, Onto the Couch." *New York Times Magazine*, August 2, 2009.

ON COOKING AS A DEFINING HUMAN ACTIVITY

Flammang, Janet A. *The Taste for Civilization: Food, Politics, and Civil Society.* Urbana, IL: University of Illinois Press, 2009. An important book, by a political scientist, on the gender politics, and implications for civic life, of "food work."

Lévi-Strauss, Claude. *The Origin of Table Manners.* New York: Harper & Row, 1978. See especially the chapter titled "A Treatise on Culinary Anthropology."

———. *The Raw and the Cooked.* New York: Harper & Row, 1975.

Wrangham, Richard, et al. "The Raw and the Stolen: Cooking and the Ecology of Human Origins." *Current Anthropology* (1999): 40, 567–94.

Wrangham, Richard W. *Catching Fire: How Cooking Made Us Human.* New York: Basic, 2009.

ON THE DIVISION OF LABOR AND SELF-RELIANCE

Berry, Wendell. "The Pleasures of Eating," in *What Are People For?* Berkeley: Counterpoint, 2010. My discussion of the division of labor and self-reliance owes a large debt to Wendell Berry's entire body of work.

Pollan, Michael. "Why Bother?" *New York Times Magazine*, April 20, 2008.

Zagat, Tim and Nina. "The Burger and Fries Recovery." *Wall Street Journal*, January 25, 2011.

ON THE CONTINUING RELEVANCE OF THE CLASSICAL ELEMENTS

Bachelard, Gaston. *Air and Dreams*. Dallas: Dallas Institute, 2011.
———. *Earth and Reveries of Will*. Dallas: Dallas Institute, 2002.
———. *The Psychoanalysis of Fire*. Boston: Beacon, 1964.
———. *Water and Dreams*. Dallas: Pegasus Foundation, 1983.
Macauley, David. *Elemental Philosophy: Earth, Air, Fire and Water as Environmental Ideas*. New York: SUNY Press, 2010.

PART I: FIRE

The literature on American barbecue is vast. The Web site of the Southern Foodways Alliance (http://southernfoodways.org/) offers a wealth of excellent material, including short films of pit masters at work and oral histories of North Carolina pit masters, such as Ed Mitchell and the Joneses. (http://www.southernbbqtrail.com/north-carolina/index.shtml)

I found these books and journals on Southern barbecue particularly illuminating:

Egerton, John. *Southern Food: At Home, on the Road, in History*. New York: Knopf, 1987.
Elie, Lolis Eric. *Smokestack Lightning: Adventures in the Heart of Barbecue Country*. New York: Farrar, Straus, & Giroux, 1996.
———, ed. *Cornbread Nation 2: The United States of Barbecue*. Chapel Hill, NC: University of North Carolina Press, 2009.
Engelhardt, Elizabeth Sanders Delwiche. *Republic of Barbecue: Stories Beyond the Brisket*. Austin, TX: University of Texas, 2009.
Kaminsky, Peter. *Pig Perfect: Encounters with Remarkable Swine and Some Great Ways to Cook Them*. New York: Hyperion, 2005.
McSpadden, Wyatt. *Texas Barbecue*. A book of photographs, with a foreword by Jim Harrison and an essay by John Morthland. Austin, TX: University of Texas, 2009.
Reed, John Shelton, and Dale Volberg Reed with William McKinney. *Holy Smoke: The Big Book of North Carolina Barbecue*. Chapel Hill, NC: University of North Carolina, 2008.
Southern Cultures, *The Edible South*, Vol. 15, No. 4, Winter 2009. Special issue on Southern food.

On the Early History and Evolutionary Implications of Cooking

Carmody, Rachel N., et al. "Energetic Consequences of Thermal and Nonthermal Food Processing." *Proceedings of the National Academy of Sciences of the United States of America* 108, 48 (2011): 19199–203.
Carmody, Rachel N., and Richard W. Wrangham. "Cooking and the Human Commitment to a High-Quality Diet." *Cold Spring Harbor Symposia on Quantitative Biology*, 74 (2009): 427–34. Epub October 20, 2009.
———. "The Energetic Significance of Cooking." *Journal of Human Evolution* 57 (2009): 379–91.
Fernández-Armesto, Felipe. *Near a Thousand Tables: A History of Food*. New York: Free Press, 2002.
Berna, Francesco, et al. "Microstratigraphic Evidence of in Situ Fire in the Acheulean Strata of Wonderwerk Cave, Nothern Cape Province, South Africa." *Proceedings of the National Academy of Sciences of the United States of America* 109, 20 (2012): E1215–20.
Jones, Martin. *Feast: Why Humans Share Food*. Oxford: Oxford University Press, 2007.
Symons, Michael. *A History of Cooks and Cooking*. Urbana, IL: University of Illinois, 2000.
Wrangham, Richard, et al. "The Raw and the Stolen: Cooking and the Ecology of Human Origins." *Current Anthropology* 40 (2009): 567–94.
Wrangham, Richard W. *Catching Fire: How Cooking Made Us Human*. New York: Basic Books, 2009.

A Few More Practical Books on Cooking with Fire

Mallmann, Francis, and Peter Kaminsky. *Seven Fires: Grilling the Argentine Way.* New York: Artisan, 2009.

Raichlen, Steven. *The Barbecue! Bible.* New York: Workman, 1998.

————. *Planet Barbecue!* New York: Workman, 2010.

Rubel, William. *The Magic of Fire: Hearth Cooking—One Hundred Recipes for the Fireplace or Campfire.* Berkeley: Ten Speed Press, 2002.

Harold McGee's books are indispensable to anyone interested in the science of cooking:

McGee, Harold. *On Food and Cooking: The Science and Lore of the Kitchen.* New York: Scribner, 2004.

————. *The Curious Cook: More Kitchen Science and Lore.* San Francisco: North Point Press, 1990. See especially chapter 17: "From Raw to Cooked: The Transformation of Flavor," a brilliant speculation on why humans like the taste of cooked food.

————. *Keys to Good Cooking.* New York: Penguin Press, 2010.

On Fire, Fire Cookery, and Sacrifice in History and Mythology

Alter, Robert. *The Five Books of Moses.* New York: W. W. Norton, 2004. See Alter's notes to Leviticus for discussion of sacrifice in the Old Testament and the kosher laws.

Bachelard, Gaston. *The Psychoanalysis of Fire.* Boston: Beacon, 1964.

Barthes, Roland. *Mythologies.* Annette Lavers, tr. New York: Hill and Wang, 1972. See the essay "Steak and Chips."

Brillat-Savarin, Jean Anthelme. *The Physiology of Taste.* New York: Everyman's Library, 2009.

Detienne, Marcel, and Jean-Pierre Vernant. *The Cuisine of Sacrifice Among the Greeks.* Chicago: University of Chicago, 1989.

Douglas, Mary. "Deciphering a Meal," accessed online: http://etnologija.etnoinfolab.org/dokumenti/82/2/2009/douglas_1520.pdf.

Freedman, Paul, ed. *Food: The History of Taste.* Berkeley: University of California, 2007. See especially the chapter on ancient Greece and Rome by Veronika Grimm.

Freud, Sigmund. *Civilization and Its Discontents.* New York: W. W. Norton, 1962. See his "conjecture" on the control of fire in the note on pp. 42–43.

Goudsblom, Johan. *Fire and Civilization.* London: Allen Lane, 1992.

Harris, Marvin. *The Sacred Cow and the Abominable Pig: Riddles of Food and Culture.* New York: Touchstone, 1985.

Kass, Leon. *The Hungry Soul: Eating and the Perfecting of Our Nature.* New York: Free Press, 1994. See especially his accounts of sacrifice, cannibalism, and the kosher laws.

Lamb, Charles. *A Dissertation Upon Roast Pig & Other Essays.* London: Penguin Books, 2011. Also available on-line at: http://www.angelfire.com/nv/mf/elia1/pig.htm.

Lévi-Strauss, Claude. *The Origins of Table Manners.* New York: Harper & Row, 1978. See especially the chapter "A Short Treatise on Culinary Anthropology."

Lieber, David L. *Etz Hayim: Torah and Commentary.* New York: The Rabbinical Assembly/United Synagogue of Conservative Judaism, 2001. See the essay on sacrifice in the Old Testament, by Gordon Tucker.

Montanari, Massimo. *Food Is Culture.* New York: Columbia University Press, 2006.

Plato. *The Phaedrus, Lysis and Protagoras of Plato: A New and Literal Translation by J. Wright.* London: Macmillan, 1900.

Pyne, Stephen J. *Fire: A Brief History.* Seattle: University of Washington, 2001.

Raggio, Olga. "The Myth of Prometheus: Its Survival and Metamorphoses up to the Eighteenth Century." *Journal of the Warburg and Courtauld Institutes,* Vol. 21, No. 1/2 (January–June, 1958).

Segal, Charles. "The Raw and the Cooked in Greek Literature: Structure, Values, Metaphor." *Classical Journal* (April–May, 1974): 289–308.

PART II: WATER

On the History and Significance of Cooking with Pots

Allport, Susan. *The Primal Feast: Food, Sex, Foraging, and Love*. New York: Harmony, 2000.

Atalay, Sonya. "Domesticating Clay: The Role of Clay Balls, Mini Balls and Geometric Objects in Daily Life at Çatalhöyük" in Ian Holder, ed., *Changing Materialities at Çatalhöyük*. Cambridge: McDonald Institute for Archaeological Research, 2005.

———, and Christine A. Hastorf. "Food, Meals, and Daily Activities: Food Habitus at Neolithic Çatalhöyük." *American Antiquity*, Vol. 71, No. 2 (April 2006): 283–319. Published by the Society for American Archaeology.

Fernández-Armesto, Felipe. *Near a Thousand Tables: A History of Food*. New York: Free Press, 2002.

Haaland, Randi. "Porridge and Pot, Bread and Oven: Food Ways and Symbolism in Africa and the Near East from the Neolithic to the Present." *Cambridge Archaeological Journal* 17, 2: 165–82.

Jones, Martin. *Feast: Why Humans Share Food*. Oxford: Oxford University Press, 2007.

Kaufmann, Jean-Claude. *The Meaning of Cooking*. Cambridge: Polity, 2010.

Lévi-Strauss, Claude. *The Origin of Table Manners*. New York: Harper & Row, 1978. The discussion of boiling versus roasting is in the chapter "A Short Treatise on Culinary Anthropology."

Rumohr, C. Fr. v., and Barbara Yeomans. *The Essence of Cookery (Geist Der Kochkunst)*. London: Prospect, 1993.

Sutton, David, and Michael Hernandez. "Voices in the Kitchen: Cooking Tools as Inalienable Possessions." *Oral History*, Vol. 35, No. 2 (Autumn 207): 67–76.

Symons, Michael. *A History of Cooks and Cooking*. Urbana, IL: University of Illinois, 2000.

Tannahill, Reay. *Food in History*. New York: Stein and Day, 1973.

Welfeld, Irving. "You Shall Not Boil a Kid in Its Mother's Milk: Beyond Exodus 23:19." *Jewish Bible Quarterly*, Vol. 32, No. 2, 2004.

On Cooking, Gender, and the Time Crunch

Clark, Anna. "The Foodie Indictment of Feminism" on *Salon*, May 26, 2010. http://www.salon.com/2010/05/26/foodies_and_feminism/.

Cognard-Black, Jennifer. "The Feminist Food Revolution." *Ms. Magazine*, Summer 2010, Vol. xx, No. 3.

De Beauvoir, Simone. *The Second Sex*. New York: Vintage, 2011.

Flammang, Janet A. *The Taste for Civilization: Food, Politics, and Civil Society*. Urbana, IL: University of Illinois, 2009.

Friedan, Betty. *The Feminine Mystique*. New York: W. W. Norton, 1963.

Gussow, Joan Dye. "Why Cook?" *Journal of Gastronomy* 7 (1), Winter/Spring, 1993, 79–88.

———. "Women, Food and Power Revisited." A speech to the South Carolina Nutrition Council, February, 26, 1993.

Hayes, Shannon. *Radical Homemakers: Reclaiming Domesticity from a Consumer Culture*. Richmondville, NY: Left to Write Press, 2010.

Hochschild, Arlie Russell. *The Time Bind: When Work Becomes Home & Home Becomes Work*. New York: Metropolitan Books, 1997.

———, and Anne Machung. *The Second Shift*. New York: Penguin Books, 2003.

Java, Jennifer, and Carol M. Devine. "Time Scarcity and Food Choices: An Overview." *Appetite* 47 (2006): 196–204.

Larson, Nicole I., et al. "Food Preparation by Young Adults Is Associated with Better Diet Quality." *Journal of the American Dietetic Association*. Vol. 106, No. 12, December 2006.

Neuhaus, Jessamyn. "The Way to a Man's Heart: Gender Roles, Domestic Ideology, and Cookbooks in the 1950s." *Journal of Social History*, Spring 1999.

Pollan, Michael. "Out of the Kitchen, Onto the Couch." *New York Times Magazine*, August 2, 2009.

Shapiro, Laura. *Perfection Salad: Women and Cooking at the Turn of the Century.* New York: Modern Library, 2001.

————. *Something from the Oven: Reinventing Dinner in 1950's America.* New York: Viking, 2004.

On Trends in American Eating and Cooking Habits

See the Web site of NPD, Harry Balzer's market research firm: https://www.npd.com/wps/portal/npd/us/industryexpertise/food. See also the U.S. Bureau of Labor Statistics "American Time Use Survey": http://www.bls.gov/tus/.

Cutler, David, et al. "Why Have Americans Become More Obese?" *Journal of Economic Perspectives.* Vol. 17, No. 3 Summer (2003): 93–118. Cutler attributes part of the increase in obesity to a decrease in the time spent preparing food.

Gussow, Joan Dye. "Does Cooking Pay?" *Journal of Nutrition Education* 20,5 (1988): 221–26.

Haines, P. S., et al. "Eating Patterns and Energy and Nutrient Intakes of US Woman." *Journal of the American Dietetic Association* 92, 6 (1992): 698–704, 707.

On the Chemistry of Flavor, Including Umami and Phytochemicals

Beauchamp, Gary K. "Sensory and Receptor Responses to Umami: An Overview of Pioneering Work." *American Journal of Clinical Nutrition* 90 (suppl) (2009): 723S–27S.

Block, E. "The Chemistry of Garlic and Onions." *Scientific American* 252 (1985): 114–19.

Blumenthal, Heston, et al. *Dashi and Umami: The Heart of Japanese Cuisine.* Tokyo: Kodansha International, 2009.

Chaudhari, Nirupa, et al. "Taste Receptors for Umami: The Case for Multiple Receptors." *American Journal of Clinical Nutrition* 90, 3 (2009): 738S–42S.

Gladwell, Malcolm. "The Ketchup Conundrum." *New Yorker*, September 6, 2004.

Griffiths, Gareth. "Onions—a Global Benefit to Health." *Phytotherapy Research* 16 (2002): 603–15.

Kurlansky, Mark. *Salt: A World History.* New York: Penguin Books, 2003.

Kurobayashi, Yoshiko, et al. "Flavor Enhancement of Chicken Broth from Boiled Celery Constituents." *Journal of Agriculture and Food Chemistry*, 56 (2008): 512–16.

McGee, Harold. *On Food and Cooking: The Science and Lore of the Kitchen.* New York: Scribner, 2004.

Rivlin, Richard S. "Historical Perspective on the Use of Garlic" in Recent Advances in the Nutritional Effects Associated with the Use of Garlic as a Supplement, proceedings of a conference published as a supplement to *The Journal of Nutrition*, 2009.

Rogers, Judy. *The Zuni Café Cookbook.* New York: W. W. Norton, 2002. Be sure to read her brilliant short essay on "salting early," pp. 35–38.

Rozin, Elisabeth. *Ethnic Cuisine: How to Create the Authentic Flavors of 30 International Cuisines.* New York: Penguin Books, 1992.

————. *The Universal Kitchen.* New York: Viking, 1996.

Sherman, Paul W., and Jennifer Billing. "Darwinian Gastronomy: Why We Use Spices." *BioScience*, Vol. 49, No. 6 (June 1999): 453–63.

Vitali, Benedetta. *Soffritto: Tradition and Innovation in Tuscan Cooking.* Berkeley: Ten Speed Press, 2004. Benedetta was one of Samin's teachers in Italy.

On the Element of Water

Bachelard, Gaston. *Water and Dreams: An Essay on the Imagination of Matter.* Dallas: Pegasus Foundation, 1983.

PART III: AIR

On the History of Wheat, Milling, and Bread

Belasco, Warren J. *Appetite for Change: How the Counterculture Took on the Food Industry.* Ithaca, NY: Cornell University, 2006. Good on the symbolism of white and brown bread in the 1960s.

Braudel, Fernand. *The Structures of Everyday Life: Civilization and Capitalism 15th–18th Century.* Vol. 1. New York: Harper & Row. 1981. See part 2, "Daily Bread."

David, Elizabeth. *English Bread and Yeasty Cookery.* Newtown, MA: Biscuit Books, 1994. Very good on the history of milling in England.

Drummond, J.G., and Anne Wilbraham. *The Englishman's Food: A History of Five Centuries of English Diet.* London: Jonathan Cape, 1939.

Eisenberg, Evan. *The Ecology of Eden: An Inquiry into the Dream of Paradise and a New Vision of Our Role in Nature.* New York: Vintage, 1999. The first few chapters offer a wonderful account of the coevolution of grasses and humankind.

Graham, Sylvester. *Treatise on Bread and Bread-Making.* Boston: Light & Stearns, 1837. In case you thought nutritional fads were something new in America.

Jacob, H.E., and Peter Reinhart. *Six Thousand Years of Bread.* New York: Skyhorse Publishing, 2007.

Kahn, E.J. "The Staffs of Life: Part III, Fiat Panis," *New Yorker,* December 17, 1984. This notorious series on grains is often mocked as a symbol of the "old" *New Yorker* at its most irrelevant—but I found it fascinating.

Kaplan, Steven Laurence. *Good Bread Is Back: A Contemporary History of French Bread, the Way It Is Made, and the People Who Make It.* Durham, NC: Duke University, 2006. Valuable for his account of the rise of white bread and the revival of sourdoughs.

Mann, Charles C. *1493: Uncovering the New World Columbus Created.* New York: Knopf, 2011. In chapter 8, "Crazy Soup," Mann tells the story of how the conquistadors brought wheat to the New World, p. 281.

Manning, Richard. *Against the Grain: How Agriculture Has Hijacked Civilization.* New York: North Point Press, 2004.

———. *Grassland: The History, Biology, and Promise of the American Prairie.* New York: Penguin Books, 1997. Manning recounts how the American prairie was transformed from grasslands to wheat fields.

Marchant, John, et al. *Bread: A Slice of History.* Charleston, SC: History Press, 2009.

McGee, Harold. *On Food and Cooking: The Science and Lore of the Kitchen.* New York: Scribner, 2004. See his chapter on bread history and technique.

Rubel, William. *Bread: A Global History.* London: Reaktion Books, 2011.

Standage, Tom. *An Edible History of Humanity.* New York: Walker & Co., 2009.

Storck, John, and Walter Dorwin Teague. *Flour for Man's Bread: A History of Milling.* Minneapolis: University of Minnesota, 1952.

Tudge, Colin. *So Shall We Reap: What's Gone Wrong with the World's Food—and How to Fix It.* London: Penguin Books, 2003. A good account of wheat's evolution.

On Baking Technique

Beard, James. *Beard on Bread.* New York: Knopf. 1974.

Clayton, Bernard. *The Breads of France.* Berkeley: Ten Speed Press, 2004.

Lahey, Jim. *My Bread: The Revolutionary No-Work, No-Knead Method.* New York: W. W. Norton, 2009.

Leader, Daniel, and Judith Blahnik. *Bread Alone: Bold Fresh Loaves from Your Own Hand.* New York: Morrow, 1993.

Oppenheimer, Todd. "Breaking Bread." A profile of Chad Robertson. *San Francisco Magazine,* November 2010.

Orton, Mildred Ellen. *Cooking with Whole Grains.* Foreword by Deborah Madison. New York: Farrar, Straus and Giroux, 2010.

Reinhart, Peter. *The Bread Baker's Apprentice: Mastering the Art of Extraordinary Bread.* Berkeley: Ten Speed Press, 2001.

———. *Whole Grain Breads: New Techniques, Extraordinary Flavors.* Berkeley: Ten Speed Press, 2007. Reinhart pioneered (or revived) the soaking of whole grains before fermenting them.

Robertson, Chad. *Tartine Bread.* San Francisco: Chronicle Books, 2010. Terrific book that manages to instruct and delight in equal measure.

Roussel, Philippe, and Hubert Chiron. *Les pains Français: evolution, qualité, production.* Vesoul: Mae-Erti, 2002.

Thorne, John. *Outlaw Cook.* New York: Farrar, Straus and Giroux, 1992. See the section "The Baker's Apprentice."

Wing, Daniel, and Alan Scott. *The Bread Builders: Hearth Loaves and Masonry Ovens.* White River Junction, VT: Chelsea Green, 1999. Contains an excellent discussion of sourdough microbiology as well as an interview with Chad Robertson done when he was baking in Point Reyes.

Wood, Ed. *Classic Sourdoughs.* Berkeley: Ten Speed Press, 2001.

On Nutrition and Bread

Cordain, Loren. "Cereal Grains: Humanity's Double-Edged Sword." *World Review of Nutrition and Dietetics.* Vol. 84. Basel, Switzerland: Karger (1999): 19–73.

Czapp, Katherine. "Against the Grain." Published on the Web site of The Weston A. Price Foundation, July 16, 2006. http://www.westonaprice.org/digestive-disorders/against-the-grain.

Di Cagno, Raffaella, et al. "Sourdough Bread Made from Wheat and Nontoxic Flours and Started with Selected Lactobacilli Is Tolerated in Celiac Sprue Patients." *Applied and Environmental Microbiology* (February 2004): 1088–96. This study suggests that a long sourdough fermentation may render wheat less toxic to people with celiac disease.

Jacobs, David R., Jr., and Lyn M. Steffen. "Nutrients, Foods, and Dietary Patterns as Exposures in Research: A Framework for Food Synergy." *American Journal of Clinical Nutrition* 78 (suppl) (2003): 508S–13S.

———, et al. "Food Synergy: An Operational Concept for Understanding Nutrition." *American Journal of Clinical Nutrition* 89 (suppl) (2009): 1543S–8S.

———, and Linda C. Tapsell. "Food, Not Nutrients, Is the Fundamental Unit in Nutrition." *Nutrition Reviews* Vol. 65, No. 10 (2007): 439–50.

———, and Daniel D. Gallaher. "Whole Grain Intake and Cardiovascular Disease: A Review." *Current Atherosclerosis Reports* 6 (2004): 415–23.

Lindeberg, Staffan. *Food and Western Disease: Health and Nutrition from an Evolutionary Perspective.* Oxford: Wiley-Blackwell, 2010.

Price, Weston A. *Nutrition and Physical Degeneration* (7th edition). La Mesa, CA: Price-Pottenger Nutrition Foundation, 2006.

Rizzello, Carlo G., et al. "Highly Efficient Gluten Degradation by Lactobacilli and Fungal Proteases During Food Processing: New Perspectives for Celiac Disease." *Applied and Environmental Microbiology* (July 2007): 4499–507.

Spiller, Gene, and Monica Spiller. *What's with Fiber?* Laguna Beach, CA: Basic Health Publications, 2005.

Taubes, Gary. *Good Calories, Bad Calories.* New York: Knopf, 2007.

Van den Broeck, Hetty C., et al. "Presence of Celiac Disease Epitopes in Modern and Old Hexaploid Wheat Varieties: Wheat Breeding May Have Contributed to Increased Prevalence of Celiac Disease." *Theoretical and Applied Genetics* 121 (2010): 1527–39.

On the Science of Sourdough Bread

Bamforth, Charles. *Food, Fermentation and Micro-organisms.* Oxford: Wiley-Blackwell, 2005.

Buehler, Emily. *Bread Science: The Chemistry and Craft of Making Bread.* Hillsborough, NC: Two Blue Books, 2006.

Ganzle, Michael G., et al. "Carbohydrate, Peptide and Lipid Metabolism of Lactic Acid Bacteria in Sourdough." *Food Microbiology* 24 (2007): 128–38.

Kitahara, M., et al. "Biodiversity of *Lactobacillus sanfranciscensis* Strains Isolated from Five Sourdoughs." *Letters in Applied Microbiology* 40 (2005): 353–57. An early study using DNA sequencing to identify the bacterial species in a sourdough culture.

Kulp, Karel, and Klaus Lorenz. *Handbook of Dough Fermentations*. New York: Marcel Dekker, 2003. Excellent anthology of scientific articles on the microbiology of sourdough bread.

MacGuire, James. "Pain au Levain: The Best Flavor, Acidity, and Texture and Where They Come From." *Art of Eating*, No. 83 (Winter 2009).

Scheirlinck, I., et al. "Molecular Source Tracking of Predominant Lactic Acid Bacteria in Traditional Sourdoughs and Their Production Environments." *Journal of Applied Microbiology* 106 (2009): 1081–92. This study found that *L. sanfranciscensis*, once thought to be native to the San Francisco Bay Area, is common in European sourdough cultures.

Sugihara, T. F., L. Kline, and M. W. Miller. "Microorganisms of the San Francisco Sour Dough Bread Process." *Applied Microbiology* 21, 3: 456–58.

Thiele, C., et al. "Contribution of Sourdough Lactobacilli, Yeast and Cereal Enzymes to the Generation of Amino Acids in Dough Relevant for Bread Flavor." *Cereal Chemistry* 79, 1: 45–51.

Weckx, Stefan, et al. "Community Dynamics of Bacteria in Sourdough Fermentations as Revealed by Their Metatranscriptome." *Applied and Environmental Microbiology* (August 2010): 5402–8. This study found that the ecosystem in a sourdough culture tended to stabilize over time.

On Air in Food, Smell, and Retronasal Olfaction

Aftel, Mandy, and Daniel Patterson. *Aroma: The Magic of Essential Oils in Food & Fragrance*. New York: Artisan, 2004.

Fincks, Henry T. "The Gastronomic Value of Odours" in *Contemporary Review*. Vol. L (July–December 1886). Early study of the relationship of taste and smell and their combined effect in producing flavor. May be the first published description of retronasal olfaction, which he calls "our second way of smelling."

Gilbert, Avery. *What the Nose Knows: The Science of Scent in Everyday Life*. New York: Crown, 2008.

Rozin, Paul. "Taste-Smell Confusions and the Duality of the Olfactory Sense." *Perception and Psychophysics* 31, 4 (1982): 397–401. One of the first analyses of retronasal olfaction and its role in detecting and cataloguing flavor.

Shepherd, Gordon M. *Neurogastronomy: How the Brain Creates Flavor and Why It Matters*. New York: Columbia University, 2012. The latest science of retronasal olfaction.

PART IV: EARTH

On Fermentation and Fermented Foods in General

Albala, Ken. "Bacterial Fermentation and the Missing Terroir Factor in Historic Cookery." In *Cured, Fermented and Smoked Foods: Proceedings of the Oxford Symposium on Food and Cookery 2010*. Devon, England: Prospect Books, 2011.

Bilger, Burkhard. "Nature's Spoils." *New Yorker*, November 22, 2010. An excellent profile of Sandor Katz and the underground food movement.

Jacobsen, Rowan. *American Terroir: Savoring the Flavors of Our Woods, Waters, and Fields*. New York: Bloomsbury, 2010. Especially the chapters on cheese and wine.

Katz, Sandor Ellix. *The Art of Fermentation*. White River Junction, VT: Chelsea Green, 2012. With a foreword by Michael Pollan. Sandor Katz's magnum opus and indispensable to anyone interested in fermented foods.

———. "Fermentation as a Coevolutionary Force." In *Cured, Fermented and Smoked Foods: Proceedings of the Oxford Symposium on Food and Cookery 2010*. Devon, England: Prospect Books, 2011.

———. *Wild Fermentation: The Flavor, Nutrition and Craft of Live-Culture Food*. White River Junction, VT: Chelsea Green, 2003. An exhilarating if somewhat rough-edged manifesto for fermentos.

Lewin, Alex. *Real Food Fermentation: Preserving Whole Fresh Food with Live Cultures in Your Home Kitchen*. Minneapolis: Quarry Books, 2012.

Margulis, Lynn, and Dorion Sagan. *Dazzle Gradually: Reflections on the Nature of Nature*. White River Junction, VT: Chelsea Green, 2007.

————. *Microcosmos: Four Billion Years of Evolution from Our Microbial Ancestors*. New York: Summit Books, 1986.

Mintz, Sidney W. "The Absent Third: The Place of Fermentation in a Thinkable World Food System." In *Cured, Fermented and Smoked Foods: Proceedings of the Oxford Symposium on Food and Cookery 2010*. Devon, England: Prospect Books, 2011.

Steinkraus, K.H. "Fermentation in World Food Processing." In *Comprehensive Reviews in Food Science and Food Safety*, Vol. 1 (2002). Published by the Institute of Food Technologists. A comprehensive survey of fermented foods and beverages from around the world.

Trubek, Amy B. *The Taste of Place: A Cultural Journey into Terroir*. Berkeley: University of California, 2008.

On Vegetable Ferments

Andoh, Elizabeth. *Kansha: Celebrating Japan's Vegan and Vegetarian Traditions*. Berkeley: Ten Speed Press, 2010. See especially the chapter on tsukémono, Japan's extraordinary pickling tradition.

Fallon, Sally, with Mary Enig. *Nourishing Traditions: The Cookbook That Challenges Politically Correct Nutrition and the Diet Dictocrats*. Washington, DC: New Trends Publishing, 2001.

Haekyung, Chung. *Korean Cuisine: A Cultural Journey*. Seoul: Korea Foundation, 2009.

Lee, Chun Ja. *The Book of Kimchi*. Seoul: J=Korea Information Service, 1999.

Madison, Deborah. *Preserving Food Without Freezing or Canning: The Gardeners and Farmers of Terre Vivante*. White River Junction, VT: Chelsea Green, 2007.

Pederson, Carl. S., and Margaret N. Albury. *The Sauerkraut Fermentation*. Geneva, NY: New York Agricultural Experiment Station, Bulletin 824, December 1969.

Plengvidhya, V., F. Breidt, Z. Lu, and H. P. Fleming. "DNA Fingerprinting of Lactic Acid Bacteria in Sauerkraut Fermentations." *Applied and Environmental Microbiology* 73, 23 (2007): 7697–702.

Yoon, Sook-ja. *Good Morning, Kimchi!: Forty Different Kinds of Traditional and Fusion Kimchi Recipes*. Elizabeth, NJ: Hollym, 2005.

On the Human Microbiome

Start with the National Institutes of Health's Web site for the human microbiome project: http://www.hmpdacc.org/. It has links to many academic articles on the subject. The articles below I found particularly helpful:

Ainsworth, Claire. "I Am Legion: Myriad Microbes Living in Your Gut Make You Who You Are." *New Scientist*, May 14, 2011.

Bengmark, D. "Ecological Control of the Gastrointestinal Tract: The Role of Probiotic Flora." *Gut* 42 (1998): 2–7.

Benson, Alicia, et al. "Gut Commensal Bacteria Direct a Protective Immune Response Against *Toxoplasma gondii*." *Cell Host & Microbe* 6, 2 (2009): 187–96.

Blaser, Martin J. "Who Are We? Indigenous Microbes and the Ecology of Human Disease." *European Molecular Biology Organization*, Vol. 7, No. 10, 2006.

Bravo, Javier A., et al. "Ingestion of Lactobacillus Strain Regulates Emotional Behavior and Central GABA Receptor Expression in a Mouse Via the Vagus Nerve." www.pnas.org/cgi/doi/10.1073/pnas.1102999108.

Desiere, Frank, et al. "Bioinformatics and Data Knowledge: The New Frontiers for Nutrition and Food." *Trends in Food Science & Technology* 12 (2002): 215–29.

Douwes, J., et al. "Farm Exposure in Utero May Protect Against Asthma." *European Respiratory Journal* 32 (2008): 603–11.

Ege, M.J., et al. Parsifal study team. "Prenatal Farm Exposure Is Related to the Expression of Receptors of the Innate Immunity and to Atopic Sensitization in School-Age Children." *Journal of Allergy Clinical Immunology* 117 (2006): 817–23.

Flöistrup, H., et al. "Allergic Disease and Sensitization in Steiner School Children." *Journal of Allergy and Clinical Immunology* 117 (2006): 59–66.

Gershon, Michael D. *The Second Brain: Your Gut Has a Mind of Its Own*. New York: Quill, 1998.

Greer, Julie B., and Stephen John O'Keefe. "Microbial Induction of Immunity, Inflammation, and Cancer." *Frontiers in Physiology*, Vol. 1, article 168 (January 2011).

Hehemann, Jan-Hendrik, et al. "Transfer of Carbohydrate-Active Enzymes from Marine Bacteria to Japanese Gut Microbiota." *Nature*. Vol. 464 (April 8, 2010). This is the study that found that genes from a marine bacterium had been taken up by gut bacteria among the Japanese, allowing them to digest carbohydrates in seaweed.

Jung, Ji Young, et al. "Metagenomic Analysis of Kimchi, a Traditional Korean Fermented Food." *Applied and Environmental Microbiology* (April 2011): 2264–74.

Kaplan, Jess L., et al. "The Role of Microbes in Developmental Immunologic Programming." *Pediatric Research*, Vol. 69, No. 6 (2011).

Karpa, Kelly Dowhower. *Bacteria for Breakfast: Probiotics for Good Health*. Victoria, BC: Trafford Publishing, 2003.

Ley, Ruth E. "Worlds Within Worlds: Evolution of the Vertebrate Gut Microbiota." *Nature Reviews*, Vol. 6 (October 2008).

O'Keefe, Stephen J.D. "Nutrition and Colonic Health: The Critical Role of the Microbiota." *Current Opinion in Gastroenterology* 24 (2008): 51–58.

Parvez, S., et al. "Probiotics and Their Fermented Food Products Are Beneficial for Health." *Journal of Applied Microbiology* 100 (2006): 1171–85.

Perkin, Michael R., et al. "Which Aspects of the Farming Lifestyle Explain the Inverse Association with Childhood Allergy?" *Journal of Allergy and Clinical Immunology* Vol. 117, No. 6.

Robinson, Courtney, et al. "From Structure to Function: The Ecology of Host-Associated Microbial Communities." *Microbiology and Molecular Biology Reviews* (September 2010): 453–76. A landmark article seeking to apply the lens of ecology to the microbial communities inhabiting the human body.

Song, Yeong-Ok. "The Functional Properties of Kimchi for the Health Benefits." *Food Industry and Nutrition* 9, 3 (2004): 27–28.

Turnbaugh, P.J., et al. "An Obesity-Associated Gut Microbiome with Increased Capacity for Energy Harvest." *Nature* 444 (2006): 1027–31.

———, et al. "The Human Microbiome Project." *Nature* 449 (2007): 804–10.

———, et al. "A Core Gut Microbiome in Obese and Lean Twins." *Nature* 457 (2009): 480–84.

Walter, Jens. "Ecological Role of Lactobacilli in the Gastrointestinal Tract: Implications for Fundamental and Biomedical Research." *Applied and Environmental Microbiology* (August 2008): 4985–96.

Zivkovic, Angela M., J. Bruce German, et al. "Human Milk Glycobiome and Its Impact on the Infant Gastrointestinal Microbiota." *Proceedings of the National Academy of Sciences*, Vol. 107, No. suppl 1 (March 15, 2011): 4653–58.

On Cheese and Cheese Making

Abdelgadir, Warda S., et al. "The Traditional Fermented Milk Products of the Sudan." *International Journal of Food Microbiology* 44 (1998), 1–13.

Behr, Edward. "Pushing to a Delicate Extreme: The Cheeses of Soyoung Scanlan." *Art of Eating*, No. 86 (2010).

Bilger, Burkhard. "Raw Faith." *New Yorker*, August 19, 2002. An excellent profile of Sister Noëlla and the controversies surrounding raw-milk cheeses.

Boisard, Pierre. *Camembert: A National Myth*. Berkeley: University of California, 2003.

Bosco, Antoinette. *Mother Benedict: Foundress of the Abbey of Regina Laudus*. San Francisco: Ignatius Press, 2007.

Culture: The Word on Cheese. Terrific quarterly magazine covering the art and science of cheese making and occasionally other fermented foods as well.

Johnson, Nathanael. "The Revolution Will Not Be Pasteurized: Inside the Raw Milk Underground." *Harper's Magazine*, April 2008.

Kindstedt, Paul S. *American Farmstead Cheese: The Complete Guide to Making and Selling Artisan Cheeses*. White River Junction, VT: Chelsea Green, 2005.

————. *Cheese and Culture: A History of Cheese and Its Place in Western Civilization*. White River Junction, VT: Chelsea Green, 2012.

Latour, Bruno. *The Pasteurization of France*. Alan Sheridan and John Law, trs. Cambridge: Harvard University, 1988.

LeMay, Eric. *Immortal Milk: Adventures in Cheese*. New York: Free Press, 2010.

Mendelson, Ann. *Milk: The Surprising Story of Milk Through the Ages*. New York: Knopf, 2008.

Montanari, Massimo. *Cheese, Pears & History*. New York: Columbia University, 2010.

Paxson, Heather. "Post-Pasteurian Cultures: The Microbiopolitics of Raw-Milk Cheese in the United States." *Cultural Anthropology*, Vol. 23, Issue 1, 15–47. Brilliant analysis of "post-Pasteurian" thinking and my first encounter with that term.

On the Microbiology of Cheese

Marcellino, R.M. Noëlla. *Biodiversity of Geotrichum Candidum Strains Isolated from Traditional French Cheese*. A doctoral dissertation, submitted to the University of Connecticut, 2003.

————, and David R. Benson. "Scanning Electron and Light Microscopic Study of Microbial Success on Bethlehem St. Nectaire Cheese." *Applied and Environmental Microbiology* (November 1992): 3448–54.

————. "Characteristics of Bethlehem Cheese, an American Fungal-Ripened Cheese," 114–20. In T. M. Cogan, P. F. Fox, and R. P. Ross, eds., 5th Cheese Symposium. Teagasc, Dublin, Cork, Ireland, 1997.

————. "The Good, the Bad and the Ugly: Tales of Fungal Ripened Cheese." (In Press: Catherine W. Donnelly, ed. *Cheese and Microbes*. Herndon, VA: ASW Press, 2013.)

Marcellino, N., et al. "Diversity of Geotrichum candidum Strains Isolated from Traditional Cheesemaking Fabrications in France." *Applied and Environmental Microbiology* (October 2001): 4752—59.

Sieuwerts, Sander, et al. "Unraveling Microbial Interactions in Food Fermentations: from Classical to Genomic Approaches." *Applied and Environmental Microbiology* (August 2008) 4997–5007.

On Disgust

Darwin, Charles. *The Expression of the Emotions in Man and Animals* (1872). Chicago: University of Chicago, 1965.

Kolnai, Aurel. *On Disgust*. Edited and with an introduction by Barry Smith and Carolyn Korsmyer. Chicago: Open Court, 2004.

Miller, William Ian. *The Anatomy of Disgust*. Cambridge: Harvard University, 1997.

Rozin, P., J. Haidt, and C. R. McCauley. "Disgust." In M. Lewis and J. Haviland, eds., *Handbook of Emotions*, second edition. New York: Guilford, 2000, 637–53.

Rozin, Paul, and April E. Fallon. "A Perspective on Disgust," *Psychological Review* 94 (1987): 23–41.

On Alcohol and Intoxication

Bamforth, Charles. *Food, Fermentation and Micro-organisms*. Oxford: Wiley-Blackwell, 2005.

Buhner, Stephen Harrod. *Sacred and Herbal Healing Beers: The Secrets of Ancient Fermentation*. Boulder, CO: Brewers Publications, 1998. Fascinating research on ancient alcoholic beverages, their psychotropic ingredients, and social role. With recipes.

Edwards, Griffith. *Alcohol: The World's Favorite Drug*. New York: St. Martin's, 2000.

Euripedes. *The Bacchae*. C. K. Williams, tr. New York: Farrar, Straus and Giroux. 1990.

Feiring, Alice. *Naked Wine: Letting Grapes Do What Comes Naturally*. New York: Da Capo, 2011.

Kerenyi, Carl. *Dionysos: Archetypal Image of Indestructible Life*. Princeton, NJ: Princeton University, 1976.

Lenson, David. *On Drugs*. Minneapolis, MN: University of Minnesota, 1995. A little-known but brilliant study of intoxication and its role in culture and the arts.

————. "The High Imagination." Delivered as the Hess Lecture at the University of Virginia, April 29, 1999. On the romantic movement and drugs.

McGovern, Patrick E. *Uncorking the Past: The Quest for Wine, Beer, and Other Alcoholic Beverages.* Berkeley: University of California, 2009. Indispensable archaeological account of early alcoholic beverages and their contribution to civilization.

Otto, Walter F. *Dionysus: Myth and Cult.* Translated and with an introduction by Robert P. Palmer. Bloomington, IN: Indiana University, 1965.

Palmer, John J. *How to Brew: Everything You Need to Know How to Brew Beer Right the First Time.* Boulder, CO: Brewers Publications, 2006. Excellent primer.

Phaff, Herman Jan, et al. *The Life of Yeasts.* Cambridge: Harvard University, 1978.

Siegel, Ronald K. *Intoxication: The Universal Drive for Mind-Altering Substances.* New York: Dutton, 1989. Especially good on alcohol use by animals.

Standage, Tom. *A History of the World in Six Glasses.* New York: Walker & Co., 2005.

Zainasheff, Jamil, and John. J. Palmer. *Classic Brewing Styles: 80 Winning Recipes Anyone Can Brew.* Boulder, CO: Brewers Publications, 2007. A somewhat more advanced guide to beer making; Shane MacKay and I had good results with several of these recipes.

INDEX

Adams, Chuck, 410
Adrià, Ferran, 120-21
Africa, 57, 60, 61, 226, 259, 384
African Americans, 46-48, 76-79, 84
agriculture, 27-28, 79, 90, 148, 153, 154, 185, 206–9, 329
   bread and, 258–59, 274, 277, 278, 279
   fermentation and, 306–7, 308, 381–82
air, 5, 13, 14, 110, 203–89
   see also bread
Air and Dreams (Bachelard), 252
Alcala, Kel, 380–81, 388, 390
alcohol, 15, 16, 73, 224, 228, 306, 372–404
   religion and, 346, 371–73, 386, 397–401
   as social drug, 396–97
   as toxin, 375, 395
   see also beer; mead; wine
Alcohol (Edwards), 397
allergies, 330, 335, 341
Allinson, Thomas, 260
amino acids, 57, 88–89, 143, 220, 224, 225n, 229, 284–85, 307, 308, 358
   glutamate, 167, 168, 169, 172, 173–74
amylase, 228–29, 284
Amy's vegetable curry, 197–200
animals, 51–55, 58–62, 110, 156, 205–6, 208, 253, 254, 316, 327, 328, 335, 348, 349
   fermentation and, 239, 306, 309, 373–75, 380

humans vs., 42, 52–54, 365–66
sacrifice of, 13, 39–42, 51–52, 55, 95–99, 411
salt in, 148
vegetable mingled with, 89–91
anthropology, 40, 57, 97, 182, 256, 303, 368
   alcohol and, 381–85, 396
   views on cooking in, 5–7
antibiotics, 296, 323, 325, 327, 329, 330, 331, 340
antimicrobial compounds, 144–45
archaeologists, 60, 153–54, 306, 375–76
Areopagite, The (Demetrius), 25
Arguinzoniz, Angel, 116
Arguinzoniz, Bittor, 114–21
Aristotle, 156
Aroma (Patterson and Aftel), 251
art, 83–84, 91, 244, 254, 288, 400, 401
Art Culinaire, L' (Cussy), 25
Art of Fermentation, The (Katz), 321
Asador Etxebarri, 115–21
Asia, Asians, 127, 153, 164, 225, 256, 259, 313n, 369
Asian dipping sauce, 421–22
asthma, 330, 335, 341
Atalay, Sonya, 153, 154
Axpe, 114–21
Ayden, N.C., 27–30, 67, 77, 82, 107, 117
   see also Skylight Inn

Bachelard, Gaston, 109–11, 177, 252
bacteria, 296–301, 309, 315–37, 365
    bread and, 209–10, 213, 215–16, 219, 220,
        221, 224, 228, 237, 240, 245, 276, 284,
        287, 304
    cheese and, 338, 342–44, 347, 349, 352,
        353, 355, 357–60, 362
    war on, 296, 300, 310–11, 323, 329, 339
Bacteria for Breakfast (Korpa), 320
Bacteroides plebeius, 326
"Balkans of Barbecue, The" (map), 66
Balzer, Harry, 129–31, 188, 193, 199
Bamforth, Charles, 386
Bane, Roger, 283
barbecue, 10, 13, 15–16, 18, 27–55, 64–109,
        156, 248, 409–12
    authenticity and, 29–30, 44, 50, 70, 71,
        78–79, 80, 82, 85, 100, 102, 103, 106,
        113, 114
    community and culture and, 29, 46–48, 79,
        83–84, 95–100, 107, 111, 412
    Pig's Revenge on, 64–65
    pit masters and, 13, 15, 29, 30, 32, 36–38,
        47, 50, 66–87, 98, 99, 102, 103, 105–8,
        113, 409–10
    pork shoulder, 418–22
    price of, 43, 45, 50
    sacrificial feast and, 95–99, 411
    seasoning of, 44, 45, 93–94, 101
    Wilson benefit and, 69, 71–72, 81–83,
        86–87, 91–94, 99–101
barley, 224–25, 226, 375, 386–87, 394, 408
Barthes, Roland, 54
Bay Village Bakers, 242, 244
Beauvoir, Simone de, 186
Becker, Jude, 108
beef, 166, 197, 423–26
    steaks, 45, 54–55, 61n, 67, 118–19
beer, 14–17, 18, 88, 306, 307, 372–73, 375,
        381–95, 396, 398n, 402–3, 405–8, 412
    barley and, 225, 375, 386–87, 408
    hops in, 382, 387–89, 394, 408
    yeast in, 219, 383–84, 387, 389, 390, 392,
        394, 408, 414
beer-before-bread hypothesis, 385
Berkshire Mountain Bakery, 237, 238,
        239, 241
Berry, Wendell, 21
Bible, 39–40, 96, 97, 107, 371–72
Big Apple Barbecue Block Parties, 69, 102–7
bitterness, 165, 168, 176
blood, 81, 97, 321, 324, 325, 334

Blue Smoke, 102
Bo-bo, 32–33, 62
boiling, 53–54, 148, 152–56, 172, 207, 208
Boisard, Pierre, 363
Boswell, James, 5, 53, 55
Bourdon, Richard, 237–44, 271–72
Brackett, Sylvan Mishima, 171–73, 421
brain, 6, 7, 56, 57, 59, 60, 110, 174, 249, 327,
        328, 329n, 407
    taste and, 167, 252
braising, braises, 12, 15–16, 53–54, 126,
        132–33, 139–40, 151, 160–66, 194, 409
    liquid for, 161–66, 173, 179–80
    maiale di latte (pork braised in milk), 174–77
    tough meat cuts and, 146
Braudel, Fernand, 226
bread, 12, 14–19, 88, 182, 203, 205–89, 304,
        310, 346, 371, 383, 385, 406, 412–13
    additives to, 268, 269, 271, 273
    biological processes in, 218, 223
    chemical processes in, 223–24, 229
    commercial production of, 209, 228,
        258–72
    ear of, 233, 234
    fortified, 260–61, 262
    health issues and, 244, 252–55, 258–62,
        267, 268, 270, 271, 274–75, 280–81
    origins of, 205–8
    perfect loaf of, 211
    religion and, 208, 225, 250, 251
    sense of accomplishment and, 234, 247–49
    unleavened, 207, 225
    whole-wheat country loaf, 427–32
    see also dough; flour
Bread Bakers Guild of America, 263, 264, 279
breast milk, 173–74, 331–32
Brevibacterium linens, 358, 359–60, 362
Brie, 350, 357
Brillat-Savarin, Jean Anthelme, 5–6, 61, 152
brine, 312–13, 315n
broth, 144, 165
Buddhists, 125, 130, 131, 195
bulk fermentation, 223, 226–30, 243, 269
Bunyan, Edward, 355
butchering, 20–21, 51–95, 109
butter, 119–20, 127

CAFOs (Concentrated Animal Feeding
        Operations), 27–28, 49, 51
Cain and Abel, 39–40
cake mixes, 187–88
Callaghan, Kenny, 102

calories, 6, 60–61, 191, 196, 226, 253, 254, 256, 263, 382
Calvino, Italo, 350
Camembert, 350, 357, 362, 363, 368
cancer, 58, 259, 307, 320, 324, 333, 334, 335, 382
caramelization, 89, 141, 143, 150, 229, 387
carbohydrates, 57–58, 144, 228–29, 324
  fermentation and, 307, 308, 386
  refined, 229, 259, 260, 270, 311, 332–33
carbon dioxide, 224, 228, 316, 384, 390, 395, 402
casein, 339, 353
cassava, 58, 302–3
casseroles, 156, 157–58, 160
Cassidy, Stephanie, 352–54, 371
cast-iron pots and pans, 151, 160, 232–33
Çatalhöyük, 153, 154
Catching Fire (Wrangham), 56
cauldrons, 156, 158, 159–60, 176–77
Cecelski, David, 76
celery, 127, 140, 143–44, 165
Certified Foods, 279–84
Chang, David, 421
charcoal, 82–83, 86, 87, 115
cheese, cheese makers, 15, 16, 18, 296n, 303, 304, 319, 338–72
  aerobes and, 355–56, 358
  "green," 354–55
  rind of, 353, 355–59, 361
chewing, 6, 57, 58, 59, 386
Chez Panisse, 134, 136–38
chicken, 81n, 130, 132, 251
  broth, soup, and stock, 144, 163, 166, 174
Child, Julia, 150, 169
children, 155, 174, 196, 309, 340–41, 370
  bacteria and, 329–32, 335
chimpanzees, 58–59, 61, 374
China, 32–33, 159, 167, 302, 306, 369
cholesterol, 333, 334
chopping blocks, 43, 46, 93, 94, 99, 100, 103–5
Churchill, Winston, 7
chymosin, 348, 353
civilization, 11, 14, 31–32, 41, 42n, 54, 154, 156, 307, 365, 368
  bread and, 209, 225, 262, 278
Civilization and Its Discontents (Freud), 31
coffee, 88, 91, 208, 304
Coleridge, Samuel Taylor, 401, 404
collagen, 58, 114, 180
comfort foods, 174, 175

Community Grains, 279, 280, 288
ConAgra, 269–70, 280
Confucius, 320–21
consumption, 21, 22–23, 131, 191, 192, 258, 300, 406–8
Continental Baking Company, 261
convenience food, 182, 191
Cook, Captain, 307
cookbooks, 132, 179, 212–15, 223, 251, 263
cooking, cooks:
  as defining human activity, 5–7, 55–62
  drudgery of, 127, 136, 181, 185
  emotional power of, 4–5, 13, 50–51
  gender politics of, 10–11, 15, 31, 128, 182–85
  home, 10–11, 13–14, 18, 125–32, 181–85, 192–201
  isolation of, 181–82
  as moral obligation, 186, 188
  myths of origins of, 40–42
  as optional, 130–31, 181
  outsourcing of, 7–10, 190
  professional, 3, 10, 15, 209
  reasons for, 1–23
  time spent, 3, 19, 128, 130, 132, 179–85, 190–93
  what constitutes, 9, 128–30, 188
cooking hypothesis, 6, 56–62, 110
Cooking Paradox, 4–5
cooking stones, 153–54
corn, 206, 224, 226, 258, 385–86
cornbread, 44, 48
cows, 338, 339, 340, 351, 352, 360
crackling, 32, 45, 62, 91, 94, 101, 104, 109, 114
cream, 119, 120
creativity, 400–402, 404
Cuisine of Sacrifice Among the Greeks, The, 95, 97
Culinary Institute of America, 237, 238, 241
culture, 6–7, 8, 13, 18, 29, 53, 56, 121, 128, 156, 164–65, 175, 193, 368–70
  alcohol and, 373, 396–97
  animal sacrifice and, 40, 52, 95, 96
  bread and, 229–30, 241
  cheese and, 351, 352
  fermentation and, 295–96, 299, 305, 309, 311, 414
  obesity rates and, 192
  smell and, 167
Curious Cook, The (McGee), 89–91
Current Anthropology, 56
Cussy, Marquis de, 25
Cutler, David, 191–92

Darwin, Charles, 364
dashi, 170–73
death, 293–94, 296, 346, 364–68
de Gaulle, Charles, 350
"Deipnosophists, The" (Athenaeus), 25
Demetrius, 25
Dennis, Skilton, 28
de Soto, Hernando, 46
dessert, 192–93, 197, 251–52
diabetes, 259, 260, 321, 333, 334, 382
diet, gut health and, 331–34
digestion, 6, 7, 57, 60, 61, 110, 140, 168, 176, 229, 240, 256, 270, 307–8
    bacteria and, 320, 327, 332
    of grasses, 206, 207
Dionysus, 367, 398–400
Dionysus (Otto), 398–99
dipping sauce, 173, 421–22
disease, 8, 229, 255, 259–60, 261, 296, 300, 382
    bacteria and, 321, 322, 333–34, 339
disgust, 360–70
"Dissertation upon Roast Pig, A" (Lamb), 32–33, 62
DNA, 323, 326, 353, 383, 385
Dostoevsky, Fyodor, 203
dough, 207, 210–11, 214–15, 217, 219, 222–24, 226–33, 235, 240, 242–45, 265, 268–69, 273, 275, 277, 281, 287
    bulk fermentation of, 223–24, 226–30, 243, 269
    scoring of, 233, 234
    shaping of, 231–32, 236, 243–46, 275
Douglas, Mary, 175
drunken-monkey hypothesis, 374–75
duck, 200–202
Dudley, Robert, 374–75
Dutch oven, cast-iron, 232–33

earth, 5, 13, 14–15, 110, 153, 291–404
    see also alcohol; beer; fermentation; mead; wine
eating, primary vs. secondary, 8, 190
eating habits, Balzer's study of, 129–31
E. coli, 325, 335, 340, 343, 347
economy, economics, 21, 23, 27, 79, 100, 191, 193, 408
    bread making and, 278–79, 280
Edge, John T., 76–77, 79, 85, 86
eggs, 61n, 139, 188, 251
Egypt, ancient, 207–8, 224
Emerson, Ralph Waldo, 51, 52, 291, 401

Empire Eats, 69, 71
endocuisine, 155–56
energy, 57–61, 110, 168, 205–6, 239, 256, 258, 274, 295, 328, 333
    fermentation and, 305, 308, 372, 375, 379, 395
English Pale Ale, 388–91
Enterobacteriaceae, 316
environment, 21, 22, 147, 331
    microbes and, 325–26, 336, 341, 343
enzymes, 126, 168, 207, 218, 222, 224, 228–29, 240, 253, 284, 326, 332, 375, 386–87
    cheese making and, 348, 357, 358
Epicure's Companion, The (Bunyan), 355
epithelium, 321, 324–25, 334–36
Erskine, Sy, 100
Escoffier, Auguste, 165
Essence of Cookery, The (Rumohr), 152–53
Ethnic Cuisine (Rozin), 164
evolution, 6, 56–60, 62, 89, 111, 168, 173–74, 207, 323–27, 332
    alcohol and, 379, 383, 384, 395
exocuisine, 155–56
Expression of the Emotions in Man and Animals, The (Darwin), 364

Facebook, 213–14
family, 8, 14, 155–58, 182, 190, 194–201
fast food, 8, 9, 43, 164, 182, 190, 191, 196, 197, 198
fat, 8, 150–51, 160, 169, 192, 307, 311, 333, 334, 351n, 357, 358
    pork, 88, 91, 114
Feminine Mystique, The (Friedan), 187
feminists, 131, 184–87
fermentation, 12, 14–16, 19, 91, 169, 291–404, 413–15
    in bread making, 215, 221, 222–23, 226–30, 232, 235, 237–41, 243–47, 269, 270, 284
    food preservation purpose of, 302–6, 309–10
    "live culture" foods and, 297, 310–11, 319–20
    Steinkraus survey of, 304–5
    of vegetables, 15, 298–99, 302, 303, 311–19, 330n, 332, 336–37
    see also alcohol; beer; mead; wine
Fermentation Festival, 298, 320–21, 328
Fernández-Armesto, Felipe, 111, 155
fiber, dietary, 259, 261, 262, 264, 267, 271, 324, 332, 333

Fielding, Henry, 42
fire, 5–6, 11, 12, 13, 16, 25–121, 208
control of, 30–33, 56, 110, 113, 120,
133, 303
in cookhouses, 30, 34
cooking with water compared with, 126,
132–34, 145–47, 152–53, 155–56
fermentation compared with, 303, 305
myths and theories about, 31–33, 39–42,
303
see also barbecue
fish, 167, 170–73
katsuobushi (cured bonito), 171, 172, 173
fish sauce, 369
Flammang, Janet A., 11
"Flavor Enhancement of Chicken Broth from
Boiled Celery Constituents," 144
flavor profiles, 163–65
flavors, 89–91, 119, 120, 121, 143, 146, 151,
160, 165, 250, 416
of bread, 208, 213, 223, 228, 235, 244, 245,
249, 273–76, 283
of cheese, 351, 352, 357, 358, 361, 369
fermentation and, 308–9, 313n
salt and, 149
Flay, Bobby, 80, 100
flour, 214–18, 222, 224, 226, 232, 234, 244,
245, 267, 269
etymology of word, 274–75
fortifying of, 253, 260–61
milling of, 209, 218, 253–54, 255, 257–60,
264–65, 269–70, 272, 273–74, 277–84
sifting of, 256–57, 285
white, prestige of, 253–59
white, problems with, 252–55, 258–61
whole-grain, 215, 218, 255–57, 259, 260,
263–65, 269–70, 272, 273–74, 277–86
Flowers, George, 79–80
food:
as commodity and abstraction, 9–10, 17
raw, 32–33, 42, 53, 57–61, 96, 156
rotted, 167, 168
senses and, 11, 38–39
see also specific topics
Food and Drug Administration (FDA), 268
Food Network, 80, 100
food processing, 8, 14, 207, 254–62, 309–10
food-service industry, 183, 185–91
food system, 1, 193, 258–59, 299–300
France, French cooking, 127, 146–47, 237,
242, 244, 256
cheese and, 349–50, 357, 360, 363, 367, 368

Freud, Sigmund, 31–32, 362, 364, 367–68
Friant, Émile, 244, 254
Friedan, Betty, 22, 186, 187
frozen food, 196–99
fruits, 89, 90, 258, 274–75
fermentation and, 307, 308, 309, 375
fungi, 365
cheese and, 349–53, 355–59

Galen of Pergamum, 59, 63
gardening, 19, 210, 218, 256, 286, 287, 413
garlic, 127, 144–45, 163, 175, 176
gelatin, 56, 88, 114, 146, 166, 233–34
genome, 322n, 326, 336, 395, 396
George Flowers Slaughterhouse, 79–80
Geotrichum candidum, 349–50, 357
German, Bruce, 174, 228
ginger-and-rose soufflé, 251–52
gliadin, 223, 225
glucose, 174, 224, 253, 270
glutamate, 167, 168, 169, 172, 173–74
gluten, 222–23, 225, 226, 227, 229, 231, 234,
243, 246, 251, 256, 265, 268, 269, 285
glutenin, 223, 225
gods, 59, 303, 373, 397–400
sacrifices to, 38–42, 51, 52
Graham, Sylvester, 260, 261
grains, 148, 154, 182, 382
fermentation and, 239, 307, 385–87, 394
whole, 215, 218, 255–57, 259–65, 269–86
grandma cooking, 132, 135
Grand Unified Theory of Diet and Chronic
Disease, 334
grapes, 295, 376–77, 399
grasses, edible, 205–7, 224–25, 258
see also flour; wheat
Great Britain, 146–47, 259, 260
Greece, ancient, 4, 51, 80, 95, 96, 97, 99, 158,
254, 398–400
grill cooking, 127–28, 156–57
guanosine, 167, 168

Hagood, Jimmy, 102, 105–6, 107
hákarl (fermented shark), 303, 307
Hastie, Lennox, 115, 116, 117, 119
Hatem, Greg, 70, 71
Hazan, Marcella, 163n
health issues, 21, 34, 35, 37, 190–93, 342–44
bacteria and, 297, 300, 342–44
bread and, 244, 252–55, 258–62, 267, 268,
270, 271, 274–75, 280–81
heart disease, 259, 260, 333, 334, 382

Helicobacter pylori, 328, 331n
heroes, 107, 133, 161
Hesiod, 41–42
HIV, 297, 321
home meal replacement, 128, 185–89
Homer, 10, 42, 51–52, 95, 107, 159
Homo erectus, 57, 60
honey, 375, 377–80, 385, 398n
hops, 382, 387–89, 394, 408
Horace, 291, 400
Hostess, 264, 265–71, 273, 274, 277, 278
Howell, James Henry, 36–38, 68, 117
Humboldt Spingo, 392–94, 405, 412
hunting, 54, 55, 58, 155, 175, 206, 382, 385, 396
Hyeon Hee Lee, 415–16
hygiene hypothesis, 330, 340

ice cream, 119, 120, 174
Iceland, 303, 307
Ikeda, Kikunae, 166–67
immune system, 320, 325, 330, 334, 335, 340, 344n
Indian cooking, 127, 145, 313n, 370
indigenous peoples, 46, 153, 154, 155, 239, 302, 385–86
inflammation, 320, 334–35
inosinate, 169, 173
inosine, 167, 168
insulin, 229, 270
International Congress for the Suppression of Fraud, 268–69
intestines, 174, 321–37
Intoxication (Siegel), 374
Italy, Italian dishes, 127, 134–35, 163n, 174–77, 229
I Yin, 123, 176–77

Japan, Japanese, 166–67, 170–73, 307, 326
Jesus Christ, 208, 250, 346, 371–72, 373, 386
Jones, Jeff (Uncle Jeff), 38, 43, 44, 48–50, 68, 77, 78, 83, 410
Jones, Pete, 28, 33
Jones, Samuel, 28–29, 33–38, 43, 44, 49, 68, 77, 78, 83, 107, 410

Kaminksky, Peter, 78–79
kashrut (kosher rules), 97, 98, 175
katsuobushi (cured bonito), 171, 172, 173
Katz, Sandor, 297–303, 308, 311–14, 317, 320–22, 378–79, 392, 413
ketchup, 164, 304

KFC, 131, 132
kimchi, 15, 19, 303, 310, 314, 318, 337, 339, 370, 415–16
Kimmons, Joel, 336
Kingsford, 82, 108
Kirby, James, 75–76
koji (Aspergillus oryzae), 171
Kolnai, Aurel, 364
kombu, 166–67, 172, 173
Korea, Koreans, 303, 314, 370, 415–16
Kosher (pet pig), 63–66

labor, division of, 154, 182, 184, 209
lachrymator (tear maker), 126
lactic acid, 301, 305, 316, 325n, 347, 353, 355, 357
lactobacilli, 297, 301, 316, 317–18, 320, 325n, 331
  cheese making and, 343, 347, 349, 353, 355
Lactobacillus plantarum, 301, 317–18, 332, 336, 337
Lactobacillus sanfranciscensis, 216, 220, 304
lactose, 339, 347, 353, 355, 357, 396
Lamb, Charles, 32–33, 34, 62
lard, 48, 50, 84
lasagna, 134, 135, 197–200
Lawrence, D.H., 123
Leuconostoc mesenteroides, 301, 316–17
Lévi-Strauss, Claude, 5, 6, 51, 53, 56, 155, 156, 368
Leviticus, 40n, 51–52, 97–98, 99
Listeria monocytogenes, 340, 341
"live culture" foods, 297, 310–11, 319–21, 332, 335, 336, 339

McDonald's, 43, 416
McGee, Harold, 89–91, 126, 142–43, 179–80, 291
McGovern, Patrick, 397–98
MacKay, Shane, 391–95, 405, 412
maiale al latte (pork braised in milk), 174–77
Maillard reaction, 88–89, 139, 143, 150, 229, 387
Malaysia, 306, 374
malting, malts, 386–87, 392, 393, 412
Marcellino, Sister Noëlla, 341–67, 371, 372, 384, 413
Margulis, Lynn, 297, 327
mead, 15, 372–73, 375, 377–81, 383, 386, 403
meals, 9, 158, 188, 191–93
  shared, 7, 8, 42, 95, 96, 97, 200–201
meat, 66, 67, 126, 144–50, 161, 197, 310
  browning of, 139, 150–51

determining doneness of, 68
glutamate in, 168–69
raw vs. cooked, 32–33, 42, 57, 60–61, 89–91, 156
scent of, 38–39
sugo and pasta, 423–26
see also barbecue; beef; pork
men, 132, 140–41, 175, 182–85, 187, 189, 193, 196, 213–14
fire cooking and, 13, 54–55, 67–68, 73, 127–28, 155
mental disorders, 321, 328–29
metabolism, 326–27, 328, 332, 336, 362
alcohol and, 375, 379, 395–96
metaphor, 56, 91, 167, 218, 323, 361, 391, 400, 404
Mexico, 225n, 237, 370
microbial ecology, 322–24
microbiome, 322n, 327
microbiota, 322–37
microcosmos, the, 297, 344
"Microorganisms of the San Francisco Sour Dough French Bread Process" (USDA study), 219–20
"Microwave Night," 196–200
microwave oven, 16, 111–12, 121, 128, 155, 158, 188, 198–99
milk, 177–78, 338–41, 347, 351n
breast, 173–74, 331–32
fermentation of, see cheese, cheese makers
pasteurization of, 339–41, 349
pork braised in (maiale al latte), 174–77
Miller, Dave, 242, 244, 266, 271–78
Miller's Bake House, 272–78
minerals, 207, 240, 253, 261, 262, 267, 271, 284, 285
fermentation and, 308, 381–82
mirepoix, 127, 141, 143–44, 150, 163, 194
miso paste, 169, 173, 304
Mitchell, Aubrey, 72, 73, 81–83, 86, 87, 91–94, 99–105
Wilson benefit and, 72, 81–83, 86, 87, 91–94, 99–101
Mitchell, Doretha, 73–74, 84
Mitchell, Ed, 69–87, 92–95, 100–105, 107, 108, 113, 114, 115, 410, 411, 412
at Big Apple barbecues, 69, 102–5
story of, 72–78
Wilson benefit and, 69, 71–72, 81–83, 86–87, 92–94, 100–101
Mitchell, Ryan, 103
Mitchell, Willie, 73–74, 84

Mitchell's Ribs, Chicken & Barbecue, 69–70, 75–76, 78, 79, 81–86
molecular gastronomy, 120–21
monosodium glutamate (MSG), 167, 169, 172, 198
Montana Flour Mills Company, 280–81
Moroccan food, 163, 164, 165
MSG, see monosodium glutamate
muscle, 57, 88, 113–14, 180
mushrooms, 167, 169, 170, 172, 173
Mythologies (Barthes), 54
myths, 40–42, 59, 62, 65, 68, 83, 84, 303

Nathaniaël, Frère, 360
natural selection, 60, 89, 174, 192, 221, 258, 326, 332, 351
nature, 2, 9, 12, 18, 21, 22, 52–54, 56, 118–19, 121, 164, 248, 365, 400, 401–2, 404
bread and, 241, 259, 262–63, 282
cheese and, 351–52, 361, 366
exocuisine vs. endocuisine and, 155–56
fermentation and, 299, 408, 413
New World, 225, 383–84
New York, N.Y., 69, 102–7
Nietzsche, Friedrich, 399, 400
North Carolina, 13, 27–30, 66–87, 91–95, 99–102, 108, 120, 410
see also Skylight Inn
Nosrat, Samin, 134–43, 146, 148–51, 165, 169, 174–76, 180, 181, 194, 198, 251, 410, 423
at Chez Panisse, 134, 136–38
chicken stock as viewed by, 163, 166
NPD Group, 129–30
nucleotides, 167, 168

Oak Barrel, 378, 380–81, 387–88, 392
obesity, 8, 61, 191–92, 328, 330, 333
Odyssey (Homer), 42
oil, 127, 165
oligosaccharides, 332
olive oil, 127
onions, 140–45, 165, 180
chopping, 125–28, 130, 131, 132, 136, 140, 141, 194
reasons for widespread use of, 142–43
orthonasal olfaction, 249
Otto, Walter, 398–99
ovens, 232–34, 242, 273
see also microwave oven
Oxford, Miss., 77–78, 79, 92
oysters, 117–18

packaged foods, 8, 9–10, 187–88
Palomar (Calvino), 350
pans, 119, 151, 155
Pansies (Lawrence), 123
Paradise Lost (Milton), 250n
PARSIFAL (Prevention of Allergy-Risk Factors
    for Sensitization Related to Farming and
    Anthroposophic Lifestyle) study, 330n
pasta, 61n, 134, 135, 423–26
Pasternak, Mark, 410
Pasteur, Louis, 219, 295, 296, 311, 322, 339, 399
pasteurization, 339–41, 349
Patterson, David, 251
Perlès, Catherine, 96
Persian food, 135
pets, 61, 63–66
P. F. Chang's Shanghai Style Beef, 197–200
philosophy, 11, 59, 109, 111
Physiology of Taste, The (Brillat-Savarin), 61, 152
phytase, 229, 284
phytic acid, 240, 270
phytochemicals, 261, 308
pickles, pickled food, 15, 298–99, 303, 310
Pig Perfect (Kaminksky), 78
pigs and hogs, 21, 27–30, 32–38, 46, 48–49
    as author's pet, 63–66
    breeds of, 78–79, 108
    roasting of, 32–33
    see also barbecue
Pit, The, 69–72
pit fermentation, 302–3, 306
pits, barbecue, 33–38, 82, 84, 86, 109, 112
plants, 57, 58, 89–91, 97, 126–27, 148, 154,
    164, 205–8, 225n, 254, 327n, 331, 351
    cell walls of, 295
    fermentation and, 306, 307
Plato, 59, 377
poetry, 91, 111, 250n, 291, 294, 400–401
Point Reyes Station, Calif., 242, 244
Pollan, Isaac, 194–201, 245, 247, 388–91, 410,
    412
Pollan, Judith, 67, 181, 182, 197, 199,
    200–201, 247, 388, 410
Pollan's Pale Ale, 390, 391, 412
Ponsford, Craig, 263–64, 279
pork, 81n, 97, 100, 166, 173
    braised in milk (maiale di latte), 174–77
    industrial production of, 28, 49–50, 85, 86
pork shoulder, 44, 45, 86, 107, 108–9, 113–14
    barbecue, 418–22
    butchering of, 20–21
    in meat sugo and pasta, 423–26

porridge, 207, 208, 225, 249
pot dishes, 126–28, 139–81, 194–96,
    200–201
    basic procedure for, 132–33
    see also braising, braises; stews
pots, 13, 54, 153–61
poverty, the poor, 146, 182, 192, 256, 339
prebiotics, 332, 337
priestly class, 96, 98–99, 133
primates, 57–62
probiotics, 320, 328, 332, 335–37
processed food, 148–49, 183, 185–92, 333
production, 23, 131, 406–8
    mass, 191, 194, 219, 258, 266–67
Prometheus legend, 41–42, 62, 303
proteases, 229, 284
proteins, 57–58, 88, 143, 168, 174, 225n, 307,
    308, 330, 334, 357, 358, 381, 385
    bread making and, 207, 220, 223, 224, 229,
    273, 284
    in milk, 339, 348, 353
Prueitt, Elisabeth, 238, 242
Psychoanalysis of Fire, The (Bachelard), 109–11

quinoa, 226

Raleigh, N.C., 69, 70, 85–86
Raw and the Cooked, The (Lévi-Strauss), 6, 53
"Raw and the Stolen, The" (Wrangham), 56
recipes, 132–33, 134, 179, 251–52, 417–36
    beer, 388–89
    bread, 212–15, 222n, 246, 277, 427–32
    meat sugo and pasta, 423–26
    pork shoulder barbecue, 418–22
    sauerkraut, 433–36
red pepper, 44, 45, 47, 93, 94
Regina Laudis, 341–48, 350–61, 363, 371–72
religion, 11, 38–42, 95–99
    alcohol and, 346, 371–73, 386, 397–401
    bread and, 208, 225, 250, 251
rennet, 347–49, 353
restaurants, 11, 19, 47–48, 136–38, 140–41,
    151, 183, 189
    see also Mitchell's Ribs, Chicken & Barbecue;
    Skylight Inn; Pit, The
retronasal olfaction, 249–50, 251
ribs, 66, 81n, 105, 107, 173
rice, 206, 224, 225n, 226, 256
roasting, 53–54, 148, 155–56, 159
Robertson, Chad, 212–16, 218, 221, 227, 233,
    235–38, 241–47, 254, 263, 272, 275, 277,
    279, 285, 286, 407, 413, 427

Bourdon and, 237, 238, 241–44
 perfectionist streak of, 241, 242, 245–46
Rogers, Will, 378
Romans, ancient, 224–25, 254, 256, 320
Rozin, Elizabeth, 164
Rozin, Paul, 164, 364–65
Rumohr, Baron Karl Friedrich von, 152–53
rye, 224, 226

Saccharomyces cerevisiae, 219, 220, 373, 379,
 382–84, 386, 395–96, 400, 402, 408
sacrifice, 13, 39–42, 51–52, 55, 95–99, 115
Safeway, 196–97
saffron, 138
Saint-Nectaire, 341–59
salmonella, 325, 335
salt, 8, 37, 38, 44, 45, 93, 94, 96, 142, 192
 bacteria and, 301
 in bread, 222–23, 269
 for meat, 148–50
 as taste, 165, 168, 169, 176
sandwiches, 43, 45, 50, 129
sauce:
 Asian dipping, 421–22
 barbecue and, 44, 45, 50, 66, 67, 105
 meat sugo and pasta, 423–26
 pot cooking and, 146, 161, 166, 176
 vinegar-BBQ, 418, 420–21
sauerkraut, 15, 17, 297–98, 300, 301–2,
 307–8, 310, 312–18, 337, 339, 343, 406
 recipe for, 433–36
scents, 89–91
Scott, Alan, 242
sea cucumbers, 116–17
seaweed, 166–67, 172, 326
Second Sex, The (Beauvoir), 186
senses, 11, 18, 91, 121, 407
 see also smell; taste
sex, cheese and, 363–67
Shapiro, Laura, 185
shit-in-milk story, 338
shopping, 189, 190n, 196–97
Skylight Inn, 28–30, 33–38, 42–50, 68
slaughter, slaughterhouses, 51–52, 79–80, 84
slaves, 46–47, 99, 100
smell, 11, 38–39, 61, 64–65, 90, 119, 157, 167,
 236, 237, 249–52, 362
 of bread and dough, 208–9, 211–12, 223,
 230, 234, 235, 249–52, 266, 267, 275
 cheese and, 351, 352, 353, 358–64, 368
 fermentation and, 317, 375
 of whole-grain flour, 273–74

smoke, 38–41, 45, 46, 50, 55, 66, 67, 82, 86,
 88, 100, 106, 112, 113, 117–21, 133
 ritual sacrifice and, 39–41, 51, 95
soffritto, 127, 141, 143, 144, 150, 175, 194
Soffritto (Vitali), 141
sofrito, 127
Something from the Oven (Shapiro), 185
soufflés, 251–52
soups, 126, 132–33, 155, 157, 160, 178
 Safeway's French onion, 197–200
 umami and, 166–67, 170
sourdough culture, 213, 215–17, 219–21,
 227–30, 234, 235, 236–37, 240, 265, 269,
 270, 276, 284–85, 287, 304, 351,
 412–13
sourness, 165, 168, 176
South America, 385–86
Southern Foodways Alliance, 69, 71, 72,
 76–78, 107
soy sauce, 164, 169, 173, 304, 307
Spain, Spanish dishes, 114–21, 127, 225n
specialization, 1–2, 19–20, 22, 407
spices, 126, 127, 138, 144–45, 149, 162–63
sponge (leaven), 217, 222, 245, 269, 284
starches, 58, 207, 222, 224, 229, 233–34, 240,
 253, 270, 284
starter, 213–17, 234, 236–37, 245, 246, 287,
 412–13
Steinkraus, K.H., 304–5, 311
stews, 126, 132–33, 139, 146, 152, 157, 160,
 161, 179, 194
Stillwaggon, James, 361, 363, 366–67
stock, 165–69
 chicken, 163, 166, 168
 dashi, 170–73
stomach, 154, 168, 174, 205, 206, 348, 349
"Stone Soup," 178
stories, 4, 21, 62, 65, 133–35, 161, 338
 bread and, 215
 Ed Mitchell, 72–78
Stouffer's lasagna, 197–200
Streptococcus cremoris, 357
sugar, 8, 57, 58, 88–89, 93, 168, 192, 255,
 258, 259, 308, 316, 325n, 339, 358
 alcohol and, 375, 385, 386
 bread making and, 220, 222, 224, 229, 253,
 269, 284
Sullivan, Steve, 279
supermarkets, 21, 187–89, 196–97, 200, 264,
 265, 311
sweetness, 165, 167, 168, 174, 176, 258,
 308, 309

take-out food, 183, 188–89
Tartine, 212, 222n, 235–36, 238, 241–42, 245–46, 247, 279
Tartine Bread (Robertson), 212–16, 230, 231, 427
taste, 11, 19, 58, 61, 90, 118, 120, 135, 143, 164–70, 250, 252, 308, 375
    of bread and dough, 223, 235, 246, 247, 271, 274, 275–76
Taste for Civilization, The (Flammang), 11
television, 59, 68, 69, 189, 190
    cooking shows on, 3–4, 5, 80, 100
terroir, 46, 350–52
texture, 58, 61, 149, 170, 351
    of bread, 208, 213, 223
TheFreshLoaf.com, 213–14, 247
Theogeny (Hesiod), 41–42
"This Compost" (Whitman), 294
time, 112, 132, 187, 189–93
    barbecue and, 66, 100, 109
    bread making and, 244, 258, 269
    spent avoiding cooking, 189–90
    spent cooking, 3, 19, 128, 130, 132, 179–85, 190, 199
technique vs., 147
tobacco, 27, 47, 79, 83–84, 92
Treatise on Bread and Bread-Making (Graham), 260
Trichothecium roseum, 352, 358
Turkey, 153, 154, 225
Tuscany, 134–35, 160

Ultrafine process, 270
umami, 143–44, 164–74, 198, 308, 309
USDA studies, 190, 219–21

Vanderliet, Joe, 265, 280–84, 286
Varieties of Religious Experience, The (James), 398
vegetable curry, Amy's, 197–200
vegetables, 126–27, 168, 197, 310, 333
    chopping of, 125–28, 140
    fermentation of, 15, 298–99, 302, 303, 311–19, 330n, 332, 336–37
vegetarian dishes, 145, 197–200
vinegar, 304, 310
    apple cider, 44, 45, 93–94
    -BBQ, sauce, 418, 420–21
vitamins, 207, 253, 259, 260–61, 262, 327
    fermentation and, 307, 308, 381–82

water, 5, 12, 13–14, 110, 123–201
    barbecue and, 67, 88, 91
    in bread, 214–17, 222, 234, 267, 269, 277, 284

fire cooking compared with, 126, 132–34, 145–47, 152–53, 155–56
    functions of, 162–63
    psychoanalysis of, 177
    skeletal recipe for cooking in, 133
    see also boiling; braising, braises; pot dishes; stews
Water and Dreams (Bachelard), 177
Waters, Alice, 136
weight, regulation of, 327–28, 331n
wheat, 205, 206, 223–26, 239, 253–54, 269, 279, 286, 375
    author's visit to field of, 288–89
    hard vs. soft, 258–59
Whitman, Walt, 294
Wild Fermentation (Katz), 298, 321
Wilson, N.C., 69–77, 81–87, 91–95, 99–102
wine, 151, 208, 295, 304, 352n, 361, 367, 376, 383
    religion and, 346, 371–73, 386, 398–99
women, 59, 99, 128, 131–32, 175, 182–87, 189, 193, 196
    fire cooking and, 67, 68, 156
    pot cooking and, 155, 156, 159
    pregnant, 168
    in work force, 183, 184, 192
Wonder Bread, 209, 261, 263–72, 278
    plants, 14, 18, 266–71, 281
wood, 106, 108, 109, 115–19, 121, 132, 273, 342–44
work, 131, 182–85, 190n
    women and, 183, 184, 192
Wrangham, Richard, 6–7, 56–62, 89, 110

Yanko, Nathan, 243
yeasts, 209–10, 213, 215–16, 218–21, 224, 234, 237, 244–45, 284, 287, 291, 306
    in beer, 219, 383–84, 387, 389, 390, 392, 394, 408, 414
    commercial, 213, 218–19, 228, 257, 264, 265, 267–70, 277, 278
    in mead, 377–81
    Saccharomyces cerevisiae, 219, 220, 373, 379, 382–84, 386, 395–96, 400, 402, 408
yogurt, 251, 304, 310, 311, 328n, 332, 406

Zagats, 19
Zawislak, Lydie, 342, 351–52
Zobellia galactanivorans, 326

ALLEN LANE

an imprint of

PENGUIN BOOKS

Recently Published

James Lovelock, *A Rough Ride to the Future*

Michael Lewis, *Flash Boys*

Hans Ulrich Obrist, *Ways of Curating*

Mai Jia, *Decoded: A Novel*

Richard Mabey, *Dreams of the Good Life: The Life of Flora Thompson and the Creation of* Lark Rise to Candleford

Danny Dorling, *All That is Solid: The Great Housing Disaster*

Leonard Susskind and Art Friedman, *Quantum Mechanics: The Theoretical Minimum*

Michio Kaku, *The Future of the Mind: The Scientific Quest to Understand, Enhance and Empower the Mind*

Nicholas Epley, *Mindwise: How we Understand what others Think, Believe, Feel and Want*

Geoff Dyer, *Contest of the Century: The New Era of Competition with China*

Yaron Matras, *I Met Lucky People: The Story of the Romani Gypsies*

Larry Siedentop, *Inventing the Individual: The Origins of Western Liberalism*

Dick Swaab, *We Are Our Brains: A Neurobiography of the Brain, from the Womb to Alzheimer's*

Max Tegmark, *Our Mathematical Universe: My Quest for the Ultimate Nature of Reality*

David Pilling, *Bending Adversity: Japan and the Art of Survival*

Hooman Majd, *The Ministry of Guidance Invites You to Not Stay: An American Family in Iran*

Roger Knight, *Britain Against Napoleon: The Organisation of Victory, 1793-1815*

Alan Greenspan, *The Map and the Territory: Risk, Human Nature and the Future of Forecasting*

Daniel Lieberman, *Story of the Human Body: Evolution, Health and Disease*

Malcolm Gladwell, *David and Goliath: Underdogs, Misfits and the Art of Battling Giants*

Paul Collier, *Exodus: Immigration and Multiculturalism in the 21st Century*

John Eliot Gardiner, *Music in the Castle of Heaven: Immigration and Multiculturalism in the 21st Century*

Catherine Merridale, *Red Fortress: The Secret Heart of Russia's History*

Ramachandra Guha, *Gandhi Before India*

Vic Gatrell, *The First Bohemians: Life and Art in London's Golden Age*

Richard Overy, *The Bombing War: Europe 1939-1945*

Charles Townshend, *The Republic: The Fight for Irish Independence, 1918-1923*

Eric Schlosser, *Command and Control*

Sudhir Venkatesh, *Floating City: Hustlers, Strivers, Dealers, Call Girls and Other Lives in Illicit New York*

Sendhil Mullainathan & Eldar Shafir, *Scarcity: Why Having Too Little Means So Much*

John Drury, *Music at Midnight: The Life and Poetry of George Herbert*

Philip Coggan, *The Last Vote: The Threats to Western Democracy*

Richard Barber, *Edward III and the Triumph of England*

Daniel M Davis, *The Compatibility Gene*

John Bradshaw, *Cat Sense: The Feline Enigma Revealed*

Roger Knight, *Britain Against Napoleon: The Organisation of Victory, 1793-1815*

Thurston Clarke, *JFK's Last Hundred Days: An Intimate Portrait of a Great President*

Jean Drèze and Amartya Sen, *An Uncertain Glory: India and its Contradictions*

Rana Mitter, *China's War with Japan, 1937-1945: The Struggle for Survival*

Tom Burns, *Our Necessary Shadow: The Nature and Meaning of Psychiatry*

Sylvain Tesson, *Consolations of the Forest: Alone in a Cabin in the Middle Taiga*

George Monbiot, *Feral: Searching for Enchantment on the Frontiers of Rewilding*

Ken Robinson and Lou Aronica, *Finding Your Element: How to Discover Your Talents and Passions and Transform Your Life*